CREATION

CREATION

A Biblical Vision for the Environment

MARGARET BARKER

t&t clark

Published by T&T Clark International
A Continuum Imprint
The Tower Building,   80 Maiden Lane,
11 York Road,   Suite 704, New York,
London SE1 7NX   NY 10038

www.continuumbooks.com

British Library Cataloguing-in-Publication Data
A catalogue record for this book is available from the British Library

ISBN: 978–0-567–44103-4 (Hardback)
          978–0-567–01547-1 (Paperback)

Typeset by Newgen Imaging Systems Pvt Ltd, Chennai, India

Printed and bound in Great Britain by CPI Antony Rowe, Chippenham, Wiltshire

For
Maria Becket

CONTENTS

FOREWORD
by
His All Holiness
Ecumenical Patriarch Bartholomew

✠ ✠ ✠

The crisis that we face is – as we all now know and as we all readily admit – not primarily ecological but religious; it has less to do with the environment and more to do with spiritual consciousness. It is a crisis concerning the way we imagine the world; it is a crisis, ultimately, over the image that we have of our planet. The starting-point, then, is our worldview, the vision that we have of creation and the environment. We are treating the earth in a senseless, even godless manner because we fail to see it as a divine gift inherited from above and owed to future generations. Unless we radically change the way that we perceive the world, then we will simply be dealing with symptoms, not their causes. We require a new image of the world if we hope for "a new heaven and a new earth." (Rev. 21:1)

Yet, far too often, we search for solutions to the environmental crisis without taking the time to explore the roots of our civilization, especially as these are revealed in the sacred texts of our Judaeo-Christian faith. Thus, we should act less hastily and search instead for fundamental connections between our vision and our praxis, between the Scriptural texts and the nature of our mission in the world. This book is precisely about the biblical vision for the environment.

For this reason, we are all indebted to Ms. Margaret Barker for her tireless efforts to articulate a Scriptural vision that will affirm the sacred bonds between Creator and creation. Indeed, Ms. Barker has sought over many years to live out and "materialize" this vision through her commitment, contribution and participation in the international, interfaith and interdisciplinary Symposia organized by the Religion, Science and the Environment committee of the Ecumenical Patriarchate.

Therefore, we extend herewith our blessing also to her research and writing in this critical and growing area with the publication of this important book.

At the Ecumenical Patriarchate, the 29th of June 2009

Your fervent supplicant before God,

✠ BARTHOLOMEW
Archbishop of Constantinople,
New Rome and Ecumenical Patriarch

PREFACE

Every product we make, every tree we fell, every building we construct, every road we travel, permanently alters creation. This reveals a fundamental difference between human, natural and divine economies. In the Orthodox tradition, the phrase 'divine economy' is used to describe God's extraordinary acts of love and providence towards humanity and creation. 'Economy' is derived from the Greek word 'oikonomia', which implies the management of an environment or household, [oikos], which is also the root of the word 'ecology' [oikologia].

Let us consider, however, the radical distinction between the various kinds of economy. Our economy tends to use and discard; natural economy is normally cyclical and replenishes; God's economy is always compassionate and nurturing. Nature's economy is profoundly violated by our wasteful economy, which in turn constitutes a direct offence to the divine economy. The prophet Ezekiel recognized this abuse of the natural co-systems when he observed:

Is it not enough to feed on good pasture?
Must you also trample the rest with your feet?
Is it not sufficient to drink clear water?
Must you also muddy the rest with your feet?
Ezekiel 34.18

His All Holiness Ecumenical Patriarch Bartholomew, addressing the conference *Climate Change and Human Security*, Athens, May 30th 2008.

For many years I have been privileged to be part of the Ecumenical Patriarch's Symposium, *Religion, Science and the Environment*. These water borne gatherings of scientists, environmentalists, journalists, policy makers and representatives of the world's main religious faiths have established an environmental ethics movement. They raise awareness of the plight of the areas they visit, strengthen local capacities for environmental protection, initiate schemes or institutions for environmental cooperation and education, and catalyse projects that will benefit the area. The core belief of the Symposium is that the analytical tools of science and the spiritual messages of religion must work in harmony if the earth's environment is to be safeguarded against further degradation.

I have heard, as a result, distinguished speakers in fields very different from biblical studies, but soon realized that what they were saying was familiar. It was another aspect of Temple Theology. On the Baltic Sea, I listened to Dr Elliott Norse talking about wasteful and destructive fishing methods, and I was hearing *tikkun 'olam*, atonement.

On the Amazon, I listened to Dr Antonio Nobre talking about the complex interdependencies of life in the rainforest, and I was hearing the creation covenant. In the Arctic, I listened to Dr Jane Lubchenco talking about marine reserves, and I was hearing the Sabbath year. Over the years, as more correspondences became clear to me, this book began to form in my mind, together with the realization that it could be a huge undertaking.

I have therefore limited the scope of the book to an outline of what the first Christians could have known, thinking as they did within the framework of Temple Theology, and set this alongside some striking parallels in today's environment discourse. The Temple Theology is reconstructed from such material as remains from the time of the early Church, and a pattern can be discerned. The other material is drawn from reading at a popular level in areas where I have no expertise, prompted by topics raised in the Symposium sessions. Time and again I found extraordinary similarities.

I should like to thank the Ecumenical Patriarch for inviting me to be a member of his Symposium. Although prompted by what I have heard in those gatherings, this book does not represent any official Symposium position. I should like also to thank my colleagues in the Symposium from whom I have learned so much, my family for their patience and the staff of the Cambridge University Library for their help. I should like to dedicate this book, with affection and admiration, to Maria Becket, the Symposium co-ordinator. Her extraordinary energy, and her ability to motivate and inspire people all over the world, have made the Patriarch's vision a reality.

Margaret Barker
Easter 2009

INTRODUCTION

It is 50 years since Rachel Carson began to write her book *Silent Spring*,[1] which alerted a wider public to what human beings were doing to the earth. In her preface she described a fictional small town in America, where there was sickness and death caused by pollution. There were no birds and no fish, and young animals did not survive. 'No witchcraft, no enemy action had silenced the rebirth of life in this stricken world; the people had done it to themselves.' For her, this nightmare was a possibility for the future. That future is almost upon us.

Isaiah had a similar vision, but he knew why it had happened and how people had done it to themselves. They had broken the everlasting covenant, and the creation was collapsing.

> The earth mourns and withers
> The world languishes and withers
> The heavens languish together with the earth
> The earth lies polluted under its inhabitants
> For they have transgressed the laws
> Violated the statutes
> Broken the everlasting covenant.
> Therefore a curse devours the earth
> And its inhabitants suffer for their guilt
> Therefore the inhabitants of the earth are scorched
> And few men are left
>
> (Isa. 24.4–6)

In the Book of Revelation, John saw beyond the disaster to the time when creation would be renewed, the Kingdom of God would be established on earth, and the destroyers would themselves be destroyed. When the first Christians prayed: 'Thy kingdom come, Thy will be done on earth as it is in heaven,' John's vision was the context for that prayer, spelling out how it would happen. Voices in heaven announced the Kingdom and the 24 elders affirmed what was unfolding before them.

---

1 Written 1958–62; published London: Hamilton, 1963.

1

The kingdom of the world has become the kingdom of our LORD and of his
Christ . . .
A the time for the dead to be judged,
    B for rewarding thy servants the prophets and saints,
    B and those who fear thy name both great and small,
A and for destroying the destroyers of the earth.

(Rev. 11.15, 18)

The ABBA structure of the last four lines shows that the servants of the
LORD were the prophets, the saints and those who feared the name of
the LORD; and that the 'dead' who faced the judgement were those
who destroyed the earth. These were the spiritually dead, those of
whom Jesus said: 'Leave the dead to bury their own dead' (Mt. 8.22;
Lk. 9.60), and Luke contrasted them with those who proclaimed
the Kingdom. The original vision of the Kingdom ranked together the
spiritually dead and the destroyers of the earth. The destruction of the
earth is a spiritual problem.

But how would the destroyers be destroyed? Here again, the Book
of Revelation has vivid images that have caught the imagination of
Christian artists over the centuries. The King of kings and LORD of
lords rides from heaven on a white horse, followed by his angel army.
He has a sharp sword to smite the nations, but the sword is *in his
mouth* – to symbolize teaching (Rev. 19.11–16). He will shepherd the
nations with an iron rod (Rev. 19.15, translating literally). John's image
here derives from Isaiah's description of the One who has received the
Spirit of the LORD: 'He shall smite the earth with the rod of his mouth,
and with the breath of his lips he shall slay the wicked' (Isa. 11.4b).
It would be a battle of beliefs, or, as we might say nowadays, a conflict
of ideologies. Nor would it be an arbitrary exercise of power: it was
power exercised on behalf of the poor and the meek. 'With righteousness shall he judge the poor, and decide with equity for the meek of
the earth' (Isa. 11.4a). The destroyers of the earth would be destroyed
by his teaching.

The battle, no matter how vividly described, was a battle of ideologies. Isaiah also described how the Warrior was prepared for this
battle; he was given the sevenfold Spirit. 'The Spirit of the LORD
shall rest upon him, the spirit of wisdom and understanding, the spirit
of counsel and might, the spirit of knowledge and the fear of the LORD'
(Isa. 11.2). All these gifts of the Spirit alter ways of knowing and
thinking; they change the mind. The empowered warrior thinks differently, and so acts differently. The result is a world in harmony, because
the world has a different attitude to knowledge – or even, different

knowledge. Isaiah's oracle ends: 'They shall not hurt or destroy in all my holy mountain; but the earth shall be full of the knowledge of the LORD as the waters cover the sea' (Isa. 11.9).

It is clear from these three passages from Isaiah and Revelation that the Bible addresses the same situation as contemporary environmentalists and economists, and even asks the same questions, but understands those questions differently and gives answers in terms of visions and symbols drawn from, and set in, the Jerusalem temple. The vision and its symbols are the key to their world view.

RE-VISION

John Zizioulas, speaking to the Symposium *Religion, Science and the Environment,* set out the distinction between *ethos* – the shared symbols (perhaps one might add the shared vision) that unite a group of people – and *ethics,* which traditionally have been based on reason, the consideration of what is right. 'Ethics has to do with principles worked out consciously or even rationally, and perhaps intellectually, whereas ethos relates to symbols, emerging from shared everyday experience in a particular community. Such symbols unite a particular community in a common attitude towards life.' Religious leaders and scientists, he said, 'must be ready to propose not simply an ethic but an ethos, and to root [our] ethical demands deep in human existence and not simply in human behaviour . . .'[2] The biblical vision for the environment is the ethos that underlies any Christian environmental ethic. Other approaches run the risk of adopting secular positions and dressing them up with a few biblical texts. They are like the seed that was not sown in good soil: some was devoured, some died because it had no depth of root, and some was choked by thorns (Mk 4.2–8).

One of the wise teachers of Israel observed: 'Where there is no vision, the people perish . . .' (Prov. 29.18 AV). A more literal translation would be: 'Where there is no vision, the people unravel . . .' The meaning is clear: without a shared vision which keeps all things together, there is no basis to inspire action. Christian attitudes to the environment must be rooted in the vision and the symbols of the Christian community. Nobody can prove a vision, and yet nobody can make a decision without one. What we choose is what we want

---

2 J. Zizioulas 'Towards an Environmental Ethic' in *The Adriatic Sea. A Sea at Risk, a Unity of Purpose,* Athens: Religion, Science and the Environment, 2003, pp. 93–101.

to be or to achieve. *For those people who have the luxury of choice,* something – often unacknowledged – determines why one option is chosen rather than another. It will certainly be the culture that has shaped their attitudes to life, and then it may be price or quality or source, or something else. Advertising and other pressures try to influence the decision-making process – for some people this will be a counterculture – offering another vision and another self-image, creating a 'need', and then making a sale. The action reveals the true ethos, the true self-image, what those people really believe about themselves and what they aspire to be. John described them as either servants of the LORD or destroyers of the earth. Actions result from the choice of vision, and with a different vision, they would have made different choices.

A contemporary secular observer might say that the reason the environment is changing rapidly is that there are increased amounts of carbon dioxide in the atmosphere and pollutants in the oceans. Data would be presented, the sources of those emissions and pollutants identified, and the consequences of their presence set out in terms of economic, social and political consequences. High-level conferences would follow; scientists would suggest ways to alter the situation, and politicians, influenced by economics and the prospect of the next election, would find reasons why such changes were not possible, or only possible much later and in a much reduced way. Or the matter would be overtaken by other more imminent pressures. Diamond noted in his book *Collapse*: 'Governments . . . regularly operate on a short-term focus . . . A friend of mine . . . found [in 2000] that our government's new leaders had what he termed a "90-day focus": they talked only about those problems with the potential to cause disaster within the next 90 days.'[3] Others have a different sense of priorities: 'Climate change is not an issue that allows the luxury of academic debates and the delay of long over due action.'[4]

The first Global Environment Outlook Report published by the United Nations Environment Programme in 1997 summarized thus:

> Significant environmental problems remain deeply embedded in the socio-economic fabric of all societies in all regions. Progress towards a sustainable

3 J. Diamond, *Collapse. How Societies Choose to Fail or Survive*, London: Penguin, 2005, p. 434.

4 'Moving Beyond Kyoto with Equity, Justice and Solidarity'. World Council of Churches discussion paper, November 2004.

future is just too slow. A sense of urgency is lacking. Internationally and nationally, the funds and political will are insufficient to halt further global environmental degradation and to address the most pressing environmental issues – *even though the technology and knowledge are available to do so.*[5]

There is the skill, but not the will. Such observations have been all too easy to find for a long time. John Taylor, in his important study *Enough is Enough* published as long ago as 1975, gave this warning:

> If this devastation of the delicate balance of nature has been carried on largely through ignorance, one might hope that the new knowledge might bring new sense. Unhappily, however, we are not dealing with sense, but with that which is insensate. For a long time men have known well enough what the score was if they continued unchecked in the modern methods . . .

He went on to describe marine life endangered by industrialized fishing.[6] More recently, Paul Stiles found this in a review of books in *The New York Times* in 2004:

> Why have Americans failed to face up to the evidence of global warming? . . . Short term interest is a powerful buffer against reality. So is the lobbying of the fossil fuel industries and the complacency of an administration that lives in thrall to them . . . What stands in the way is custom, ignorance, sloth, greed and fear . . . We continue to live in the assumption that we can ride out the changes without changing ourselves, coasting, as we have always coasted, on the historic wave of human development . . .[7]

Stiles commented: '*The true puzzle is human nature.* In every one of these accounts [that is, the books reviewed] of climate change and environmental degradation, the authors note the inertia of the global system.'[8]

Biblical prophets such as Isaiah or John would address the same question differently. Instead of: 'Why is the environment changing?' they would ask: 'Why is the creation collapsing?' Their reply would be: creation is collapsing due to human choices. People have chosen to ignore the divinely given law, and the prophets called such actions sin. There were lifestyles that were out of harmony with the Creator's laws,

---

5   GEO 1, Executive Summary: Global Overview.

6   J. V. Taylor, *Enough is Enough*, London: SCM Press, 1975, p. 32.

7   V. Klinkenborg, 'Chronicle Environment; Be Afraid, Be Very Afraid', *The New York Times*, May 30th 2004, section 7, p. 19.

8   P. Stiles, *Is the American Dream Killing You?*, New York: HarperCollins, 2005, p. 151, my emphases.

and these laws were not negotiable. The prophets and wise ones of Israel had a vision of the creation held in existence by a system of divine bonds, and when these were broken, creation began to disintegrate. Since human society and the natural order were bound in one system, human behaviour could and did contribute to the destruction of creation. Instead of data about emissions and pollutants, the prophets would declare what human sins had caused the creation to collapse. Or, as we say nowadays, what lifestyle choices had impacted adversely upon the environment.

The vision of the biblical prophets was creation held in place by a web of bonds, which they described as the covenant, meaning the 'binding'. Whatever broke those bonds was not an alternative life style; it was sin – the ethic arising from the ethos. In his vision, Isaiah saw a curse devouring the earth. In other parts of this vision he saw the social and economic system of his time collapsing and everyone affected: ' . . . as with the maid, so with her mistress, as with the creditor, so with the debtor . . .' (Isa. 24.2). Crops fail – 'the vine languishes' (Isa. 24.7) – 'and the gladness of the earth is banished' (Isa. 24.11). There are floods and earthquakes: 'the windows of heaven are opened, and the foundations of the earth tremble . . .' (Isa. 24.18). Why? Because the earth's transgression lies heavy upon her (Isa. 24.20). As with so many sayings of the prophets, there are other meanings echoing here. The Hebrew words could also mean: 'Her rebellion is honoured upon her.' The Greek translator, working in the second century BCE, understood it to mean: 'Lawlessness prevails upon the earth.'

Nowadays, a disaster is likely to prompt the question: 'Why does God allow such things to happen?', but the ancient prophets had a different view. When Joel saw his people suffering disasters – locusts, drought, crop failure, enemy invasions (Joel 1.4–2.11) – he did not call in question the existence of God. 'Rend your hearts and not your garments,' he proclaimed in the name of the LORD. 'Return to the LORD your God' (Joel 2.13). Joel's world view may seem hopelessly unrealistic today, but set in the broader context of the biblical vision for the creation, it is one to ponder. Many of the eco-disasters of our time are the result of human activity, choices made without the biblical vision, and so choices made with a vision other than that of the original unity. The alternative vision or visions have not proved to be valuable or even viable. Presented as freedom – the free market, democracy, consumer choice – they have produced what Paul called the creation going nowhere ('subjected to futility', Rom. 8.20), and in 'bondage to decay'.

It was long ago recognized by religious leaders that the real cause of the environmental crisis was spiritual, resulting from human attitudes towards the world we live in and to the other living beings who share the same planet. The Ecumenical Patriarch Bartholomew I has made this the theme of his international symposia *Religion, Science and the Environment*: 'We often refer to an environmental crisis' he said, 'but the real crisis lies not in the environment, but in the human heart. The fundamental problem is to be found not outside but inside ourselves, not in the ecosystem, but in the way we think.'[9] 'What is required is an act of repentance on our part and a renewed attempt to view ourselves, one another, and the world around us, within the perspective of the divine design for creation.'[10] Pope Benedict XVI, in his inauguration homily on April 24th 2005, said:

> There is the desert of God's darkness, the emptiness of souls no longer aware of their dignity, or the goal of human life. The external deserts of the world are growing, because the internal deserts have become so vast. Therefore the earth's treasures no longer serve to build God's garden for all to live in, but they have been made to serve the powers of exploitation and destruction.

A spiritual problem needs a spiritual solution, one determined by the heart. Cardinal Newman, writing in the midst of the nineteenth-century debates about science and religion, said this:

> We have to take [science's] facts and to give them a meaning and to draw our own conclusions from them. The heart is commonly reached, *not through the reason but through the imagination,* by means of direct impressions, by the testimony of facts and events, by history, by description . . . Many a man will live and die upon a dogma; no man will be a martyr for a conclusion.[11]

The biblical vision for the creation appeals to the heart and to the imagination, and offers what would nowadays be called a 'theory of everything', including the special role of human beings in the complexity of creation.

---

9 HAH Bartholomew I, Ecumenical Patriarch, 'Sacrifice. The Missing Dimension', in *The Adriatic Sea. A Sea at Risk, A Unity of Purpose,* Athens: Religion, Science and the Environment, 2003, p. 218.

10 The Venice Declaration, 2002, in *The Adriatic Sea,* p. 226.

11 J. H. Newman, *An Essay in Aid of a Grammar of Assent,* 2nd edn, London: Burns and Oates, 1870, pp. 89–90.

In the Book of Revelation, John recorded his vision of the Kingdom established and everything put right: the destroyers of the earth destroyed, and the servants of the LORD rewarded. A sign appeared in the temple: a woman clothed with the sun, whose son was taken up to the throne of God in heaven. The woman was Wisdom, whose sacrament in the ancient temple had been the anointing oil. The anointed ones were her children, those human beings who received from their Mother the gift of wisdom that enabled them to see the world differently. She opened their eyes. John then saw the battle to establish on earth the Kingdom proclaimed in heaven. It was a battle between truth and deception, described as the archangel Michael and his army of angels driving Satan the great deceiver from heaven (Rev. 11.19–12.10). Satan's first appearance in the biblical story had been in Eden, when he had tempted Eve to take the forbidden knowledge that led to the loss of Eden and a curse upon the earth (Gen. 3.14–9). He had appeared as a snake, the ancient symbol of Wisdom, and this was his first deception in the biblical story. Paul knew that Satan could disguise himself as an angel of light (2 Cor. 11.14).

Creation and its distress are themes running all through the Bible, from the first disobedience of the Garden of Eden, to the vision in the Book of Revelation where everything is restored. Scholarly study of the Old Testament, however, has tended to emphasize the sacred history and to neglect the other aspects of Scripture such as the ongoing concern for the creation. The call of Abraham, Moses and the Exodus from Egypt, conquering Canaan, building the temple in Jerusalem and the story of the Davidic kings, exile and restoration are, for many people, what the Old Testament is about. Thus the cosmologist Paul Davies, in his brief survey of the history of 'reason and belief', represented the Hebrew Scriptures as based on God's revelation through history, 'as expressed in the historical record of the Old Testament, and represented most obviously in Genesis with the account of God's creation of the universe at a finite moment in the past. And yet the Jewish God was still declared to be transcendent and immutable'.[12] It is true that there is little in the history books that could be the basis for creation theology, except perhaps Adam and Eve, the promise to Noah after the flood (Gen. 9.12–7), and Solomon's songs and wise sayings about the creation (1 Kgs 4.32–3), but Davies' final observation –

---

12 P. Davies, *The Mind of God. Science and the Search for Ultimate Meaning*, London: Penguin, 1993, p. 36.

that God was still declared to be transcendent – shows that he sensed gaps in what he had been told about the Old Testament.

The missing element was the so-called Wisdom writings in the Hebrew Scriptures, which bear witness to another tradition.[13] The wise ones may have been the priests; scholars have reached no conclusion as to the origin of these writings and their characteristic theology, but they do recognize that, in common with similar writings from neighbouring cultures, they assume a world order[14] and an all-seeing deity. They gave harmony as their reason for observing the Sabbath: 'In six days the LORD made heaven and earth, the sea and all that is in them, and rested on the seventh day; therefore the LORD blessed the Sabbath day and hallowed it' (Exod. 20.11). Their literary forms are found throughout the other books of the Old Testament – clearly they shared a common culture – and yet they mention neither the history of Israel nor the Sinai covenant. There is a widespread suspicion that the current Wisdom texts in the Hebrew Scriptures have been drastically edited, and prophets such as Jeremiah attacked 'the false pen of the scribes' who had rejected the word of the LORD and could no longer claim to be wise' (Jer. 8.8–9). We shall return to this question of Wisdom.[15] For now, suffice it to say that the two traditions existed side by side, and those who emphasized Moses and the Exodus claimed that the Law had superseded Wisdom, implying that Wisdom was the older way. In the complex symbolism of the ancient storytellers, they said that Moses the Lawgiver had replaced Miriam, *his older sister*, who represented Wisdom.[16]

Those who emphasized and promoted the Moses traditions set out their characteristic viewpoint in Deuteronomy. They declared: '[The Law] will be your wisdom' (Deut. 4.6), that is, the law will replace the older Wisdom. Their form of the fourth commandment was based on memories of the Exodus: 'Observe the Sabbath day . . . You shall remember that you were a servant in the land of Egypt, and the LORD your God brought you out thence with a mighty hand and an outstretched arm; therefore the LORD God commanded you to keep the Sabbath day' (Deut. 5.12, 15). These were the teachers who

---

13 In the Hebrew Scriptures they are Proverbs, Ecclesiastes and Job. In the Greek Old Testament there are also the Wisdom of Solomon, the Wisdom of Jesus ben Sira and Tobit.

14 The Egyptians called this *maat.*

15 See below, pp. 241–3.

16 Thus *Exodus Rabbah* XLVIII.4.

appealed to history and promoted nationalism; they denied the vision of God (Deut. 4.12); they were unhappy with any mystical theology (Deut. 29.29); and they left no account of the creation and had no place for angels. The land was a gift to them in return for their obedience, and 'All these blessings shall come upon you' (Deut.28. 2) was the preface to a catalogue of prosperity. Some of their laws showed respect for the justice and balance of creation – it was forbidden to fell fruit trees even in time of war (Deut. 20.19–20), to take a mother bird and her eggs or young (Deut. 22.6–7) or to muzzle the ox who threshed the grain (Deut. 25.4) – suggesting that there was more to the basis of their world view than memories of the Exodus, but 'prosperity as reward' could and did give rise to the expectation of constant progress measured in terms of increased consumption. 'Prosperity Gospel' is a recent example of this.

The creation-based element did not disappear. It re-emerged in the middle ages as the Kabbalah, a name meaning 'tradition'. Working with the usual paradigm – that the original religion of Israel was that of Moses and sacred history – scholars of the Kabbalah have written about the re-emergence of 'age-old archaic elements.' The distinguished Jewish scholar Gershom Scholem made some interesting observations about the difference between a history-based religion and this 'other', and they are relevant here:

> This history saturated ritual was accompanied by no magical action. The rites of remembrance produce no *effect*, they create no natural bond between the Jew and his natural environment, and what they conjure up, without the slightest gesture of conjuration, is the memory, the community of generations, and the identification of the pious with the experience of the founding generation which received the Revelation. The ritual of Rabbinical Judaism makes nothing happen and *transforms* nothing.[17]

The same can be said of the Christian history-based approach to the Bible. Some of the great controversies over the Eucharist have centred on this very issue: remembering or transformation. The temple insights preserved in the Kabbalah will prove very relevant to this enquiry, because Christianity also grew from the creation-based element of Hebrew tradition, and the Church saw itself as the new temple.

Modern biblical scholarship – and especially Protestant Old Testament scholarship – has been preoccupied with 'the Bible as History',

---

17 G. Scholem, *On the Kabbalah and Its Symbolism*, London: Routledge, 1965, p. 121, emphases in the original.

and has concentrated on the stories of Moses and the Exodus, on the kings of Israel and Judah, and how archaeology can (or cannot) show that these stories are true. B. W. Anderson, in his *The Living World of the Old Testament*, a book that was foundation reading for most students in the second half of the twentieth century, wrote this: '(The) biblical faith . . . is fundamentally historical in character. It is concerned with events, social relationships and concrete situations, not abstract values and ideas existing in a timeless realm.'[18] Another influential scholar was G. E. Wright, whose *Biblical Archaeology* also became a standard work in that period. He wrote: 'The Bible, unlike the other religious literature of the world, is not centred on a series of moral, spiritual and liturgical teachings, but in the story of a people who lived in a certain time and place.'[19] Whatever had happened to the Law, the Prophets and the Psalms in their Old Testament? Wright, and others, were concerned to distinguish biblical theology from the world of Canaanite mythology. Israel was little interested in nature, said Wright, in a book entitled *The Old Testament against its Environment*: 'The basis [of Israel's religious literature] was history, not nature . . .,' the angels and concern for creation were signs of 'the paganizing of Yahwism.'[20] If the religion of Israel is defined in one particular way, it is easy to identify 'other' elements as alien accretions. The conclusion follows from the premise.

The emphasis on history, and the power of the scholarly networks who promoted it, has had serious consequences for biblical study and for the churches, especially in the area now recognized as crucial: the biblical teaching about the creation. It was, then, hardly surprising that when the world began to wake up to the question of the environment – 1970 was World Environment Year – Bible users had very little to contribute. Christians were very slow to adopt a responsible attitude towards the current environmental crisis. It is this 'history' school that has dominated popular perception of the Old Testament – as shown by the conclusion of Davies mentioned above – and it is the creation theology – living in harmony with the Creator – that we need to recover.

18 B. W. Anderson, *The Living World of the Old Testament*, 4th edn., Harlow: Longman, 1988, p. 13.

19 G. E. Wright, *Biblical Archaeology*, revised edn., London: Duckworth, 1962, p. 17.

20 G. E. Wright, *The Old Testament against Its Environment*, London: SCM, 1950, p. 28, 36.

Being careless with the truth, as Alister McGrath observed, opens the way to enslavement by falsehoods.[21]

Things are changing, and scholars are reflecting on how creation theology came to be so neglected. Apart from the emphasis on the salvation history of the chosen people, and the aversion to anything Canaanite on the grounds that it was a fertility cult or nature worship, there had been an increasing tendency to leave the natural world to scientists, 'not least in view of the controversies generated by the creationists'. There has also been the growth of political theology centred on the liberation of human beings (but not of creation); the emphasis on the other worldly and 'spiritual' dimensions of religious life; the widely believed 'end-of-the-world scenarios, wherein God is soon going to blow everything up anyway'; the neglect of the Old Testament in the teaching and preaching of the Church; and the evident patriarchalism in biblical interpretation that stressed the intervention of mighty acts, rather than the gentler themes of creation and blessing.[22]

There is an urgent need for new thinking, for Christians to articulate their characteristic views in the current crisis, because now, as never before, what we believe about the creation is a matter of life and death. It is *forty years* since Hugh Montefiore observed: 'It is small wonder that theology is regarded by so many as irrelevant if it does not concern itself with what is happening to the real world in which we all live.'[23] The Bible teaching is clear: the Kingdom is established on earth by destroying the destroyers of the earth. So how do we help to bring about what we pray for? No single text sets out the biblical view of creation, and the relevance of a talking snake and a missing rib is not immediately obvious to problems of the third millennium. The Bible does, however, have a beautiful and sophisticated account of the creation and the role of human beings within it. It is, in a very real way, a theory of everything: politics, economics, social cohesion, justice, the integrity and the security of the creation. Reconstructing this biblical vision of the creation entails a journey into the very heart of the Hebrew genius and the Christian good news.

21 A. McGrath, *Glimpsing the Face of God*, Oxford: Lion, 2002, p. 37.

22 These are some of the reasons listed in T. E. Fretheim, *God and World in the Old Testament*, Nashville: Abingdon Press, 2005, pp. ix–x.

23 H. W. Montefiore, *The Question Mark. The End of Homo Sapiens?* London: Collins, 1969, p. 44.

Reading Biblical Texts

The Bible is the record of revelation, received and recorded over many centuries; it has many human authors, and many contexts. Over time there have been interpreters of the original texts, all trying to relate biblical teaching to their own situations. As a result, a vast amount of material has accumulated, fascinating as a historical record, but often of no immediate relevance today. Although 'natural theology' and biblical 'creation theology' are different ways of theology, what McGrath wrote recently of natural theology applies also to biblical creation theology.

> The lengthening shadows of half forgotten historical debates and cultural circumstances have shaped preconceptions and forged situation specific approaches to natural theology that have proved singularly ill-adapted to the contemporary theological situation . . . there is much to be said for beginning all over again . . .[24]

And so we return to the sources in the quest for biblical creation theology, which for Christians must be the Bible as it was and as it was understood in the time of Jesus.

This is not easy: the text of the Hebrew Bible that we use today differs in some important ways from the one (or ones) known in the time of Jesus. The great Isaiah scroll found at Qumran, for example, although remarkably like the text used today, has a few differences that are important for Christians.[25] And even where the consonants are the same, the way of reading them may have been different. Rabbi Joḥanan ben Zakkai, a younger contemporary of Jesus, understood Ezekiel 48.35 in the same way as did John, but not in the way it is read today. John read the verse as 'From that time, the name of the city shall be "the LORD"', whereas today it is read as : 'The name of the city henceforth shall be "The LORD is there"'. What else might we be reading differently? The great Jewish commentary on Leviticus, probably compiled in the fifth century CE, but preserving older Palestinian material, says: that 'A law will go forth from me' (Isa. 51.4), was understood to mean 'A new law will go forth from me,'[26] and this was

---

24 A. E. McGrath, *The Open Secret. A New Vision for Natural Theology,* Oxford: Blackwell, 2008, p. 3.

25 See my book *The Great High Priest,* London: T&T Clark, 2003, pp. 301–6.

26 *Leviticus Rabbah* XIII.3.

eventually understood to mean that the LORD would show the true meaning of the Hebrew letters.[27] What then did Mark mean when he recorded the reaction to Jesus' teaching: 'They were astonished at his teaching, for he taught them as one who had authority, and not as the scribes' (Mk 1.22). And why were other meanings 'fixed' into the text when the vowels were added, other meanings that have passed into the translations used by the Church? Recovering the Bible Jesus knew and how he understood it is fraught with problems.

'What would Jesus drive?' was a successful way to make people stop and think about their driving habits, pollution and consumption. This awareness campaign initiated by the Evangelical Environmental Network in 2002, emphasized that transportation was a moral issue: 'Pollution from cars hurts people and the rest of God's creation.' 'Tailpipe pollution from cars and trucks accounts for almost one third of outdoor air pollution in the United States, including approximately half the pollution that creates smog.' A selfish choice of vehicle was no way to show love for your neighbour. There were predictable hostile responses in some sources: Jesus would have chosen a donkey, he would have walked, and so forth. But the question raised is important: it highlighted the need for Christians to consider how fundamental biblical principles apply to the way we live today. 'Love of neighbour' is an obvious and simple principle to apply.

For some Christians, however, care of the creation was a less obvious duty, since they believed that the end of the material creation was imminent. A recognizable parody of the Evangelical position was set out by Peter Harris in his response to the Evangelical Declaration on the Care of Creation (1994):

> The conventional argument is that now that creation has fallen, God has lost interest in everything but salvaging the souls of human beings: all we need to know is how to live in the creation meantime, and to extract what we can of God's good gifts from it before it all burns in the final judgement.[28]

This expectation of the final fiery judgement has encumbered much Christian thinking about the environment by people, who, knowing they will die one day, would not hesitate to see a doctor if they were ill. The *Preaching of Peter*, an early Christian text quoted by Clement of

27 G. Scholem, *On the Kabbalah and Its Symbolism*, p. 75.

28 Peter Harris, 'A New Look at Old Passages' in R. J. Berry, ed., *Care of Creation*, Leicester: InterVarsity Press, 2000, pp. 132–9, p. 134. This volume also has the text of the Declaration.

Alexandria, shows that the early Church was well aware that the creation was finite 'Know then that there is one God who made the beginning of all things, and holds the power of the end . . .'[29]

Nobody denies that the New Testament verses in 2 Peter about the judgement by fire are difficult, but this is because they are not clear, nor are there any other biblical texts for comparison if they are understood to mean the final destruction of all things. The cultural context of the time suggests that the fire of judgement would destroy evil so that the Kingdom could be established. Malachi likened the day of the LORD's judgement to a refiner's fire, purifying the sons of Levi (Mal. 3.2–4); and Jesus said that when the Kingdom was established, the devil and his angels would be sent to their fiery judgement (Mt. 25.41). John the Baptist spoke of the One to come who would gather his wheat into a granary, and then burn the chaff (Mt. 3.12). Paul knew that the day of the LORD would burn up evil and reveal the truth about each person's deeds (1 Cor. 3.12–5). John saw in his vision that when the Kingdom was established, the destroyers of the earth would be destroyed, presumably in the fire that Jesus prophesied for the devil and his angels (Rev. 11.18).

Establishing the Kingdom was the limit of the biblical vision, except for a few lines about the state beyond the Kingdom. Paul implies this with his enigmatic description of the Son triumphing over all his enemies, and then returning all things to the original Unity with the Father (1 Cor. 15. 24–28, if that is what v. 28 means). John saw 'the great white throne' at the end of the era of the Kingdom, when 'heaven and earth fled away and no place was found for them' (Rev. 20.11). Philo, the contemporary of the early Christian writers, set out what he saw as the two possibilities for the future:

> Nothing is so foolish as to raise the question whether the world is destroyed into non-existence. The point is whether it undergoes a transmutation from its ordered arrangement through the various forms and combinations of the elements, *stoicheia*, being resolved into one and the self same conformation, or being reduced into complete confusion as things are when broken or shattered.[30]

The future change would either be the disintegration of the covenant structure or its return to the original Unity.

29 Quoted in Clement, *Miscellanies* 6.5.

30 Philo, *Eternity* 6.

The overall biblical picture and contemporary Jewish evidence should perhaps be the context for reading 2 Peter, rather than the Zoroastrian or Stoic expectation of a final world conflagration. 'The day of judgement and the destruction of ungodly men' is clear enough (2 Pet.3.7), but 'the elements will be dissolved with fire' (2 Pet.3.10) is not. The most likely understanding is that elements, *stoicheia*, means what it meant for Paul: the hostile 'elemental spirits' from which Christians have been set free (Gal. 4.3; Col. 2.8, 20). Peter's picture of the judgement would then be the destruction of evil powers, 'destroying the destroyers of the earth' (Rev. 11.18). Nor is 'The earth and the works that are upon it will be burned up' (2 Pet. 3.10) the best attested reading in the ancient manuscripts, even though it is favoured by the English versions. The earliest texts[31] have 'the earth and the works on it will be found,' in the Hebrew sense of being caught for punishment: 'As the thief is ashamed when he is found . . .' (Jer. 2.26) or '[Babylon], you are found, you are caught' (Jer. 50.24). Peter would then be in agreement with Paul, that the fire would test the works of each person: 'Each man's work will become manifest; for the Day will disclose it, and the fire will test what sort of work each man has done' (1 Cor. 3.13).[32]

'What did Jesus think about the creation and the role of human beings in the creation?' is therefore an important question. Nothing is set out in the gospels and there are no easy-to-quote proof texts. We have to reconstruct what he and the first Christians could have believed, and see how this fits with the allusions and symbolism of the New Testament and the earliest Christian writings. This means drawing on all available contemporary evidence to illuminate the familiar texts, and, in effect, starting again. It is not wise to prejudge what could have been widely available and what were 'esoteric' texts, since our ideas of canon and Judaism are formed by the results of later labelling, and by using the canon of a later age we could be guilty of massive anachronism. As we shall see, it is unlikely that Jesus knew exactly the same Isaiah text as we use today,[33] or that he understood the first chapter of Genesis in the way that some creationists understand it today. People at that time were asking: How could there be days and nights before the sun was created on the fourth day? The Christians concluded from Psalm 90.4

31 Codex Sinaiticus, Codex Vaticanus.

32 For detailed discussion, see R. Bauckham, *Jude, 2 Peter*, Waco: Word Books, 1983, pp. 296–322.

33 See below, pp. 157–8.

that a day in the sight of God meant a thousand years: 'With the LORD, one day is as a thousand years, and a thousand years as one day' (2 Pet. 3.8). The *Letter of Barnabas*,[34] attributed to Barnabas, the Levite from Cyprus (Acts 4.36) who was a companion of Paul (Acts 13.2) shows this was widely believed: 'With him one day means a thousand years' (*Barn.* 15).

The truth of the Bible is not the same as literal accuracy, and real fundamentalism – holding fast to the truths of the Bible – is not literalism. The earliest Christian teachers found the truth of the Scriptures in many ways: in the fulfilment of prophecy, for example, and the symbolism of the temple and its rituals. The earliest detailed interpretation of the death and resurrection of Jesus was given in terms of the temple: the day of atonement was the pattern by which they came to understand what had happened (Heb. 9.11–14). So too with the actual shape of the temple: the outer part was symbolic of 'the present age', and the Holy Spirit revealed truths to them by means of the temple services (Heb. 9.8–10). Dionysius, for many centuries thought to be a first generation Christian (Acts 17.34)[35] and thus witness to the formative years of the Church, explained that some biblical images, especially the descriptions of heaven, were only a concession to the limits of the human mind. 'The Word of God makes use of poetic imagery when discussing these formless intelligences . . . using scriptural passages in a way, provided for us from the first, to uplift our mind in a manner suitable to our nature.'[36]

Irenaeus, bishop of Lyons at the end of the second century, was in touch with the apostolic teaching since he was a pupil of Polycarp, the martyr bishop of Smyrna who had been a disciple of John.[37] Irenaeus wrote a short summary of Christian teaching as it was in his time; he dealt first with the heavens and the angels, and said this was all encoded in teaching about the seven branched lamp, the temple menorah.[38] Early Christian teaching was based on temple symbolism – something that we have almost lost today. The temple furnishings were described in the Scriptures, but not explained. There is no indication in the Old Testament why the curtains, the lampstand or the incense had to be

34 Included in the fourth-century Sinai Codex, one of the oldest copies of the New Testament.

35 But now recognized as a fifth-century writer.

36 Dionysius, *Celestial Hierarchy* 137AB.

37 Eusebius, *Church History* 5.20.

38 Irenaeus, *Demonstration* 1–3.

made in a particular way. Origen, writing in the early third century, knew that all the temple furnishings described in Exodus had been symbolic of teaching that was known only to the high priests. This, he said, was why the furnishings were carefully wrapped and concealed before even the Levites were allowed to carry them in the desert (Num. 4. 4–15).[39] Any literalist reading of Numbers would probably not draw this conclusion, but Origen, the greatest biblical scholar in the early Church, taught that this was the true meaning of the passage. *And since the temple represented the creation, this high priestly teaching must have concerned the creation.*

The deeper way of reading Scripture was well known in the time of the first Christians. Philo, a contemporary of Jesus, described a religious community in northern Egypt known as the Therapeuts who studied the Scriptures 'allegorically'. His Greek text at this point is not entirely clear, but seems to mean: 'They think that the words of the literal text are symbols of something whose hidden nature is revealed by studying the underlying meaning.'[40] Eusebius, the bishop of Caesarea in Palestine, who studied in the great library there, was convinced that these Therapeuts were the earliest Christian communities. Many recent scholars have doubted this, but Eusebius knew a lot more about the early Church than we do, and he saw enough similarities to conclude that they had been Christian. Origen adopted their ascetic life style as well as their allegorical way of reading Scripture.[41] Whatever the truth of the matter, it is clear that the early Christians adopted a figurative way of reading the Old Testament, and attached great importance to the ritual and symbolism of the temple, which represented the creation.

Biblical scholarship in recent generations has concentrated on the 'pre-Bible',[42] trying to recover the sources and component parts of the ancient texts, and this is a fascinating occupation. Such investigation, however, was not part of the intellectual world of the first Christians, nor can it really be called theology; it is textual archaeology, a literary discipline. Essential for entering the world of the first Christians is

39 Origen, *On Numbers*, Homily 5.

40 Eusebius, *Church History*, 2.17; Philo, *On the Contemplative Life*, 21–38, 65–90, this quotation being F. H. Colson's translation of the obscure Greek original of #28 in LCL *Philo* vol.X.

41 Eusebius, *Church History*, 6.3

42 The term used by J. L. Kugel in *Traditions of the Bible. A Guide to the Bible as It was at the Start of the Common Era*, Cambridge, MA: Harvard University Press, 1998, p. 894.

recovering what the Old Testament was in their time, the mixture of ancient text and interpretation, their way of reading and understanding scripture. 'The pioneers of modern biblical scholarship did not, by and large, address themselves to the subject of ancient biblical interpretation, save, of course, to denounce its conclusions as fanciful and wrong headed.' They were looking for the real Bible, which they understood to be the earliest component parts that they could recover. It is now being recognized that 'the decisive part played by the anonymous biblical interpreters of the centuries just before and just after the start of the common era must ultimately be recognised in any new disposition of biblical theology's forces.'[43]

Anyone coming to these biblical texts with no knowledge of the fabric of interpretation that had been woven around them, and their system of images and wordplay would ask, quite rightly: what is all this about? The windows of heaven and the pillars of the earth are not expressions used today. A lamb with seven eyes and seven horns (Rev. 5.6) is a creature from science fiction. In the Bible, these images belong with talking snakes and missing ribs; they are part of a pre-philosophical way of describing the world. The strange visions of the biblical prophets and wise ones do in fact point to a beautiful, sophisticated and coherent account of the creation and human lifestyles, with an extraordinary relevance to our present situation.

Much harm has been done by those with well-intentioned but misguided commitment to the actual words of the biblical text, and their loyal refusal to study anything other than the biblical texts. Such good-hearted people call themselves fundamentalists, when they are in fact literalists, reading the symbolic and visionary texts of the Bible in a way that would have been strange to their authors because they have been wrenched from their literary and cultural context. The true fundamentalists are all those who accept the fundamentals of the biblical world view, not in the sense of a flat earth floating on water, with the windows of heaven opening to allow rain to fall, which used to appear in text books as a diagram of the biblical world view. The view that underlies the Bible recognizes that the world is the work of the Creator. The biblical world view is a vision of the unity of all things, and how the visible material world relates to another dimension of existence that unites all things into one divinely ordained system known as the eternal covenant, the creation covenant.

---

43 J. L. Kugel, *Traditions of the Bible. A Guide to the Bible as it was at the Start of the Common Era*, Cambridge, MA: Harvard University Press, 1998.

Even more disastrous has been the rush to appear relevant and modern by adopting the so-called postmodern approach to biblical studies, well defined by John Barton:

> Applied to literary and cultural theory, post-modernism is to be understood as a hypothesis about epistemology and the philosophy of knowledge. It maintains that knowledge does not form a unified body of data, held together by girders of shared scientific or humanistic vocabulary and a framework of striving for universal truth. Post modernists express this by saying that there are no true meta narratives (sometimes master narratives), only piece meal information, bits and pieces of temporarily valid ideas.[44]

It may well be true that we cannot give an overall view of the literary history of the biblical texts; but it is possible to glimpse the 'vision', the 'meta-narrative' that is fundamental to the biblical view of creation. The authors of Genesis 1 were probably priests, who began with the vision of creation they had inherited. *Their portrayal of an ordered cosmos helped to create one, and their liturgies maintained it.* This was the function of any temple in the ancient near east: it represented the identity of the community and was the epitome of their social order.[45] There was no idea of religion as a private matter, or the position promoted so much today, of no binding ideology to be the structure of society. Without any binding ideology, as is all too clear, we live in a fragmented, even broken, society, that cannot be healed by retail therapy.

The biblical world view was very like that depicted by Walter Wink:

> The world is, to a degree at least, the way we imagine it. When we think it to be godless and soulless, it becomes for us precisely that. And we ourselves are then made over into the image of godless and soulless selves. If we want to be made over into the image of God – to become what God created us to be – then we need to purge our souls of materialism and the other world views that block us from realising the life God so eagerly wants us to have.[46]

The storytellers of ancient Israel knew that our attitude to the creation is shaped by the way we speak about it. If we use only the language of politics or economics, that will shape our attitude. If we have only a few words to choose from, we are limited in what we can express and,

---

44 J. Barton, *Reading the Old Testament. Method in Biblical Study*, London: Darton, Longman and Todd, 1996, p. 234.

45 N. Wyatt, *Space and Time in the Religious Life of the Near East*, Sheffield: Sheffield Academic Press, 2001, p. 162.

46 W. Wink, *The Powers that Be*, New York and London: Doubleday, 1998, p. 14.

in the end, how we can think. George Orwell, in his book *Nineteen Eighty-four*, described a frightening future world in which thought was controlled by reducing the words available for use. He imagined a time when only one way of thinking was allowed, and the language was altered to make sure that words for other ideas were removed. Other ways of thinking became impossible, because nobody could understand the words. Some of these words could still be found in strange old books (like the Bible?) but nobody could think the thoughts because they did not know the words.[47] Strong pressures from influential but often unrepresentative voices in the media have attempted to banish religious language from public discourse. Writing in the midst of the economic crisis that began in late 2008, a well-known journalist commented: 'The theological language which would have recognised the collapse of the credit bubble as "the wages of sin", the come-uppance for prodigious profligacy, has become unusable. But the come-uppance has come, nevertheless.'[48] Only time will show the impact on society, and on the whole creation, of this refusal to use theological or even moral language. So far, the signs are not good. The latest edition of the Oxford Junior Dictionary has even removed such dangerous words as bishop, disciple and sin. 'Vineeta Gupta of OUP said that the changes had been made to reflect the UK's multicultural society.'[49]

Nobody can prove a vision, but this biblical vision of the creation underlies the Christian culture of Europe (and elsewhere), and has nowadays been largely lost due to aggressive secularism, and the mistaken notion that scientific method is the only path to truth. Many biblical scholars and theologians have tried to 'modernise' their methods by turning to history and archaeology to prove that the Bible was true because it was historically accurate. This has been another disaster. Since the discoveries of the nineteenth century, some biblical scholars have reacted to the new claims of science, by forcing the story of creation in Genesis into the new time scales proposed by geologists and zoologists. So concerned were they to protect the literal truth of the words that one major fact was overlooked: Genesis was the product of a pre-philosophical culture. The six days of creation was a vision of the Creator's works, as we shall see, and not the historical record of something that happened before there was anyone around to record it.

47 G. Orwell, *Nineteen Eighty-four*, London: Secker and Warburg, 1949.

48 Robert Skidelsky 'Where do we go from here?' in *Prospect Magazine*, 154, January 2009.

49 *The Church Times*, 19/26 December, 2008, p. 6.

All those conflicts in so-called fundamentalist Christian communities have been misguided. Even if the story of the six-day creation was literally true, the story had a function in the biblical revelation other than being a record of history.

The biblical world view is assumed throughout the Bible, and so it was the background to early Christian thought. The creation stories in Genesis are the most obvious expression of the view, but they are by no means the only texts. The design of the desert tabernacle that Moses was told to build reflected the pattern of creation, as did the design of Solomon's temple. The worship in both tabernacle and temple was about the well-being of creation and human society. The shape of the tabernacle/temple expressed a world view that had God enthroned at the centre, built so that the LORD had a holy place in the midst, not just in the midst of the tabernacle/temple, but in the midst of their whole world view (Exod. 25.8). The pattern of the worship there both shaped and expressed the attitude of the worshippers towards the creation.

Stephen Hawking began his best selling book *A Brief History of Time*, with the story of a public lecture on astronomy and the structure of the universe, after which an old lady corrected the speaker. His theory was completely wrong; the world was a flat plate, she said, supported on a giant tortoise, with others underneath it. It was 'turtles all the way down.'[50] It would be a great mistake to dismiss the biblical world view as another 'tower of turtles' proposal. It may well be that in context – whatever it was – the old lady's description was part of a highly sophisticated world view, but there it served, out of context, to introduce a book on recent theories about cosmology. The author did graciously admit that his current proposals might also, one day, seem as 'ridiculous as a tower of tortoises.'

So too with biblical imagery. The Hebrews communicated with parables, stories, symbols and word play, not with data and scientific papers. Jesus' parables are some of the best-known texts in the Bible, but the truth they convey is not in their literal accuracy. Jesus may have been recounting recent incidents to illustrate his teaching, or he may simply have created stories to help people remember what he was teaching. What if there never was a good Samaritan? Would his teaching be invalid? Could all later sermons about helping those in need be dismissed as based on something we now know to be untrue? Knowing

---

50 S. Hawking, *A Brief History of Time. From the Big Bang to Black Holes*. London: Bantam, 1988, p. 1.

the story to be fiction, could we then reason that helping people in need is an outmoded world view, the product of an ancient superstition? Something similar is done with the Genesis stories, and accepted without comment. *No amount of research into the age of the universe or the origin of life on earth can invalidate the special truths conveyed by those stories.*

The purpose of the stories was (and is) to address other questions: what is the value and purpose of the creation, where does each individual person fit into its vast complexity, and how can each person recognize that the present state is not as good as it could be – what has gone wrong? Fred Hoyle concluded his popular book *The Nature of the Universe* by saying: 'Perhaps the most majestic feature of our whole existence is that while our intelligences are powerful enough to penetrate deeply into the evolution of this quite incredible universe we still have not the smallest clue as to our own fate.'[51] He had been describing the Steady State model of the universe, and coined the phrase Big Bang to describe and reject the alternative models.[52] The model he rejected was later accepted as more likely than the one he was advocating, and so, in one generation, cosmology moved on. Nevertheless, he was sure that the biblical view of creation was 'the merest daub, compared with the sweeping grandeur of the picture revealed by modern science'.[53] The ancient Hebrews were ignorant of modern science, and so, he was confident, their ideas about the creation could be dismissed. But he was still left with the question that the Bible addressed: what is the place of the human being in this incredible universe?

Science has radically reorientated our society, and so 'the biblical perspective of the world seems largely irrelevant . . . Any comprehensive philosophy based on ancient concepts faces a hard task in adapting to the space age.'[54] Thus the cosmologist. But is this necessarily so? *The ancient concepts of the Bible, properly understood, are remarkably relevant to our present situation.* How did those ancient prophets know what they knew and describe so accurately what is now being recognized by those who have travelled by another route only to reach the same conclusion? The Lamb with seven eyes and seven horns sitting on a throne in heaven (Rev. 5.6) encapsulates in one startling image,

---

51 Fred Hoyle, *The Nature of the Universe*, Oxford: Basil Blackwell, 1960, p. 103.

52 Ibid. p. 86.

53 Ibid. p. 100.

54 P. Davies, *God and the New Physics*, London: Penguin 1990, p. 2.

as we shall see,[55] a whole complex of theology about the nature of human beings and their intended role in the creation, about their relationship to the Creator and the natural forces, about their use of knowledge and the consequence of choices they freely made. The talking snake and the missing rib, the bonds of creation and the collapsing covenant are similar symbols, which, together – *but only together and in context* – enable us to glimpse the biblical vision of the creation and for the creation.

Wordplay, too, was an important part of Hebrew literary and theological style, but this completely disappears in translation, and the detailed explanations necessary to reveal some of the patterns are rather like having to explain a joke. Much of the impact is lost. Wordplay was important, and where important reconstructions depend upon it, we shall pursue the links to reveal patterns that would have been obvious to people in the time of Jesus. There is, as we shall see,[56] evidence that the early Christians used the same style. When Isaiah compared a way of living that brought justice and righteousness with one that brought bloodshed and a cry of despair, he chose this contrasting pair of words because in Hebrew they sound very similar (Isa. 5.7), and he delivered his oracle in the form of a parable about a vineyard. Those who heard him knew what was meant by the vineyard and its fruit. Jesus could take this parable seven centuries later and update it for the chief priests, scribes and elders of his own time. They knew what he was saying because they shared a cultural heritage of biblical imagery and literary style, and they 'perceived that he had told the parable against them' (Mk 12.12). So too with the common cultural heritage of stories about creation and about Adam and Eve; when Adam was set in Eden, did he serve and preserve it – the literal meaning of the Hebrew – or did he destroy and despoil it? (Gen. 2.15). The pairs of Hebrew words sound similar, and the contrast is clear in the words that John heard as the kingdom was established on earth: rewarding the servants, and destroying the destroyers (Rev. 11.18). It would be possible and very relevant to preach Isaiah's sermon today, to contrast lifestyles and political systems that lead to justice and righteousness, with those that lead to bloodshed and cries of despair; or to ponder the contrast between the servants and the destroyers of the earth. There is more use for

---

55 See below, pp. 180–1.

56 See below, p. 250.

such scholarly investigations than just the reconstruction of an ancient Hebrew literary style.

There was also the actual shape of the stories and sayings. Clear patterns can be seen in, for example, the story of Eden and the story of Noah's ark. Both were shaped around a central verse that was the key to the story. The story of Eden centres on the section where the snake tempts Eve with the forbidden fruit (Gen. 3.1–6). Before and after this point there are matching themes – a structure called a chiasm. Adam formed from the dust (Gen. 2.7) and then returning to the dust (Gen. 3.19), Adam forbidden the tree of knowledge (Gen. 2.17) and then forbidden the tree of life (Gen. 3.22), Adam as male and female in harmony (Gen. 2.21–4) and then Adam ruling over his wife (Gen. 3.16), Adam and Eve naked and not ashamed (Gen. 2.25) and then naked and ashamed (Gen. 3.7–10). The story of Noah turns around Genesis 8.1: 'God remembered Noah.' The story in the Book of Revelation turns around the vision of establishing the Kingdom, destroying the destroyers of the earth, and seeing the woman clothed with the sun. These were the keys to John's vision of establishing the Kingdom, and they were about the restoration of the creation.

In Hebrew poetry, the lines formed parallel couplets, or sometimes triplets: 'transgressed the laws, violated the statutes, broken the everlasting covenant' (Isa. 24.5) shows that these were three aspects of the one offence. 'The LORD is in his holy temple, the LORD's throne is in heaven' (Ps. 11.4) shows that the holy of holies in the temple was, to their way of thinking, heaven. The golden chariot throne in the holy of holies (1 Chron. 28.18) was the throne of the LORD (1 Chron. 29.23), and it was Solomon who sat on it. He must have been the human presence of the LORD. Deducing this from several Old Testament texts is hugely important for understanding how the first Christians, who were good Jews and steeped in the Hebrew Scriptures, recognized Jesus as the LORD. With similar processes, it is possible to recover something of what they believed about the creation.

SEEING AND BELIEVING

Jesus said: 'The eye is the lamp of the body. So, if your eye is sound, your whole body will be full of light; but if your eye is not sound, your whole body will be full of darkness. If then the light in you is darkness, how great is the darkness.' (Mt. 6. 22–3). This is part of the Sermon on the Mount, often said to be Matthew's own collection of the sayings of

Jesus that were uttered at different times during the ministry. The location of this saying is significant: before it is the saying about treasure in heaven, and not storing up earthly riches; after it, the saying about serving two masters: 'You cannot serve God and Mammon.' Even if this was Matthew's own ordering of the sayings, he could have known their traditional pattern and sequence. Did Jesus specifically link attitudes to money to ways of seeing, knowing that money can bring great darkness to the human mind?

Creation is not just seen, but seen as something. What is seen depends on how it is seen, and this in turn depends on presuppositions, whether acknowledged or not. Perception is always from the point of view of the perceiver; the creation will be seen by a poet and by a potential developer in very different ways. We learn a language by being trained to listen for certain sounds and patterns. Without that training, the language is heard as a stream of meaningless noises and communicates nothing. The language might have been learned as a child, as one's mother tongue, or it might have been acquired by study and practice, by conversing with native speakers. Nobody dismisses a language she/he does not understand as meaningless babble, nor does she/he consider its native speakers as lesser beings because they do not speak – say English. And yet something very similar is happening when the 'religious' way of seeing the world is dismissed, and everything is seen in terms of its potential for profit.

Those with the 'biblical' way of thinking saw the creation as the work of God, and felt that people who saw it in any other way were not liberated, but deprived. Theophilus, a Christian teacher writing in Antioch about 180 CE, emphasized that seeing creation as the work of God was a special gift: 'For God is seen by those who are enabled to see Him, when they have the eyes of their soul opened. For all have eyes, but in some they are overspread, and do not see the light of the sun. Yet it does not follow . . . that the light of the sun does not shine.'[57] Jesus warned his disciples that 'those outside' did not understand parables (Mk 4.11), and Isaiah had seen that those who rejected Wisdom were condemned to live with the world view they had chosen. In the enigmatic verses that follow his vision of the glory of God filling the whole earth, he hears the warning that people will hear and not understand, see and not perceive, and eventually will suffer the results of their own ways of seeing and hearing: 'Until cities lie waste without

57 Theophilus, *To Autolycus* I.2.

inhabitant, and houses without men, and the land is utterly desolate' (Isa. 6.1–11).

Someone – we know not who or when or where – was inspired to describe the creation in the particular ways we find in the Bible. Over the years, this was developed and refined, detail was added, poetry was written, a temple was constructed. To recover that initial vision of the creation we have to work in reverse: to distil the images from the poetry, to reconstruct the thought that shaped the building of the temple. The meaning of the psalms, even where the Hebrew can be read with some confidence, is not always clear. And the temple, described with such frustrating lack of detail in both Kings and Chronicles, can never really be reconstructed by archaeologists and their comparisons with neighbouring structures. 'As the pigments are but the vehicle of painting' wrote William Lethaby in his classic exploration of religious architecture,

> so is building but the vehicle of architecture, which is the thought behind form, embodied and realised for the purpose of its manifestation and transmission . . . The main purpose and burthen of sacred architecture . . . is thus inextricably bound up with people's thoughts about God and the universe.[58]

Ancient religions were essentially practical. They set out the framework within which human beings could live safely and understand their place in an otherwise unknowable world. 'Ancient religions were . . . concerned primarily with the management of this world, contrary to many studies in religion, which emphasize their otherworldly, transcendental and even eschatological concern, as though their purpose was . . . always to provide a means of escape from the material world.'[59] Ancient cosmology was the mental construction that brought order, the way that human beings orientated themselves with reference to the external world.[60] In this respect ancient cosmology, such as we find on the Old Testament, differed markedly from the modern scientific discipline that has the same name. No ancient cosmology was irrelevant to human existence; none would have concluded, as did Fred Hoyle: 'Perhaps the most majestic feature of our whole existence is that while our intelligences are powerful enough to penetrate

---

58 W. R. Lethaby, *Architecture, Mysticism and Myth*, (1891), Bath: Solos Press, 1994, pp. 11–12.

59 Wyatt, *Space and Time*, p. 31.

60 Wyatt, *Space and Time*, p. 53.

deeply into the evolution of this quite incredible universe we still have
not the smallest clue as to our own fate.' He declared: 'Religion is but
a desperate attempt to escape from the truly dreadful situation in
which we find ourselves', [61] although in his later work he concluded
that there must have been a 'superintellect' to produce such a complex system.[62] Comparing ancient and modern cosmologies is an
unfruitful occupation.

The Old Testament seers glimpsed a creation centred on the
Creator, and the initial moment of vision was also the moment from
which they created, by their words, the world view of their people.
They described God creating by words ('Let there be light', Gen. 1.3;
'Let there be a firmament', Gen. 1.6), and they replicated their mystical
experience in their instructions for building a place of worship or
setting up a system of social order. A description of how Einstein
worked is remarkably similar to the workings of an ancient seer:

> [His] entire working procedure is surprisingly analogous to that of an artist.
> Once he has come upon a problem, his path towards a solution is not a matter
> of slow, painful stages. He has a definite vision of the possible solution, and con-
> siders its value and the methods of approaching it. If he is fortunate enough to
> remove all difficulties in the way of a clear, certain and accurate solution, he is
> moved not only by the sum of new scientific proof, but by aesthetic pleasure. His
> difficulty is now simple; he has created a clear, harmonious world of thought.[63]

We see a similar process in the thought of Isaiah. He had something
on his mind ('I am a man of unclean lips' Isa. 6.5), and then he received
a vision. He stood in before the LORD on his throne, and then he
learned that the whole world was full of divine glory. 'My eyes have
seen the King, the LORD of Hosts' (Isa. 6.5). In one moment, he saw
the LORD at the heart of the temple and of the creation, and this
moment of vision shaped all his teaching about the political situation
of his time and the future of his people. Everything depends on how
we see things. Looking at something is one thing; how we see it is
another, because 'seeing' implies setting what comes to us within an
existing framework, so that it makes sense. Revelation happens in a

61 Hoyle, *The Nature of the Universe*, p. 103.

62 Fred Hoyle, 'The Universe: Past and Present Reflections', *Engineering and Science*,
November,1981, pp. 8–12.

63 A. Reiser, *Albert Einstein. A Biographical Portrait*, London: Butterworth, 1931,
p. 6.

culture and a context, and, in the case of biblical revelation, this is the vision of God enthroned at the heart of creation.

In our present situation, 'the "meaning" of nature is not something that is self-evident, but something that requires to be discerned,'[64] yet even to ask about the 'meaning' of the natural world (rather than just 'how does it work' or 'how can we work it?') implies an awareness of something other than scientific knowledge. John Polkinghorne, 20 years ago, observed a renewed interest in a theological approach to the creation, but not from theologians.

> [Natural theology] is undergoing a welcome revival in our time. This is not so much at the hand of theologians, (whose nerve, with some honourable exceptions, has not yet returned), but at the hands of scientists. There has grown up a widespread feeling, especially among those who study fundamental physics, that there is more to the world than meets the eye. Science seems to throw up questions which point beyond itself and transcend its power to answer. They arise from recognising the potentiality inherent in the structure of the world, its interlocking tightly knit character, and, indeed, its very intelligibility, which makes it open to our enquiry.[65]

Creation theology is also being explored by people who are redis-covering angels, and we shall return to angels many times in this book. There is huge interest in angels, not least because so many people have experienced something 'other' that they feel sure was an angel presence; and the media love angels, because they can be certain of a large audience.[66] The rush to rationalism in religion has left people, even church-going people, with little or no framework in which to understand what they have experienced, and this lack of framework extends to the cosmos as a whole. Matthew Fox used to tell his students to think Einstein when they thought about angels:

> Einstein was once asked, 'What's the most important question you can ask in life?' And his answer was , 'Is the universe a friendly place or not?' . . . I tell my students that every time you see angels mentioned in the Bible, you should think Einstein because you're dealing with the same issue. It's the ultimate cosmologi-cal issue. Can we trust the cosmos? Is the cosmos benign?[67]

64 McGrath, *The Open Secret*, p. 148.

65 J. Polkinghorne, *Science and Creation. The Search for Understanding*, London: SPCK, 1988, p. 15.

66 I have done radio phone-in programmes about angels.

67 M. Fox and R. Sheldrake, *The Physics of Angels. Exploring the Realm where Science and Spirit Meet.* HarperSanFransisco 1996, p. 12.

The 'scientific' view of the cosmos has excommunicated the angels or transformed them. The cherubim, for example, are now depicted as small children, the playful putti who frolic around grand ceilings, but in temple cosmology, the cherubim represented mighty divine powers. They appeared throughout the temple: they formed the throne of the LORD in the of the holy of holies, they were embroidered on the veil and they were carved on the walls of the great hall (1 Kgs 6.23–36; 2 Chron. 3.10–14). Since the temple represented the whole cosmos, and the cherubim appear throughout, they must have functioned in all parts of the cosmos. In the time of Jesus, Philo said the two cherubim on the ark in the tabernacle symbolized 'great recognition' and 'knowledge poured out in abundance'.[68] They were also the two aspects of the LORD, who both creates and rules the world, and their outspread wings were the sign that the powers of the LORD overshadowed and protected the universe. Thus the cherubim – and indeed all angels – have a twofold aspect: their nature, and the power to reveal their nature. They teach about themselves. They are the creating and ruling powers of the LORD, and communicate these to the human mind. Philo's words seem at first sight fanciful, but decoded, he was saying that heavenly knowledge poured out in abundance *and recognized as such* was the LORD's way of protecting the creation.

In biblical discourse, the angels are the unseen forces in the creation, connecting the material world to the Source of all life whom we call God. They are one, because the divine is One, but we perceive them separately, a measure of how far our human perception of the cosmos is from the reality. Angels – the name means messengers – are the only means by which we can have a complete knowledge of the creation. They reveal what human minds could not work out for themselves, and enable new insights by joining together human knowledge in the way they themselves bind together the cosmos. As they reveal themselves, so they reveal the unified knowledge that is called Wisdom. In the Bible the angels worship and praise the Creator; they symbolize and they are the harmony of creation. In the Book of Revelation, all the angels and all creatures in heaven and earth honour and praise the Creator. 'Let all God's angels worship him' was an important proof text (Heb. 1.6). We do not know how Philo understood: 'Thou who art enthroned upon the cherubim, shine forth . . . Come to save us!' (Ps. 80.1–2); but if he thought of the cherubim as 'great recognition'

---

68 Philo, *Questions on Exodus*, II.62–5; *Life of Moses* II.97–9.

and 'knowledge poured out in abundance', this shining forth could well have been recognizing the source and nature of knowledge about the creation, and its role in protecting and preserving.

The sense of awe was fundamental. 'When I look at the heavens, the work of thy fingers . . . What is man?', was coupled with a sense of responsibility towards the creation: 'You have made [the human] a little less than the *'elohim* . . .' (Ps. 8.3–5). Job in his suffering, recognized the power of the Creator and how little he could understand: 'These are but the outskirts of his ways; and how small a whisper do we hear of him!' (Job 26.14). Isaiah contemplated the power of the Creator, who measured the waters, marked out the heavens, enclosed the dust of the earth and weighed the mountains (Isa. 40.12), and then assured his people that such a Creator did not grow weary and would renew their strength too (Isa. 40.28–31). The Psalmist sang: 'O LORD how manifold are thy works! With Wisdom thou hast made them all' (Ps. 104.24, my translation). The power of the Creator and the glory of the creation were not just an object of awe and an inspiration for poets; they were always linked to the role of human beings: they mattered, they had a special place and special responsibilities. When the early Christians were instructed before baptism, they had to learn 'the order of the several parts of creation . . . why the world was made and why man was appointed to be a citizen therein'.[69] *Why* the world was made, not how. They kept every Sabbath as a memorial of the creation.[70]

'Religion is founded on revelation and received wisdom; religious dogma that claims to contain an unalterable Truth can hardly be modified to fit changing ideas.'[71] This is true, but first one needs to clarify what the Bible offers as eternal truth, and then set this alongside the changing ideas of our time. It is remarkable just how much of the biblical revelation that has been 'imposed' on the world has proved to correspond with what is there, how so much that has been 'discovered' had been expressed, long ago and in a different way, by our mystics. One of the great but largely unacknowledged problems that hinders any 'religion and environment' discussion is the irrelevance of much recent biblical scholarship to this issue. Time and again one sees serious efforts on the part of scientists who want to engage with the Judaeo-Christian tradition. They have had to rely on what biblical

---

69 *Apostolic Constitutions* 7.39.

70 *Apostolic Constitutions* 7.23.

71 Davies, *God and the New Physics*, p. 6.

scholars told them about the Bible, and they found very little that was any use to them. This is not because the Bible has nothing to reveal, but because many of those entrusted with expounding it have not engaged with the really important issue of our time – the state of the planet. They have indulged themselves in fashionable diversions and have missed 'the many splendoured thing.'

People in the time of Jesus were contemplating the shape of the temple and how it represented not only the creation but also human attitudes towards the creation. Philo, explaining how the holy of holies at the heart of the temple represented the LORD at the centre of the worshipper's world view, wrote this: 'God always appears in his work, which is most sacred; by this I mean the world. For his beneficent powers are seen and move around in all its parts . . .' He then explained how the vision of holiness comes only after self-discipline, after the mind has been cleansed of selfish desires, injustices and related evils. Those not prepared to change themselves live their whole lives unable to see the divine light.

> If, however, you are worthily initiated, and can be consecrated to God and in a certain sense become an spiritual shrine of the Father, (then) instead of having closed eyes, you will see the First (things), and in wakefulness you will cease from the deep sleep in which you have been held. Then will appear to you that manifest One, Who causes incorporeal rays to shine for you, and grants vision of the unambiguous and indescribable things of nature and the abundant sources of other good things. For the beginning and end of happiness is to be able to see God. But this cannot happen to him who has not made his soul, as I said before, a sanctuary and altogether a shrine of God.[72]

Could the early Christians have known such ideas? Apollos, 'a native of Alexandria . . . an eloquent man, well versed in the Scriptures . . .' became a Christian. He was in Ephesus for a while around 50 CE, and then moved on to teach in Corinth (Acts 18.24–19.1). He had become a learned man when Philo, who died about 50 CE, was a leading thinker in his native city. Did he know his ideas? Were those ideas part of the general intellectual scene in Alexandria, and not unique to Philo? There is no way of knowing. What is interesting is that Paul, writing to Corinth when Apollos had been teaching there, could assume that the Church knew 'Philo's' teaching about the body as a temple. 'Do you not know that your body is a temple of the holy Spirit?' (1 Cor. 6.19).

---

72 Philo, *Questions on Exodus* II.51.

Reconstructing what the first Christians could have known and thought about the creation means looking closely at the familiar words and images of the New Testament and asking why they spoke in that way. 'Jesus is LORD' (Rom. 10.9); 'the Holy and Righteous One . . . the Author of Life' (Acts 3.14–15); 'He is before all things and in him all things hold together . . . making peace by the blood of his cross' (Col. 1.17,20) are all rooted in the early Church's belief about the creation, but not always read that way.

Chapter 1

VISION OF CREATION

The story of the creation at the beginning of Genesis, one of the best known chapters in the Bible, tells how God created heaven and earth in six days. It described the relationship between God, heaven and earth, the visible world of material things and living creatures, and above all, human beings. An identical, or very similar, set of relationships was expressed in the layout and rituals of the tabernacle that Moses built, as described in Exodus, and later in the Jerusalem temple. To understand what Genesis is saying about the creation and relationships within the creation, it is important to know about the temple: how it was built and what happened there. This has been neglected, but it is the key to recovering what the Bible really teaches about the creation.

The creation story in Genesis has instead given rise to fierce controversies which continue to this day, and can even affect what is taught in schools. How and when was the world made? In the nineteenth century, developments in the natural sciences and an increased knowledge of the ancient world caused people to question the biblical story of the creation. Many, including biblical scholars, had long accepted that the six days were not to be understood literally, that they represented long periods of time, and so the theories of geologists such as Lyell[1] about the age and formation of the earth could be accommodated. The real difficulties came with the theories about evolution, especially as they challenged the biblical teaching that humans were a special and unique creation.

Archaeologists had made discoveries in the lands once called Mesopotamia: ancient libraries had been found, and some of their stories were very like Genesis. They told how the first human being was formed from clay and then brought to life, just as the Bible says Adam

---

1 Charles Lyell, *Principles of Geology*, London: John Murray, 1835.

34

was created (Gen. 2.7). The Mesopotamian Adam, however, was brought to life by the blood of the god Kingu, who had been defeated by Marduk, and the human race was created from blood and clay to serve the triumphant gods. This is very different from the Genesis picture, where Adam was formed from dust and brought to life by the breath of the LORD, who then set him in Eden to serve it and keep it (Gen. 2.15).

Nor were the evolutionists agreed as to how their evidence should be related to Christian theology. Darwin was cautious, and claimed he had been misrepresented. 'I placed in a most conspicuous position . . . the following words: "I am convinced that natural selection has been the main, but not the exclusive means of modification." This has been of no avail. Great is the power of steady misrepresentation . . .'[2] T. H. Huxley, a most vocal supporter, rejected the revealed religion of the Bible, but recognized that the theory of evolution posed a problem for ethics.

> The practice of that which is ethically best – what we call goodness or virtue – involves a course of conduct which in all respects is opposed to that which leads to success in the cosmic struggle for existence. In place of ruthless self-assertion, it demands self-restraint . . . The ethical progress of society depends not on imitating the cosmic process, still less in running away from it, but in combating it.[3]

He meant, of course, the cosmic process as he then understood it. More recent study is reaching the conclusion that co-operation is an element in evolution.[4] Darwin's co-proposer of evolution, however, A. R. Wallace, reached a conclusion not unlike Philo's description of the powers that sustain the creation.

> There are now in the universe infinite grades of power, infinite grades of knowledge and wisdom, infinite grades of influence of higher beings upon lower. Holding this opinion, I have suggested that this vast and wonderful universe, with its almost infinite variety of forms, motions and reaction of part upon part, from suns and systems up to plant life, animal life and the human living soul, has ever required, and still requires, the continuous co-ordinated agency of myriads of such intelligences.[5]

---

2 C. Darwin, *The Origin of Species*, London: Dent, Everyman edition 1959, p. 454.

3 T. H. Huxley, *Evolution and Ethics*, New York: Appleton and Co., 1896, pp. 81, 83.

4 See below, pp. 161–2.

5 A. R. Wallace, conclusion of *The World of Life*, London: Chapman and Hall, 1910.

He was, in effect, talking about angels.[6]

Although the effects of these debates are still with us, the current need is not to prolong them or even try to resolve them. The need is to recover the original vision, uncluttered by the fashions in natural sciences or cosmologies that have prompted earlier discussions and confident claims in this area, and informed by a real knowledge of what the earliest Christians could have thought about the creation. *The Bible that has featured in recent debates has not been the Bible as the first Christians understood it.* For the early Church, the six days of Genesis were historical insofar as they indicated six eras of time. God completed the creation on the seventh day and then rested, according to the Hebrew text of Genesis 2.2. The other ancient versions[7] say that God completed the work in six days and then rested on the seventh. The *Letter of Barnabas* explained that the six days represented six thousand years, one day being a thousand years in the sight of the LORD (Ps. 90.4). The sixth day was the present era, and the seventh would be the great Sabbath, when the Son would return. In other words, the Sabbath was the time of the Kingdom.[8] We shall return to this teaching about the Sabbath.[9]

The description of the six days of creation is the opening of the five books of Moses,[10] and in the time of Jesus, people believed that Moses had written all but the last chapter of Deuteronomy, which describes his death. How, then, had he been able to describe the process of creation, before there was anyone to see what happened? One clue lies in the *Book of Jubilees*, a parallel version of Genesis which has been preserved by the church in Ethiopia. Nobody knows when it was written, but fragments found among the Dead Sea Scrolls show that it was known in Palestine some two hundred years before the time of Jesus. The first Christians probably knew it. The importance of *Jubilees* for the question of Moses and the first chapter of Genesis is that it describes how Moses had a vision on Sinai of everything that had happened before he lived, including the creation. *In other words, the first chapter of Genesis is a record of Moses' vision.*

---

6 See below, p. 115.

7 Samaritan, Greek, Syriac.

8 *Letter of Barnabas* 15.

9 See below, p. 189.

10 Genesis, Exodus, Leviticus, Numbers, Deuteronomy.

The biblical story does not present Moses as a visionary, but after the demise of the monarchy in Jerusalem in the sixth century BCE, popular imagination gave to Moses more and more of the role of the ancient kings who were remembered as divine figures. Philo, a contemporary of Jesus, described Moses as the God and King of his people. 'He was named God and King of the whole nation, and entered, we are told, into the darkness where God was, that is into the unseen, invisible and incorporeal and archetypal essence of existing things. Thus he beheld what is hidden from the sight of mortal nature . . .'[11] He was not the first to say this, because he says: 'we are told.' In the third century BCE, for example, Ezekiel (not the biblical prophet) had written a play about the life of Moses, in which he described how a figure on the summit of Sinai rose from his throne and gave it to Moses.[12] From a high place – in Moses' case Sinai – the temple visionaries had learned about the creation and the history of their people. Scholars realized long ago that memories of Sinai had fused with memories of the holy of holies, and so what Moses 'saw' on Sinai was what the ancient royal high priests 'saw' in the holy of holies. The final scene in Revelation shows all the servants of the LORD in the holy of holies, seeing the face of the LORD (Rev. 22.3–5), which means seeing his presence. And we know from Isaiah that seeing the face of the LORD meant recognizing the glory of the LORD in the whole earth. The Christians adapted the words that Isaiah heard: 'Holy, holy, holy . . . heaven and earth are full of his glory' (Isa. 6.3), and they became the heart of the eucharistic prayer when they celebrated the renewal of the covenant. Why did they associate the visible glory of the LORD in creation and the atonement effected by the death of the LORD? *This is the fundamental question that Christians have to address when setting out what they believe about the environment.*

Traces of these visions survive. Enoch, who was the seventh from Adam and therefore an early patriarch, was a high priest figure. His name means 'the dedicated one'. One collection of Enoch traditions known in the time of Jesus, says he was taken up by angels to a high tower, so that he could see the future (*1 En.* 87.3–4). Another collection of Enoch traditions, of uncertain date, says that when he had been taken up to stand before the throne, he was anointed and transformed into an angel, and then he was taught about the process of creation. There is far more detail about the creation narrative here than in

11 Philo, *Life of Moses* I.158.
12 Quoted in Eusebius, *Preparation of the Gospel* IX.29.

Genesis, but what is significant for us is the setting; Enoch was shown all this while he was standing in the holy of holies as an angel high priest (*2 En.* 22–30). Habakkuk had looked out from a tower and received a vision of the future (Hab. 2.1–4). R. Yosi, early in the second century CE, taught that the tower was the holy of holies: 'He built a tower in the midst of his vineyard (Isa. 5.2) . . . this is his sanctuary.' These visions in the holy of holies were also a part of the early Christian world. John was summoned: 'Come up hither, and I will show you what must take place after this' (Rev. 4.1). John 'went up' and found himself in the holy of holies, before the heavenly throne, where he learned about the past and the future; and Jesus himself saw 'all the cities of the world in a moment of time' when the devil 'took him up' (Lk. 4.5). John heard the voice from the throne declaring that he would renew/restore the whole creation (Rev. 21.5).

MOSES

Moses on Sinai saw the creation. The vision lasted six days, and these days became the six days of Genesis: 'The glory of the LORD settled on Mount Sinai, and the cloud covered it *six days*; and on the seventh, (the LORD) called to Moses out of the midst of the cloud' (Exod. 24.16). In the time of Jesus, this was understood to be when he received the vision 'what was in the beginning and what will be'.[13] Moses was then told to gather in offerings from the people to make a place of worship. 'And let them make me a sanctuary, that I may dwell in their midst. According to all that I am causing you to see, the pattern of the tabernacle and the pattern of its furnishings, thus you shall make them' (Exod. 25.8–9. my translation). *It was the creation that Moses had to replicate in the tabernacle, and so both the tabernacle, and later, the temple, represented the creation, and the worship there both preserved and renewed the creation and human society.*

The patterns of creation and temple building were ancient and in the biblical text they are often fragmented, or supplemented with later explanatory material. The clearest surviving text about building the tabernacle is the final section of Exodus (Exod. 40.16–33), which should be read alongside Genesis 1, the six days of creation. In the Exodus account, the stages of tabernacle building are marked by 'As the LORD commanded Moses'. There are complications in the text

13 *Jubilees* 1.2–4.

here because the Greek translation differs slightly from the Hebrew, the Greek seeming to preserve the older tradition where there was no giant bronze sea full of water in the desert tabernacle compound. Thus Exodus 40.7, 11, 30–32 do not appear in the Greek text. Apart from that, the pattern has survived the centuries. It is easy to forget just how old these texts are, but the pattern of creation and tabernacle is older than the damage and dislocations.

On the first day of the first month Moses erected the framework of the tabernacle, as the LORD commanded him (Exod. 40.17–19), corresponding to the beginning of creation, what Genesis 1.5 calls Day One. Later interpreters understood this curious expression to mean that Day One was the state (rather than the time or place) when all was a unity, when God was one with the creation, and so before the visible creation has been separated out from God into its distinct forms. (We shall return to this fundamental aspect of biblical creation theology). There was no division in the tabernacle and no furnishing; it was simply a tent. Similarly there was no division in the creation, except the division of light from darkness, but this light must have been the heavenly light since the sun was not made until the fourth day. Those who preserved the ancient temple traditions about creation said that there had once been a book of Torah about this state of light described in Genesis 1.3. The Talmud says that the seven pillars of Wisdom (Prov. 9.10) meant seven books of the Torah, not the five we have today,[14] and the teaching concealed in Genesis 1.3 was one of the missing books. Teaching about the state where there was no light but no darkness, they said, would one day be restored.[15] This was one of the earliest Christian claims about Jesus; that he revealed this teaching.[16]

Tabernacle and temple building was a new year ritual, marking the renewal of the year and the renewal of the creation. Moses began to erect the tabernacle on the first day of the first month (Exod. 40.17); Solomon dedicated the temple at the autumn festival (1 Kgs. 8.2).[17] New year rituals in the ancient near east had for centuries celebrated together the process of creation and the building or rededication of a

14 Babylonian Talmud *Shabbath*, 116a.

15 G. Scholem, *On the Kabbalah and its Symbolism*, London: Routledge, 1965, p. 81, where Sholem deals with the mediaeval *Book Temunah*.

16 See below, p. 74.

17 Here described as the seventh month because it was written after the calendar had changed to a spring new year.

temple. This was not unique to Hebrew tradition, although they brought their own characteristic insight to the established practice. In Babylon, for example, the new year was marked by eleven days of celebration; on the fourth day they read their story of the creation, and on the fifth they purified the temple, using the severed head of a sheep, which was then thrown into the river. Some aspects of this ritual resemble the day of atonement, which was part of the Hebrew new year festival (Lev. 23.26–32; the ritual is described in Lev.16).

As the second stage of erecting the tabernacle, Moses took the ten commandments and put them in the ark, set the *kapporet* (usually translated mercy seat) over the ark and then set up the veil to screen the ark. Thus the tabernacle was divided into two parts: the holy place and the most holy place (Exod. 40.20–21; Exod. 26.33). This corresponded to the second day of creation, when God set the firmament to separate the waters above from the waters below (Gen. 1.6–8). The firmament corresponded to the veil of the tabernacle, and this is why the Hebrew storytellers described the birds flying 'in front of the firmament of the heavens' (Gen. 1.20, translating literally). They had in mind the tabernacle model of the creation, and the birds flying in front of the curtain.

The holy and the most holy were important distinctions between the two 'houses' of the tabernacle and what they represented, and holiness was closely linked to the gift of life.[18] Anything described as 'most holy' had the power to impart holiness and so was actively holy. The perfumed oil imparted this power of 'active holiness', and so anything anointed became 'most holy' and acquired the power to transmit holiness. Anything described simply as 'holy' had received holiness but did not impart it. All the furnishings and vessels for the tabernacle were anointed and became 'most holy': 'You shall consecrate them that they may be most holy; whatever touches them will become holy' (Exod. 30.29). This is well illustrated by an incident recorded in Haggai; the prophet asked the priests if an item that was simply holy imparted holiness, and they said it did not (Hag. 2.12), but impurity was much more easily spread. The veil of the tabernacle/temple separated the most holy from the holy; the high priests who passed between the two states were the means of bringing holiness into the material world. If the material world lost contact with the holy of holies, it lost the capacity to be holy and ultimately lost contact with the source

18 The hymn in Rev. 4.8,11 shows that the thrice holy LORD God Almighty was the source and sustainer of the creation.

of its life. Anointed knowledge, as we shall see, was also transformed and acquired the capacity to transmit holiness. It was known as 'wisdom'.[19]

As the third stage, Moses put the table on the north side of the holy place and set bread on it. The fuller description says that the table also held plates and dishes for incense, flagons and bowls for libations, and the Greek version of the Old Testament says there was also salt (Exod. 40.22–3; 25.23–30). There were bread, wine and incense on a table in the tabernacle – something that must be of significance for Christians – but we are told very little about this table or how it featured in worship. The corresponding day of the creation was the third, when the earth put forth vegetation, 'plants yielding seed and fruit trees bearing fruit in which is their seed, each according to its kind' (Gen. 1.12), a prophetic and disturbing definition of vegetation in the light of the genetically modified crops. When the Egyptian king Ptolemy II (285–274 BCE) gave a magnificent gift to the second temple in Jerusalem, he sent a table made of solid gold, decorated with precious stones to represent fruits and grain, flowers and leaves, and the vessels were also decorated with fruits and leaves.[20]

As the fourth stage, Moses set the seven branched lamp, the menorah, on the south side of the holy place (Exod. 40.24–5), corresponding to the lights of heaven created on the fourth day: the sun, the moon and the five planets known at that time. But the seven branched lamp must have had another meaning as it was made in the form of an almond tree (Exod. 25.31–7). Zechariah, at the end of the sixth century BCE, remembered it as the seven eyes of the LORD (Zech. 4.2,10) and this must be the explanation of Jeremiah's vision. When the prophet saw an almond branch, the LORD said to him, ' You have seen well, for I am watching . . .' (Jer. 1.12). Jeremiah would have known that the menorah was a golden almond tree, the symbol of the LORD's watching presence in the temple, and so the almond tree became for him a sign. The incident is often explained as simply a play on the sound of the Hebrew words, and such similarities of sound were an important feature in the teaching of the prophets and wise ones. Here, almond is *shaqed* and watching is *shoqed*, almost indistinguishable in sound. The fluidity of sounds and words indicated patterns of perception, but we can only guess which was cause and which was effect. Did the words give rise to the ideas or vice versa?

19 See below, p. 270.
20 *Letter of Aristeas* 57–82.

After the installation of the lamp as the fourth stage, the sequence in Exodus 40 is interrupted by mention of the incense altar, the fifth stage, which seems to be an addition to the pattern. The fuller account of the tabernacle in Exodus chapters 25–29 does not mention the incense altar but adds it at the end, in chapter 30. If the incense altar was a later addition to the furnishings, this would explain the interrupted pattern in Exodus 40. This means that the sixth stage, but probably the fifth in the original scheme, was the altar of burnt offerings (Exod. 40.28–9), which would have represented the creation of the animals and birds that were offered there, just as the table represented the offering of the plant life that was created on the third day. The pattern in Genesis 1 is not clear at this point either: sea life and birds appeared on the fifth day and the creatures of the land, including human beings, appeared on the sixth day.

The final problem is the bronze laver, which does not appear in the Greek text. A bronze laver of water is unlikely in the desert, but this final stage in the erection of the tabernacle could have been influenced by memories of the temple furnishings. The bronze laver corresponded to the creation of the human being on the sixth day. The laver was to purify the high priests (Exod. 40.30–31), and Adam, as we shall see, was created as the high priest of the temple of creation. Despite the text problems for the fifth and sixth days in Genesis 1 and the later stages of the tabernacle construction in Exodus 40, the pattern for the first four days is clear, and is unlikely to have been coincidence, especially as the correspondence between tabernacle and creation is found in other texts both Jewish and Christian.

The creation is described as a building in the Old Testament, presumably because the temple 'was' the creation. The earth had foundations and a cornerstone (Job 38.4–6); the LORD 'builds his upper chambers in the heavens and founds his vault upon the earth' (Amos 9.6; Ps. 104 1–6 is similar); 'My hand laid the foundation of the earth, and my right hand spread out the heavens (Isa. 48.13; 51.13 is similar). These images do not come directly from the Genesis account, which simply describes the various parts of the creation being separated out and called into being. The tabernacle/temple is the link between the Genesis creation story and the imagery of the creation as a building. Rabbi Abbahu, teaching in Palestine in the late third century CE, said that 'In the beginning God created' referred to the temple; the unformed earth represented the destroyed temple, and the light symbolized the rebuilt temple in the time of the

Messiah: 'Arise, shine for your light has come, and the glory of the
LORD has risen upon you' (Isa. 60.1).[21]

In the time of Jesus, the Jews were still thinking of the creation in
terms of the temple. Philo described the whole universe as a temple:

> 'the highest, and in the truest sense, the holy temple of God is, as we must believe,
> the whole universe, having for its sanctuary the most sacred part of all existence,
> even heaven, for its votive ornaments the stars, for its priests the angels . . .'[22]

Josephus, a younger contemporary of Jesus, was of a high priestly
family,[23] and wrote thus of the tabernacle:

> The proportion of the measures of the tabernacle proved to be an imitation of
> the system of the world, for that third part thereof [which is within the veil] is, as
> it were, a heaven peculiar to God, but the area twenty cubits long is, as it were,
> sea and land, on which men live . . .[24]

The 'measures' of the temple were an important part of the symbolism.

As early as Ezekiel, who was a temple priest at the beginning of the
sixth century BCE, the dimensions of the temple represented the
correct proportions in creation and human society. Distortions in the
temple indicated rebellion against the divine plan, the Hebrew word
translated 'distortion', '*awon*, being from the same root as the word
translated 'iniquity'. Iniquity understood as distortion is an important
element in our enquiry. Ezekiel described (in a text that is now almost
opaque) an anointed guardian angel, who was 'the seal of proportion/
plan', wise and beautiful, but one who corrupted the wisdom and grew
proud from the beauty. Through corrupt trade and many iniquities/
distortions, the holy places became unholy and were destroyed with fire
(Ezek. 28.12–19).[25] In his vision of how the temple was to be restored
after the exile, Ezekiel saw an angel 'with a line of flax and a measuring
reed in his hand' (Ezek. 40.3). Three chapters of temple measurements
follow, after which, the angel tells Ezekiel: 'Tell the house of Israel about
the house, that they may be ashamed of their distortions/iniquities,
and measure the proportion' (Ezek. 43.10; or measure the plan, since

---

21 *Genesis Rabbah* II.5.

22 Philo, *Special Laws*, I.66.

23 Josephus, *Life*, 1.

24 Josephus, *Antiquities* III.180–81.

25 My awkward English reflects the awkward Hebrew.

'plan' is a very similar Hebrew word).[26] After the vision, the prophet's message to the rulers was: 'Put away violence and oppression, and execute justice and righteousness; cease your evictions of my people, says the LORD God. You shall have just balances, a just ephah and a just bath' (Ezek. 45.9–10). This was no exhortation to a better temple-building project; it was a demand for a just society, followed by a detailed list of what the weights, measures and currency should be. The fixed order of the creation, represented by the temple, extended to commercial transactions, and so trade and currency distortions were the concern of a temple priest-prophet. The angel set on the holy mountain as the 'seal of proportion' had been corrupted through unjust trade, and the holy places had been destroyed as a result.

The biblical vision linked 'economics' with the temple vision of the creation, but nowadays, the two have become separated. Whether or not this is progress is debateable. Consider the words of Larry Rasmussen, scrutinizing 'the classic texts in the study of economics'. There is, he said, typically no mention of the environment. Instead, there is 'a huge mismatch between the Big Economy [the present globalising human economy], and the Great Economy, [the economy of nature]'. Two quotations follow, the first from Thomas Berry:

> The difficulty of contemporary economics is its effort to impose an industrial economy on the organic functioning of the Earth . . . [H]uman economics is not integrated with the ever-renewing economics of the natural world. This ever-renewing productivity of the natural world is the only sustainable economics. The human is a subsystem of the Earth system.

We know this has to be the case; if there is conflict between ecology and economics, ecology has to 'win', for we have only one earth. Rasmussen's second extract was from Lawrence Summers, one time chief economist of the World Bank and later part of the Clinton administration:

> There are . . . no limits to the carrying capacity of the Earth that are likely to bind at any time in the foreseeable future . . . The idea that we should put limits on growth because of some natural limit is a profound error.[27]

---

26 *tknyt* or *tbnyt*, k and b being almost identical Hebrew letters.

27 L. L. Rasmussen, *Earth Community, Earth Ethics*, Geneva: World Council of Churches Publications, 1996, pp. 111–12.

This is how some people were thinking a few years ago; the contrast with the biblical view is clear, and it is also clear that these recent ways of relating to the creation are bringing disaster. 'How do we imagine our future, when our commercial systems conflict with everything nature teaches us?'[28] In the Sermon on the Mount, Jesus was more succinct: 'No one can serve two masters . . . You cannot serve God and mammon [money]' (Mt. 6.24, also Lk. 16.13).

This idea of heaven determining the shape and function of earth can be seen in the words used to describe their relationship: one of them is *mašal.* The Hebrew lexicon lists three apparently distinct meanings for this word: to rule or have dominion; to be like, or cause to be like; and to speak in parables or poetry – the two latter clearly aspects of the same meaning. But in fact all three are the same: the one who 'rules' in this sense is the one who determines how and what things are, and does this by making or maintaining the correspondences. This was Adam's intended role, as we shall see.[29] An approximate equivalent in English might be 'ruler' which can mean governor, but also the instrument for measuring and laying out a plan. The sun and moon 'rule', that is determine, the day and night (Gen. 1.18). The Hebrew world view envisaged the ruler emerging with the divine law from eternity that is, from the holy of holies, and ensuring that the earth prospered because it was in harmony with heaven. The Deuteronomists who emphasized only the ten commandments, questioned this belief in the laws brought down from heaven: '[This commandment] is not in heaven that you should say, "Who will go up to heaven, and bring it to us that we may see it and hear it?"' (Deut. 30.12). Jesus did claim to have learned in heaven: how, he asked, could Nicodemeus understand the heavenly things of which he spoke? (Jn 3.12–13); people did not believe the things he had seen and heard there (Jn 3.31–3). The older belief and prophecy was that the shepherd 'ruler', *mošel,*[30] would come forth 'from everlasting, from eternity', that is, from the holy of holies (Mic. 5.2). Isaiah's mysterious servant would bring forth justice (Isa. 42.1).[31] Punishment for the faithless would be that they lost their dignity and status; the LORD 'from everlasting' judges the faithless by depriving them of 'rule' so that they become like 'crawling things' (Hab. 1.14). In contrast, the faithful man prays that sins may not 'rule'

28 P. Hawken, *The Ecology of Commerce,* London: Phoenix, 1995, p. 5.

29 See below, p. 215.

30 A noun from *mašal.*

31 The second half of the verse associated with Jesus' baptism.

him (Ps. 19.13). The LORD has 'rule' and rules over the nations (Ps. 22.28); 'the LORD has established his throne in the heavens, and his kingdom "rules" over all' (Ps.103.19).[32]

It is likely that the first Christians inherited these ways of thinking. They prayed 'Thy Kingdom come. Thy will be done on earth as it is in heaven'; and the measurements and proportions of the creation and what they represented, were part of contemporary temple discourse. At that time the exact measurements of the temple were recorded and later preserved in the *Mishnah*, in the tractate *Middoth*, a word that means measurements, but is also translated 'mysteries'. Rabbi 'Akiba, the great teacher at the time of the second war against Rome (135 CE), was remembered as a temple mystic who ascended to stand before the heavenly throne, where the LORD spoke to him: 'Akiba, my son, descend and bear witness of this mystery/measurement to the creatures.' Then R 'Akiba descended and taught the creatures this mystery/measurement.'[33] Philo described the Logos as the 'pre-measurer of all things',[34] and the *Gospel of Philip* said that the title Messiah had two meanings: 'the anointed one' and 'the measurer'.[35] Both these examples echo the old idea of the 'ruler' coming forth from the eternity as the strong shepherd who gives his people security because cosmic order is maintained (Mic. 5.3–4). John was told to measure the temple (Rev. 11.1), presumably because the dimensions were wrong. Then it was destroyed, the temple being the harlot city of his later vision, condemned because of its trading practices (Rev. 18.1–24). John's description of her burning has clear echoes of the fate of the fallen angel in Ezekiel 28. Christian prophets and visionaries were the direct cultural descendents of the old temple prophets, and prophesied with the same world view. The words of Al Gore in 1992 are relevant here:

> Ecology is the study of balance, and some of the same principles that govern the healthy balance of elements in the global environment also apply to the healthy balance of forces making up our political system. In my view, however, our system is on the verge of losing its equilibrium . . .[36]

32 My translations, to emphasize where the word occurs.

33 *Merkavah Rabbah* # 686, quoted in P. Schäfer, *The Hidden and Manifest God*, New York: State University of New York Press, 1992, p. 119.

34 Philo, *Questions on Genesis*, I.4.

35 *Gospel of Philip*, Coptic Gnostic Library II.3.62. In rabbinic Hebrew, *mšḥ* can mean measure or anoint.

36 A. Gore, *Earth in Balance. Ecology and the Human Spirit*, Boston: Houghton Mifflin, 1992, p. 11.

The Creator had made the world both visible and invisible, the outer and the inner, which was represented by the shape of the temple. The outer part, corresponding to the nave of a traditional western church, represented the material world, and the inner part, the holy of holies behind the veil, represented the invisible world of God and the angels. The outer part existed in time as we know it, and the inner part was beyond time, a state known as 'eternity'. The writer to the Hebrews assumes that the readers know this temple world view: '...as long as the outer tent is still standing, which is symbolic for the present age . . .' (Heb. 9.8–9). The *Clementine Recognitions* is a Christian text originally attributed to Clement, bishop of Rome at the end of the first century. Most now date the text somewhat later, but recognize that it incorporates early Jewish-Christian material, some of which described the creation: 'In the beginning, God made heaven and earth . . . and he divided into two portions that fabric of the universe, although it was but one house. The reason of the division was this, that the upper portion might provide a dwelling place to the angels and the lower to men . . .'[37] Cosmas Indicopleustes ('the man who sailed to India') was a sixth-century Egyptian Christian who wrote an account of his travels with observations on geography. He knew about Moses' vision of the creation, and that the tabernacle was to represent what he had seen. Moses, he said, had built the tabernacle to represent the whole world because he had seen the creation in his vision on Sinai.

> Since therefore it had been shown to him how God made the heaven and the earth, and how on the second day he made the firmament in the middle between them, and thus made the one into two places, so Moses, in like manner, in accordance with the pattern he had seen, made the tabernacle and placed the veil in the middle, and by this division he made the one tabernacle into two, the inner and the outer.[38]

The Jews remembered that the tabernacle had replicated the creation. Rabbi Tanḥuma bar Abba, who lived in Palestine in the latter part of the fourth century CE, collected many of the ancient traditions and his work formed the basis of the Tanḥuma-Yelammedenu midrashim. Nobody can date the component parts of this with certainty, but one section has a detailed comparison of the tabernacle and the creation. 'I love the habitation of thy house, and the place where thy glory dwelleth' (Ps. 26.8), is said to show that 'the tabernacle is equal

---

37 *Clementine Recognitions*, I.27.

38 Cosmas, *Christian Topography*, 2.35.

to the creation of the world itself.' 'In the beginning God created the heaven and the earth' (Gen. 1.1) was linked to 'Thou shalt make curtains of goats hair' (Exod. 26.7); the firmament (Gen. 1.6) was linked to the veil (Exod. 26.33); the gathering of the waters (Gen. 1.9) was linked to the brass laver (Exod.30.18); the lights in the firmament (Gen. 1.14) were linked to the menorah (Exod. 25.31); the birds created on the fifth day were linked to the winged cherubim (Exod. 25.20); and the creation of the human was linked to anointing the high priest (Exod. 29.1–7).[39] These correspondences are not exactly those of Exodus. Louis Ginzberg surveyed the 'tabernacle as creation' traditions and summarized thus: until the sanctuary was erected, the world was not stable, but once it was erected, 'the world stood firmly grounded.' The firmament corresponded to the veil; the great sea gathered together on the third day corresponded to the laver; the plants corresponded to the table for the bread; the sun, moon and five known planets were the seven lamps of the menorah; the birds of the fifth day corresponded to the cherubim; and the human, Adam the image of God, was the anointed high priest.[40]

The creation was sustained by the liturgies of the temple: Simeon the Just, the last of the spiritual heirs of men of the Great Synagogue,[41] was high priest about 280 BCE, and he was remembered for teaching: 'The world is sustained by three things: by the Law, by the temple service, and by deeds of loving kindness.'[42] Ben Sira described him officiating in the temple on the day of atonement, emerging 'glorious . . . as he came out of the house of the veil' (Ben Sira 50.5). The music and the prayers continued until 'the LORD's cosmos [*kosmos kuriou*] was completed' (Ben Sira 50.19, translating literally); the liturgy created the cosmos, and both were completed together by the high priest who 'was' the LORD.[43] Thus the Qumran *Temple Scroll* linked the building of the temple to the renewal of the creation: 'I will dwell with

39 *Midrash Tanḥuma–Yelammedenu*, English translation by S. A. Berman, New Jersey: KTAV Publishing, 1996, pp. 648–9. A verse no longer in the Hebrew text is given here for anointing the high priest. I have substituted another.

40 L. Ginzberg, *The Legends of the Jews*, vol.2, Philadelphia: Jewish Publication Society of America, 1913, p. 151.

41 Those who had come back from Babylon with Ezra in the fifth century BCE.

42 Mishnah *Aboth* 1.2. Simeon may have been the later high priest of that name, about 200 BCE.

43 C. T. R. Hayward, *The Jewish Temple: A Non-biblical Sourcebook*, London: Routledge, 1996, pp. 79–80.

them for ever and ever, and will sanctify my [sa]nctuary by my glory. I will cause my glory to rest on it until the day of creation on which I shall create my sanctuary . . .'[44] The text is broken, but it seems to link the creation of the temple to the six days between the day of Atonement and Tabernacles.

Memories of the temple services in the time of Jesus show this too. When the Zealots and the Idumeans together began the uprising against Rome, they killed the high priest and his deputy; Josephus described them as men who had 'but lately worn the sacred vestments, led those cosmic ceremonies and been venerated by people who came to the city from all over the world . . .'[45] In happier times, each of the 24 courses of priests took turn to officiate in the temple, and when it was their week, some went up to Jerusalem and the rest stayed at home and recited, day by day, the six days of creation. 'The priests and the Levites therefore went up to Jerusalem and the Israelites that were of the same course came together in their own cities to read the story of Creation.'[46] They added appropriate intercessions, praying, for example, for seafarers on Monday, when the waters were separated (Gen. 1.6), and for land travellers on Tuesday when the dry land appeared (Gen. 1.9). If Jesus thought that the temple represented the creation, his words as he drove out the traders have an added significance: 'It is written, "My house shall be a house of prayer"; but you have made it a den of robbers' (Lk. 19.46), serving not God but mammon.

GOD IN THE MIDST

The original command to Moses on Sinai was: 'Let them make me a sanctuary, that I may dwell in their midst' (Exod. 25.8), and so they imagined the Creator enthroned 'in the midst', looking out from the throne onto the earth: 'The LORD looks[47] from heaven, he sees all the sons of men; from where he sits enthroned he looks forth on all the inhabitants of the earth' (Ps. 33.13–14, my translation). This accurate rendering appears in the AV and in the NEB, but the transla-

---

44 *Temple Scroll*, 11QT XXIX.

45 Josephus, *War*, IV.324, my translation.

46 Mishnah *Ta'anit* 4.2–3.

47 Some translations say 'looks down', introducing a different world view. The Hebrew says 'looks'.

tors of several English versions import their own idea of heaven at this point, and say: 'The LORD looks *down* from heaven . . .' (RSV, NRSV, GNB, JB), thus altering the biblical view. The LORD reigned *in the midst*, which explains Jesus' much debated saying about the Kingdom: 'Behold, the Kingdom of God is in the midst of you' (Lk. 17.21), meaning that the LORD is enthroned and reigns in the midst of the world. This is how they constructed their world, and so they built the holy of holies at the heart of the temple.

At the centre of the creation, and so of the temple, was the 'foundation stone', the *'eben shetiyah*, a great rock that represented stability and security in the midst of threatening chaos. This belief was not unique to Israel. In Egypt, the first dry land emerging from the watery abyss became the location of the sanctuary of the temple. Later Jewish tradition remembered the foundation stone as the embryo from which the creation grew. 'A child starts to grow . . . and then develops in all directions, and the Holy One, Blessed be he, began the creation of the world at the foundation stone and built the world upon it.'[48] An island surrounded by sea was a secure place, a temple surrounded by chaos.[49] When an ancient poet described the Exodus, she/he described the wind that parted the sea as the breath of the LORD, who then led his people safely to his own mountain, and planted them there in his sanctuary, safe from the hostile waters (Exod.15.4, 17).

The foundation stone of creation is often depicted in ikons of the Holy Wisdom, probably inspired by the Greek translation of Proverbs 8.23, which has Wisdom say of herself: 'In the beginning [the LORD] set me in place as the foundation, before the present age, before he made the earth.' Wisdom, and everything this represented, enthroned on the foundation of the earth, was essential for the security of the creation, as we shall see.[50]

Temple legends accumulated around this rock: it was there that the LORD had appeared to David, and so David moved the ark to Jerusalem from Gibeon, and the rock became the site of the temple (1 Chron. 21.14–22.1). Dust from this rock had created Adam; Abraham and Melchizedek had met there; and it was the place where Abraham had prepared to sacrifice Isaac.[51] The rock secured the

48 See Berman, op.cit. n.39 above, p. 652.

49 N. Wyatt, *Space and Time in the Religious Life of the Near East*, Sheffield: Sheffield Academic Press, 2001, p. 147.

50 See below, p. 247.

51 There are many such stories, see Babylonian Talmud *Yoma* 54a.

waters of chaos under the throne of the LORD: 'The LORD sits enthroned over the flood,' sang the psalmist, 'the LORD sits enthroned as king for ever' (Ps. 29.10). When king David began to dig the foundations for the temple, the subterranean waters of chaos threatened to well up and submerge the world, but a potsherd bearing the Sacred Name was thrown into the waters and they subsided.[52] John saw the throne in heaven, set in a sea of crystal (Rev. 4.6), and beneath the throne there would have been the foundation stone. The temple and the LORD enthroned in the temple symbolized and ensured the order of creation, and on the rock they set the ark of the covenant that held the ten commandments, or they depicted Wisdom enthroned.

The king, who represented the LORD on earth, was given power over the waters and what they represented. 'I will set his hand on the sea and his right hand on the rivers. He shall cry to me "Thou art my Father . . ."' (Ps. 89. 25–6). When Jesus calmed the waters of Galilee, his disciples asked, rhetorically: 'Who then is this, that even the wind and sea obey him?' (Mk 4.41). Calming the stormy waters was, for the first Christians, a sign that they recognized. Temple cosmology was their cultural heritage, and shaped their way of thinking. This can be seen in the early Christian Psalter included in the fifth century Bible known as the Codex Alexandrinus. In addition to the familiar psalms, there are several biblical songs such as the Nunc Dimittis and the Magnificat, and one otherwise unknown: the Prayer of Manasseh. The wicked king (2 Kgs 24.3–4) repented and the early Church prayed his prayer: 'O LORD Almighty . . . who hast shackled the sea by thy word of command, who hast confined the deep and sealed it with thy terrible and glorious name . . .' (Prayer of Manasseh 3). They thought in terms of chaos subdued by the Name of the LORD.

Trying to locate the rock is another matter. In Roman times, Jewish pilgrims used to return once a year to their ruined city, to visit a great rock. A Christian pilgrim in 333 CE reported: 'Two statues of Hadrian stand there, and, not far from them, a pierced stone which the Jews come and anoint every year. They mourn and rend their garments and then depart.'[53] Had the rock been the altar of sacrifice (1 Chron. 22.1), it would have been east of the temple building, but the ground here

---

52 This story is told in Babylonian Talmud *Sukkah* 53b.

53 *The Pilgrim of Bordeaux* in J. Wilkinson, *Egeria's Travels*, Warminster: Aris and Phillips, 2002.

slopes away towards the west, and would not have been an ideal site for the temple building. So perhaps the rock was under the holy of holies, as the later teachers recalled. In the absence of any decisive evidence, we are left only with what the rock represented: the foundation stone of the creation.

In the time of Jesus, it was said to be the rock under the holy of holies that protruded through the floor to a height of 'three finger-breadths'. The high priest rested the incense there when he entered on the day of atonement, and people remembered that the ark of the covenant had formerly stood on that spot.[54] In other words, at the heart of the Christian vision of the temple as creation was the Law. Philo emphasized this: when Moses set out the Law he began with

> an account of the creation of the world, implying that the world is in harmony with the Law, and the Law with the world, and that the man who observes the Law is constituted thereby a loyal citizen of the world (literally 'cosmopolitan'), regulating his doings by the purpose and will of nature, in accordance with which the entire world itself is also administered.[55]

Jesus accepted that the Law could be summarized by the two great commandments – to love God and to love your neighbour (Lk. 10.25–8) – but the ten commandments were never abandoned or superseded (Mt. 5.17–20; Rom. 13.8–10). They remained at the heart of the Christian view of creation, and, as if to emphasize this, John saw the ark restored to the holy of holies. The real ark had disappeared centuries earlier, but would be restored, it was said, in the time of the Messiah. In John's vision of establishing the Kingdom on earth, he saw the servants of the LORD rewarded, the destroyers of the earth destroyed, and the ark restored to the holy of holies (Rev.11.15–9), an important conjunction of ideas. Restoring the Law and removing the destroyers were part of the one process.

Cosmology in the contemporary sense of the word is a relatively new branch of physical science, exploring deeper and further into the universe, but not, as we have seen, discovering anything new about the question that concerns most people: 'Where do I fit into all this?' 'What about me?' Answers to our current environmental crisis are not likely to come from greater attention to current theories about cosmology. A recent survey of the history of cosmology began with the confident statement: 'The first such theories or models were myths

54 Mishnah *Yoma* 5.2.

55 Philo, *Creation*, 3.

that we nowadays regard as naïve or meaningless. But these primitive speculations demonstrate the importance we as a species have always attached to thinking about the Universe.'[56] For most people, the discoveries in outer space, and theories about the ultimate origin of the universe are fascinating, but of no immediate relevance to the business of daily living. When the people of ancient Israel described their LORD enthroned over the threatening flood of chaos and thus securing their world, they rejoiced: 'The LORD sits enthroned over the flood; the LORD sits enthroned as king for ever. May the LORD give strength to his people. May the LORD bless his people with peace.' (Ps. 29.10–11). Biblical cosmology prescribes the place for people, offers them security and makes clear their responsibilities.

THE TEN COMMANDMENTS

Temple theology recognized only one Law for the natural order and for human society, and the ten commandments spelled this out in practical terms.[57] They serve as a summary of the creation theology that will be set out in the rest of this book. The prophet Hosea, when he described the LORD's controversy with his people, summarized the commandments and the effect of breaking them. It was not just human society that was damaged.

> There is no faithfulness, or kindness, and no knowledge of God in the land;
> There is swearing, lying, killing, stealing and committing adultery;
> They break all bounds and murder follows murder.
> *Therefore the land mourns*
> And all who dwell in it languish,
> And also the beasts of the field,
> And the birds of the air,
> And even the fish of the sea are taken away.

Hosea blamed the priests for what had gone wrong.

> With you is my contention O priest . . .
> My people are destroyed for lack of knowledge;
> Because you have rejected knowledge,
> I reject you from being a priest to me.

56 P. Coles, *Cosmology. A Very Short Introduction*, Oxford: University Press, 2001, p. 1.

57 The Ten Commandments occur twice in the Old Testament (Exod. 20.1–17; Deut. 5.1–21) with differences in the reason for observing the Sabbath.

(Hos. 4.1–4, 6)

The first commandment was that there were to be no other gods in addition to the LORD. This did not necessarily exclude a plurality within the one deity; the ambiguity of the plural Hebrew word for God, *'elohim,* suggests this, as does the complex of beliefs about angels, to which we shall return.[58] No other god meant no other independent focus of deity, as in the Greek or Roman systems, no other centre and therefore no conflicting laws within the creation. There could be only one source of laws for both human society and the wider creation. Human systems – political, economic, social, religious – which did not recognize this would in the end destroy the unity since they offered a false centre, or a plurality of centres, an obvious contradiction in terms.

Second, there were to be no graven images as objects of worship This cannot have been the prohibition of all statues, since Moses was commanded to put two golden cherubim over the ark of the covenant to mark the place where the LORD would meet with him (Exod. 25.18–22), and the entire tabernacle/temple was built to represent the creation. The prohibition was the *worship* of anything made by human hands. Thus Isaiah had denounced the practices of his time: 'Their land is filled with idols; they bow down to the work of their hands, to what their own fingers have made' (Isa. 2.8). Jeremiah too: 'They burned incense to other gods and worshipped the works of their hands' (Jer. 1.16). Paul took up this theme at the beginning of his letter to Rome, because it was still a relevant issue as they took the Christian message into the Greek and Roman world. Those who worshipped 'images', he said, 'exchanged the truth about God for a lie, and worshipped and served the creature rather than the Creator, who is blessed for ever' (Rom. 1. 25). The result was a 'base mind and improper conduct' (Rom.1.28). Worshipping the work of human hands – think of this now in the sense of current human achievements and aspirations such as political systems, economic systems, management methods – is the certain way to destroy the bonds of creation, since the object of worship is a variety of human achievements and aspirations rather than the underlying and unifying glory of God. This is a distorted perspective in a system that the human does not control, because human beings do not make the laws that give life itself its structure.

58 See pp. 97–8.

The result of idolatry was a barren land (Deut. 29.22–8). It was not bad management that destroyed the land, but false gods, and to see the relevance of this insight we have only to look at the devastation caused by modern industries, driven by the need to make vast profits rather than the desire to be in harmony with the creation. Harvey Cox, in his classic article 'The Market as God' made some chilling comparisons between the market and the structures and processes of religion. He showed 'that in fact there lies embedded in the business pages an entire theology, which is comparable in scope, if not in profundity, to that of Thomas Aquinas or Karl Barth . . . In this new theology, [the] celestial pinnacle is occupied by "The Market."' This has now become the First Cause. Market has redefined the power to create, and 'there is no conceivable limit to its inexorable ability to convert creation into commodities.' The human body has become the latest sacred vessel to be converted into a commodity. 'The diviners and seers of the Market's moods are the high priests of its mysteries,' pronouncing it 'nervous' or 'jubilant' or whatever, and, 'on the basis of this revelation, awed adepts make critical decisions about whether to buy or sell.' 'The Market has become the most formidable rival [to other religions] because it is so rarely recognised as a religion.' No longer can we say 'The earth is the LORD's,' and only those with decent ways of running a business – clean hands and a pure heart, no false or deceitful practices – can stand in the holy Presence (Ps. 24.4). In the religion of the market, human beings own anything they can buy, and they can then act with very little to restrict them.[59]

Or consider the idolatry of the global food business, and worshipping the god of the GNP. Raj Patel gave many examples in his book *Stuffed and Starved*; this one was about 'the supermarket to the world' Archer Daniels Midland and its CEO: 'When agribusiness gives money to politicians, it sometimes buys politicians themselves . . .' [They] think of political donations as tithing and politics as like the church.

> The national interest has no self-evident form or substance, but it has its high priests and oracles, to whom a tithe can secure a more favourable dispensation.

---

59 All quotations from H. Cox, 'The Market as God', in *The Atlantic Monthly*, 283.3.(1999), pp. 18–23.

And as with the medieval grace of the Almighty, the national interest has tended
to bestow itself on the rich rather than on the poor.[60]

Idolatry affects not only those who break the commandment, but
also their whole society and their descendents. The chilling words
attached to this commandment *and to no other* – 'visiting the iniquity of
the fathers upon the children to the third and fourth generation of
those who hate me' – emphasize the consequences of idolatry. False
gods in one generation would affect future generations. It is in this
context that we should set the remarks of Gro Harlem Brundtland
more than twenty years ago: 'A new cultural ethos is the main thing.
That ethos, I believe, is inter-generational responsibility . . . If we cannot make people realise that living as we do will make it impossible
for their grandchildren to live at all, they won't change';[61] and the definition given by Paul Hawken: 'Sustainability is an economic state where
the demands placed upon the environment by people and commerce
can be met without reducing the capacity of the environment to
provide for future generations.'[62]

Iniquity, *'awon,* is the significant word.[63] It meant both the wrong
action and its consequence and was closely related to the Hebrew word
for distortion or bending. Hebrew Dictionaries list these as two separate
words which are spelled in the same way, but one wonders if that
distinction has been imposed. 'Distortion' is exactly what idolatry
entails. The Book of Job had Elihu describe the penitent man as one
who confesses: 'I sinned, I *perverted* what was right . . .' (Job 33.27).
Jeremiah described the faithless ones 'who have *perverted* their way and
forgotten the LORD their God' (Jer. 3.21). Isaiah described the LORD's
response to his people's wickedness; he would *distort* the surface of the
earth and make it desolate, the effect matching the cause (Isa. 24.1).
The reason for the destruction, said Isaiah, was the pollution of the
land caused by breaking the covenant laws (Isa. 24.5). And here
'polluted' is an interesting word, because it also means to be profaned
or godless.

---

60 R. Patel, *Stuffed and Starved. Markets, Power and the Hidden Battle for the World Food
System,* London: Portobello Books, 2007, pp. 112–3.

61 Gro Harlem Brundtland, 'The Test of our Civilisation' in *New Perspectives Quarterly*
6.1 (1989), p. 5.

62 Hawken, *The Ecology of Commerce,* p. 139.

63 See below, p. 150.

The distorted values – 'I will visit the perversions of the fathers upon the children' – which affect the third and fourth generation are contrasted with the result of keeping the commandments, which would result in 'steadfast love' for thousands. Here is another interesting word: 'steadfast love', *ḥesed*, is the one used to describe the LORD's acts in redeeming and preserving, that is in maintaining the great covenant, a fundamental of creation theology, as we shall see.[64] Isaiah gave this oracle of hope to the devastated Jerusalem: 'For the mountains may depart, and the hills be removed, but my steadfast love shall not depart from you, my covenant of peace shall not be removed, says the LORD who has compassion on you' (Isa. 54.10). 'Steadfast love' was the Creator's response to keeping the covenant commands. The picture is vividly presented in Psalm 25:[65] 'All the paths of the LORD are steadfast love and faithfulness, *'emet*, for those who keep, *nṣr*, his covenant and his testimonies' (Ps. 25.10).

The Book of Revelation suggests that the early Christians described themselves as 'keepers/guardians of the covenant and the testimonies', and the high priest's envoy described Paul as a leader of the Nazorenes,[66] the 'keepers' (Acts 24.5). The dragon waged war on those who kept the commandments and had the testimony of Jesus (Rev. 12.17), and the dragon's agent was the beast from the earth, who controlled commerce – the contrast again between God and mammon. 'No one can buy or sell unless he has the mark [of the beast]', a mark worn on the right hand and the forehead. Such marks must have replaced the phylacteries worn by observant Jews, which held sacred texts including the ten commandments.[67] In other words, the mark of the beast was incompatible with the Law. 'Mark', in Greek *charagma*, was literally the mark left by a snake bite, and in the Hebrew of the first Christians, this would have been the word *nešek*, the word used for interest. The righteous man who could stand on the LORD's holy hill did not lend his money at interest (Ps. 15.5); he did not take the mark of the beast. The followers of the beast who wore his mark instead of the Law are mentioned six times in the great drama of Revelation (13.7; 14.9,11;16.2; 19.20; 20.4); they are the 'destroyers of the earth' who are contrasted with the servants of the LORD (Rev. 11.18).

---

64 See below, pp. 162–4.

65 An acrostic with each of its 22 verses following the 22 letters of the Hebrew alphabet.

66 Not *Nazarenes* as in many translations.

67 Traditionally, they held Exod. 12.43–13.16; Deut. 5.1–6.9; Deut. 10.12–11.21.

The third commandment said that the Name of the LORD was not to be borne ('take' is the customary translation here for the Hebrew word *nasa'*, meaning bear or carry) in vain. This was a commandment for the high priests, who wore the Name of the LORD to indicate that they were the presence of the LORD in the visible world, and that they were his messengers, his angels – the same word in Hebrew. The Christians received the Name on their foreheads at baptism; they all became high priests when they were marked with the cross, the ancient symbol for the Name (Rev. 5.10; 14.2). The role of the ancient high priests became the role of the Christians: to maintain the unity of their people and the unity of the whole creation, visible and invisible. Wearing the Name, as we shall see, enabled the high priests to bear the sins of their people which would otherwise have fractured the covenant bonds. They were also the teachers, whose instruction ensured that the covenant bonds were not broken even through ignorance (Mal. 2.7). Those who failed to fulfil this high calling were in grave danger, and they were described as fallen angels, destined for a fiery judgement.

The fourth commandment was to observe the Sabbath day. Rest was part of the created order, and life was not to be given over entirely to work and production. Enough was enough. The 'Sabbath principle', as we shall see, has recently become an important part of Christian environment discourse.[68] The fourth commandment was an obligation on employers to ensure that everyone and everything had day of rest:

> In it you shall not do any work, you, or your son or your daughter, or your manservant or your maidservant, or your ox or your ass, or any of your cattle, or the sojourner who is within your gates, that your manservant and your maidservant may rest as well as you. (Deut. 5.12–15)

The Sabbath rest, now abandoned, ostensibly in the cause of freedom from outmoded superstitions and restraints, but in fact in the interests of the retail trade, was an early example of employee protection, animal rights and a good deal more. The language we use still bears the imprint of this commandment; we have a time of re-creation on our holidays, that is holy days.

The fifth commandment was to honour parents. The stability and continuity of any society lies with the family; and human parents, a male and a female, were jointly the image of the Creator. The family line was important. Look, for example, at 1 Chronicles 1–9, and consider the work of the scribes in collecting and preserving all those

---

68 See below, p. 181–2.

names in the genealogies. This was the order and structure of society just as much as the other laws. Fragmenting the family, with its network of support and obligations, was the breaking of a fundamental bond. We used to hear much about alternative lifestyles, but more recently the talk has been of a broken society, and the loss of family structures is a significant factor in this. In the biblical Jubilee year, when the great atonement was realized by the healing of human society,[69] slaves were released and debts were cancelled. We have heard a lot about this recently, with campaigns to remit the debt of developing countries, but have heard less about other aspects of the Jubilee – that people should be able to return to their own land and property, and be reunited with their families (Lev. 25.1–12). Fragmented families are a symbol of a greater fragmentation. The increased awareness of domestic violence and child abuse explain why, for some people, 'Father' is no longer an acceptable image for God.

Murder was forbidden, and elsewhere the reason was given. Since the human was made in/as the image of God, human life was given special protection (Gen. 9.6). In fact, all life was respected, and when an animal had to be killed for food, the blood, which was the symbol of its life, could not be consumed, but had to be poured into the earth (Deut. 12.23–5). Respect for blood was important for the early Christians too. Shedding blood was a sign of the broken covenant, and often set as a contrast to justice, a pair of Hebrew words that sound similar (*mišpat*, justice/ *mišpaḥ*, bloodshed). The *Book of Jubilees* says that some of commandments had been known even before Moses. They were originally given by Enoch and handed down to his heirs, one of whom was Noah. Noah warned his sons against consuming any blood, and against fornication, pollution and injustice. They had to dress modestly, bless their Creator, honour their parents and love their neighbours (*Jub.* 7.20–25). These Noahic commandments formed the basis of early Christian practice, as can be seen from the decision of the Council of Jerusalem: 'Abstain from what has been sacrificed to idols, and from blood and from what has been strangled and from unchastity' (Acts 15.29).

Seventh, the marriage bond could not be broken. Jesus saw this as the original pattern of creation, and taught that divorce was wrong, except where the bond had already been broken (Mt. 5.31–2; Mk 10.10–12). Divorce was permitted under Jewish law at that time, but Jesus taught that this was Moses' concession to human 'hardness of

---

69 See below, pp. 184–9.

heart' (Mt. 19.8). The original vision for creation had been for one man and one woman to become one flesh, joined together by God. Thus the basis for the sanctity of human life – that humans were made in/as the image of God – was also the basis for the sanctity of the lifelong marriage of male and female. The human male–female couple was the earthly image of the Creator.

Eighth, there was to be no theft. Humans had the right to own property, but also the duty to share it. Tithing was part of the temple law, and although the detail of tithing law is complicated, it is clear that this sacred giving was to support not only the temple worship, but also strangers, orphans and widows (Deut. 26.12). A part of what was owed to the Creator was caring for the less fortunate, as can be seen in Jesus' parable of the sheep and the goats who faced the judgement. They were not asked about the complexities of theology, and what they had believed; they were asked what they had done to help others, since in them, they should have been able to see and so to serve, the divine image (Mt. 25.31–46). Hence the question put to US politicians by Bono, the Irish rock star and debt relief campaigner, and even reported in the Financial Times: 'There is something eerily effective about an Irish rock star who can look conservative American religious politicians in the eye and say: "The Bible says we will be judged according to how we treat the poor. I believe that I will be judged. Do you?"'[70]

There was no expansion or qualification of the commandment not to steal, and so we can only speculate about its application. Was it just about theft of property, or theft of dignity and time as well? Today there is theft of identity, and also the sense that we are stealing from the creation if we take for ourselves irresponsibly, and without care and recompense. The laws in Deuteronomy to protect the environment and non-human creatures concern theft in that broader sense: it was forbidden to fell fruit trees even in time of war (Deut. 20.19–20); it was forbidden to take a mother bird and her eggs or young (Deut. 22.6–7); it was forbidden to muzzle the ox who threshed the grain (Deut. 25.4).

Modern equivalents might be some of the practices of big business. Paul Stiles assembled a chilling catalogue of examples in a culture ruled by the Market:

> One needs to look no further than the tapes from the Enron trading floor to understand the culture that the unbridled Market has created. "One energy trader boasts about cheating poor grandmothers. Another suggests shutting

---

70 Jamie Drummond, quoted in the *Financial Times* 13 May 2002, p. 24.

down a power plant in order to drive up electricity prices . . ." Certainly financial
crime is nothing new . . . What is new today is the nature, scope and efficiency of
that crime, the wholesale adoption of it as a common business practice, the types
of people involved in it, and the sheer audacious scale of it.[71]

And when the banks collapsed, as they did in the autumn of 2008, it
was the savings of those poor grandmothers that vanished, and their
taxes were used to rescue the banks from the consequences of their
own practices as they continued to reward their failures with huge
bonuses. But there was no Amos to fulminate against those who
'trample on the needy and bring the poor of the land to an end'
(Amos 8.4), just fine minds paid handsomely to justify what was happening. The prophet demanded justice and righteousness (Amos 5.24),
two words that were key to understanding the biblical world view.

Or one might consider the exploitation and destruction caused
by over-fishing and the use of wasteful methods such as bottom trawl-
ing, the destruction of forests for short-term gain, or the assumption
that natural resources are there for the taking because they do not
belong to anyone. The cost of destroying the earth – could that be
measured – has been absent for far too long from the prices set in
the marketplace. Should payments be made to preserve the rainforests
of the Amazon by those whose livelihoods depend on their continued
existence, for example those who benefit from the rainfall on their
cattle ranches? Forest keeping and forest management could become
recognized occupations, rather than forest destruction, but there are
fears that such schemes would be made unworkable by the corruption
of those involved in handling the funds. Obviously these particular
examples would not have been issues in iron age Palestine or in Roman
Judea, but if the temple vision is for all time, its fundamental insights
will be relevant to other very different situations. Isaiah had looked for
a time of justice and righteousness in the whole creation – for 'the
forest and the fruitful field' – but he knew this would only come
when there was good government, a king ruling in righteousness
(Isa. 32.1, 16–7).

And could the commandment now mean theft from future generations, using up non-renewable resources by living on the earth which
is our capital, rather than managing on our income from that capital?
In October 2008, the republic of Ecuador voted to give legal rights to
rivers and forests. 'Natural communities and ecosystems possess the

71 P. Stiles, *Is the American Dream Killing You?* New York: HarperCollins, 2005,
p. 184.

unalienable right to exist, flourish and evolve within Ecuador.'[72] Until
that time all legal frameworks had been people based, and governments (not just in Ecuador) permitted a certain amount of pollution
in the interest of business. It is now the duty of the government and
citizens to enforce the rights of the environment. No longer is damage
to be measured in terms of injury to humans beings; in future, it would
be measured according to the damage to the creation.

Free access to 'the commons' – forests, water, air – is no longer possible in a heavily populated world. What used to be 'free for all' can no
longer be so. We cannot all increase the number of our grazing animals
on the same patch of 'public' pasture, nor all draw an infinite quantity
of water from what used to be a more than abundant supply, or extract
limitless amounts of minerals from the earth or fish from the sea.

> Each man is locked into a system that compels him to increase his herd without
> limit – in a world that is limited. Ruin is the destination toward which all men
> rush, each pursuing his own best interest in a society that believes in the freedom
> of the commons.[73]

Such freedom was formerly exercised in the right to gather food, to
graze cattle, to mine ores and to dispose of waste. With increased
population, those ancient freedoms – including the freedom to breed
– bring ruin to all, and so extraction, pollution and the increased consumption that inevitably follows breeding are all forms of theft.

Ninth, there was to be no false witness, no half truth and ambiguity.
Satan is described as 'the deceiver of the whole world' (Rev. 12.9), and
his fall from heaven and eventual defeat is the theme of the Book of
Revelation. There is no place for Satan and his angels in the Kingdom.
This calls into question the whole culture of public relations and
advertising, the ways in which, for example, the legitimate concerns of
environmentalists have been transformed by the wordsmiths of commerce and given what is called a 'greenwash'. The concepts of sustainable development, meaning a more efficient use of existing resources
to produce a better outcome, 'has been reinterpreted by business to
become synonymous with sustainable growth – an oxymoron which
reflects the conflict between a trade vision of the world and the
environmental, social and cultural vision. It has become a mantra for

---

72 *The Guardian*, September 24th 2008, Society Guardian p. 8.
73 G. Hardin, 'The Tragedy of the Commons', *Science*, 162.13 (1968), pp. 1243–8.

big business and multi-national corporations'.[74] Official reports of ecological degradation are notorious for their inaccuracy. There is the double standard that sustains much big business.

> Millions of us now lead a schizophrenic existence, caught between the public, surface world of the American dream – the realm of family, of God, of country and of moral principle – and the hidden subterranean world of Market America, a dog-eat-dog world run by major corporations, where everyone does what they can get away with. It is the secret fact of American life, the one we are all not supposed to admit.[75]

The autumn of 2008 saw the great collapse of the world's financial systems. Having been told for years that there was 'no alternative' to those systems, they were exposed as a system based on a dubious mythology, demanding trust and faith from people who really did have no alternative, and ridiculing those who said they were unjust and destructive of the creation and human society. Hawken opened his book *The Ecology of Commerce* by saying: 'Making money is, on its own terms, totally meaningless, an insufficient pursuit for the complex and decaying world we live in.'[76] A journalist, reflecting on the deepening financial crisis early in 2009, wrote this:

> Adair Turner, the chairman of the Financial Services Authority, last week attributed the crisis to ' an intellectual failure' that ran though the whole system. But this was not a failure of brain power; rather it shows how intellect must always be married to morality if it is to prove conducive to the common good. It's not enough to be clever.[77]

So too with so many environmental disasters; it is not lack of knowledge or planning or management skills that brings disaster. It is lack of morality.

Tenth, there was to be no envy. The biblical word 'covet' has been re-branded as 'aspiration', and presented as something positive. Mockers have said the Bible is irrelevant because few people nowadays have the temptation to covet their neighbour's ox, but in the time of

---

74 Sadruddin Aga Khan, 'Is Sustainable Sustainable?' in *Symposium IV: The Adriatic Sea*, Athens: Religion Science and the Environment, 2003, pp. 103–8, p. 103.

75 Stiles, *Is the American Dream Killing You?*, p. 193.

76 Hawken, *The Ecology of Commerce*, 1995, p. 1.

77 Madeleine Bunting in *The Guardian*, January 26th 2009, p. 29.

Jesus, it was said that coveting was Adam's first sin.[78] A series of articles in the *New York Times* in 2002 examining the 'personal struggles to comply with the directions of ancient laws in the modern world', dealt with this commandment on Christmas Eve, in the context of the fashionable programmes offered by self-improvement gurus, self-improvement being the ability to make more money:

> The commandment against coveting warns against devoting energy to acquiring goods and possessions. Yet, the message to achieve wealth is the engine of the modern consumer society. The conflict between the commandment and the drive to consume is as much a conflict between the ethical demands of the ancient world and the practical reality of living in the modern one.[79]

This could be read as assuming that the ten commandments are of historic interest only, that the modern world in essence is different from the ancient. The laws of nature have not changed; it is only human attitudes that have changed, and what the tenth command-ment forbids has become the very basis of the marketing and advertising industries, the fundamental of economic prosperity. The result is so often consumption for the sake of consumption, success measured by the power to consume and growth for its own sake. Stimulating consumer demand is a key element in modern economic systems. A journalist commenting on the financial crisis of late 2008, wrote this:

> The crisis also represents a moral failure: that of a system built on debt. At the heart of the moral failure is the worship of growth for its own sake, rather than as a way to achieve the "good life." As a result, economic efficiency – the means to growth – has been given absolute priority in our thinking and policy. The only moral compass we now have is the thin and degraded notion of economic welfare.[80]

To have a few months without economic growth is, by definition, a recession, and the system is now collapsing. Such growth cannot go on for ever. There is only one earth.

---

78 See below, p. 221.

79 Chris Hedges, 'Path to Riches (But No Coveting): Seeking, After Rough Stretch, to Unlock the Inner Tycoon', *New York Times*, December 24th 2002.

80 Robert Skidelsky 'Where do we go from here' in *Prospect Magazine*, 154, January 2009.

ONE WORLD

The 'temple as creation' separated the holy of holies from the great hall of the temple by a curtain, often called the veil of the temple, which was woven from threads of four colours. In the time of Jesus these were said to symbolize the four elements from which the world was made: red for fire, blue for air, white linen for the earth, because linen was made from a plant, and grew in the earth and purple for the sea, because purple dye was made from sea shells.[81] In other words, the fabric of the veil represented matter which hid the glory of God from human eyes. Nobody knows the age of this explanation; the original description in Exodus just stipulates the four colours. No reason is given in the Bible for any of the prescriptions for the tabernacle and its furnishings, except for the purpose of the tabernacle itself; that the LORD might dwell in the midst. Philo commented: 'He thought it right that the divine temple of the Creator of all things should be woven of such and so many things as the world is made of, the universal temple which was before the holy temple.'[82]

The creation that the temple represented was both visible and invisible, material and non-material, and this has become the Christian view. Knowledge that encompasses only the material world is incomplete and dangerous. It is the authentic Christian voice that says:

> Orthodox theology asserts that reality, understood in a wide theological sense, is much wider than that which is known to human beings through their reason and scientific research. If human reason is subjected to this lure of all-embracing knowledge and disregards the human spiritual experience of contemplating realities that are above and beyond the visible and intellectual, it inevitably arrives at the idol of scientific progress, which can only know this reality 'objectively' (that is, not from within its inward existence), and manipulate it technologically, so that humility in grasping the sense of existence is lost.[83]

In the time of Jesus, they understood the two parts of the temple to represent not only the visible, and the invisible creation, but also two aspects of time. Hidden within the veil was the holy of holies, which represented eternity, the state beyond time as we know it. This was not the remote past, but the ever-present divine reality beyond the mate-

---

81 Thus Josephus, *Jewish War*, V.212–13.

82 Philo, *Questions on Exodus*, II.85.

83 A. V. Nesteruk, *Light from the East. Theology, Science and the Eastern Orthodox Tradition*, Minneapolis: Fortress, 2003, p. 9.

rial world. The Hebrew words for 'hidden' *'alum*, and 'eternity' *'olam*, are from the same root *'lm*, which is usually said to have two distinct meanings: hidden or eternal. In temple cosmology these were not distinguished. The one creation had an inner and an outer aspect: the inner was the origin of all things, the unity of the divine presence; the outer was the constantly changing material world, where everything existed in time. The hidden world was 'within' the creation, not beyond it. The divine unity was continually related to the visible world, and all the 'depths' of the holy of holies could be perceived from and through the material world. When Jesus spoke of the Kingdom of God in the midst (Lk. 17.21), this is what he meant, and Thomas's Jesus explained: 'The Kingdom of the Father is spread out upon the earth and men do not see it.'[84] *There was more to creation than just the world we see around us.* There was only one 'system' and so only one truth that included both aspects of the creation. The separation of the two can be seen today in the way that science and theology have so often gone their separate ways: 'Science and theology for a long time seemed to be in search of different sorts of truth, as if there were not one truth in existence as a whole. This resulted from making truth subject to the dichotomy between the transcendent and the immanent . . .'[85] The writer of Genesis indicated this by describing the days of the visible creation in a numbered sequence – second, third, fourth, fifth, sixth – but the origin was described as Day One, not part of that sequence, but underlying the whole. The Old Greek translation kept this form, 'Day One', showing that it was a significant distinction.

Philo explained the function of the veil: 'It speaks mysteriously of the changeable parts of the world . . . which undergo changes of direction, and the heavenly part, which is without transient events and is unchanging.'[86] Philo used the same language to describe the creation: the first book of Moses, he said, was aptly named Genesis, meaning 'becoming', because 'everything that is an object of sensible perception is subject to becoming and constant change. . .'[87] Philo was clear that the 'beginning' was outside time, rather than the earliest part of time: '[Moses] says that "in the beginning" God made the heaven and the earth, taking "beginning" not, as some think, in a chronological sense,

84 *Gospel of Thomas*, 113.

85 John Zizioulas, *Being as Communion. Studies in Personhood and the Church*, London: Darton, Longman and Todd, 1985, p. 119.

86 Philo, *Questions on Exodus*, II.91.

87 Philo, *Creation*, 12.

for there was no time before there was a world.'[88] He concluded that 'beginning' indicated that the heaven had been made before the earth.

Nor did they believe that the Creator had completed the creation in the remote past and then left it to run its course. They imagined the LORD enthroned in the midst as the continual source of all creation. The text of Psalm 104.29 found at Qumran (11QPs³) is slightly but significantly different from the later Masoretic Hebrew that underlies the English translations. This psalm describes the creation, the manifold works of the LORD, and the familiar 'When you take away *their* spirit they die and return to their dust' appears as in the Qumran text as 'When you take away *your* Spirit, then they die and return to their dust' (My translations). The Qumran text says that the life of the creatures is the Spirit of the LORD, and when he withdraws it, they perish. The Spirit of the LORD holds them in existence. The following verse affirms: 'When you send forth your Spirit they are created, and you renew the face of the earth.' This follows more naturally from the Qumran version of the text – a comparison of the LORD withdrawing and sending forth his Spirit – and suggests that the Spirit of the LORD maintaining the life of all things was the original form of this Psalm.

There is also good reason to believe that 'The One who causes to be' was the meaning of the name Yahweh. At the burning bush, the Hebrew text says that the Name revealed to Moses was a special form of Yahweh: *'ehyeh 'ašer 'ehyeh,* usually translated 'I am who I am,' and the Greek had the very similar *ho ōn,* 'I am the One who is.' This name appears in ikons of Christ, to identify him as the LORD. The Targums, however, the Aramaic translations of the Hebrew Scriptures, rendered the repeated *'ehyeh,* (that is, the double 'I am'), as: 'He who said, and the world was there from the beginning, and is to say to it, "Be there" and it will be there . . .'[89] They must have thought that Yahweh meant 'He who causes to be,' the one who created in the past and will create in the future. Old Testament scholars have been suggesting for centuries that Yahweh means 'He who causes to be,'[90] despite the popular hymn that proclaims 'Jehovah great I AM.' The Targumists expanded the Name into its past and future aspects because this is how it was understood in their time. The LORD was continually creating.

---

88 Philo, *Creation*, 26.

89 Thus the *Neofiti* Targum to Exodus 3.14. Targum Pseudo-Jonathan is similar.

90 First suggested by Clericus in 1700. For a brief history of this interpretation, see W. H. Brownlee 'The Ineffable Name of God', *Bulletin of the American Schools of Oriental Research,* 226 (1977), pp. 39–46.

The first Christians had this same understanding, and in the earliest known Christian description of worship, John heard the song of the living creatures around the throne. They were praising the LORD God Almighty 'who was and is and is to come', an expansion of the Name (Rev. 4.8); and the elders responded by singing praise to the Creator: 'For thou didst create all things, and by thy will they existed and were created' (Rev. 4.11). This is praise of the Creator at the source of creation, and the expanded form of the Name meant the One who was continually creating. Thus Jesus could say: 'My Father is working still and I am working' (Jn 5.17); creation was not completed while there were still people in need of healing. One of the fragmented Qumran hymns had similar ideas: 'By thy wisdom [ ] eternity, and before creating them thou knewest thy works for ever and ever . . . All things [ ] according to [ ], and without thee, nothing is done.'[91] Life came forth from the presence of the LORD, that is from the holy of holies. Peter explained this in his sermon in Solomon's porch. 'Times of refreshing' would come from the presence of the LORD when Christ returned (Acts 3.19). This, as we shall see, was imagery from the Day of Atonement, the time when the creation was cleansed and renewed by the self-offering of the great high priest.[92]

The biblical writers were aware that creation was held in existence and could return to a state of chaos, but they did not identify this as simply a physical process; it was caused by human activity. Just as obeying the Law helped to sustain the creation, so too abandoning the Law could bring its destruction. Jeremiah had a vision of everything returning to the pre-created state because ' . . . my people are skilled in doing evil, but how to do good they know not.' He saw the creation disintegrate: 'I looked on the earth, and lo it was waste and void, and to the heavens, and they had no light' (Jer. 4.22–3). 'Waste and void' *tohu wabohu*, are the words used in Genesis 1.2 to describe the earth before the Spirit began to move and God began to create. In other words, Jeremiah saw evil actions destroying everything that God had created and made. The creation existed because the Creator maintained it, but the creation could be destroyed. The pre-created light of the holy of holies was the source of life and of the bond that held everything together in good order. In the biblical accounts, this state is known as righteousness, and those who establish and maintain it are the righteous. The Word, said John, was in the beginning, that is, in

91 1QH IX.
92 See below, pp. 156–8.

the state represented by the holy of holies: 'All things were made through him, and without him was not anything made that was made. In him was life, and the life was the light of men' (Jn 1.3–4). The early Church called Jesus 'The Holy and Righteous One', 'the Author of Life' (Acts 3.14–5), not just in the sense of being the Creator in the remote past, but in the sense of being the continuous source of life.

Set these theological statements alongside a brief description of the second law of thermodynamics, which says much the same, but without the ethical dimension.

> The second law of thermodynamics informs us that as energy is dissipated, systems tend to descend into reduced states of organisation and ultimately to chaos and entropy. Only life prevents entropy from extending to all things in nature: the intricate, mysterious interaction of organisms that captures sunlight and evolves into higher levels of order and complexity. This state of organisation and succession, the opposite of entropy, is called negentropy.[93]

'In him was life, and the life was the light of men.'

Some of the Qumran texts show that in the time of Jesus, the faithful were being exhorted to ponder 'the mystery of existence', if that is what the phrase *raz nihyeh* means. This seems – one can say no more – to be an exhortation to gaze on the holy of holies, and there to learn the secrets of the source of life: 'Gaze upon the *raz nihyeh* and understand the birth-time of salvation and know who is to inherit glory and trouble . . .'[94] 'Gaze upon the *raz nihyeh* and know the paths of everything that lives.'[95] These 'paths' were probably the orbits and patterns prescribed for all creation, and held in place by the eternal covenant. Harrington commented: 'The [*raz nihyeh*] appears to be a body of teaching that involves creation, ethical activity and eschatology.'[96] Creation could not truly be understood without the concept of righteousness, the human choices that contribute to holding all things together or to their eventual dissolution.

The temple visionaries who ascended in their visions into the holy of holies, show the 'view' from that perspective, just as Isaiah had seen the LORD enthroned and then that his glory filled the earth (Isa. 6.1–5).

---

93 Hawken, *The Ecology of Commerce*, 1995, p. 19.

94 4 Q417.1.

95 4Q418.43.

96 D. J. Harrington, *Wisdom Texts from Qumran*, London: Routledge, 1996, p. 83.

Two who lived in the early years of the second century CE, and so in the formative years of the Church, described the pattern of the whole creation: Rabbi Neḥunyah ben Hakanah saw the very bonds of creation, 'the mysteries and secrets, the bonds and wonders, the weaving of the web that completes the world . . .', and Rabbi 'Akiba saw the whole world.[97] This was a temple tradition: the LORD reminded Isaiah that he had known the future 'from the beginning . . . from the foundations of the earth.' (Isa. 40.21). Isaiah had known the whole creation – the heavens stretched out, the host of heaven created – and also human history: princes and rulers brought to nothing. (Isa. 40.23). We shall return to this.

Such a person was an 'Adam', who had returned to the presence of God and so learned the secrets of the creation, and this was promised to the Christians. When the disciples asked: 'Tell us how our end will be' – the question the modern cosmologists have failed to answer – Thomas's Jesus said:

> Have you discovered the beginning, that you look for the end? For where the beginning is, there will the end be. Blessed is he who will take his place in the beginning; he will know the end and will not experience death.[98]

Seeing all things 'from the beginning' was an ancient belief: Job was mocked for claiming that he understood the ways of God: 'Are you the first man that was born? Or were you brought forth before the hills? Have you listened in the council of God? And do you limit wisdom to yourself?' (Job 15.7–8). The psalmist knew he would understand the future fate of the wicked when he 'went into the sanctuary of God' (Ps. 73.17). 'Abraham', in the *Apocalypse of Abraham*, ascended with his angel guide and saw the whole creation beneath him, as well as the whole course of history.[99] Most significant in our quest for what the early Christians knew, is the fact that Jesus himself spoke of such experiences: after his time alone in the desert, he spoke of the experience of being taken up to see all the cities of the world in a moment of time (Lk. 4.5), and John the Baptist could say: 'He who comes from heaven is above all. He bears witness to what he has seen and heard, and yet no one receives his testimony' (Jn 3.31–2). The early Church remembered that Jesus had taught the secrets of the holy of holies,

---

97 Texts in P. Schäfer, *Synopse zur Hekhalot Literatur*, Tübingen: Mohr, 1981, ## 201, 496.

98 *Gospel of Thomas*, 18.

99 *Apocalypse of Abraham*, 21–29.

presumably the *raz nihyeh* that the Qumran writers knew, the lost Torah of the state of light. Ignatius, bishop of Antioch early in the first century CE, wrote: 'To Jesus alone, as our high priest, were the secret things of God committed.'[100]

Jesus was proclaimed as the incarnation of Yahweh, the Lord, and so as the human presence of the One who causes to be. Old Testament texts describing appearances of the Lord were recognized as pre-incarnation appearances, and the Lord whom Isaiah saw enthroned was identified as Jesus (Isa. 6.1–5; Jn 12.41). The psalms were also sung as hymns, praising Jesus Christ. The earliest reference to Christian worship outside the New Testament is a letter written in about 112 CE by Pliny, the governor of Bythinia, who described the Christians assembling before dawn to sing a hymn to Christ as to a god.[101] They were probably singing a psalm. 'I will sing and make melody to the Lord' (Ps. 27.6), in the NT means singing to Jesus: 'Singing and making melody to the Lord . . . giving thanks in the name of our Lord Jesus Christ to God the Father' (Eph. 5.19–20). 'You have tasted the kindness of the Lord' followed by the exhortation to 'reverence Christ as Lord', that is Yahweh, (1 Pet. 2.3, 15) is a quotation from Psalm 34.8 'O taste and see that the Lord is good.' The collection of texts at the beginning of Hebrews includes Psalm 45.6–7, 'Your divine throne endures for ever and ever'; here, it is applied as a proof text, to Jesus: 'But of the Son he says: "Thy throne, O God, is for ever and ever"' (Heb. 1.8). These few examples – there are many more[102] – of psalms used to describe Jesus are taken from a spectrum of sources: Paul (or whoever wrote Ephesians), Peter and the author of Hebrews.

The first Christians proclaimed Jesus as the incarnate Lord described in the Psalms. He was the Lord, the Creator of the heavens, the moon and the stars (Ps. 8.3). They would have sung: 'The earth is the Lord's and the fullness thereof, the world and those who dwell therein' (Ps. 24.1); they would have proclaimed the Lord enthroned over the flood, ruling over the powerful forces of nature (Ps. 29.5–10), reflected in the disciples' question as Jesus stilled the storm: 'Who is this that even the wind and sea obey him?' (Mk 4.41).

---

100 Ignatius, *Letter to the Philadelphians*, 9.

101 Pliny, *Letter* 10.

102 See M. Daly-Denton, 'Singing Hymns to Christ as to a God', in *The Jewish Roots of Christological Monotheism*, ed. J. R.Davila, G. S Lewis and C. C. Newman, Leiden: Brill, 1999, pp. 277–92.

They would have proclaimed: 'By the word of the LORD the heavens were made' (Ps. 33.6); 'The LORD reigns, he is robed in majesty . . . Yea, the world is established; it shall never be moved' (Ps. 93.1); 'The sea is his and he made it; for his hands formed the dry land. O come let us worship and bow down, let us kneel before the LORD our Maker' (Ps. 95.5–6). The glorious works of creation described in Psalm 104 would have been attributed to the LORD, as would the praises in Psalm 147: 'He covers the heavens with clouds . . . he gives snow like wool . . . He declares his word to Jacob, his statutes and ordinances to Israel' (Ps. 147. 8, 16, 19). 'Praise the LORD, Praise him all his angels . . . For he commanded and they were created' (Ps. 148.1,2,5). *Singing psalms such as these cannot but have shaped the early Church's view of the creation.* John wrote: 'All things were made through him, and without him was not anything made that was made' (Jn 1.3); and Barnabas 'He is the LORD of all the earth, to whom at the foundation of the world God addressed the words, "Let us make man in our own image and likeness."'[103]

The *Letter to Diognetus*, written in the late second century, shows how the Church depicted Christ as the Creator.

[God sent] the universal Artificer and Constructor himself, by whose agency God made the heavens and set the seas their bounds; whose mystic word the elements of creation submissively obey; by whom the sun is assigned the limits of his course by day, and at whose command by night the obedient moon unveils her beams, and each compliant star follows circling in her train. Ordainer, Disposer and Ruler of all things is he; of heaven and all that heaven holds, of earth and all that is in the earth, of sea and every creature therein; of fires, air and the abyss; of things below and things in the midst. Such was the Messenger God sent to men,[104]

but we hear little of this today.

103 *Letter of Barnabas* 5.
104 *Letter to Diognetus* 7.

Chapter 2

BEGINNING CREATION

Day One was the holy of holies, the state beyond time and matter, and the earliest picture of Christian worship is set in the holy of holies. John was summoned to enter the holy of holies – 'Come up hither' (Rev. 4.1) – and there he saw the throne and the host of heaven worshipping the Creator.

> Holy, holy, holy, is the LORD God Almighty
> Who was and is and is to come . . .
> Worthy art thou, our LORD and God,
> to receive glory and honour and power,
> for thou didst create all things,
> and by thy will they existed and were created.
>
> (Rev. 4.8, 11)

Christian worship joined the heavenly host in their praises, and still does:

> Therefore with Angels and Archangels, and with all the company of heaven, we laud and magnify thy glorious Name; evermore praising thee, and saying: Holy, Holy, Holy, LORD God of Hosts, heaven and earth are full of thy glory: Glory be to thee O LORD most High.

From the beginning, Christian worship expressed praise of the Creator and shaped the Christian attitude to the creation, because it joined with the worship in Day One.

DAY ONE

Everything beyond the veil of the temple was forbidden, except to the sons of Aaron (Num. 18.7). This means that the teaching about Day

One – the origin of the creation and how the invisible world related to the visible – was known only to the high priests. In the time of Jesus it was forbidden to reveal this knowledge, or to expound certain texts: the first verses of Genesis that described Day One; Ezekiel's vision of the Chariot throne in the holy of holies that represented Day One; and the high priestly blessing about the shining face/presence of the LORD, that is, seeing beyond the veil into the light of the glory of Day One (Num. 6.24–6).

> The story of creation may not be expounded before two people, nor the Chariot before one alone, unless he is a sage that understands of his own knowledge. Whosoever gives his mind to four things, it were better for him if he had not come into the world – what is above? What is beneath, what was before time? and what will be hereafter?[1]
> The blessing of the priests may be read out but not interpreted.[2]

Since the temple represented the creation in both time and eternity, this secret knowledge must have been about the creation, and what was at the heart of it: its origin, its nature and its destiny.

In contrast, *the early Christians claimed to have this knowledge,* and expressed it in their worship. The tradition of the LORD, said Clement of Alexandria, was learned by 'drawing aside the curtain'.[3] Ignatius of Antioch claimed that Jesus, the great high priest, had been entrusted with the secret things of God.[4] Origen, as we have seen, said that only the high priests saw the temple furnishings, and so they alone knew what they meant. The mysteries of the Church, he said, had been handed down by the high priest and his sons, presumably Jesus and those who had kept his teachings.[5] These mysteries were the teachings symbolized by the furnishings and by the holy of holies. Deuteronomy emphasized that such teachings were not for everyone: 'The secret things belong to the LORD our God . . .' What mattered for most people was just keeping the Law (Deut. 29.29), that is, dealing with the affairs of the visible world. The Christians claimed more: they knew of 'things into which angels long to look' (1 Pet. 1.12). The Book of Revelation made public precisely the knowledge that was forbidden to synagogue

---

1 Mishnah *Ḥagigah* 2.1.

2 Mishnah *Megillah* 4.10.

3 Clement, *Miscellanies* 7.7.

4 Ignatius, *To the Philadelphians*, 9.

5 Origen, *On Numbers*, Homily 5.

congregations: teaching about the chariot throne, about what was before and after, about what was above and below. John heard the heavenly song in the holy of holies, declaring that the LORD was the Creator and Sustainer of all (Rev. 5.11) and that when his Kingdom was established, the destroyers of the earth would be destroyed (Rev. 11.18).

The problem with trying to reconstruct the meaning of the holy of holies is that the teaching was secret and did not appear in the public scriptures. Where there was even a hint of it, those texts were not expounded. The Book of Revelation, however, shows that the holy of holies, and thus the invisible creation, was full of heavenly beings. The closing vision of Revelation shows the Christians there too, presumably among the angels, bearing the Name on their foreheads and serving him (Rev. 22.4). Genesis says nothing about angels on Day One, only that God commanded light into being, and then separated light from darkness. *Jubilees* was another version of Genesis known in the time of Jesus, and it revealed much more about Day One. When Moses was on Sinai, the angel of the presence told Moses to record what he was about to see, just as John was told, 'Write what you see, what is and what is to take place hereafter' (Rev. 1.19). At the beginning, according to the *Jubilees* account, the LORD God, that is, Yahweh, created the heavens, the earth, the water, and *all the spirits who serve him*. He was the LORD of Hosts.

> The angels of the Presence, the angels of sanctification, the angels of the spirit of fire, the angels of the spirit of the winds, the angels of the spirit of the clouds, darkness, snow, hail and frost, the angels of the sound of thunder, and lightning, the angels of the spirits of cold, heat, winter, springtime, harvest, and summer, and all the spirits of the creatures which are in heaven and on earth.[6]

None of these angels is mentioned in Genesis – although there may be a hint of them: 'Thus the heavens and the earth were finished, *and all the host of them*' (Gen. 2.1). 'The spirits of the creatures which are in heaven and on earth' implies that the various beings in the material world had their corresponding spirits in Day One. This is important evidence. The spirits of the invisible creation are also mentioned in the Song of the Three children, Shadrach, Meshach and Abednego who were thrown into the fiery furnace by King Nebuchadnezzar.[7]

6 *Jubilees* 2.2.

7 The Song is not in the Aramaic text that is the basis of the English translations, but appears in the Greek text which has more detail at this point. In the English translation, the Song would fit after Daniel 3.23.

The central section of the Song is better known as the Benedicite, a song calling on all creation, both invisible and visible, to praise the LORD. The less familiar opening lines of the Song show the original setting of this praise; it was the holy of holies.

> Blessed are you LORD, the God of our fathers, praised and glorified for ever. Blessed is the holy name of your glory . . . blessed are you in the temple of your holy glory . . . blessed are you who sit enthroned on the cherubim, looking out upon the abysses . . . blessed are you on the throne of your kingdom . . . Blessed are you in the firmament of heaven . . .

And then the familiar lines follow: 'All you works of the LORD, bless the LORD . . .' All creation is listed and summoned to praise. First the powers: angels, heavens, waters, powers, sun, moon and stars, showers and dew, winds, fire and heat, winter and summer, dews, frosts and cold, ice and snow, nights and days, light and darkness, lightnings and clouds. Then the visible creation: earth, mountains, green things, wells, seas and floods, water creatures, birds, beasts and cattle, mankind – thus far the order is the same as Genesis 1 – then Israel, priests, servants of the LORD, spirits and souls of the righteous, the holy and humble, and finally the three children themselves. All are exhorted to praise the LORD enthroned in the holy place of his Kingdom. The Sanctus of the Jacobite Liturgy has kept this fuller form: 'Who is praised by the heavens and the heavens of heavens, and their entire power, the sun and moon and the entire choir of stars, earth and sea and all that is in them.'

It is easy to imagine the holy of holies static, our ideas being shaped by pictures, but in fact the holy of holies was described as a state of movement and the powers as moving around the throne. Romanus (died 556 CE), the Jewish born hymn writer in Constantinople, composed a *kontakion* in praise of the Three Children, and emphasized that the context of their song was both the furnace and the holy of holies, and that they formed a *choros*, which often meant a circular singing and dancing group, imitating the invisible angels:

> In the midst of the furnace the children formed a *choros,* and made the furnace a heavenly church, singing with the Angel to the Maker of the angels, and imitating the whole hymnody of the immortals (literally the ones without flesh).[8]

---

8 Quoted in E. Wellesz, *A History of Byzantine Music and Hymnography*, Oxford: Clarendon Press, (1949) 1980, p. 59.

Just as the visible form faithfully reproduced the invisible, so too the earthly music made audible its heavenly original. We shall return to this.[9]

Much of the list of the powers in the Benedicite corresponds to the list in *Jubilees*: fire, winds, clouds, darkness, snow, frost, lightening, cold, heat, winter and summer, and all the creatures in heaven and on earth. Something very similar to this *Jubilees* list was used by bishop Epiphanius, the great denouncer of heresies in the late fourth century, in his treatise *On Measures and Weights*. The Christians knew and used these texts, and such lists of all creation worshipping the enthroned LORD are the background to brief references in the New Testament. Paul, citing what seems to be a formula or even a hymn, said:

> God has highly exalted him and bestowed on him the Name which is above every name [that is, the name Yahweh], that at the Name of Jesus, every knee should bow, in heaven and on earth and under the earth, and every tongue confess that Jesus Christ is LORD [that is Yahweh], to the glory of God the Father. (Phil. 2.9–11)

Jesus had been given the Name, and so all creation praised him. He was the LORD of Hosts. The same scene, but with more of the context, is found in Revelation: when the Lamb had been enthroned, 'every creature in heaven and on earth and under the earth and in the sea' began to praise the-One-who-sits-on-the-throne-and-the-Lamb, one figure, the human who had become the LORD: 'Blessing and honour and glory and might for ever and ever.' (Rev. 5.13). This is the exhortation in the Benedicite: 'Bless the LORD, praise him and magnify him for ever.' We have to think of the LORD, as did the first Christians, enthroned at the midst of the angel powers in the holy of holies – the source of creation.

Whoever was singing the Psalms found at Qumran had this same world view; the texts are fragmented, but the gist is clear.

> . . . all thy works, before ever creating them: the host of thy spirits and the Congregation . . . their hosts and the earth and all it brings forth. For Thou hast established them from before eternity.[10]
> By thy wisdom . . . eternity, and before creating them Thou knewest their works for ever and ever . . . Thou hast created all the spirits . . . and law for all their works . . . eternal spirits in their dominions, the heavenly lights to their mysteries, the stars to their paths . . . to their tasks, the thunderbolts and lightnings to their duty . . .[11]

9 See below, p. 286.

10 1QH V.14,16.

11 1QH IX.7–12.

He divides light from obscurity; he establishes the dawn by the knowledge of his
heart. When all the angels saw it, they sang, for he showed them that which they
had not known . . .[12]

This vision of the origin of creation was probably the *raz nihyeh*, the
mystery of existence, meaning the angels of the holy of holies, the
powers of creation. At the end of the *Community Rule* there is a poem:

For my light has sprung from the source of his knowledge, my eyes have beheld
his marvellous deeds, and the light of my heart the ***raz nihyeh*** . . . My eyes have
gazed on that which is eternal, on wisdom concealed from the sons of Adam, on
knowledge and wise design: on a well of righteousness, a reservoir of strength
with a spring of glory . . .[13]

This resembles the teaching that 'Ezra' had to restore to his people:
the 94 books of which only 24 could be made public. The other 70
were only for the wise, because they were 'the spring of understanding,
the fountain of wisdom and the river of knowledge' (2 Esd. 14.47).
Since this is a thinly veiled account of defining the Hebrew canon at
the end of the first century CE, the 70 books were probably the Jewish
texts excluded from the canon that were preserved by the Church.[14]
Aramaic fragments of Enoch texts found at Qumran give the earliest known form of some of these angel names. The ones that can be
deciphered include *Ramt'el* 'burning heat of God', *Kokab'el*, 'star of
God', *Ra'm'el*, 'thunder of God', *Zeqi'el*, 'lightning flash of God',
Baraq'el, 'lightning of God', *Matar'el*, 'rain of God', *'Anan'el*, cloud of
God', *Sᵉtaw'el*. 'winter of God'.[15] The Ethiopic Enoch (*1 Enoch*) has
additional names, and it has been proposed that the originals behind
the Ethiopic were 'sun of God', and 'moon of God'.[16] At this distance
the details are lost, but the pattern can be seen; the angel names
indicated their role in the creation. The list in *1 Enoch* is the names of
the rebel angels, those who broke away from the Great Holy One and
came to corrupt the earth.[17] The names of the angels were part of the

12 *Hymn to the Creator*, from 11Q Psᵃ.

13 1QS XI.3, 5–6.

14 See my book *The Great High Priest*, London: T&T Clark, 2003, pp. 298–9.

15 As reconstructed by J. T. Milik, *The Books of Enoch. Aramaic Fragments of Qumran
Cave 4* Oxford: Clarendon Press 1976, p. 152. They correspond to the names in *1 Enoch*
8.3.

16 Thus R. H. Charles, *The Book of Enoch*, Oxford: Clarendon Press, 1912, p. 16.

17 See below, p. 166.

secret lore of the Essene community, where the initiate had to swear to preserve the books of the sect and the names of the angels.[18] The angel lore in *1 Enoch* described an attempt by a rebel angel to obtain the hidden Name from Michael, because this Name was the key to binding creation together. We shall return to this.[19] Suffice it to say here that the faithful follower of the risen LORD was promised 'a white stone, with a new name written on it, which no one knows except him who receives it (Rev. 2.17), and that Peter reminded the Christians that they had learned 'things into which angels long to look' (1 Pet. 1.12). Angel lore about the creation is never far from the surface of the New Testament.

Angel lore was in effect the natural science of that time. When Moses was on Sinai, as we have seen, he learnt the ten commandments and was shown the vision of creation. He also learned, according to texts known in the time of the early Church, detailed knowledge about the creation,[20] possibly what the Qumran writer called 'wisdom concealed from men, knowledge and wise design.'[21] A Jewish text written in the early second century CE by 'Baruch' said that Moses learned the measures of fire, the depths of the abyss, the weight of the winds, the number of the raindrops . . . the height of the air . . . the multitude of the angels which cannot be counted, the powers of the flame, the splendour of lightnings, the voice of thunders, the orders of the archangels, the treasuries of the light and a good deal more. Moses learned about angels and natural phenomena but also about the abundance of long-suffering, the truth of judgement, the root of wisdom, the richness of understanding and the fountain of knowledge.[22] These revelations gave the *measurements* of the natural phenomena: depths, weights, numbers and heights, as well as moral guidance. Enoch also learned these secrets: the depths of the earth, the division and weight of the winds, the power of the moon and the division of the stars. But Enoch tells us something more: the natural phenomena were/had angels or spirits. He learned about the angel of the frost and the angel of the

---

18 Josephus, *Jewish War* II.142.

19 See below, pp. 117–19.

20 For a survey of this material see M. E. Stone, 'Lists of Revealed Things in the Apocalyptic Literature' in *Magnalia Dei; The Mighty Acts of God*, ed. F. M. Cross and others, Garden City NY: Doubleday, 1976, pp. 414–52.

21 1QS XI.

22 *2 Baruch* 59.4–11.

hail, the spirits of mist, dew, rain and so forth, and how they related to each other and acted together.[23]

Both Moses and Enoch learned the secrets of creation as they stood in the presence of the LORD, either in the holy of holies, or on Sinai which, as we have seen, was often described in terms of the holy of holies. This was the vision of the Kingdom. Thus when Jacob fled from Esau, according to the Wisdom of Solomon, his dream at Bethel was not just of a ladder between earth and heaven; Wisdom showed him the Kingdom of God and gave him knowledge of angels (Wis. 10.10). What, then, did Jesus promise Nathanael when he said that he would see the heavens opened and angels ascending and descending upon the Son of man? (Jn 1.51). A similar experience to Jacob's? This would have meant knowledge of the angels, and all that implied by way of knowledge of the creation. Another text, *2 Enoch*, has him learning everything from the angels in the holy of holies. Once he had become one of them, that is, had been anointed as a high priest and transformed, he could say: 'I know everything either from the lips of the LORD, or else my eyes have seen from the beginning to the end.'[24] The account is remarkable. Nobody can date this text, but whoever remembered the inner detail of the high priest's anointing also remembered the revelation about the creation that was given when he was anointed. It was the LORD himself who revealed to Enoch how he created the world.

The Christians were similarly anointed, and John saw them all, bearing the Name, standing in the holy of holies (Rev. 22.3–5). He also reminded his flock what this meant:

> You have been anointed by the Holy One and you know all things . . . But the anointing which you received from him abides in you and you have no need that anyone should teach you; as his anointing teaches you about everything, and is true, and is no lie, just as it has taught you, abide in him. (1 Jn 2.20.27)

The knowledge imparted by anointing and unity with the LORD was the knowledge revealed to Enoch: the heavens, angels, stars, seasons and weathers, timekeeping, knowledge of plants and measuring the earth. Enoch also heard the songs of the angels, as did John, an important point to which we shall return.[25] The angel song symbolized

---

23 *I Enoch* 60.11–22.

24 *2 Enoch* 40.1.

25 See below, pp. 284–5.

the harmony of all creation, and when Adam was first created, the heaven was open, and he was able to look in and to hear the heavenly song.[26] When the new Adam was born in Bethlehem, the shepherds heard again the song of the angels – glory to God, peace on earth – showing that the original state of creation had been restored. But if the nature of the angels and their song was revealed to the anointed ones, would they have claimed to 'own' that knowledge? The claim to 'own' the knowledge of the creation, and then the right to patent it for commercial purposes, is one of the greatest examples of modern hubris.

The Enoch tradition preserved an ancient stylized account of Israel's history now known as the *Apocalypse of Weeks*, parts of which have been found at Qumran.[27] Since there are the remains of some twenty copies of *1 Enoch*, it was widely known in the time of Jesus. The *Apocalypse of Weeks* describes the second temple period as a time of apostasy, falling away from the true faith. At the end of that week, however, sevenfold wisdom would be given to those chosen 'to serve as witness to righteousness.'[28] Those reading Enoch texts – and one of them was the author of the Letter of Jude because he quotes Enoch – were expecting sevenfold wisdom to be restored to the righteous in the time of Jesus. This may be why third generation bishops could claim knowledge of celestial secrets and angel hierarchies and the dispositions of heavenly powers and much else both seen and unseen;[29] or pray 'to hope in thy Name, which is the source and fount of all creation'.[30]

The invisible creation was concealed from the material world by the veil, but was very much 'within' the creation rather than beyond it. Thomas's Jesus said: 'The Kingdom of the Father is spread out upon the earth and men do not see it.'[31] Philo described the angels as the invisible powers that extend through the whole creation. When Moses was on Sinai, he asked to see the glory of the LORD (Exod. 33.18), and when Philo expounded this passage, he showed how the glory and the powers were understood in the time of Jesus. 'By thy glory' said Philo's Moses, 'I understand the powers that keep guard around thee, of

26 *2 Enoch* 31.1–2.

27 4Q En^g.

28 *1 Enoch* 93.10.

29 Ignatius, *Letter to the Trallians* 5.

30 *1 Clement* 59.

31 *Gospel of Thomas* 113.

whom I would fain gain apprehension . . .' The LORD told Moses that
the powers were not seen by human sight, but rather could only be
'seen' by a pure mind. 'But while in their essence they are beyond your
apprehension, they nevertheless present to your sight a sort of impress
and copy of their active working.' The Exodus story continued with
the LORD saying to Moses: 'You shall see my back; but my face/pres-
ence shall not be seen' (Exod. 33.23), and in Philo's account the LORD
explained that his powers were not unlike Plato's 'forms' or 'ideas',
'since they bring form into everything that is, giving order to the disordered, limit to the unlimited, bounds to the unbounded, shape to the
shapeless, and in general changing the worse into something better.'
Moses would be able to see the back, that is, what lies behind the
powers, and this meant seeing how they were manifested in the material world.[32] Paul summarized this view, when he explained how God
was revealed in the creation: 'For what can be known about God is
plain to them, because God has shown it to them. Ever since the
creation of the world, his invisible nature, namely his eternal power
and deity, has been clearly perceived in the things that have been
made' (Rom. 1.19–20). Similar thinking seems to underlie his reasoning in 1 Corinthians, where he explains the distinction between material and resurrection bodies: 'There are celestial bodies and there are
terrestrial bodies . . . It is sown a physical body, it is raised a spiritual
body. If there is a physical body, there is also a spiritual body'
(1 Cor. 15.40, 44).

Since Paul had the same view about angels and creation as did Philo,
it is likely that Philo's more detailed teaching about the powers was
part of the original Christian world view. The Powers were the bonds
of the creation:

> God is everywhere because he has made his powers extend through earth and
> water, air and heaven, and has left no part of the universe without his presence.
> Uniting all with all, he has bound them fast with invisible bonds that should
> never be loosed. His power, by which he made and ordered all things, embraces
> all things and runs right through every part of the universe. The divine which is
> everywhere we can neither see nor understand, and what we can see and under-
> stand is nowhere near the truth.[33]
> Moses teaches us that everything is held together by unseen powers, which the
> creator made reach from the furthest parts of the earth to the furthest parts of

32 Philo, *Special Laws*, I.41–50.

33 Philo, *Confusion of Tongues* 136.

heaven, thinking wisely beforehand that what was bound should not be unbound. For the powers in everything are bonds which should not be broken.[34]

The angels as the powers in the creation remained part of the Christian world view, as can be seen, for example in the writing of Cardinal Newman:

> Persons commonly speak as if the other world did not exist now but would after death. No: it exists now, though we see it not. It is among us and around us . . . We are, then, in a world, of spirits as well as in a world of sense. And we hold communion with it and take part in it, though we are not conscious of doing so.[35]

The 'forms' are usually identified as an element from Platonism, but something very similar is found in the ancient temple tradition. There is, however, good reason to believe that the teachings of Pythagoras, many of which passed into the teachings of Plato, were very similar to temple lore.[36] Josephus, an educated man from 'the chief family of the first course of the priests',[37] said the Essenes, who guarded the names of the angels, had a lifestyle like the Pythagoreans[38] – but he did not elaborate on the extent of the comparison. He said that Pythagoras not only knew Jewish teachings, but adopted them as his own teaching: 'It is very truly affirmed of this Pythagoras that he took a great many of the laws of the Jews into his own philosophy.'[39] Viewing creation 'from above' or 'from within' – the temple world view – could well be what Aristotle had in mind when, in effect, he accused the Pythagoreans of an unscientific way of investigating the natural world: 'They do not seek accounts and explanations in conformity with appearances, but try by violence to bring the appearances into line with accounts and opinions of their own.'[40] He also considered it strange that they 'attribute generation to eternal things',[41] which is very like the temple belief that all life comes forth from the eternity in the midst.

34 Philo, *Migration of Abraham* 181.

35 Cardinal Newman. *Parochial and Plain Sermons*, Cambridge: Rivingtons, 1868, 4.13.

36 See my book *The Great High Priest*, pp. 262–93.

37 Josephus, *Life* 1.

38 Josephus, *Antiquities* XV.371.

39 Josephus, *Against Apion* I.22.

40 Aristotle, *On the Heavens*, 293a.

41 Aristotle *Metaphysics* N3 1091 a.

The Pythagoreans had had two fundamental principles, one of which was the 'Limit', described as unity, goodness and rest,[42] and which sounds very like the holy of holies, and the other the belief that a fiery cube was at the centre of the universe. This was the number One and the present moment,[43] and was 'the creative force which gives life to the whole earth . . . Some call it Zeus' tower, or Zeus' watch tower, or Zeus' throne.'[44] This must have been the holy of holies: the ever present eternity, the source of life, the throne of the LORD, and the tower from which he looked out. According to Iamblichus, the Pythagoreans called Unity 'the Chariot', which can only have derived from the chariot throne in the holy of holies.[45] Since educated Jews in Jesus' time recognized that Pythagoras had adopted their ancient forms of belief into his own system, whence they passed into the teaching of Plato, it is not accurate to say that the early Christians adopted elements from Plato, or his world view; the characteristic Christian world view, as depicted in Revelation and implied in the rest of the New Testament, is that of the temple.

Philo was careful to distinguish between Plato's 'forms' and the powers. He was working with the original temple cosmology, and it is likely that the Christians also knew the older temple scheme. The Qumran *Songs of the Sabbath Sacrifice* and the *Thanksgiving Hymns* are the best contemporary evidence for how Jesus and his disciples might have imagined the holy of holies. Several technical terms are used in the *Sabbath Songs* for what exists in the *d^ebir*, the holy of holies, and it is not easy to compare these with Philo's Greek. There are *'elohim*, here meaning gods, there are *surot*, shapes or forms, and there is *tabnit*, another word meaning form or pattern. The *'elohim* who serve the Presence in the *d^ebir* of glory are the priests of the highest heights, figures of fire who move swiftly. Note that they are moving. They are chiefs of the pattern of the *'elohim*, and they know the mysteries.[46] A better preserved piece of text reads: 'Spirits of the knowledge of truth [ ] righteousness in the holy of holies, forms, *surot*, of the living

42 See Burkert, tr. E. L. Minar, *Lore and Science in Ancient Pythagoreanism*, Cambridge, MA: Harvard UP, 1972, p. 43.

43 P. Kingsley, *Ancient Philosophy, Mystery and Magic. Empedocles and the Pythagorean Tradition*, Oxford: Clarendon, 1995, p. 183.

44 Simplicius, *On the Heavens*, 511.26 quoting Aristotle's lost work *On the Pythagoreans*.

45 Iamblichus, *Theologumena Arithmeticae* 6, ed. V de Falco, Leipzig, 1927.

46 Phrases from 4Q 400.1.1; 4Q 403.1.2; 4Q 405.3.2.

'elohim, forms, *ṣurot*, of luminous spirits, figures of forms, *ṣurot*, of *'elohim* engraved [the verb *ḥqq*] round their glorious brickwork.' They all bless the enthroned Creator and serve in his Presence. The precise meaning of the technical terms is probably beyond recovery, but something can be reconstructed. The singer of the hymns declared: 'All things are graven before Thee, on a written reminder, for everlasting ages, and for the numbered cycles of the eternal years in all their seasons they are not hidden or absent from Thee.'[47]

In the holy of holies, Day One, what Philo called the powers around the LORD are thought of as 'engraved', distinguishable but without solidity. They are 'flat'. Philo explained this briefly: the number 1 indicated a point, 2 a line and 3 a flat surface with length and breadth; 4 then indicates depth and solidity, a solid object. 'The result of all this is that "4" is very important, because it has led us from the realm of bodiless existence known only to the mind, to a body of three dimensions, which by nature we can perceive with our senses.'[48] Trying to describe the world of 'forms' cannot have been easy, but the gist is clear enough. The fundamentals of the creation existed 'flat' in the holy of holies and determined the visible creation. Plato taught that maths was discovered and had an independent reality, that numbers transcended the physical reality known to our senses, and in a similar way, the 'mystery' of the holy of holies was also described as measurements or numbers. In the Hebrew tradition, these powers of the Creator were personified because they were one with the living God.

A modern equivalent might be the 'laws of nature' or principles expressed as mathematical formulae.

> Modern science itself is based on the idea that the universe is governed by invisible principles, the laws of nature. These laws are essentially intellectual, because mathematical equations are things that exist in minds. They're not physical things you actually encounter in the world. You don't look though an electron microscope and see Schrödiger's equation among the molecules, or look through a telescope and see Einstein's equations written in the sky. They are invisible governing principles, but they are conceived of in an extremely limited and non-creative sense, as abstract mathematical equations rather than as living minds with creative power. Creativity is supposed to come into the creative process by blind chance.[49]

47 1QH IX.

48 Philo, *Creation*, 49.

49 R. Sheldrake and M. Fox, *The Physics of Angels*, HarperSanFransisco, 1996, p. 81.

Roger Penrose, the Oxford mathematician suggested something very similar, when writing on 'Platonic Reality of Mathematical Concepts':

> How 'real' are the objects of the mathematician's world? From one point of view, it seems there can be nothing real about them at all . . . Can they be other than mere arbitrary constructions of the human mind? . . . There often does appear to be some profound reality about these mathematical concepts, going quite beyond the deliberations of a particular mathematician. It is as though human thought is, instead, being guided towards some eternal, external truth – a truth which has a reality of its own, and which is only revealed partially to any one of us . . . a profound and timeless reality.
>
>   . . . I cannot help feeling that with mathematics, the case for believing in some kind of ethereal, eternal existence, at least for the more profound mathematical concepts is a good deal stronger than in these other cases. There is a compelling uniqueness and universality in such mathematical ideas which seems to me to be of quite a different order from that which one could expect in the arts or engineering.[50]

Modern scientific investigation would probably part company with temple cosmology over the question of what the eternal, external truth might be: is it limited to descriptions of how the universe 'works', or does it have a moral dimension? In temple cosmology, the Creator's laws encompassed both; there was no distinction between understanding the physical world and accepting rules for how one should live in it. The human mind needs patterns to make sense of experience, and recognizes that these patterns are discovered, not invented. As Paul Davies observed, the order of the world is not logically necessary:

> It is a synthetic property of the world, one for which we can rightly demand some sort of explanation . . . The various forces of nature are not just a haphazard conjunction of disparate influences.[51]
>
> Scientists frequently experience a sense of awe and wonder at the subtle beauty and elegance of nature . . . The study of the atom revealed the same sort of mathematical regularities that occur in the organisation of the solar system. This is surely a surprising fact and has nothing to do with the way we perceive the world.[52]

Temple cosmology recognized the unity of everything, including the powers of good and evil, which were named as such. There were 'fallen' angels who used their knowledge and power in the creation to bring

---

50 R. Penrose, *The Emperor's New Mind. Concerning Computers, Minds and the Laws of Physics*, Oxford: OUP 1999, p. 123–4, p. 127.

51 P. Davies, *The Mind of God*, London: Penguin, 1992, pp. 195–6.

52 P. Davies, *God and the New Physics*, London: Penguin, 1990, p. 145.

corruption and destruction, as we shall see.[53] A recent writer on the subject of the invisible powers in our contemporary context said this: 'The powers that be are more than just the people that run things. They are the systems themselves, the institutions and structures that weave society into an intricate fabric of power and relationships.'[54]

The 'engraved world' of the powers or 'forms' is found in the earliest strata of the Old Testament, but is obscured by the inconsistency of modern translations. Ezekiel was a priest in the first temple, and when he described the chariot throne leaving the holy of holies and appearing in Babylon (Ezek. 1 and 10), he distinguished between the 'form' of what he saw, and how it actually appeared to him. The AV translation of these chapters does consistently use 'likeness' for the inner reality (here the Hebrew word *d*mut*) and 'appearance' for the Hebrew word *mar'eh*. Thus: 'From the midst of [the fire] the likeness of four living creatures, and this was their appearance . . .' (Ezek. 1.5); 'the likeness of a throne as the appearance of a sapphire stone . . .' (Ezek. 1.26) and 'a sapphire stone as the appearance of the likeness of a throne' (Ezek. 10.1); 'the likeness as the appearance of a man above upon it . . .' (Ezek. 1.26); 'This [a rainbow] was the appearance of the likeness of the glory of the LORD' (Ezek. 1.28). Ezekiel was expressing the temple world view of his time: the invisible reality manifesting itself in certain appearances, just as Philo explained that Moses could see only the 'back' of the powers. Seeing the 'likeness' came to be associated with knowledge of how the heavens and earth were created.

An exposition of *The Sayings of the Fathers*, attributed to Rabbi Nathan who lived in the mid-second century CE, but compiled several centuries later, said that man could not know the likeness, *d*mut,* on high because of sin. 'Were it not for [sin], all the keys would be given to him, and he would know how the heavens and earth were created.'[55] Seeing the likeness initiated the beholder into the mysteries of creation, which may explain a difficult verse in the Prayer of David. 'You have caused me to see the man on high, the LORD God [or O LORD God]' (1 Chron. 17.17, the gist of an almost opaque text). The Chronicler, who wrote within temple tradition, attributed to David the privilege of seeing the vision of the Man enthroned, just as Ezekiel saw the appearance of the likeness of the glory. Isaiah also saw the LORD enthroned, and he

53 See below, p. 166.

54 Walter Wink, *The Powers that Be*, New York and London: Doubleday 1998, Introduction.

55 *Abot de Rabbi Nathan* A 39.

heard the heavenly voices: 'Holy, holy, holy is the LORD of Hosts, the whole earth is full of his glory.' This suggests two things: that seeing the one enthroned was from the very beginning associated with knowledge of the creation; and that this knowledge concerned the angelic presence of the glory throughout the creation. John saw the One enthroned and heard the angel song praising the Creator (Rev. 4.1–11).

There are many examples in the Old Testament of the 'engraved' world underlying the visible creation, but this owed nothing to Plato. Ezekiel lived two centuries before Plato. The LORD comforted Zion with the words: 'I have *graven* you on the palms of my hands; your walls are continually before me' (Isa. 49.16). Closer to our enquiry about the creation are the examples in Proverbs 8, where Wisdom describes how the creation was engraved before the mountains and hills were made, in other words, how the 'form' preceded the visible manifestation. Translating literally: 'When he prepared the heavens, I was there, when he *engraved* a circle on the face of the deep . . . when he set down for the sea its *engraved* mark . . . when he *engraved* the foundations of the earth . . .' (Prov. 8.27–9). The date of Proverbs is disputed – this poem could conceivably have been influenced by Platonism – but Ezekiel is a witness to the first temple world view, and Jeremiah, his contemporary, also knew an engraved creation: the sand was set as 'an *engraving* of eternity' to limit the sea (Jer. 5.22, RSV 'perpetual barrier'); the sun, moon and stars had 'engravings' that determined their movements (Jer. 31.35–6; RSV 'fixed order'); 'the engraved things of heaven and earth' (Jer. 33.25; RSV 'ordinances'). 'He made an engraving for the rain' (Job 28.26; RSV 'decree'); 'Do you know the engravings of the heavens?' (Job 38.33; RSV 'ordinances'), this latter followed by 'Can you establish their rule on earth?' Job was asked if he could order the creation according to the heavenly pattern.

The engravings for the intended order of the creation included the rules for human behaviour. The same word 'engraving' is used for the statutes that Moses had to teach to Israel: 'all the engraved things which the LORD has spoken to them by Moses (Lev. 10.11; RSV 'statutes'); these are the engraved things that the LORD commanded Moses' (Num. 30.16; RSV 'statutes'). In fact, words deriving from 'engrave' are the usual way to describe the divinely given laws and customs of Israel. Ignoring them caused the whole creation – not just human society – to collapse.[56] Living out of harmony with the heavenly pattern brought disaster.

56 See below, pp. 139–48.

The patterns in the holy of holies and their appearance in the visible world probably underlie the familiar but enigmatic passages in Philippians 2 and Colossians 1, both of which are thought to be based on early hymns with the same theme: the invisible one becoming human in order to restore the creation. 'Christ Jesus, who, though he was in the form of God . . . emptied himself, taking the form of a servant, being born in the likeness of men. And being found in human shape . . .' (Phil. 2.6–8, my translation). This was what Ezekiel described: 'The appearance [visible manifestation] of the likeness [invisible reality] of the glory of the LORD' (Ezek. 1.28). So, too, using different words: 'He is the image of the invisible God . . .' (Col. 1.17), bringing back to their former state of harmony 'all things', making peace, that is *šalom*, though his blood. It is consistent with this that Jesus' most characteristic form of teaching was the parable, where he compared the Kingdom of heaven, that is, the state of the holy of holies, to the visible world. 'The Kingdom of heaven is like . . .', he taught, but warned his disciples that this referred to secret things that outsiders would neither perceive nor understand (Mk 4.11–12). The spirit came on Jesus in the *form* of a dove, and Luke emphasized that this was a bodily form (Lk. 3.22).

Theodotus was a teacher in the second century CE, a disciple of Valentinus. Their interpretation of Christianity was eventually rejected by the main Church, but there are elements in the writings of Theodotus that show knowledge of temple tradition and the angel priesthood.[57] He described the Son as 'drawn in outline in the beginning', just as the 'outline forms', the *ṣurot*, were described in the Qumran *Songs*. Jewish scholars have shown how *ṣurot* was a key term for angels in their mediaeval texts, and how the 'measures'[58] corresponded to the *ṣurot* that serve before the throne of Glory.[59] These were the fundamental structures of the creation. A singular form of this word often appears in the Hebrew Scriptures, but in the English versions it becomes 'Rock', because the two words are written in the same way. In most instances, the translators of the Old Greek did not include the word 'Rock', showing that they gave the word another meaning. 'The "Rock" his work is

57 For example, the high priest's entering the holy of holies, and the hierarchy of the archangels and angels as a heavenly priesthood, *Excerpts from Theodotus* 27.

58 See above, pp. 46–7.

59 See M. Fishbane, 'The "Measures" of God's Glory in the Ancient Midrash', in *Messiah and Christos, Studies in the Jewish Origins of Christianity. Presented to David Flussner*, ed. I Gruenwald, S. Shaked and G. G. Stroumsa, Tübingen: Mohr, 1992, pp. 53–74.

perfect; for all his ways are justice' (Deut. 32.4); 'You were unmindful of the Rock that begot you, and you forgot the God who gave you birth' (Deut. 32.18); 'O Lᴏʀᴅ my God, my Holy One . . . O Lᴏʀᴅ . . . O Rock . . .' (Hab. 1.12) are all examples of texts where there is no 'Rock' in the Greek, and 'Unseen One' would make more sense.[60] The Old Greek of Isaiah 30.29 has 'the God of Israel' where the English has 'the Rock of Israel', and the familiar 'Rock of Ages' was the invisible form in eternity.

It would seem, then, that the Lᴏʀᴅ had long been described as the 'form', showing why Paul described Jesus as 'in the form of God' (Phil. 2.6); and that the 'form' was equivalent to the 'measure' of the creation. This explains the sequence of Paul's thought in Ephesians 4:

> . . . until we all attain to the unity of the faith and of the knowledge of the Son of God, to mature manhood [?in the sense of mature Adamhood?] to the measure of the stature of the fullness of Christ . . . from whom the whole body, joined and knit together by every joint with which it is supplied, when each part is working properly, makes bodily growth and upbuilds itself in love. (Eph. 4.13–16)

'Working properly' is a reference to each part being in accordance with its 'engraving', and the whole is a unity. The body of Christ here is the living temple, which in turn was a microcosm of the creation.

Tʜᴇ Uɴɪᴛʏ

The many angels/powers/'forms' of the holy of holies were One and were Day One. This was the mystery at the heart of the creation, the origin, outside time and matter, but the centrality of this temple insight has been neglected in much recent theology, and consequently is not often linked to the work of scientists. Cardinal Newman observed long ago:

> The sin of what is called an educated age, such as our own . . . is to account slightly of [the angels] or not at all; to ascribe all we see around us, not to their agency, but to certain assumed laws of nature . . . So [the vain man] goes on, tracing the order of things, seeking for causes in that order, giving names to the wonder he meets with, and thinking he understands what he has given a name to.[61]

---

60 For a fuller list see my book *The Great High Priest*, London: T&T Clark, 2003, pp. 183–4.

61 J. H. Newman, *Plain and Parochial Sermons*, vol.2. no.29.

More recently, an Orthodox scientist and theologian wrote: 'Faith as the expression of belief in unity of orders in the universe, provided by the Logos, has been nearly eliminated from the diverse, extremely specialized scientific fields we see today.'[62]

In the early years of the Church, this unity was expressed in several ways. R Judan, who lived in the fourth century CE, taught that Day One was 'the day in which the Holy One, blessed be he, was One with his universe'.[63] Day One was the state of unity before the visible creation had been separated out from the divine source. It was outside time as we know it. Ben Sira, part of the Greek Old Testament, and thus known to the early Christians, shows how this was understood in Jerusalem about 200 BCE. The translation 'He who lives for ever created the whole universe . . .'[64] (Ben Sira 18.1, RSV) does not represent the Greek *koine,* which the Vulgate understood as *simul,* 'at the same time'. A more accurate rendering would be: 'He who lives for ever created all things at the same time.' All life originated together in Day One, and all life was One in origin. This accords with *Jubilees,* which knew that 'all of the spirits of his creatures which are in heaven and on earth' were created on Day One.[65]

It could also explain some of the detail in Ezekiel's vision of the throne chariot, where the Hebrew text is almost opaque.[66] Ezekiel saw the throne and its retinue, that is, the holy of holies as he knew it in the first temple. On the throne was the likeness of the glory, and beneath it there was a fourfold Living One known as the Spirit of Life, or perhaps it was the Spirit of Life within a fourfold group of Living Ones. The Hebrew is impossible, and any English translation that seems to make sense is not accurate. The AV is the most accurate. Consider the description in Ezekiel 10.1–22: A Living One, singular (vv. 15, 17, 20) is surrounded by wheels and something whirling and eyes (or points of light). There are three references to a whirling, ('whirling wheels', vv. 3,6,13) distinguished from the wheels of the throne. The prophet goes among them, v. 2, and takes out fire, v. 6. Then what? The words translated 'their whole body' (thus v. 12, AV; the RSV omits them)

62 A. V. Nesteruk, *Light from the East. Theology, Science and the Eastern Orthodox Tradition,* Minneapolis: Fortress Press, 2003, p. 201.

63 *Genesis Rabbah* III.8.

64 This verse has not survived the Hebrew.

65 *Jubilees* 2.2.

66 For detail see my book *The Great High Priest,* pp. 168–87.

elsewhere in the Hebrew Scriptures mean 'all flesh' in the sense of 'all created things' (e.g. Ps. 136.25; Job 34.15; Num. 18.15).

Beneath the throne was a whirling and all created things? This could explain Philo's account of the heavenly ascent, where the human mind [which for Philo is the image of God in each person], goes up into the circuit of heaven, where it is whirled around 'in accordance with the laws of perfect music' and then sees 'the patterns and the originals' (literally the paradigms and ideas) of the things it had seen on earth.[67] This is certainly how the later temple mystics described the scene in the presence of the Holy One: '. . . the souls of the righteous which have already been created in the "body" of created things and have returned to the presence of God, and the souls of the righteous which have not yet been created in the "body."'[68] This was the mystic's understanding of Isaiah 57.16b, which can be read as: 'The Spirit clothes itself proceeding from my Presence/Face, and all the souls I have made.' It is likely that the first Christians imagined Day One as the source and destination of all life. They knew their LORD as the upholder of all creation,[69] who declared himself to be 'the Alpha and the Omega, the first and the last, the beginning and the end' (Rev. 22.13).

According to R. Yannai, teaching in Palestine in the early third century CE, and R Judah ben Rabbi Simon, teaching in the fourth century CE, Day One was the Day of Judgement, that is, the Day of Atonement.[70] 'The whole idea underlying atonement, according to the rabbinical view, is regeneration – restoration of the original state of man in his relation to God . . .'[71] The temple ritual for the Day of Atonement must have expressed the restoration of the original state; in other words, atonement concerned the renewal of the creation and so was at the heart of the Christian message. The *Community Rule* at Qumran said something very similar. It prescribed what the community had to learn, and this included recognizing the role of every part of creation:

> From the God of knowledge comes all that is and shall be. Before ever they existed, he established their whole design, and when, as ordained for them, they come into being, it is in accord with his glorious design that they accomplish

67 Philo, *Creation*, 71.

68 *3 Enoch* 43.3.

69 See below, pp. 121–6.

70 *Genesis Rabbah* III.8; II.3.

71 *The Jewish Encyclopedia* , New York: Funk and Wagnalls, 1901.

their task without change. The laws of all things are in his hand, and he provided them with all their needs.[72]

At first sight, exploring the visions of the temple mystics may seem, like the talking snake and the missing rib, to be of little relevance to current problems. Read in their cultural and theological context, however, they set out a world view that is all too relevant.

Forty years ago, Hugh Montefiore was calling for a greater Christian awareness of the environment, for theology to be relevant to everyday concerns, but there was little response.[73] When he became a member of the Church of England's Board for Social Responsibility, and tried to promote concern for the environment: 'I was told that it had enough to do without that'[74] Christians were thinking differently, because biblical fundamentals had been lost. Dillistone, in his influential work on atonement published at that time, had completely missed the significance of the temple world view. He wrote: 'From the New Testament there come hints, suggestions, even daring affirmations of a comprehensive cosmic reconciliation' but he doubted this had Hebrew roots. 'It was not until early Christian witnesses found themselves confronted by pagan systems in which a full theory of cosmic redemption played a prominent part that the effect of the work of Christ upon the cosmos at large began to receive serious consideration.'[75] He was yet another victim of the all pervasive emphasis on the Old Testament as history. Hugh Montefiore suggested that most Christians focused not on creation but on salvation,[76] but in the original temple world view creation and re-creation were one and the same.

Far from being just hints and suggestions, the restoration of the original unity seems to be the culmination of Paul's outline of the future: 'And when all things shall be subjected unto him, then shall the Son also himself be subject unto him, that put all things under him, that God may be all in all' (1 Cor. 15.28, AV). This is a literal rendering of the Greek *ho theos panta en pasin*, and is Paul at his most opaque. It seems to be a summary of what John described in

72 *The Community Rule*, 1QS III.

73 See above, p. 12.

74 'Why Aren't More Church people Interested in the Environment?' in *A Christian Approach to the Environment*, special issue of Transformation 16.3 1999, pp. 5–18, p. 7.

75 F. W. Dillistone, *The Christian Understanding of Atonement*, Philadelphia: Westminster press, 1968, p. 47.

76 Montefiore, *A Christian Approach to the Environment*, p. 15.

Revelation 21: 'He who sat on the throne said: "Behold I make all things new"' (Rev. 21.5), the re-creation that followed the great atonement. A voice had announced: 'Behold, the tabernacle of God is with men and he shall tabernacle with them . . .' (Rev. 21.3). The *Book of Jubilees* described the end of this era as the time when the LORD would descend to his people 'and dwell with them in all the ages of eternity.'[77]

The *Gospel of Thomas* uses unfamiliar language but expresses familiar ideas: he has Jesus say: 'Where the beginning is, there the end will be. Blessed is he who will take his place in the beginning; he will know the end and will not experience death.' These are the resurrected, those who have entered the holy of holies, and so returned to the beginning at their end. 'You are from [the kingdom] and to it you will return' needs no explanation if set in the world of temple theology. Thomas' Jesus said:

> I am he who exists from the undivided . . . If [he] is undivided he will be filled with light, but if he is divided he will be filled with darkness.[78]
> It is I who am the light which is above them all. It is I who am the All. From me did the All come forth and unto me did the All extend.[79]

Theodotus, who knew and used temple symbolism, taught this about the angels:

> They say that our angels were put forth in unity and are one in that they are from the One. Now since we existed in a state of separation, Jesus was baptised so that the undivided should be divided until he should unite us with them [the angels] in the fullness. Thus we many having become one might all be mingled in the One, which was divided for our sakes.[80]

The 'fullness' here is the holy of holies, and Jesus entered the 'divided' world in order to reunite the faithful with the One. This is familiar teaching, albeit expressed differently by John in Jesus' prayer after the last supper: 'That they may be one even as we are one . . . that they may be with me where I am, to behold my glory which thou hast given me in thy love for me before the foundation of the world' (John 17.11, 24).

77 *Jubilees* 1.26.
78 *Gospel of Thomas* 18, 49, 61.
79 *Gospel of Thomas* 77.
80 *Excerpts from Theodotus* 36.

Philo explained that the golden ornament worn on the forehead of the high priest and bearing the four letters of the Name (that is Yahweh, meaning 'He who causes to be') represented: 'The original principle behind all principles, after which God shaped or formed the universe.' The rebel angels tried to learn the secret sacred Name, says one very difficult piece of text in *1 Enoch*. This Name was the key to the great oath that bound all creation in its order: 'This oath is mighty over them, and through it their paths are preserved and their course is not destroyed.'[81] It was the unifying power of the Name that upheld the creation. This became a fundamental of later Jewish mysticism: the Name was the supreme concentration of divine power, and through the creative powers (which they called the *sephirot*) the Creator was revealed.

> The Name contains power, but at the same time embraces the secret laws and harmonious order which pervade and govern all existence.
> The hidden dynamic of this [divine life insofar as it moves toward creation] fascinated the Kabbalists, who found it reflected in every realm of creation.

The *sephirot* were both the powers and, literally, the letters by which the world was made and through which divine revelation was given.[82]

Thus no *letter* of Scripture could be changed. Rabbi Meir, who was teaching in the mid second century CE, recalled a warning he had been given by Rabbi Ishmael, the 'high priest' who ascended to heaven and talked with Enoch/Metatron in *3 Enoch* – in other words, who was remembered as a temple mystic: 'He said to me: " My son, be careful in your work, for it is the work of God; if you omit a single letter, or write a letter too many, you will destroy the whole world."'[83] This idea seems to underlie Jesus' saying about the Law: 'For truly, I say to you, till heaven and earth pass away, not an iota, not a dot, will pass from the law until all is accomplished' (Mt. 5.18).

Philo also said that all the powers were 'given the Name of the LORD',[84] just as another Enoch text names sixteen great princes in heaven, who bear names compounded with Yahweh: for example, Tatrasi'el Yahweh, 'Atrugi'el Yahweh, Na'ari'el Yahweh.[85] When Josephus wrote the story

81 *1 Enoch* 69.25.

82 G. Scholem, *On the Kabbalah and its Symbolism*, London: Routledge, 1965, pp. 40, 35.

83 Babylonian Talmud *Erubin* 13a.

84 Philo, *Migration of Abraham* 103; *Who is the Heir?*, 170.

85 *3 Enoch* 18.9–11.

of the LORD and two angels appearing to Abraham at Mamre (Gen. 18), he did not mention the LORD, but said simply that three angels appeared. This must have been how people at that time read the story: the LORD appeared in his angels.[86] It explains what the LORD promised the faithful Christian: 'I will write on him . . . my own new name' (Rev. 3.12); and what John saw on Mount Zion: 'a hundred and forty four thousand who had his name and his Father's name written on their foreheads' (Rev. 14.1). 'Where two or three are gathered in my name, there am I in the midst of them' (Mt. 18.20).

'The Name' was the cross marked on the forehead at baptism, and Philo's evidence that all the powers were given the Name may account for one of the ways baptism was described: '*into* the Name' (thus Mt. 28.19; Acts 8.16). Paul asked the Christians at Corinth: 'Were you baptised *into* the name of Paul?' (1 Cor. 1.13), and explained to the Christians in Rome that they had been baptized *into* Christ Jesus (Rom. 6.3). Jesus prayed for the unity of his disciples, which would be proof of his own divinity: '. . . that they may all be one, even as thou, Father, art in me, and I in thee, that so they also may be in us, so that the world may believe that thou hast sent me' (Jn 17.21). The unity of the LORD and his followers was that of the LORD and his powers: the fundamental belief about the unity of all the baptized in Christ was part of the wider belief that all the powers of creation were One. Hence the 'hymn' in Colossians: 'For in him all things were created . . . all things were created through him and for him. He is before all things, and in him all things hold together.' (Col. 1.16–7); and the logic behind Clement of Rome's appeal to the factions in Corinth at the end of the first century, when he appealed for unity, and reminded them of 'the total absence of any friction that marks the ordering of his whole creation'. He described the sun, moon and stars keeping to their paths, the sea staying within its bounds, the seasons and the winds performing their duties, all obeying the decrees of the Creator. Good order and harmony in the Church were part of that greater cosmic order, the harmony of creation.[87]

Clement of Alexandria distinguished the teaching of heretics from genuine Church tradition, by saying that they had not entered in 'by drawing aside the curtain'.[88] When Enoch was transported in his vision beyond the curtain and into the holy of holies, he was taught the

---

86 Josephus, *Antiquities* I.196–7.

87 *1 Clement* 20

88 Clement, *Miscellanies* 7.17.

secrets of creation – presumably what the early Christian writers claimed had been taught by Jesus their great high priest, who had received 'the secret things of God'.[89] Enoch first learned the names of the four presences around the LORD of Spirits and was shown all the hidden things; then he saw 'all the secrets of the heavens' and how the Kingdom was divided, presumably the secret of how the One could also be the plurality of the powers. Then he saw the secrets of the invisible powers listed in *Jubilees* – lightning, thunder, wind – and how they functioned in accordance with the great oath of the Name that bound them together, the many functioning as One (1 En. 40.2; 41.1–6). Thus too Ben Sira, writing in Jerusalem about 200 BCE:

> The works of the LORD have existed from the beginning by his creation, and when he made them, he determined their divisions. He arranged his works in an eternal order, and their dominion for all generations . . . *After this*, the LORD looked upon the earth, and filled it with his good things . . . (Ben Sira 16.26, 27, 29)

The most familiar example of all must be the Shema', that fundamental statement of belief: 'Hear O Israel, the LORD our God is one LORD' (Deut. 6.4), where 'God', *'elohim*, is the noun in plural form that is also used to describe angels. In the Qumran *Sabbath Songs* there are *'elohim* who are clearly angels, and phrases such as 'the praises of all the *'elohim*, the living *'elohim*, the moving *'elohim* run like coals of fire'.[90] These 'elohim also appear in the Psalms: a son of Adam has been made a little less than *'elohim* (Ps. 8.4). Less than God, or less than the angels? The problem of meaning is very obvious in Psalm 82. 1, 6: *'elohim* has taken his place (a singular verb) in the midst of the *'elohim*, who are then described as 'sons of the Most High'. This statement, whatever it has come to mean, says that Yahweh the LORD was the *'elohim* and was One. Jesus applied this fundamental belief to the unity of all his disciples in Him. He was the LORD and they were One.

The unity of the angels in the LORD was later expressed as the unity of the *logoi* of creation in the Logos, for example, by Maximos the Confessor, (died 662 CE). What Nesteruk wrote of Maximus' teaching about the Logos and the *logoi* is temple theology, if one uses the terms 'the LORD' and 'the angels' in place of Logos and *logoi*.

> Maximus considered the contemplation of the *logoi* of created things to be a mode of communion with the Logos, leading ultimately to mystical union with

---

89 Ignatius, *Letter to the Philadelphians*, 9.

90 4Q 403 1 i 32,44; 4Q 403.1 ii 6.

God. The fundamental aspect of this union is that, because it is exercised through the purified intellect (*nous*), the contemplation of the *logoi* is not the same as either empirical perception or mental comprehension. It is a mode of spiritual vision of reality in which the ontological roots of things and beings have their grounds beyond the world. This Christian contemplation of creation as if it were 'from above' or 'from within' and not through external sensible or internal mental impressions, is significantly different from what is now normally accepted as taking place in scientific experience.[91]

The angels in the state of unity, being one and yet many, was part of the mystery of the holy of holies. This fundamental statement of belief was the premise of temple theology. The process of creation must somehow how have described both the separation and the unity, and this can be seen in Proverbs 8, and in the way Genesis 1 was interpreted in the ancient Palestinian Targums. Proverbs 8.22–31 describes creation with the imagery of engraving, as we have seen, and Wisdom declares herself to be the one who 'holds all thing together' (Prov. 8.30). The meaning of the Hebrew letters *'mn* is not clear: it could be 'When he marked out the foundations of the earth I was beside him *holding firm* or *as an artist*,' but the Greek understood that she was 'the one who holds all things together in harmony'. The Targum incorporated this into its rendering of Genesis 1.1: 'In the beginning with Wisdom the LORD created . . .' suggesting that the 'separation' that characterizes the six days (e.g. Gen. 1.4; 1.7; 1.14; 1.18) was balanced by the presence of Wisdom who joins all things together.[92]

Now in the time of Jesus, Philo was teaching that the Logos had both these functions: the Logos separated and the Logos held all things together. 'The Logos of Him that Is is the bond of all things, and holds together all the parts . . .'[93] The Logos was also called the covenant, another way to describe binding together.[94] The Logos both bound together and separated: 'The Father begat the Logos an unbreakable bond of everything' but also set the Logos to keep the elements separate, such that earth was not overwhelmed with water, nor the air ignited fire.[95] Thus the Logos was 'the Severer of all things',[96] a role illustrated by the form of the menorah, where the Logos was the

91 Nesteruk, *Light from the East,* p. 25.

92 Lxx Prov. 8.30.

93 Philo, *On Flight,* 112.

94 Philo, *On Dreams,* II.237.

95 Philo, *On Planting,* 9–10.

96 Philo, *Who is the Heir?* 130.

central stem, both separating the branches and also holding them together.[97] This is what John saw: 'I saw seven golden lampstands, and in the midst of the lampstands, one like a Son of man, clothed with a long robe and with a golden girdle round his breast' (Rev. 1.12–13). The opening scene of Revelation has the Logos high priest[98] upholding the created order. We shall return to this image of the bonds of creation, and their unity.[99]

The angels of Day One and their roles in creation had long been controversial, as too the claim that human beings could ascend to learn the knowledge of the angels. The very existence of angels in Day One, and their role in the creation, was denied by some Jewish teachers, which may explain why the Song of the Three children with its list of angel powers is only found in the Greek version of Daniel and not in the Hebrew/Aramaic. Whatever Rabbi one followed on this matter, 'all agreed that [no angels] were created on the first day, lest you should say that Michael stretched out the south and Gabriel the north while the Holy One, blessed be he, measured it in the middle.'[100] Deuteronomy compared the Law brought by Moses with some other form of teaching that had to be brought down from heaven (Deut. 30.11–12). The LORD asked Job if he had this angel knowledge. 'Where were you when I laid the foundations of the earth? . . . On what were its bases sunk, or who laid the cornerstone, when the morning stars sang together, and all the sons of God shouted for joy' (Job 38.4, 6, 7). In his speech from the whirlwind, the LORD had asked Job if he knew even the first things about the world around him, let alone the secrets of the inner working of creation (Job 38–41). 'Ezra', a contemporary of 'Baruch', learned from the archangel Uriel that such knowledge as 'Baruch' described was not possible: 'Weigh me the weight of the fire or measure me the measure of the wind, or call back for me the day that is past.' 'Ezra' could not answer, nor could he answer about the streams at the source of the deep nor the exits of hell nor the entrances of Paradise. Uriel said that if 'Ezra' could not understand the affairs of the world he lived in, how much less the depths and the heights where he had never been. 'You cannot understand the

97 Philo, *Who is the Heir?*, 215–25.

98 Philo often describes the Logos as the high priest and the Firstborn, for example *On Dreams*, I.215; *On Flight*, 118.

99 See below, pp. 121–3.

100 *Genesis Rabbah* I.3.

things with which you have grown up; how then can your mind comprehend the ways of the Most High?' (2 Esd. 4.5–11).

Given the sophistication and complexity of the secrets of the holy of holies and the angel lore, the vision of unity and the relationship between the visible world of matter and the invisible world of the powers, it is remarkable to set beside them some statements from physicists and cosmologists writing, as far as I know, with no knowledge of temple tradition. Paul Davies, in his books *God and the New Physics*, and *The Mind of God* said:

- Science is only possible because we live in an ordered universe which complies with simple mathematical laws. The job of the scientist is to study, catalogue and relate the orderliness of nature, not to question its origin.
- It appears hard to escape the conclusion that the actual state of the universe has been 'chosen' or selected somehow from the huge number of available states, all but an infinitesimal fraction of which are totally disordered.[101]

Of the state outside time and matter which temple theology described as the holy of holies, physicists use language such as:

- The very threshold of existence, where space and time themselves become intermingled with the fundamental forces . . . Within this supreme era, all four forces of nature would have been indistinguishable, and spacetime would not yet have jelled into a coherent form.[102]
- Thus the material singularity is also a space-time singularity. Because all our laws of physics are formulated in terms of space and time, these laws cannot apply beyond the point at which space and time cease to exist. Hence the laws of physics must break down at the singularity.[103]

Having recovered something of the temple world view, it is astonishing to read about:

- . . . a programme of theoretical work aimed at unifying the forces of nature into a single descriptive scheme . . . [according to which] the present profusion of physical laws is purely a low temperature phenomenon. As the temperature of matter is raised, so the varied forces that act upon it begin to merge their identity until . . . all the forces of nature should merge into a single superforce with a remarkably simple mathematical form.
- At a singularity, matter may enter or leave the physical world, and influences may emanate therefrom that are totally beyond the power of physical science

101 Davies, *God and the New Physics*, pp. 144, 168.

102 Davies, *God and the New Physics*, p. 160.

103 Davies, *The Mind of God*, pp. 49–50.

to predict, even in principle. A singularity is the nearest thing that has been found to a supernatural agent.[104]

SEEING THE FACE OF THE LORD

The glory of the LORD could be discerned in many ways, and was described as seeing the presence of the LORD, or seeing the face of the LORD, since face and presence are the same Hebrew word *panim* which has, like *'elohim*, God, the plural form. Seeing the face or presence of the LORD had been the greatest gift from the LORD, who had instructed Moses to teach Aaron and his sons, the high priests, to bless the people thus:

> The LORD bless you and keep you:
> The LORD make his *face* to shine upon you and be gracious to you:
> The LORD lift up his *countenance* upon you and give you peace.
>
> (Num. 6.24–6)

Thus the familiar translation: 'face' and 'countenance' both translate the same Hebrew word, *panim*, meaning face or presence.

In the early Christian era these words had become controversial: the *Neofiti* Targum did not translate them into Aramaic but left them in the original Hebrew, and it was forbidden to explain them: 'The Blessing of the Priests [is] read out but not interpreted.'[105] There were places in the Hebrew Scriptures too, where it was customary to read the text in a new way, in order to avoid the expression 'seeing the face of the LORD'.[106] The original sense of the command to make the pilgrimage to the temple – 'Three times in the year shall all your males appear before the LORD God.' (Exod. 23.17) – was 'Three times in the year shall all your males *see* the LORD God.' Whatever it was that had been the greatest blessing of temple worship could not be mentioned.

Part of the problem was the ban on images of any kind. The Deuteronomists denied that the LORD had been seen even on Sinai: 'You saw no form; there was only a voice' (Deut. 4.12). Part may have been the Christian claim to have seen the LORD: 'We have beheld his glory' (Jn 1.14) – using the word 'glory' to avoid the anthropomorphism. The Targums made similar changes, using the Shekinah, or the

---

104 Davies, *God and the New Physics*, pp. 54–5.

105 Mishnah *Megillah* 4.10.

106 F. Brown, S. R. Driver, C. A. Briggs, *A Hebrew and English Lexicon of the Old Testament*, Oxford: Clarendon Press, 1962 edition, pp. 816, 908.

Shekinah of your Glory, the brightness or the splendour.[107] 'When shall I come and behold the face of God?' (Ps. 42.2b) became: 'When shall I come and see the splendour of the Shekinah of the LORD?' (Targum Ps. 42.2b). Seeing the face or presence of the LORD was associated with the temple, where the presence of the LORD was represented by the high priest; but there was another sense in which the LORD was seen in the temple and this is found in the mystical experiences of those who 'ascended' to stand before the throne and thereby came to understand the inner working of the creation. Targum *Pseudo Jonathan* rendered 'May the LORD make his face shine on you' as 'May the graciousness of his countenance shine on you in your study of the Torah and reveal to you obscure things . . .,' and in the time of Jesus, the Qumran *Community Rule* knew this version of the blessing: 'May he enlighten your heart with life-giving wisdom and give you eternal knowledge.'[108] Seeing the presence gave wisdom, a knowledge of eternity. This was probably how the first Christians understood it: seeing the face/presence brought grace and peace, hence the greeting: 'Grace and peace to you from God our Father and from the LORD Jesus Christ' (e.g. Rom. 1.7; 1 Cor. 1.3). They blessed themselves with the ancient words of the high priesthood, understood at that time as the gift of life-giving wisdom and eternal knowledge.

Seeing the face or presence meant seeing or being beyond the veil of the temple to the glory of the LORD. The climax of John's vision was the servants of the LORD seeing his face, being in the light, and reigning (Rev. 22.4–5), which means that seeing the Kingdom or seeing the pre-created light or seeing the glory were all ways of describing the presence of the LORD. Philo described the pre-created light as 'that invisible light, perceptible only by mind, which was created as an image of God's Logos, who made its creation known . . .' This was the 'complete light' whose pure radiance was dimmed as it passed into matter.[109] Jesus promised some of his disciples that they would see the Kingdom before they died, and then they saw him transfigured, the pre-created light (Mk 9.1 and parallels). Theodotus, a second-century teacher in Egypt, later labelled as Gnostic, knew a different version of Jesus' words in Luke 9.27. Instead of 'There are some standing here who will not taste death before they see the kingdom of God,' he

---

107 For a fuller discussion of this, see my book *Temple Themes in Christian Worship*, London: T&T Clark, 2007, pp. 146–9.

108 1QS II.3.

109 Philo, *Creation* 31, 55.

quoted: 'There are some standing here who will not taste death until they see the Son of Man in Glory.'[110] The Kingdom of God was the vision of the Son of Man in glory, and when John's Jesus spoke of seeing the Kingdom (Jn 3.3) this was the same as seeing him in his pre-created glory (Jn 17.24). The writer to the Hebrews spoke of drawing near to the throne, which meant seeing the face (Heb. 4.14–6). John himself also proclaimed that Christians had seen the glory (Jn 1.14), and Theodotus knew that the Son was the Presence of the Father: 'The Son is the beginning of the vision of the Father, being called the "face" of the Father.'[111]

The Book of Revelation shows that the early Church knew much more about the holy of holies and the angels round the throne than is immediately obvious elsewhere in the New Testament. Other texts preserved and even augmented by the early Church show the importance of the angel world and what it represented. The *Ascension of Isaiah*, a text expanded by Christians at the end of the first century, described the early community as a group of prophets who 'believed in the ascension into heaven'.[112] There is a vivid account of how 'Isaiah' ascended. Disciples sitting round the prophet 'ascribed glory to the One who had thus graciously given a door in an alien world', and when he returned to normal consciousness, Isaiah described the vision 'from the world which is hidden from the flesh'.[113] This text says nothing about the angels and the creation – it deals with the mystery of the incarnation – but shows that the Christians not only knew but also preserved and adapted such texts. A collection known as the *Testament of Adam* incorporates a detailed list of when each of the angel powers and each element of the creation offers praise: 'At the first hour of the day is the petitions of the holy ones, at the second is the prayer of the angels, at the third is the praise of the birds, at the fourth the praise of the beasts . . .'[114] This list is thought to be Jewish, and from the end of the second temple period.

110 *Excerpts from Theodotus* 4, in R. P. Casey, *Excerpta Ex Theodoto*, London: Studies and Documents 1, 1934.

111 *Excerpt* 12.

112 *Asc. Isa.* 2.9.

113 *Asc.Isa.*6.9, 15.

114 *Testament of Adam*, 2.1–4.

There are collections of Jewish angel texts, known as *hekhalot* texts,[115] that claim to come from this formative period of the Church. Three rabbis – Rabbi Yoḥanan ben Zakkai, Rabbi Neḥuniah ben Hakanah, and Rabbi Ishmael – represent respectively the first, second and third generation of rabbis, corresponding to the first hundred years of the Church. Each of them – and they are remembered as a succession of masters and pupils – was associated with the lore of the holy of holies. Rabbi Yoḥanan and his disciple Rabbi Eleazar ben Arak were surrounded by fire from heaven, and the ministering angels danced before them as the younger man expounded the mysteries of the *merkavah* (the chariot throne) before his master.[116] Rabbi Neḥuniah used to sit on a marble bench in the temple precincts, and his disciples, an inner and an outer group, saw fire playing around him.[117] Many sayings in the *hekhalot* texts are attributed to him, and even more to his pupil Rabbi Ishmael, who was sometimes described as Rabbi Ishmael the high priest.[118] He could not have functioned as a high priest as he was too young when the temple was destroyed, but he came from a priestly family,[119] and like Isaiah, he had a vision in the holy of holies and was given teaching there.[120] Whatever the actual date of the *merkavah* texts, they show first, that the tradition was linked to Rabbi Yoḥanan ben Zakkai, who was the leader of the Rabbinic school that preserved Judaism after the destruction of Jerusalem; and second, that this is how the *temple* teaching was remembered.

These *merkavah* texts are full of angels' names and descriptions of heavenly liturgies. It is not difficult to imagine them coming from the same tradition as the Qumran *Sabbath Songs*. Both describe the fiery angels around the throne, and how they worshipped the King. The fragments from Qumran show that such hymns were known and used in the time of Jesus; the *hekhalot* texts show the fuller extent of such hymns. There is no proof that the content of the *merkavah* hymns was

115 The name means 'palaces' or temples. The outer part of the temple was the *hekhal*.

116 This story is found in Babylonian Talmud *Ḥagigah* 14b, Jerusalem Talmud *Ḥagigah* 77a, and elsewhere. For a good introduction to this area, see C. C. Rowland, *The Open Heaven*, London: SPCK, 1982, pp. 282–305.

117 *Hekhalot Rabbati*, ## 202–4, Schäfer's numbering as in P Schäfer, *Synopse zur Hekhalot-Literatur*, Tübingen: Mohr, 1981.

118 Thus *3 Enoch* 1.1.

119 Babylonian Talmud *Ketuboth* 105b and *Hullin* 49a.

120 Babylonian Talmud *Berakoth* 7a and 51a.

known in the time of Jesus, but they do seem to be the direct descendents of hymns that were sung in his time, and the few lines of heavenly hymnody in the Book of Revelation show similar concerns. The *merkavah* texts bear witness to an aspect of Hebrew heritage very different from rabbinic Judaism as usually reconstructed, but clearly of great importance to Christians, especially as it is now being recognized that rabbinic Judaism represented a substantive change from second temple Judaism.

> Far from being trustees of the accepted tradition of Israel, the sages were leaders of a bold reform movement that developed in the aftermath of the destruction of the Jerusalem temple, and took its shape in the first centuries of the Common era.[121]

The *merkavah* texts show how the angels respond to the hymns sung on earth: 'All the ministering angels . . . when they hear the sound of the hymns and praise which Israel speaks from below, begin from above with "Holy, Holy, Holy . . ."'[122] They praise the One who rules the hidden things and invoke his name with their songs. Anyone who knows and invokes the Name gains access to knowledge, and wisdom that is otherwise unknowable.[123] The mystic does not ascend simply to glimpse the vision; he always returns to the earthly community with new teaching and new power, and above all, with a new way of seeing the world. These texts are far from easy to read, but they do seem to be saying that to change the world you have to change how you see it. When the mystic has stood before the throne and seen the face/presence of the LORD, he sees everything else differently. After he had seen the LORD, Isaiah learned that his glory filled the whole creation. The blessing of the high priests linked seeing the face with the gifts of wisdom, grace and peace, and a saying attributed to Rabbi Ishmael shows how this altered perception of the whole world was central to the *merkavah* tradition.

> When my ears heard this great mystery,
> The world was transformed over me in purity,
> And my heart was as if I had arrived in new world

---

121 G. Boccaccini, *Roots of Rabbinic Judaism*, Grand Rapids: Eerdmans, 2002, *passim*, but quotation from p. xiii.

122 *Hekhalot Rabbati* #179, in P. Schäfer, *The Hidden and Manifest God*, New York: SUNP, 1992, p. 47.

123 Schäfer, *The Hidden and Manifest God*, p. 98.

Every day it appeared to my soul
As if I was standing in front of the throne of glory.[124]

This describes his new way of being in the world: he stands before the throne, and sees the creation as the Creator sees it.

One of the collections of texts linked with Rabbi Ishmael shows just how close the beliefs of the *merkavah* mystics were to Christianity. The Hebrew Enoch (*3 Enoch*) probably reached it current form in the fifth century CE, but it incorporates material so ancient that it is found in both Judaism and Christianity – but not obviously in the Hebrew Scriptures. There were beliefs common to both faiths that were not in the scriptures. In *3 Enoch*, Rabbi Ishmael describes how he ascended to heaven and was led in to stand before the King by Metatron, the prince of the divine Presence. He told Ishmael that on earth he had been Enoch, but the Holy One had taken him up and appointed him as prince and ruler of the angels.[125] He was enthroned, and then the Holy One revealed to him

all the mysteries of wisdom, . . . all the mysteries of the world, and all the orders of nature stand before me as they stand revealed before the creator. From that time onward I looked and beheld deep secrets and wonderful mysteries.[126]

Then he was crowned and given the name 'the lesser Yahweh', 'as it is written "my name is in him."'[127] His crown bore 'the letters by which heaven and earth were created', in other words, the Name. When the Holy One placed the crown on his head, all the ranks of angels trembled before him, recognizable as the angels of Day one who are listed in the Song of the Three Children:

The angel of fire, the angel of hail, the angel of wind, the angel of lightning, the angel of whirlwind, the angel of thunder, the angel of snow, the angel of rain, the angel of day, the angel of night, the angel of the sun, the angel of the moon, the angel of the stars . . .[128]

---

124 *Merkavah Rabbah* 680 in Schäfer, *The Hidden and Manifest God*, p 114, attributed to R Ishmael, see p. 52.

125 *3 Enoch* 4.5.

126 *3 Enoch* 11.1–2.

127 *3 Enoch* 12.5.

128 *3 Enoch* 14.2.

They all fell prostrate when they saw me, and could not look at me because of the majesty, splendour, beauty, brightness, brilliance, and radiance of the glorious crown which was on my head.[129]

Most of this is in the New Testament, but often without its context. Paul seems to be quoting to the Philippians a text they recognize:

> God has highly exalted him, and bestowed on him the name which is above every name, that at the name of Jesus every knee should bow, in heaven and on earth and under the earth, and every tongue confess that Jesus Christ is the LORD, to the glory of God the Father. (Phil. 2.9–11)

This is a brief summary of Metatron receiving the Name and then being worshipped by all the powers. The hymns that John heard in heaven are part of the same scene:

> And I heard every creature in heaven and on earth and under the earth and in the sea and all therein saying: 'To him who sits upon the throne and to the Lamb be blessing and honour and glory and might for ever and ever!'

The name Metatron was understood by the early Christians to means 'the throne sharer': 'He who was the beloved of the Father and his Offspring and the Eternal Priest and the Being called the Sharer of the Father's throne.'[130] Presumably this was the title for the Lamb enthroned in Revelation 5.13, the One who promised a similar status to the faithful Christian: 'I will grant him to sit with me on my throne, as I myself conquered and sat down with my Father on his throne' (Rev. 3.21).

---

129 *3 Enoch* 14.15.

130 Eusebius, *Preparation of the Gospel* IV.15.

Chapter 3

WEAVING CREATION

The biblical view of creation is rarely questioned, not in the sense that people have never taken issue with the seven day scheme, but in the sense that the seven day scheme, as usually understood, is assumed to be *the* biblical view. We are asking the question: How might Jesus and the first Christians have understood the creation? And already we have seen that their understanding of Genesis was a sophisticated and far from literal reading of the text. Material available in the time of Jesus and from the era of the early church shows that they saw creation as one intricately woven system that could be destroyed by human action. In this chapter we shall recover something of that picture; most of the evidence has been well known for a long time, but it has been read differently.

First, they knew the 'pre-Genesis' story about the origin of the angels and the 'engravings' in the invisible world. Second, Jesus himself and the first Christians read the Hebrew Scriptures as texts about more than one deity: there was El Elyon, whom the Christians were to designate 'the First Person'; there was Yahweh, the firstborn of the sons of God, whom the Christians were to designate 'the Second Person'; and there was the Spirit. Since Philo also read the Scripture in this way, it was not a Christian innovation or deviation. Yahweh the LORD was the Creator, 'through whom all things were made'.[1] Third, they knew that the invisible unity held the visible world in an ordered state, and that without that vision, 'the people unravelled' (Prov. 29.18, translating literally). And fourth, when they sang the Psalms, they understood that they were singing about the Second Person, and so they knew that it was the work of the LORD, whom they had known incarnate, to create the visible world by bringing the engraved patterns to the visible world and thus shaping it. Hence the LORD's question to Job: 'Do you know

---

1 See my book, *The Great Angel. A Study of Israel's Second God*, London: SPCK, 1992.

the engraved pattern of the heavens and can you set up its pattern/ rule on earth?' (Job 38.33, the gist of an obscure verse).

In the time of Jesus and in the early years of the Church, Jewish temple teachers and their heirs spoke of seeing how the world was made. Rabbi 'Akiba, early in the second century CE, ascended to heaven in a vision and there saw the whole inhabited world.[2] There is no detail of what he actually saw. Rabbi Neḥuniah, who lived in Emmaus at the end of the first century CE, ascended and saw 'the mysteries and the secrets, the bonds and wonders . . . the weaving of the web that completes the world.'[3] Again, there is no detail of what he saw, but he looked out and saw that the world was *woven*. Literally, he would have been looking at the reverse of the temple veil, an elaborate fabric woven from four colours that represented the four elements of matter.[4] It is impossible to date much of the material in the collections of mystical texts, but there is a consistent pattern of images, for example: 'Your throne is a hovering throne, since the hour when you fastened the weaver's peg and wove the fabric upon which the completion of the world and its ladder stand.'[5] When the mystic had seen the great mystery of the holy of holies, his own view of the material world was changed. Rabbi Ishmael, as we have seen, looked at the world each day as though standing before the throne of glory.[6] He was seeing as Isaiah saw: the whole world full of the glory.

This sense of seeing the world from above, seeing as God saw it and understanding differently as a result, has been repeated recently in an extraordinary way, and was linked to the pictures of the earth from space in 1968.

> When the earth was first seen from outside, and compared as a whole planet with its lifeless neighbours, Mars and Venus, it was impossible to ignore the overwhelming sense that the earth was a strange and beautiful anomaly. Its evolution could not be explained solely in terms of conventional biology or geology.[7]

2 P. Schäfer, *Synopse zur Hekhalot Literatur*, Tübingen: Mohr, 1981, *Hekalot Zutarti* # 496.

3 *Synopse, Hekalot Rabbati* # 201.

4 Red for fire, blue for air, purple for water and white for earth, thus Josephus, *War* V.212–13.

5 *Hekhalot Rabbati* # 98, in Schäfer *Synopse zur Hekhalot Literatur*, p. 12.

6 See above p. 105.

7 L. Margulis and J. E. Lovelock, 'Gaia and Geognosy', in *Global Ecology. Towards a Science of the Biosphere*, ed. M. B. Rambler, L. Margulis, R. Fester, London and San Diego: Academic Press, Inc., 1989, pp. 1–30, p. 6.

Perhaps it was the image of the Earth that led to what seems to have been a quantum leap by scientists and environmental action groups . . . many other science symposia and public forums *have begun to think of the Earth as a whole,* a dynamically functioning collection of ecosystems and biomes connected through atmosphere, oceans and sediments . . . This new awareness fostered a new approach to the science of the biosphere, *a holistic approach to the Earth* . . . directly stimulated by the magnificent image of the living earth from space . . . all of us must continue to recognize *the inextricable linkage among solar, atmospheric, oceanic and surface processes* modulated by life.[8]

Only in the last few years has there been a recognition of a dynamic earth, where the biota is *inextricably linked* to atmospheric, oceanic, and terrestrial processes, where ecosystems are connected to globally by the atmosphere, oceans and sediments. (my emphases)[9]

Seeing the whole earth prompted thinking in terms of connected ecosystems, a holistic approach, inextricable linkage among all aspects of creation – something not so very different from the mystics' image of the weaving of the world.

Seeing the whole earth in this way also affected thought about human society, co-operation and regulation. T. H. Huxley, although an admirer of Darwin's work, had expressed concern about evolution; goodness and virtue involve acting with self-restraint, and so were totally opposed to the self-assertion necessary for the evolutionary struggle.[10] The new ways of seeing, however, mean that the dangerous 'survival of the fittest' is not the whole story. Something more than competition is needed for human society or for any system to succeed. To those formed by a Christian culture (I can only speak for my own), this has seemed obvious, but biologists have now reached the same conclusion:

The principal additional statement [i.e. additional to evolution] made within the biotic regulation concept is that increased competitiveness (and hence, increased number of progeny) is only possible when the new species that appeared in the course of evolution enhances the regulatory potential of the community. In other words, with the biotic regulation concept, competitiveness of individuals and the regulatory potential of the community to which they belong are tightly coupled. By contrast, within the traditional paradigm, an increased competitiveness (or fitness) is considered to be sufficient condition for evolutionary changes *per se.*[11]

8 M. B. Rambler and L. Margulis 'Global Ecological Research and Public Response', in *Global Ecology,* 1989, pp. 143–7, 143, 146.

9 Ibid., pp. 143–7, p. 145.

10 See above p. 35.

11 V. G. Gorshkov, V. V. Gorshkov and A. M. Makarieva, *Biotic Regulation of the Environment. Key Issue of Global Change,* Chichester: Praxis, 2000, p. 316.

Evolutionary dynamics, and the idea that co-operation is essential for life to evolve to new levels, is now a recognized area for theological exploration.[12]

This idea had long been embedded in Christian teaching:

> Things then of conflicting and opposite nature, would not have reconciled themselves, were there not One higher and LORD over them, to unite them, to whom the elements themselves yield obedience as slaves that obey a master. And instead of each having regard to its own nature, and fighting with its neighbour, they recognise the LORD who has united them, and are at concord with one another, being by nature opposed, but at amity by the will of him who guides them.[13]

Thus Athanasius in the fourth century, but the roots of this were part Christianity's temple heritage. The covenant of creation bound everything in one system: the material world, living beings, human society, and the invisible forces they called angels or powers.

LIVING THE VISION

One characteristic of the temple mystics was that they saw everything from 'outside time', in the timeless state of the holy of holies. 'Temple' time was neither a linear progression – 'history' – nor cyclic. It enabled the link between the visible world of change and the invisible world of the divine. Paul Davies, who has written much on the subject of time, issued an interesting challenge in his book *The Mind of God*:

> No attempt to explain the world either scientifically or theologically, can be considered successful until it accounts for the paradoxical conjunction of the temporal and the atemporal, of being and becoming. And no subject confronts this paradoxical conjunction more starkly than the origin of the universe.[14]

In an earlier work he had written:

> Time is so fundamental to our experience of the world that any attempt to tinker with it meets with great scepticism and resistance.
> Today time is seen to be dynamical. It can stretch and shrink, warp, and even stop altogether at a singularity.

---

12 See M. A. Nowak and S. Coakley, *Evolution, Games and God: the Principle of Co-operation*, Cambridge MA: Harvard University Press, 2009; also p. 160–1 below.

13 Athanasius, *Against the Heathen*, 37.1.

14 P. Davies, *The Mind of God*, London: Penguin, 1992, p. 38.

The abandonment of a distinct past, present and future is a profound step, for the temptation to assume that only the present 'really exists' is great . . . Our psychological perception of time differs so radically from the physicist's model that even many physicists have come to doubt whether some vital ingredient has been omitted.

Davies then speculated about the problem of acquiring knowledge, which is an activity in time, and the manner of God's 'knowing' which is outside time. 'To know timelessly must therefore involve [God's] knowing all events throughout time.'[15]

This was exactly the experience of the temple mystics, and their attempt to articulate the effect of their visions deals with this paradox of the relationship between the temporal and the atemporal, between the world of everyday life and the timeless state of the origin of all things. The language of the temple mystics is almost opaque, but they are describing a single moment of vision when they saw the whole of creation and all history. A Jewish text, preserving Palestinian material from the second temple period, tells how the heavenly high priest Enoch/Metatron took Rabbi Ishmael into the holy of holies and showed him in a moment all history on the reverse of the veil: 'I will show you the curtain of the Omnipresent One . . . on which are printed all the generations of the world and all their deeds, whether done or to be done . . .'[16] Another Jewish text from about 100 CE had Abraham ascend to heaven and stand before the throne. The Eternal One told him to look down and see the whole of history beneath him, from the Garden of Eden to the final 'age of justice'.[17] Isaiah had this experience in the sixth century BCE: 'Has it not been told you from the beginning? Have you not understood from the foundations of the earth? It is he who . . . stretches out the heavens like a curtain . . . who brings princes to naught and makes the rulers of the earth as nothing' (Isa. 40.21–2). Isaiah must have stood 'in the beginning', that is, in the holy of holies, and seen all history.

According to Philo, the invisible, atemporal state 'contained within itself all things *equally*'.[18] Ben Sira has: 'He who lives for ever created the whole universe *koinē*,' which in Latin became *simul*, meaning 'at the

15 P. Davies, *God and the New Physics*, London: Penguin, 1990, pp. 119, 123, 124, 134.

16 *3 Enoch* 45.1.

17 *Apocalypse of Abraham*, 20–29.

18 Philo, *Questions on Genesis* I.64; 'equally' could have been *isōs* or *koinē* in Philo's original. This particular passage has survived only in Armenian.

same time.' (Ben Sira/Ecclus. 18.1) Since the eternal state is outside time, all the forms/bonds/angels must have come into being simultaneously, exactly as in the *Jubilees* account of Day One: '. . . he created the heavens . . . and all the spirits which serve before him . . . all the spirits of his creatures which are in heaven and on earth.'[19] Philo wrestled with this: all things were made simultaneously but described as a sequence, he said, because a numbered sequence indicated good order. He also said that the six days of creation (Gen. 1.1–2.3) described the invisible creation, the pattern for the material world. 'In the beginning God created the heaven' meant that he created the heaven first, because it was both the purest of all creations, and the home of the heavenly beings. 'The Maker made an incorporeal heaven and an invisible earth, and the pattern/form of air and void.'[20] He quoted the Old Greek text of Genesis 'This is the book of the genesis of heaven and earth, when they came into being, in the day in which God made heaven and earth and every herb of the field *before it appeared upon the earth*, and all the grass of the field before it sprang up.' (Gen. 2.4–5), and said it described 'the incorporeal ideas present only to the mind, by which, as by seals, the finished objects that meet our senses were moulded.'[21] Since Genesis 1 was Moses' vision on Sinai, Philo could well have read 'See that you make them after the pattern which is being shown you on the mountain' (Exod. 25.40) as the key to understanding the first creation story. The heavenly patterns were not Plato's archetypes since Exodus 25 was written long before the time of Plato. Justin said Plato derived the theory of forms from this very passage, but had not properly understood it, since he had not been instructed by the initiated: 'Without mystic insight it is impossible to have distinct knowledge of the writings of Moses.'[22]

The inspiration came to the mystics in an instant, and its implications were then worked out. One said he felt 'a light in my heart like the light of a flash which goes from one end of the world to the other'.[23] The singer of the Qumran hymns knew he had been enlightened so that he could bring light to the face of his congregation.[24] Uriel

19 *Jubilees* 2.2.

20 Philo, *Creation*, 28–9.

21 Philo, *Creation*, 129.

22 Justin, *Exhortation to the Greeks*, 29.

23 *Merkavah Rabbah* # 656 Schäfer, *Hidden*, p. 114.

24 1QH XII.24.

(whose name means 'the light of God') taught Enoch the secrets of astronomy, even revealing the details of the calendar to him: 'Uriel, the holy angel who is [the stars'] guide, showed me all their laws exactly as they are.'[25] Fragments of one such calendar have survived at Qumran and in more detail in Ethiopic: they must have formed a complex treatise. Presumably the ancient astronomer had the necessary skills to calculate in the same way as others at that time, but he had already 'seen' the answer. So too, the call vision of Saul on the road to Damascus, when he saw a great light and heard the voice: 'Why do you persecute *me*?' (Acts 9.4). This one moment of revelation became the great theme of his subsequent teaching, which was that the Christians whom he had persecuted were the body of Christ. This was revealed to him in a vision, but he could not have worked out its implications without his great knowledge of Jewish tradition.

It is characteristic of people who are inspired, who recognize that something comes to them from outside themselves, to see 'the whole'. The initial insight is given in a moment, and then the mystic or artist or thinker works out what this means. Musicians and poets tell of a complete composition coming suddenly and unexpectedly, and then having to work it out in detail. They have a sense of possession and compulsion, the feeling of absolute certainty that then has to be tested. Tchaikovsky described the origin of his music thus:

> Generally, the germ of a future composition comes suddenly and unexpectedly . . .
> It would be vain to try to put into words the immeasurable sense of bliss which comes over me directly a new idea awakens in me and begins to assume a definite form. I forget everything and behave like a madman. Everything within me starts pulsing and quivering; hardly have I begun to sketch ere one thought follows another. What has been set down in a moment of ardour must now be critically examined, improved extended or condensed as the from requires . . .[26]

Sometimes this 'breaking through' is sudden and dramatic, and affords what is sometimes called 'mathematical inspiration'.[27] This is how Paul Davies reported a mathematician's experience, but such inspiration in the time of Jesus was attributed to angelic revelation.

The temple mystics stood in their visions among the angels and the angels taught them. John stood among the angels and was instructed

---

25 *1 Enoch* 21.5; 71.1.

26 Tchaikovsky, 'Letters to Frau von Meck' in *The Life and Letters of Peter Ilich Tchaikovsky*, ed. and tr. R. Newmarch, London: Bodley Head, 1906, pp. 274–5, 311–2.

27 Davies, *The Mind of God*, p. 145.

by them (Rev. 5.5; 7.13); Enoch was guided by 'the angel of peace'. Now the name of an angel reveals its function, and, since 'peace', *šalom*, means wholeness, completeness, integrity, the angel of peace was revealing to Enoch the secret of wholeness. This was an ancient belief. Isaiah had proclaimed: 'The angels of peace weep bitterly' as the covenant was breaking and the land was mourning and languishing (Isa. 33.7b, 8b,9a, translating literally). Isaiah knew of a covenant that sustained the creation, and the angels of 'wholeness' wept as it was broken. This is what Enoch saw; the angel showed him 'everything that is hidden . . . all the secrets of the heavens, and how the Kingdom is divided and how the actions of men are weighed in a balance.'[28] Learning how the Kingdom was divided meant learning the roles of the angel powers and how they functioned in the creation,[29] how the One was manifested in these many powers, how the visible creation was, at its source, a unity. The judgement on human actions was vital to maintaining the system. As the angels revealed themselves they made possible new ideas, because angels, by definition, join things together, and so those who encountered them made connections about how the world works. In other words, they saw it whole.

Many scientists have written about meeting angels, but under another name. 'No one who is closed off from mathematics can ever grasp the full significance of the natural order that is woven so deeply into the fabric of physical reality' – an interesting choice of words.[30]

The truly basic laws of nature thus establish deep connections between different physical processes. The history of science shows that, once a new law is accepted, its consequences are rapidly worked out, and the law is tested in many novel contexts, often leading to the discovery of new, unexpected and important phenomena. This leads me to believe that in conducting science, we are uncovering real regularities and linkages, that we are reading these regularities out of nature, not writing them into nature.[31]

The seemingly miraculous concurrence of numerical values that nature has assigned to her fundamental constants must remain the most compelling evidence for an element of cosmic design.[32]

28 *1 Enoch* 41.1; this is thought to be a summary of Enoch's whole experience, described in detail later.

29 *1 Enoch* 60.11–22.

30 Davies, *The Mind of God*, p. 93.

31 Davies, *The Mind of God*, p. 82.

32 Davies, *God and the New Physics*, p. 189.

Or, as was known in the time of Jesus: 'Thou hast arranged all things by measure and number and weight' (Wis. 11.20). The temple mystics knew that the mysteries of creation were its measurements; they had one word, *middoth,* for both.[33] In the words of Alister McGrath: 'We would argue that Christian theology provides an ontological foundation which confirms and consolidates otherwise fleeting, fragmentary glimpses of a greater reality, gained from the exploration of nature without an attending theoretical framework.'[34]

The clearest ancient Jewish account of the structure of creation is found in Philo, who described 'the bonds', *but no conventional study of Philo been able to explain why he used the image of bonds*:

> Neither the Middle Platonist use of Timaeus 41ab nor the Stoic doctrine of cosmic cohesion can fully explain Philo's frequent use of the image of the *desmos,* (bond) in relation to the Logos and the powers of God. So it is difficult to determine whether we are dealing with a personal predeliction (at least partly resulting from his reading of the Timaeus), or with one of the many gaps in our knowledge of Philo's philosophical reading material.[35]

Or maybe – and this is not considered – he was just writing as a Jew of his time. For him the bonds of creation were the presence of God, who, by his powers fills all things, and 'uniting all with all, has bound them fast with invisible bonds that they should never be loosed'.[36] The next few words here are damaged; they seem to mean: 'on account of which I will celebrate it in song',[37] which would be a reference to the song of the angels that represents the divine harmony, another sign of Philo's cultural heritage. Furthermore, to the Jewish way of thinking, the 'vision of God' and 'harmony' were imagined as equivalent terms. The Hebrew text of Exodus 24.11 says the elders ascended Sinai and saw *'elohim* (God or angels) in a vision, but the Greek text has: 'not one of them sang in discord.' The vision and the song were equivalents.

---

33 See above, pp. 45–6.

34 A. McGrath, *The Open Secret, A New Vision for Natural Theology,* Oxford: Blackwell, 2008, p. 248.

35 D. T. Runia, *Philo of Alexandria and the Timaeus of Plato,* Leiden: Brill, 1986, p. 240.

36 In contemporary language, we might say that the presence of God is recognized in an enormous collection of interacting ecosystems.

37 LCL Philo vol.4, note to p. 84.

The Bethlehem shepherds saw the glory of the Lord and they heard the song of the angels (Lk. 2. 8–14). We shall return to this.[38]

Philo also said that the bonds were held in place (i.e. the creation was secured) by the Logos, the Power by which God made and ordered all things, who 'holds the whole in its embrace and has interfused itself through all parts of the universe.'[39]

> God is one, but he has around him numberless powers which all assist and protect created being . . . Through these powers the incorporeal and intelligible world was framed, the archetype of this phenomenal world, that being a system of invisible ideal forms, as this is of visible material bodies.[40]

This looks like Platonism, but Ezekiel knew a similar system some two centuries before Plato, so it would be wiser to say that since Philo was writing Greek, he inevitably used some of the same words as Plato.[41] Elsewhere, Philo claimed his teaching as characteristic of his own people, and distinguished between the teaching of Moses, and that of the 'Chaldeans'. Others said the Greeks had taken from the Hebrews: Aristobulus, for example, a Jewish scholar in Egypt in the mid second century BCE, said that Pythagoras, Socrates and Plato had followed Moses 'when they were contemplating the arrangement of the universe so accurately made and indissolubly combined by God.'[42] Josephus said Pythagoras had been influenced by Jewish teaching,[43] and Clement of Alexandria (died 214 CE) quoted the Pythagorean philosopher Numenius: 'What is Plato but Moses speaking Attic Greek?'[44]

Scholars have admitted to being puzzled about the origin of Plato's account of creation, but the possibility that it came from Hebrew sources is not seriously considered, despite the considerable witness of ancient sources.

38 See below, pp. 282–7.

39 *Philo, Tongues,* 137.

40 *Philo, Tongues,* 171.

41 I have argued in my book *The Great High Priest,* London: T&T Clark, 2003, pp. 262–93 that the claims made in the time of Jesus, namely that Plato drew his ideas from Hebrew tradition, were correct.

42 Quoted in Eusebius, *Preparation of the Gospel,* tr. Gifford, E. H., Oxford: Oxford University Press, 1903, XIII.12.

43 Josephus, *Against Apion,* I.22.

44 Clement of Alexandria, *Miscellanies* 1.15, 22.

> [Plato] introduced, for the first time in Greek philosophy . . . the scheme of creation by a divine artificer, according to which the world is like a work of art designed with a purpose. The Demiurge is a necessary part of the machinery, if the rational ordering of the universe is to be picture as a process of creation in time.[45]

So how much of Plato did the Jews of Jesus' time recognize as their Hebrew heritage? Moses, said Philo, teaches that the complete whole around us 'is held together by invisible powers, which the Creator has made to reach from the ends of the earth to heaven's furthest bounds, taking forethought that what was well bound should not be loosened, for the powers of the universe are bonds that cannot be broken.'[46] This looks like Plato's Timaeus, but where does Moses say it? Justin, who had studied philosophy before he became a Christian,[47] was certain that Plato's account of the bonds of creation *and their seal* was drawn from Moses. In the Timaeus, he said, Plato wrote of the process of creation:

> [God] then took the whole fabric and cut it down the middle into two strips, which he placed crosswise at their middle points to form a shape like the letter X; he then bent the ends round in a circle and fastened them to each other opposite the point at which the strips crossed . . .[48]

Justin then gave a rather strange interpretation of the story of the bronze serpent (Num. 21.8).[49] However odd Justin's exegesis may seem, he is witness to the early Christian claim that Plato had even taken an X shaped seal of creation from 'Moses'.

Here is the problem. If the bonds and forms and seal of creation were not borrowed from Greek philosophy, where did they originate? The Jewish context in which Christianity arose knew there were bonds in creation that Rabbi Neḥuniah saw woven together and that Philo knew as the invisible framework of the creation, but Moses' account of the creation in Genesis 1 does not mention them. There are, however, accounts of the creation in the Hebrew Scriptures that do imply bonds: texts about the 'engraved' boundaries imply bonds or definitions of the creation.[50] It may be, too, that the bonds appear in the Old Testament

---

45 F. M. Cornford, *Plato's Cosmology*, London: Routledge and Kegan Paul, 1937, p. 31.

46 Philo, *The Migration of Abraham*, 181.

47 Justin, *Trypho* 1–2.

48 Plato, *Timaeus*, 36.

49 Justin, *Apology* I.60.

50 See above, pp. 84–5.

as the 'ways' of the LORD; a word whose older usage has been overlaid by later developments.[51] In some creation texts, it is interesting to substitute 'bond' for 'way' and glimpse Philo's world in familiar texts. God binds up the waters engraves a circle on the face of the waters: 'these are outer edge of his *way(s)*...' (Job. 26.14, my translation). God saw everything on earth that he had made, he gave the wind its weight, and measured the waters, '... he made a decree/engraving for the rain and a *way* for the lightning ...' (Job 28.26, my translation). The LORD with Wisdom founded the earth; Wisdom's *ways* are the '*ways* of pleasantness' and all her paths are peace (Prov. 3.17). 'I have taught you the *way* of Wisdom' (Prov. 4.11). 'The LORD fathered me [Wisdom], the beginning/chief/first of his *way* ...' (Prov. 8.22, translating literally). 'Happy are those who keep my [Wisdom's] *ways*' (Prov. 8.32). Extolling the power of the Creator, who measured the waters and weighed the mountains, Isaiah asked: 'Who taught him the path of justice ... and showed him the *way* of understanding?' (Isa. 40.14).

The fragmented Wisdom material from Qumran seems to describe the bonds as the paths or ways of the creation:

> You have fashioned every spirit and [ ]the judgement of all their works ...
> the mighty spirits/winds according to their 'engravings'
> before they became angels of holiness
> ... and eternal spirits in their dominions;
> the heavenly lights to their mysteries
> the stars to their paths,
> [ ] to their tasks,
> the thunderbolts and the lightnings to their duty ...[52]

The same images are found in an early Christian hymn:

> He fixed the creation and set it up,
> then he rested from his works.
> And created things run according to their courses,
> and work their works,
> for they can neither cease not fail.[53]

---

51 The word *dbk* changed meaning; in Gen. 2.24 a man *cleaves* to his wife, but in Deuteronomy 10.20; 11.22; 13.4 etc. *cleaving* to the LORD was understood as obeying. R.'Akiba taught that *cleaving* to the LORD meant being joined to the LORD, Babylonian Talmud *Sanhedrin* 64a.

52 1QH IX.8.

53 *Odes of Solomon*, 16.12–13.

The clearest picture of the bonds of the creation covenant is a fragment of poetry that survives in *1 Enoch*. It follows the (now confused) episode when one of the fallen angels tried to learn the hidden Name and thus gain the power of the Name over the creation. The poem uses the imagery of courses and paths, and links the hidden Name to the great 'oath' that secures the creation.

> They are strong through his oath: and the heaven was suspended before the world was created, and for ever.
> And through it the earth was founded upon the water, and from the secret recesses of the mountains come beautiful waters, from the creation of the world unto eternity.
> And through that oath the sea was created, and as its foundation he set for it sand . . .
> And through that oath the depths are made fast
> And through that oath the sun and moon complete their course . . .
> And through that oath the stars complete their course, and he calls them by their names, and they answer him from eternity to eternity.

There follows a section about the weathers, and the poem concludes:

> This oath is mighty over them, and through it they are preserved and their paths are preserved, and their course is not destroyed. (*1 En.* 69.16–25)

A commentary on this passage observes:

> The Cosmic Oath, intimately associated with the Name of God, functions as a creative force, in that it bound chaos in the beginning and enabled the delicate structures of life to exist. It is an organisational force in that it orders all things into their proper niche in creation, and it is a preservational force in that it continues to keep destructive chaos sealed and bound.[54]

The poem of the Oath occurs in *1 Enoch* just as the Man is enthroned and sinners are bound and taken away; it is part of the restoration of the creation, which happened on the day of judgement ritualized on the Day of Atonement. Enthronement linked to securing the bonds of creation and binding sinners was part of the original Adam imagery, as we shall see.[55] *The same pattern - creation, enthronement, judgement – is found in the Book of Revelation*: the elders praise the Creator: 'Thou didst create all things and by thy will they existed and were created.' (Rev. 4.11);

---

54 D. Olsen, *Enoch. A New Translation*, North Richland Hills: Bibal Press, 2004, p. 130.

55 See below, p. 216.

then the Lamb is enthroned and the judgement begins. When the seventh angel sounds his trumpet, the Kingdom is established and the destroyers of the earth are destroyed (Rev. 11.18). So too with the letter of Jude, which has a long quotation from the beginning of *1 Enoch* to show that judgment is imminent.

> Behold the LORD came with his holy myriads, to execute judgement on all, and to convict all the ungodly of all their deeds of ungodliness, which they have committed in such as ungodly way, and of all the harsh things which ungodly sinners have spoken against him. (Jude 14–5, quoting *1 En.* 1.9)

The passage in Enoch that Jude quotes continues with observations from the well-ordered creation: how nothing transgresses its appointed order, nothing changes, the seasons keep their pattern, the trees bear leaves and fruit, the sea and the rivers keep their appointed roles – but people have chosen to go their way.[56] It is possible that Jude was quoting out of context, but more likely that he set his warnings in a context that the early Christians knew well: the well-ordered creation and the judgement.

One generation later, Clement of Rome made a similar appeal when writing to the quarrelsome Christians in Corinth.

> The heavens, as they revolve beneath his government, do so in quiet submission to him, the day and night run the course he has laid down for them . . . Nor does the illimitable basin of the sea . . . overflow at any time the barriers encircling it, but does as he has bidden it – for his word was 'Thus far shall you come; at this point shall your waves be broken within you . . .' even the minutest of living creatures mingle together in peaceful accord. Upon all these the great Architect and LORD of the universe has enjoined peace and harmony . . .[57]

The letter cites examples of people who preached repentance or did repent, which may have been drawn from Jewish penitential practice, and so Clement could have had the Day of Atonement in mind when he was writing.[58]

Philo said that the bonds of creation were held in place by the Logos, the Power by which God made and ordered all things. So too the opening of John's gospel: 'The [Logos] was in the beginning with God; all things were made through him, and without him was not anything made that was made' (Jn 1.2–3). John did not mention the bonds, but others did. The great 'hymn' in Colossians says of the Son:

---

56 *1 Enoch* 1.4–7.

57 *1 Clement* 20.

58 A. Jaubert, *Clément de Rome, Épître aux Corinthiens*, Sources Chrétiennes 167, Paris: Édtions du Cerf, 1971, pp. 50–2.

'All things were created through him and for him. He is before all things and in him *all things hold together*' (Col. 1.16b–17). The Church at Ephesus knew of 'a plan for the fullness of time, to *unite all things in him*, things in heaven and things on earth' (Eph. 1.10). The church in Ephesus also knew what was meant by: 'maintaining the unity of the Spirit in the bond of peace' (Eph. 4.3). Unity, Spirit, bond and peace, found together in what seems to be a recognized formula, suggest that the early churches knew about the bonds and their role in the creation.

The bonds and the binding were the covenant. The verb 'create', *bara'* is used in Genesis 1 (and elsewhere) only for divine activity. People never 'create'. The verb is similar to the word for covenant, *b'rith*, suggesting that the uniquely divine activity of creating was the binding of creation,[59] which was extended to mean any creative divine act. This was the creation covenant, sometimes called the everlasting covenant and sometimes the covenant of peace. Adam, created as the image, was told to subdue the earth and have dominion over other living creatures (Gen. 1.28), but the word *kbš*, translated 'subdue', means literally to harness or to bind, suggesting that binding was part of the image. Adam was to maintain the bonds of creation. Throughout the Hebrew Scriptures a creation covenant is assumed, but little noticed nowadays because scholarly interest has been largely confined to the 'historic' covenants: with Abraham, with Moses and with David.[60] The creation covenant appears as the climax of the Noah story: 'my covenant which is between me and you and every living creature of all flesh' 'the everlasting covenant' (Gen. 9.15–16). This was the covenant that bound heaven and earth together, as the Lord declared through Jeremiah: 'my covenant of day and night and the ordinances of heaven and earth . . .' (Jer. 33.25), and it was proof of the Lord's faithfulness to his people. Signs of the everlasting covenant were the rainbow (Gen. 9.16) and the bread of the presence (Lev. 24.8).

The 'covenant of peace', was shown to Enoch by the angel of peace. One of the stranger stories in the Pentateuch gives its context. When Phineas the high priest killed two people who had broken the covenant rules, the Lord entrusted to him 'my covenant of peace . . . the covenant of the priesthood of eternity' (Num. 25.12–3 translating

---

59 But K-H Bernhardt in *Theological Dictionary of the Old Testament*, Grand Rapids: Eerdmans 1974, vol. 2. p. 245 says *bara'* probably meant separate or divide.

60 The first notable exception was R. Murray, *The Cosmic Covenant*, London: Sheed and Ward, 1992.

literally), because he had 'made atonement for the people of Israel.'
(Num. 25.13). Breaking the covenant put everyone in danger, and so
the covenant had to be repaired. The covenant was seen as a protection, and when breached, there was the danger of 'wrath'. Repairing
the breach was called 'atonement', and this story, barbaric though it is,
shows clearly the link between the covenant of peace and the high
priestly rite of atonement. This is why the creation was restored on the
Day of Atonement, and explains why two rabbis teaching in Palestine
early in the Christian era taught that the Day of Atonement was Day
One when the original state was restored.[61]

The bonds of the covenant were secured by the Name, represented
in temple tradition by a diagonal cross. This was the X shaped seal of
creation that Justin said was known by Plato. In the ancient alphabet
used in the first temple, the letter *tau* was written as a diagonal cross,
which is why Ezekiel saw the faithful marked with a *tau*: 'Touch no one
upon whom is the *tau*' (Ezek. 9.6, translating literally). The high priest
was anointed with the Name, but by the time of the Babylonian Talmud,
the ancient alphabet was no longer used, and so the sign of the Name
was not described as a *tau* but as the Greek letter *chi*.[62] The high priest
also wore the Name on his crown, and Enoch/Metatron told Rabbi
Ishmael the significance of the letters:

> He wrote with his finger, as with a pen of flame, upon the crown which was on
> my head, the letters by which heaven and earth were created; the letters by which
> seas and rivers were created; the letters by which mountains and hills were
> created; the letters by which stars and constellations, lightning and wind, thun-
> der and thunderclaps, snow and hail, hurricane and tempests were created; the
> letters by which all the necessities of the world and all the order of creation were
> created.[63]

Rabbi Ishmael then saw all the elements of the creation held in order
by the Name, so that, for example, fire did not destroy snow.[64]

The Name as the seal was widely known. In *Jubilees*, for example, Isaac
has his sons Jacob and Esau swear to love each other, 'by the great oath . . .
by the glorious and honoured and great and splendid and amazing
and mighty name which created heaven and earth and everything

---

61 See above, p. 92.

62 Babylonian Talmud *Horayoth* 12a.

63 *3 Enoch* 13.3.

64 *3 Enoch* 42.2–3.

together . . .'⁶⁵ A story in the Talmud told how King David encountered
the cosmic deep when he was digging the foundation for the temple.
He was advised to write the Name on a potsherd and throw it into the
waters. They subsided.⁶⁶ Thus the LORD, in his Name, was enthroned
over the flood (Ps. 29.10). The Prayer of Manasseh, which has been dated
anywhere between the second century BCE and the second century CE,
is a prayer of penitence used by the Church that begins by describing the
great power of the creator: 'O LORD Almighty . . . thou who hast made
heaven and earth with all their order, who hast shackled the sea by the
word of command, who hast confined the deep, and sealed it with
thy terrible and glorious Name.'⁶⁷ Clement of Rome prayed: 'to hope in
thy Name, which is the source and fount of all creation. Open the eyes of
our hearts to know thee . . .'⁶⁸ Hermas, a Christian prophet in Rome early
in the second century, had an angel explain a vision to him: 'Listen. The
Name of the Son of God [i.e. the LORD] is great and incomprehensible
and supports the whole cosmos . . .'⁶⁹

The person who bore the Name had the power of the Name: 'Save
us, [*hosanna*] . . . Blessed is he who comes with the Name of the LORD
. . .' (Ps. 118.25–6, translating literally), was the cry of the crowd as
Jesus entered Jerusalem (Mk 11.9). He bore/was the seal of creation
and so could restore the protecting covenant. The earliest reference
is in Ezekiel, where the corrupted cherub was thrown from Eden:
'You were the seal of measurement/proportion,' *tknyt*, or 'the seal of
the pattern/image', *tbnyt*.⁷⁰ The cherub wore the jewelled regalia of
a high priest, and so Ezekiel was describing the corruption and fall
of a high priest figure who wore, and so was, the seal. The cause of his
fall was unrighteous trade, violence, pride, the corruption of wisdom
for the sake of splendour, and 'the multitude of your iniquities', that
is, distortions, deviations from the divine plan (Ezek. 28.16–8). It
left the holy places unholy, and they were destroyed. Aaron the
high priest was able to 'reseal' the creation by the power of the Name
he wore. He stopped the plague by 'thy majesty on the diadem
upon his head.' (Wis. 18.24). This must have been the Name. The

65 *Jubilees* 36.7.

66 Babylonian Talmud *Sukkah* 53b.

67 Prayer of Manasseh 1–3; The Prayer is found in a collection of Odes appended
to the Psalter in the fifth century Codex Alexandrinus.

68 *1 Clement* 59.

69 *Hermas*, Parable 9.14.

70 The Hebrew letters *k* and *b* are similar.

original story says that Aaron 'made atonement' to stop the plague (Num. 16.47), which was envisaged as attacking the people through the breach in the covenant. Aaron repaired the covenant and thus stopped the wrath by his incense – the sign of priesthood – and by the Name he wore on his forehead. In response to Peter's sermon at Pentecost that they were living in the last days, many people sought baptism as protection from the impending wrath. Once marked on the forehead with the Name – the diagonal cross which was the original mark of baptism – they believed that 'they would be kept unhurt from the destruction of war which impends over the unbelieving nation and [Jerusalem] itself.'[71]

Philo knew about the figure who was the seal, but he thought of it as impressed into the creation to shape it, rather than impressed on the bonds to seal them. 'The Logos of him who makes [the world] is himself the Seal, by which each thing that exists has received its shape . . .'[72] 'When the substance of the universe was without shape or figure, God gave it shape and figure, he formed it and when he had perfected it, he sealed the whole universe with likeness and ideal form, namely, his own Logos.'[73] This was the figure Ezekiel knew, and Philo described him as 'His Logos, which he calls his covenant . . .'[74] Isaiah's Servant was also called 'covenant'. When the LORD, who created the heavens and stretched forth the earth, was reassuring his people, he gave the Servant as 'a covenant to the people' (Isa. 42.6, also 49.8). This whole complex of imagery is important for understanding the Adam figure, as we shall see.[75]

The early Christians claimed to have learned secrets from the holy of holies: what did Peter mean by 'the things into which angels long to look' (1 Pet. 1.12); or Paul by 'a secret and hidden wisdom of God, which God decreed before the ages for our glorification' (1 Cor. 2.7) and 'the mystery hidden for ages and generations' (Col. 1.26)? There are more details in Ephesians: '[God] has made known to us in all wisdom and insight the mystery of his will, according to his purpose which he set forth in Christ, a plan for the fullness of time, to unite all things in him, things on heaven and things on earth' (Eph. 1.10). All

---

71 *Clementine Recognitions* I.39.

72 Philo, *On Flight* 12.

73 Philo, *On Dreams* II.45 my translation.

74 Ibid., II.237.

75 See below, p. 203.

suggest something revealed to the Christians: 'into which angels long to look' and 'before the ages' both imply the holy of holies and the high priestly knowledge; and uniting all things was the role of the Logos in securing the creation covenant.

Jesus, like Rabbi Ishmael, was described as 'a great high priest'; he appeared to John in the temple wearing the golden sash of a high priest (Rev. 1.13). His followers had confidence to enter the holy of holies and approach the throne (Heb. 4.14–6), just as John was summoned to the holy of holies (Rev. 4.1) where he saw the slain Lamb enthroned amidst the living creatures, receiving the worship of all creation (Rev. 5.6–14). This is the scene in Philippians 2: Jesus was exalted and given 'the name which is above every name', and so in the presence of this Name, all creation gave homage and recognised that Jesus Christ was the LORD, that is, he was Yahweh (Phil. 2.9–11). For the Qumran community, such a vision meant seeing the *raz nihyeh*, the mystery of existence. The *Gospel of Philip*[76] has cryptic descriptions of the holy of holies, described as the bridal chamber.

> At the present time we have the manifest things of creation . . . The mysteries of truth are revealed, though in type and image. The bridal chamber, however, remains hidden. It is the holy in the holy. The veil at first concealed how God controlled the creation . . . If some belong to the order of the priesthood, they will be able to go within the veil with the high priest.[77]

Ptolemy[78] wrote a *Letter to Flora* explaining that the original law was not given by God the Father, but by the 'craftsman and maker of the universe', that is the Second Person.[79] Clement of Alexandria said this too: Jesus, as Son of God, revealed the sure knowledge of 'things present, future and past' (Where is this in the New Testament as usually read?). Since he was the One through whom all things were created, Clement implied that he revealed a sure knowledge of the creation,[80]

---

76 Now thought to be a deposit of first or second generation teaching from the Palestinian community.

77 *The Gospel of Philip* CG II.3.84–5.

78 A disciple of Valentinus in the mid second century CE, remembered as a Gnostic but in his own time recognized as a great biblical scholar.

79 *Letter of Ptolemy to Flora*, in Epiphanius, *Against Heresies*, 33.

80 Clement, *Miscellanies* 6.7.

and Christians received what the LORD handed on, because they too had 'drawn aside the curtain'.[81]

All this suggests that the early Christians proclaimed Jesus as the Logos in the same way as Philo understood that role, but would Jesus have recognized himself? The earliest interpretations of his life and death cannot, surely, have been completely at variance with Jesus' own understanding of himself. Hebrews says that he was the great high priest making the self-sacrifice of the final Day of Atonement, the sacrifice that renewed the creation covenant (Heb. 9.11–26); and the great hymn in Colossians claims that 'in him all things hold together.' (Col. 1.17), the sign of the restored creation covenant. John said that Jesus bore witness to what he had seen in heaven, but people did not believe his testimony (Jn 3.32). The Book of Revelation says it is the heavenly visions of Jesus, even though the opening lines are not usually read that way: 'The revelation of Jesus Christ which God gave to him [i.e. to Jesus] to show to his servants what must soon take place' (Rev. 1.1). The two focal points of Revelation are the Christians' great high priest revealing how the Kingdom would be established – 'destroying the destroyers of the earth' – and how the creation would be renewed – 'Behold I make all things new' (Rev. 11.18; 21.5).[82]

Jesus saw the heavens open at his baptism, which means that he saw into the holy of holies; what followed – the vision and his subsequent struggle in the wilderness – may hold the key to his teaching. When he was tempted by the devil, he had three visionary experiences; in two he was 'taken up': onto a pinnacle of the temple, and onto a place where he could see all the kingdoms of the world in a moment of time (Lk. 4.5). Only Luke gives the detail that links Jesus' experience to the temple mystics, and since Jesus was alone in the wilderness, he must have told his disciples about the visions. Mark records, cryptically: 'He was with the wild beasts and the angels served him' (Mk 1.12–13). The association of beasts[83] and angels suggests the vision in Revelation 5 – the slain lamb enthroned in the midst of the living creatures, receiving the worship of the angels and the whole creation. Did Mark and the other early Christians know that Jesus had received temple visions, and not only seen them but had himself become part of them? Perhaps this is what John meant

81 Ibid., 7.17.

82 Luke had Jesus say: 'I saw Satan fall like lightning from heaven', and described how he had amazed the temple teachers with his knowledge. Luke 10.18; 2.46–7.

83 In Hebrew – it is unlikely that the first stories were told in Greek – the word *ḥayyoth* means both wild animals and the living creatures of the throne.

when he said that Jesus bore witness to what he had seen in heaven. Perhaps too this explains the distinction Jesus made between seeing the Kingdom – seeing the *raz nihyeh*, the secret of life – and entering the Kingdom – being himself the process (Jn 3.3–5). The early Church must have had a reason for describing him as the Author of Life (Acts 3.15).

THE MATTER OF CREATION

The forms, the bonds and the seal of creation were part of the temple tradition, and Jews in the time of Jesus claimed that Plato has copied them. But what of matter itself, the stuff that was formed, bound and sealed? Was it just 'there' and so co-eternal with God? Or was it created by God, the first stage of creation? The Christians believed that God created matter, 'one God who made the beginning of all things and holds the power of the end . . .'[84]

It is not clear what Plato envisaged as the raw material that the Demiurge, the divine Craftsman, shaped, and 'there is no point more obscure or more vehemently disputed that the nature of the so-called Platonic matter.'[85] Plato described how the Demiurge,

> when he took over all that was visible, seeing that it was not in a state of rest but in a state of discordant and disorderly motion, he brought it into order out of disorder . . .[86]
>
> [The four kinds, *genē*] were without proportion [*alogos*] and measure. Fire, water, earth and air possessed indeed some vestiges of their own nature, but were altogether in such a condition as we should expect for anything when deity is absent from it. Such being their nature at the time when the ordering of the universe was taken in hand, the god then began by giving them a distinct con-figuration by means if shapes and numbers.[87]
>
> These things were in disorder, and the god introduced into them all every kind of measure in every respect in which it was possible for each one to be in harmonious proportion both with itself and with all the rest . . . But all these he first set in order, and then framed out of them this universe . . .[88]

84 Clement of Alexandria, *Miscellanies* 6.5.

85 R. G. Bury, *Plato*, vol. IX, LCL, p. 10.

86 Plato, *Timaeus*, 30A.

87 Ibid., 53B, Cornford's translation.

88 Ibid., 69B, Cornford's translation.

Plato's divine Craftsman worked with existing materials: 'His task is to bring some intelligible order into a disorder which he "takes over", not to create the material before he fashions it.'[89] Plato admitted that he did not know the origin of the material,[90] and so Timaeus could be said to correspond to the 'second stage' of the biblical creation process.

The Nicene creed describes the two aspects of the biblical creation as the work of Father and Son. The English translation uses the same verb to describe both roles, whereas the Greek distinguishes between them. In English, both are 'makers': 'God the Father Almighty, Maker, [Greek *poiētēs*] of heaven and earth' and 'Jesus Christ the LORD, by whom all things were made, [Greek *egeneto*]'. Paul, describing Father and Son, said there is one God, the Father, from, *ex*, whom are all things and for whom we exist, and one LORD, Jesus Christ, through, *dia*, whom are all things and through whom we exist (1 Cor. 8.6). The vexed question of whether or not the Bible teaches creation from nothing, *creatio ex nihilo*, can only be addressed if the work of the two Persons is distinguished for the purpose of elucidation, though in reality the work is inseparable: *from* whom and *through* whom. This statement by Paul suggests creation in two stages: the making of matter, which comes from the Father, and the formation of the creation, which comes through the LORD, that is through Yahweh. Thus the work of Plato's Craftsman corresponds to the work of the LORD, except that his Craftsman was constrained by his materials, and so was not omnipotent.

There are complications here: most recent expositors of the Hebrew Scriptures do not read them with the eyes of the first Christians, and so do not see in them the work of *the Second Person*, the LORD who was incarnate as Jesus; and second, the early Christian sources are in Greek, not Hebrew, and the equating of key terms is not always clear or consistent. For example, Proverbs describes how Wisdom was 'brought forth' in the sense of 'birthed', and this is paired in Hebrew with the verb *qanah*. Poetic parallelism would require the same meaning, so this verb should also mean 'birthed', but it is usually translated 'created.' 'The LORD *created* me at the beginning of his works . . . When there were no depths I was *brought forth* . . . before the hills, I was *brought forth*' (Prov. 8.22,24, 25). Now the distinction between being 'birthed' and being 'created' is crucial, which is why the Creed emphasizes 'begotten not created'. The Greek text of Proverbs, however, has Hebrew

89 Cornford, *Plato's Cosmology*, p. 165.

90 Plato, *Timaeus*, 47B.

qanah, birthed/brought forth, translated by 'created', *ektise,* and the two instances of 'brought forth' are not represented in the text at all. Thus the Hebrew text says that Wisdom was 'birthed', the Greek that she was created. The origin of Wisdom is therefore unclear – and this is but one example of the problem of origins.[91]

If *qanah* implied a process like birthing, then Deuteronomy 32.6, which uses the same word, would mean: 'Is he not your Father who *begot* you, who made you and established you?' And Melchizedek would have been the priest of 'God Most High, *Begetter/Father* of Heaven and Earth' (Gen. 14.19). In each case the Greek text has 'Creator'.[92] Philo at one point says: 'God, when he gave birth, *gennēsas,* to all things, not only brought them into sight, but also made things which before were not, not just handling the material as a Demiurge, but himself being its Creator.'[93] This implies God 'giving birth' to matter, and the Demiurge shaping material that was already there. Most of the references to 'creation' in the Hebrew Scriptures refer to the work of the Second Person, the Craftsman, and are therefore not evidence one way or the other for *creatio ex nihilo,* creation out of nothing. It has long been recognized that the teachers of the second temple period were not concerned with this.[94]

There is also the problem of what was meant by 'nothing'. Did it mean formless matter, or did it mean literally nothing? The Greek term *mē on,* literally 'not being', was used by Plato to mean matter, but Philo used the term in the plural, suggesting that he did not use it in the same sense.[95] Whether or not Philo taught 'creation out of nothing', and what sense he gave to those words, is an ongoing debate in which there is no sign of agreement.[96] Certain passages do suggest

91 B. Vawter 'Prov. 8.22: Wisdom and Creation', *Journal of Biblical Literature* 99 (1980), pp. 205–16 argues that *qanah* means only acquire or possess, and that no text *compels* us to adopt another meaning, p 205. The arguments are not convincing. C. Westermann, *Genesis 1–11, A Commentary,* tr. J. J. Scullion, London: SPCK, 1984 argues that *qanah* means create.

92 The Aramaic of the *Genesis Apocryphon* described Melchizedek's God as the 'Lord, *mrh,* of heaven and earth'.

93 Philo, *On Dreams,* I.76.

94 G. F. Moore, *Judaism in the First Centuries of the Christian Era: The Age of Tannaim,* repr. Peabody, MA: Hendrickson, 1997. vol.1, p. 381: ' . . . there are few utterances that bear on it in any way.'

95 For an outline of this problem, see G. May, *Creatio Ex Nihilo,* tr. A. S. Worrell, Edinburgh: T&T Clark, 1994, p. 17.

96 See Runia, *Philo of Alexandria,* p. 152.

strongly that he believed in the pre-existing matter. Thus, commenting on 'And God saw everything that he had made, and behold it was very good' (Gen. 1.31), he said:

> God praised not the formed matter, material soulless, discordant and dissoluble, and indeed in itself perishable, irregular, unequal, but he praised the works of his own art, which were consummated through a single exercise of power equal and uniform, and through knowledge over one and the same. And thus by the rules of proportion everything was accounted similar and equal to everything else.[97]

Elsewhere there is: 'The Maker of the World , *poiētēs*, when he began to order refractory and unordered and passive substance, made use of cutting and division . . .'[98]

At the centre of the problem are the opening words of Genesis: 'In the beginning, God created the heavens and the earth.' 'Created' in Hebrew is *bara'*, the uniquely divine activity, but the Old Greek translated it 'made', *epoiēsen*. Josephus, however, and Aquila both used 'created', *ektisen*, which may indicate some controversy over the best word to describe the Creator's first work. Then we learn that 'the earth was *tohu* and *bohu*, and darkness was on the face of the deep . . .' (Gen. 1.1–2a). Does this mean: 'In the beginning, God made heaven and earth. And the earth was *tohu* and *bohu*,'? Or does it mean: 'In the beginning, when God made heaven and earth, the earth was *tohu* and *bohu*' implying that something *tohu* and *bohu* was already there on which God set to work? The former is creation out of nothing, the latter is creation out of pre-existing matter. This is a vital difference. It is interesting to compare the New English Bible (1970) and the Revised English Bible (1985). The NEB, translated during the 1950s and 1960s when popular cosmology favoured the steady state theory, has 'In the beginning of creation, when God made heaven and earth,[99] the earth was *tohu* and *bohu*,' which implies pre-existing matter; the REB, translated when the Big Bang had become popular as the way to explain the origin of the universe, has: 'In the beginning, God created the heavens and the earth. The earth was *tohu* and *bohu*,' implying a moment of creation. The modern translators, consciously or not, were influenced by current intellectual fashion. When the translators of the Old Greek opted for: 'In the beginning, God made the heaven

---

97 Philo, *Who is the Heir?* 160.

98 Philo, *Questions on Genesis* I.64.

99 With a footnote offering 'in the beginning, God created heaven and earth' as an alternative.

and the earth. The earth was unseen and unprepared . . .', were they influenced by the popular form of current ideas? The Greek 'unseen and unprepared' could well have been influenced by Platonic *descriptions* of the original matter, without raising the question of whether or not God created it.[100]

To see what the first Christians might have thought, it is necessary to look at texts from their time and place, at ideas they could have known, even if they did not know the texts themselves. Josephus certainly, and the Targum *Neofiti* probably, reflect how the beginning of Genesis was understood in Palestine in the first century CE. Josephus simply expanded the Old Greek 'In the beginning, God made the heaven and the earth, but the earth was unseen and unprepared . . .' when he wrote:

> In the beginning, God created the heaven and the earth; but when the earth did not come into sight, but was covered with thick darkness, and a wind moved upon its surface, God commanded that there should be light; and when that was made, he considered the whole mass, and separated the light and the darkness . . .[101]

The Targum *Neofiti* has: 'And the earth was waste and unformed, desolate of man and beast, empty of plant cultivation and of trees.'[102] The (later) Targum *Pseudo-Jonathan* has: 'The earth was without form and void, desolate of people and empty of all animals.'[103]

These texts suggest the two stage creation implied by Paul: 'One God the Father, *from* whom are all things . . . and one LORD, Jesus Christ, *through* whom are all things . . .' (1 Cor. 8.6). The Father created the basic material, and the LORD shaped it into the ordered creation. Paul, in the context of Abraham's hope for a son, said: 'God . . . who calls into existence the things that do not exist' (Rom. 4.17). He was alluding to a story in 2 Maccabees, where a young man faced martyrdom and his mother said: 'Recognise that God did not make [heaven and earth] out of things that existed' (2 Macc. 7.28). In other words, God created matter, and this is how the human race comes into being. The martyr's mother hoped for bodily resurrection, just as childless

---

100 Plato's Demiurge is very similar to the Hebrew Yahweh, see my book *The Great High Priest*, pp. 262–93.

101 Josephus, *Antiquities*, I.27–28.

102 Thus M. McNamara, *Targum Neofiti Genesis*, Edinburgh: T&T Clark, 1992, p. 52.

103 Thus M. Maher, *Targum Pseudo-Jonathan Genesis*, Edinburgh: T&T Clark, 1992, p. 16.

Abraham had faith that he would eventually have a son. Some of the prayers in the *Apostolic Constitutions* which are thought to have pre-Christian roots imply the 'double creation', God creating matter and the Second Person shaping it: '. . . the one who is truly God, the one who is before things that have been made . . . For you, eternal God, have made all things through him . . .'[104] The Wisdom of Solomon, on the other hand, described creation simply as forming the formless, without raising the question of the origin of the formless matter: 'Thy all powerful hand which created the world out of formless matter . . .' (Wis. 11.17). All these are compatible with the ancient Hebrew tradition that God created matter and the 'Second God' shaped it.

The debate between Jewish thought and Platonism was the context for an exchange attributed to Rabbi Gamaliel II and an unnamed philosopher. The former was the patriarch of the academy at Javneh from about 80 CE, and so one of the great authorities in the generation that was rebuilding Jewish life after the destruction of the temple. The philosopher asked him: 'Your God was indeed a great artist, but surely he found good materials which assisted him?' – implying Plato's view of the creation. 'What were they?' asked Gamaliel. '*Tohu, bohu,* darkness, water, wind/spirit, and the deep', said the philosopher, who must have known Genesis well. 'Woe to that man' exclaimed Gamaliel, and then showed him how all the 'materials' are said elsewhere in Scripture to have been created.[105] Creation from nothing was important to a Jewish teacher in that context.

Justin, a boy growing up not far from Javneh at that time, claimed that Plato's thought was Christian. He had studied philosophy[106] and was certain that Plato, in addition to his teaching about the forms, the bonds and the seal, had taken his teaching about matter from Moses. He quoted Genesis 1.1–3, and then said: 'So that both Plato and those who agree with him, and we ourselves have learned . . . that by the word of God the whole world was made out of the substance spoken of before by Moses.' In other words, Plato's pre-existent matter was created by God at the very beginning, and was not an independent substance.[107] The book of the early Christian prophet Hermas, which Justin would have known when he lived in Rome, is not clear on this point: 'Believe

104 *Apostolic Constitutions* 8.12.

105 *Genesis Rabbah* I.9, quoting Isa.45.7; Psalm148.4–5; Amos 4.13; Proverbs 8.24.

106 Justin, *Trypho*, 1–2.

107 Justin, *Apology* I.59.

that God is one, who made all things and perfected them and made all things to be out of that which is not, *mē on*.'[108] There is no way of knowing if *mē on*' here meant 'nothing', meaning that God created matter out of nothing; or if it meant the formless matter that Plato called *mē on*. But if Justin understood Plato's *mē on* as the formless matter created by God at the very beginning, then he and Hermas were in agreement.

It was probably the crisis caused in the mid second century by the growth of Gnosticism and the popularity of Marcion's teaching that prompted attention to the question of origins, and the emphasis that matter was created by God and did not have an eternal independent existence. Marcion taught that matter was evil, and so the divine could not dwell in an earthly body; Christ was not born of a woman and did not have a material body. Theophilus, writing in Antioch about 180 CE, explained the origin of matter: '[the prophets] taught us that God made all things out of nothing; for nothing is coeval with God . . .' He understood 'In the beginning God created the heaven and the earth' to mean the creation of matter: '. . . sacred scripture teaches at the outset, to show that matter, from which God made and fashioned the world, was in some manner created, being produced by God.'[109] Athanasius would eventually pen the classic statement about the universe:

> [The Christian faith] teaches that the world did not come into being of its own accord because it did not lack providence [*apronoēta*] and neither was it made from pre-existent matter, since God is not weak, but that through the Word, God brought the universe, which previously in no way subsisted at all, into being from non-existence, as he says through Moses: 'In the beginning God made heaven and earth.'[110]

Since the first Christians knew the Scriptures in Hebrew, they would have known that *tohu* and *bohu* occur elsewhere. The LORD had found his people in 'a desert land, and in the howling waste, *tohu*, of the wilderness' (Deut. 32.10). The city of Bozrah in Edom, said Isaiah, would be demolished as punishment, and the role of the builder in measuring and constructing would be reversed: the LORD would mark it out with the line of *tohu* and the stones of *bohu*

---

108 Hermas, *Mandate* 1.

109 Theophilus of Antioch, *To Autolycus*, II.10.

110 Athanasius, *On the Incarnation*, 3, tr. R. W. Thomson, Oxford: Clarendon Press, 1971.

(Isa. 34.11b translating literally). Isaiah said: 'Thus says the LORD who created [*bara'*] the heavens (he is God), who formed the earth and made it, he established it; not *tohu* did he create it, he formed it as a dwelling place' (Isa. 45.18 translating literally). Jeremiah saw the future state of his land: 'I looked on the earth, and lo it was *tohu* and *bohu*; and to the heavens and they had no light . . .' (Jer. 4.23). Significant here is the reason for his country's reversion to this state of disordered matter: the people were skilled in doing evil, and did not know how to do good. Doing good must have been a factor in keeping the creation in its intended state. The Psalmist knew that the LORD had made all his many works with wisdom (Ps. 104.24), and so presumably, without wisdom, the works were no more. The role of wisdom and knowledge in sustaining the creation was an important theme, as we shall see.

Chalcidius was an early fourth century Christian who translated the first half of *Timaeus* into Latin and wrote a commentary relating it to Genesis. The 'heaven and earth' of Genesis 1.1, he said, were not the heaven and earth that we see, but rather 'other things that are older and should rather be perceived by the intellect than by the senses.' The creation of heaven and earth was the primal division of spirit from the matter used to make the world. He cited a passage from Origen to show that the Hebrews believed matter was created and then amazed as it was formed into the world. The original Hebrew of Genesis 1.2a, *tohu* and *bohu*, could mean 'the earth was somewhat *stunned* with *amazement.*'[111] Origen's text is lost, but he had contact with Jewish scholars in Caesarea who knew the same way of reading Genesis. Rabbi Abbahu[112] taught that the *tohu* and *bohu* of Genesis 1.2a meant: 'The earth sat *bewildered* and *astonished*, saying, "The celestial beings and the terrestrial ones were created at the same time yet the celestial beings are fed by the radiance of the Shekinah, whereas the terrestrial ones, if they do not toil, do not eat."'[113]

There is abundant evidence in the time of Jesus for the second stage of the creation, the 'bonds' that Philo often mentions and

---

111 Chalcidius, *In Timaeum* 276: '*silvam generatam esse*'.

112 Rabbi Abbahu became head of the academy at Caesarea at the end of the third century.

113 *Genesis Rabbah* II.2. Hebrew *tohu* and *bohu* are similar to Aramaic words meaning astonished and perplexed. Targum *Neofiti* Gen. 1.2a could also mean 'the earth was astonished and perplexed.' See H. Jacobson, 'Origen's Version of Genesis 1.2' *Journal of Theological Studies*, 59.1 (2008), pp. 181–2.

which are not found in the way the Hebrew Scriptures are read today. Thus in his treatise *On Planting*, Philo he wrote:

> For when the Framer of the World, *kosmoplastēs*, finding all that existed confused and disordered of itself, began to give it form. Bringing it out of disorder into order, out of confusion into distinction of parts . . .
>
>   This world of ours was formed out of all that there is of earth, and all that there is of water and air and fire, not even the smallest particle being left outside . . .
>
>   For the Father who begat him constituted his Word such a bond of the universe as nothing can break. Good reason, then, have we to be sure, that all the earth shall not be dissolved by all the water which has gathered within its hollows, nor fire be quenched by air; nor, on the other hand, air be ignited by fire.[114]
>
>   For the Logos of Him that is . . . the bond of all existence, holds and knits together all the parts, preventing them from being dissolved and separated.[115]

The Logos, as we have seen, was known as the covenant, which also meant the binding.[116]

It is important to remember that John chose to describe Jesus as the incarnate Logos, and the only information about the Logos at this time is from Philo. Although there can be no proof that John used those ideas, they are the only contemporary evidence for the nature and role of the Logos. Jesus the bond of all creation and the covenant is not the way the New Testament is usually read, but how else can John's gospel be set in context? Begotten of his Father as the unbreakable bond of the creation? 'All things were made through him and without him was not anything made that was made' (Jn 1.2–3a). The words Jesus heard at his baptism – 'With you I am well pleased' (Mk. 1. 11) – are the beginning of a passage in Isaiah that describes the Servant as the covenant, or even as the eternal covenant.[117] Jesus as the [eternal] covenant gives additional meaning to the words at the last supper, which could have been 'the blood of my covenant . . .' rather than 'my blood of the covenant . . .'[118] The Logos was renewing his covenant.

---

114 Philo, *On Planting*, 3, 6, 9–10.

115 Philo, *On Flight*, 112.

116 Philo, *On Dreams* II.237.

117 Isaiah 42.6 has the unusual 'covenant of the people' *bryt l'm*, but 4Q Isa^h has 'eternal covenant', *bryt 'lm*, which makes more sense.

118 There are several problems over the original meaning of these words, see M. Casey, 'The Original Aramaic Form of Jesus' Interpretation of the Cup', *Journal of Theological Studies* 41 (1990), pp. 1–11.

The next question is: how were the invisible bonds and patterns combined with the matter so that the visible world was made? The New Testament has one enigmatic verse, which suggests that the linking is a matter of faith: 'By faith we understand that the world was perfected/ completed by the spoken word* of God, so that what is seen was made out of things which are not seen' (Heb 11.3, my translation; *rhēma*, not *logos*). The original temple world view had the LORD commanding the creation into good order; hence the question to Job: 'Do you know the engraved pattern of the heavens and can you set up its pattern/rule on earth?' (Job 38.33, the gist of an obscure verse). Enoch learned that the pattern for the stars was the pattern for the holy ones on earth.[119] Philo knew that the Logos was 'the original seal . . . the first principle, the archetypal idea, the pre-measurer of all things,'[120] and John said that the Logos became flesh (Jn 1.14). The 'archetypal idea and pre-measurer of all things' sounds very like the 'seal of proportion, full of Wisdom' (Ezek. 28. 12), the anointed high-priest figure whom Ezekiel saw driven from Eden. The *Gospel of Philip* said that Messiah meant both Christ and 'the measured one',[121] and there is similar language in the New Testament: 'The measure of the stature of the fullness of Christ' (Eph. 4.13). Throughout the temple world view, and especially in the role of the high priest, there is the sense of pattern and proportion, and it may be that 'Thy will be done on earth as it is in heaven' refers to the whole pattern of creation, not just human conduct.

Some of the ancient theological questions about the origin and formation of the creation are still with us; others are neglected.[122] The cosmologist Paul Davies observed:

> Many thinkers baulk at [the issues of the origin of the world and infinity] and turn instead to the scientific evidence. What can science tell us about the origin of the universe? These days most cosmologists and astronomers back the theory that there was indeed a creation . . . popularly known as the "big bang."[123]

---

119 *1 Enoch* 43.4.

120 Philo, *Questions on Genesis* I.4.

121 *Gospel of Philip*, CG II.3.62.

122 The Pope addressed a group of cosmologists in Rome in 1981 and reminded them that science alone could not answer the question of the origin of the universe, *Acta Apostolicae Sedis*, 73 (1981), pp. 669–70.

123 P. Davies, *God and the New Physics*, p. 10.

Many laymen, compelled these days to dismiss so much of the Old Testament as fiction, find comfort in the apparent support that modern scientific cosmology brings to the Genesis story.[124]

The point of the Genesis story, however, is not that details of the process correspond with recent scientific discovery, but that *the cosmos was and is created by the Creator, and all that that implies.* The older wisdom that everything in creation, including human beings, has its appointed place, and that there are laws to limit human behaviour, has been neglected. So too the wisdom of harmony and moderation.

Eusebius, reflecting on creation, noted the sufficiency of all things: 'God estimated for the creation of the world just sufficient matter that there would be neither deficiency nor excess . . .' He was quoting a lost work of Philo, ideas that were available to the first Christians.[125] Compare this with the current problem of waste that cannot be recycled, the plastic bags in the world's oceans that choke seabirds, the islands of floating rubbish that are the by-product of the fast-food lifestyle, the landfill sites that are full. Shipping and dumping it in a distant land is not a solution; in one world there is no 'away' for throwing away. The problem of our way of living is not waste, but waste that cannot be re-absorbed into the natural order. The waste is a symptom of the disease; our intervention in the creation has distorted the system. 'We call ourselves consumers, but the problem is that we do not consume . . .' 'The environment can absorb natural waste, but just as the earth has limited capacity to produce renewable resources, its capacity to receive waste is similarly constrained.'[126] Nobody with an eye to business growth would have designed the world that way, but the limits of the creation cannot be renegotiated. It was created for another purpose.

This is the great gulf. The Bible does not simply assert that creation had a beginning; it explores the issues of purpose – why is there anything here at all? – and relationships – how do we fit into all this? The recurring theme of the creation story is that the Creator saw that his work was very good. Adam as we shall see, was created to fill the world with the glory of God,[127] and we are filling it with waste.

124 Ibid. p. 20.

125 Philo, *On Providence*, fragment 1, in Eusebius, *Preparation of the Gospel* VII.21.

126 P. Hawken, *The Ecology of Commerce*, pp. 12, 37.

127 See below, pp. 193–4, 203–4.

BREAKING THE BONDS

The pictures of cosmic catastrophe in the New Testament indicate the collapse of the covenant system. When Jesus predicted that the sun would be darkened, and the moon not give its light; that the stars would fall from heaven and the powers would be shaken (Mk 13.24–5), he was describing the day of wrath. The fuller account of his teaching is preserved in Revelation, as the signs of the sixth seal:

> There was a great earthquake; and the sun became black as sackcloth, and the full moon became like blood, and the stars of the sky fell to earth as the fig tree sheds its winter fruit when shaken by a gale; the sky vanished like a scroll that is rolled up, and every mountain and island was removed from its place.

Everyone tried to hide from the disaster, which they knew was 'the great day of wrath' (Rev. 6.12–14, 17). Wrath was the result of breaking the covenant, what happened when its protection had been breached. The episode of the high priest Phineas and the Midianite woman shows how the words wrath, atonement and covenant of peace were used (Num. 25.6–13). On another occasion when wrath threatened the people, the high priest Aaron made atonement and the plague was stopped (Num. 16.41–50). The words would probably be understood differently nowadays, especially in those communities who associate wrath and atonement with appeasing an angry God. The biblical picture is different: wrath breaks in when there is no more covenant protection; atonement repairs the covenant bonds and restores the protection. Atonement protects the creation and human society.

Philip Pullman gave a graphic description of the broken covenant bonds and the incursion of wrath, albeit in a fictional context. Many places, he wrote in his book *The Subtle Knife*, had been invaded by Spectres, who fed on human souls and left them like them like living dead. A prosperous and happy world had been destroyed. 'All the trust and all the virtue fell out of our world when the Spectres came.' The old man told the children the story of the Tower of the Angels, and how the Spectres came because

> men of learning were making enquiry into the deepest nature of things. They became curious about the bonds that held the smallest particles of matter

together. You know what I mean by a bond? Something that binds. Well, this was a mercantile city. A city of traders and bankers. We thought we knew about bonds. We thought a bond was something negotiable, something that could be bought and sold and exchanged and converted . . . But about these bonds we were wrong. We undid them and let the Spectres in.

He did not know where they came from. 'What matters is that they are here and they have destroyed us.'[128] It is dawning upon a frightened world that Pullman's fiction is rather familiar.

The bonds of creation cannot be renegotiated, and so some man-made systems – moral, political, economic – will have to change, since the bonds of creation are breaking. The seven sins – pride, envy, gluttony, lust, anger, greed and sloth – have now been rebranded and become socially acceptable. What Paul listed as the works of the flesh are now promoted as the good life (Gal. 5.19–21). Sin has been rede-fined. The Liberation theologians in south America, although taking their starting point in the story of Exodus and the freedom from slavery, could as easily have spoken of the broken covenant when they condemned the 'structural sins' in society, the economic and social policies established and maintained by injustice. Above all, there is the global money system which aspires to be a separate creation, making its own laws.

The dominant theory of markets . . . fails to take account of the constraints on economic or market activity represented by the biophysical environment. This is a failing of *all* the neoclassical economists, both capitalist and Marxist. They all treat the economic system as a sphere of value creation which is independent of natural systems.[129]

The human economy requires for its long-term success that its architects acknowledge their dependence on the greater economy of nature, preserving its health and respecting its benefits. By this standard every modern economy, whether built on the principles of Adam Smith or Karl Marx is an unmitigated disaster . . . The ecological crisis we have begun to experience in recent years is fast becoming *the* crisis of modern culture, calling into question not only the ethos of the market place or industrialism, but also the central story we have been telling ourselves over the past two or three centuries: the story of man's triumph of reason over the rest of nature.[130]

128 Philip Pullman, *The Subtle Knife*, London: Scholastic, 1998, pp. 141, 196.

129 M. S. Northcott, 'Christians, Environment and Society', in Carling, ed. *A Christian Approach to the Environment*, The John Ray Initiative, 2005, pp. 105–32, p. 115.

130 D. Worster, *Nature's Economy: A History of Ecological Ideas*, Cambridge: Cambridge University Press, 2nd edn, 1994, pp. 217–8.

These are biblical insights: that creation and all spheres of human activity are one, and that the human attitude to knowledge has broken the bonds of creation. And so the earth is filled with waste and pollution, violence and corruption, far removed from the song of the angels: 'The whole earth is full of his glory.'

The picture language of the Bible describes what happens as the covenant collapses. There is a great judgement, when sinners are punished by the angels – *who represent the forces of nature*.[131] Isaiah left a vivid description of the creation covenant collapsing (Isa. 24.4–6), affecting human society as well as the wider creation: all joy gone from human life, desolation in the city, floods and earthquakes, the earth swaying like hut; and then the LORD punishing the powers of heaven and earth and establishing his rule on Mount Zion (Isa. 24.7–23). Embedded in the wrath and judgement sequence is: 'From the ends of the earth we hear songs of praise, of Glory to the Righteous One. But I say, "I pine away, I pine away. Woe is me! . . ." The sense of this passage is probably better represented by the Targum, which understood 'I pine away' to mean 'My mystery' (Isa. 24.16).[132] Now a saying based on this verse was attributed to Jesus: 'My mystery is for me and the sons of my house,'[133] and the Targum shows how this was understood in his time.[134]

> From the sanctuary, whence joy is about to come forth unto all the inhabitants of the earth, we have heard a song of praise for the righteous. The prophet said, 'The mystery of the reward of the righteous is visible to me, the mystery of the retribution for the wicked is revealed to me. Woe to the oppressors for they shall be oppressed, and to the spoiling of the spoilers, for they shall be spoiled . . .' For the Kingdom of the Lord of Hosts shall be revealed in the mountain of Zion, and in Jerusalem, and before the elders of his people in glory.[135]

The sequence is: breaking the everlasting covenant that caused cosmic disaster; then the expected song of praise from the sanctuary; and finally the mystery of the judgement revealed together with

---

131 See above p. 116.

132 The Isaiah Targum understands this verse as 'the mystery of the reward of the Righteous One . . .' which led to the revelation of the Kingdom. See my book *Temple Themes in Christian Worship*, London: T&T Clark, 2007, pp. 192–3.

133 Clement of Alexandria, *Miscellanies* 5.10; also in *Clementine Homilies* XIX. 20.

134 The Isaiah Targum has some early material, and parts of it are the most obvious background to Revelation. See my book *The Revelation of Jesus Christ*, London: T&T Clark, 2000, for example, pp. 253–4.

135 *Targum of Isaiah* 24.16, 23b.

the Kingdom. *This is the sequence the Christians knew in Revelation 11,* when, after the horrors of the opening seals and the six trumpets, the angel sounded the seventh trumpet. The elders around the throne praised the LORD and announced the coming of the Kingdom on earth, the time for rewarding the saints and for destroying the destroyers of the earth (Rev. 11.15–18). Isaiah pictured the collapsing covenant followed by the judgement and the revelation of the Kingdom. John's vision shows that this was fundamental to the early Christian hope.

The Hebrew Scriptures have other pictures of the collapsing covenant. Jeremiah saw the land returned to its original state, *tohu* and *bohu*, and the heavens without light. There were no people, no birds, no cities, and the cultivated land had returned to desert. The reason? People were skilled in doing evil, and did not know how to do good (Jer. 4.22–6; there is a similar passage in Jer. 12.4). Hosea, too, knew that lack of knowledge destroyed the creation and human society (Hos. 4.1–3). He blamed the priests who had neglected to teach the law of God, priests whom the much later prophet Malachi would describe as the angels (that is messengers, it is the same Hebrew word) of the LORD who had failed to teach well. As a result, they had corrupted the covenant of peace and caused many to stumble (Mal. 2.5–8). These priests were the fallen angels on earth.

The story of the fallen angels was widely known in the time of Jesus; in Genesis they were called the 'sons of God' (Gen. 6.2). Jesus spoke of the fire prepared for the devil and his angels (Mt. 25.41); Peter wrote of the angels who sinned (2 Pet. 2.4); Jude wrote of the angels who left their proper dwelling place (Jude 6). The gospel writers knew the story: according to the Enoch tradition, the fallen angels were imprisoned in the time of Enoch, and would stay there for seventy generations, until the day of judgement.[136] Luke assumes his readers know this, because in his genealogy of Jesus, there are seventy generations from Enoch to Jesus (Lk. 3.23–37). The demons, children of the fallen angels, complained that Jesus had come to drive them out 'before the time' (Mt. 8.29); and John recorded in Revelation how and why the angels fell from heaven and were eventually defeated and destroyed (Rev. 12.4–12; 19.11–21). In the *Damascus Document* the fallen angels were the model for all those who did not keep the commandments and so brought disaster, from the time of Noah until their own time. 'The Heavenly Watchers fell . . . because they did not keep the

136 *1 Enoch* 10.12.

commandments of God . . . his wrath was kindled against them . . .' The faithful remnant held fast to the commandments and were taught the mysteries; they would live for ever and be restored to all the glory of Adam.[137]

The fallen angels is the one of the two themes in the Enoch tradition; the other is his ascent to heaven. In other words, Enoch saw the creation and learned its secrets in his heavenly visions, and he also learned how the creation had been corrupted by the fallen angels. There is a brief reference to the story in Genesis 6.1–4, where the rebel angels are called the sons of God, sons of the *'elohim.* The fullest form of the story is already a conflation of two versions, with the leader of the rebel angels named 'Azazel/Shemḥazah, the strong angel.[138] This is the strong one mentioned by Jesus: 'No one can enter the house of the strong one and plunder his goods unless he first binds the strong one . . .' (Mk 3.27, translating literally). Isaiah knew the strong one who would burn together with his works (Isa. 1.31). Shem'azah persuaded 200 angels to bind themselves by an oath and to descend from heaven to take human wives. 'Azazel then taught men to work metal into weapons and jewellery, and to make eye cosmetics[139] that led to fornication. Other fallen angels taught magic and medicine, astrology, writing and much more. Although the lists have not survived in a clear form – the present text may have been translated from Aramaic to Greek and then to Ethiopic – the gist is clear enough.[140] Isaiah described his land under the influence of fallen angels: full of diviners and soothsayers, full of gold and silver, people engaged in the arms trade of the time, worshipping the work of their own hands and indulging in the current fashions (Isa. 2.6–8; 3.16–23).

The result of this knowledge was corruption of the earth. 'As men perished, their cry went up to heaven . . . [the four archangels] looked

---

137 *The Damascus Document*, CD II-III.

138 Spelled various ways, for example Asael. The double name is two aspects of the same angel: 'Azazel could mean 'strong angel' and the other form, Shem'azah, could mean mighty name. Enoch's angel lists do have these paired angels: Malkiel inverts to Elimelek, meaning 'my king is El/my El is king'; and Yosiphel inverts to Eliyasaph meaning 'God adds/my God adds', see *1 Enoch* 72.15–20 and notes in R. H. Charles, *The Book of Enoch*, Oxford: Clarendon Press, 1912, pp. 177–8.

139 Significant because Wisdom anointed the eyes of her children to make them 'see'.

140 *1 Enoch* 8.1–4.

down from heaven and saw much blood being shed upon the earth
. . .'[141] The Great Holy One then commanded the archangels to warn
Noah of the imminent destruction, to bind the leaders of the rebel
angels and to kill their offspring. Then the archangels had to 'heal the
earth' because the whole earth had been corrupted through the works
of 'Azazel. In other words, it was powerful knowledge used in rebellion
against the Great Holy One, used without the restraint of his law, that
destroyed the earth. Secular science has now reached the same
conclusion:

> Humanity is facing two contradicting phenomena – the inevitability of the devel-
> opment of civilisation and the impossibility of an equally rapid development of
> the biosphere. In other words, while civilisation develops, the biosphere
> degrades. . . . One needs to confine civilisation's development within such limits
> that would make it possible to ensure the safe existence of the biosphere . . .[142]

The Bible described these limits as the creation covenant, and warned
that breaking through them brought the wrath.

Enoch's story of the fallen angels concluded with the restored earth
'tilled in righteousness' and producing huge crops. The store chambers of blessing would be opened, and there would be truth and peace
on earth.[143] Righteousness, as we shall see, was a key word in covenant
discourse; its meaning is almost the same as 'sustainable'. Consider
here the words of Paul Stiles, writing about a world ruled by the market, the very opposite of a world 'tilled in righteousness':

> There are many repercussions that follow removing God from a society, but
> perhaps the most inhuman is that it eradicates the spirit of life, which is love.
> This is pure market dynamics. Love is the binding force, the creator of *us*, while
> the market is the dividing force, *me vs.you*. That is what competition is all about.
> While individuals and businesses may co-operate, based on a legal contract, no
> one confuses that with love. Hence, as the power of the market increases in
> a society, society fragments . . .[144]

Creation collapses too.

141 *1 Enoch* 8.4; 9.1.

142 Gorshkov, Gorshkov and Makarieva, *Biotic Regulation of the Environment*,
p. 329.

143 *1 Enoch* 10.7–11.2.

144 P. Stiles, *Is the American Dream Killing You?*, New York: HarperCollins, 2006,
p. 215.

The story of the fallen angels has sometimes been compared to the story of Prometheus, the Titan who stole fire from the chariot of the sun, hid a piece of glowing charcoal in a hollow fennel stalk, and then gave human beings fire and taught them the skills for civilized life: writing, mathematics and astronomy to make a calendar; medicine and house building, metal working and the domestication of animals. Zeus was angry,[145] and took revenge by chaining him to a rock and sending a vulture to tear out his liver. The story has been told with various emphases; Aeschylus in *Prometheus Bound*,[146] depicted him as the hero who resisted the tyranny of the gods at great cost to himself, and thereby secured for human beings the possibility of civilization. Prometheus has become a hero figure for those who put their faith in the ever increasing power of technology:

> In principle, all can be mastered and controlled. This desire for liberation was often linked with the mythical figure of Prometheus, who came to be seen as a symbol of liberation in European literature. The rise of technology was seen as paralleling Prometheus' theft of fire from the gods. Limits were removed, Prometheus was now unbound, and humanity poised to enter a new era of autonomy and progress . . . without the need to respect natural limitations.[147]

Although superficially similar – metalworking, medicine and writing were taught by the fallen angels – the purpose of the Enoch story was very different. Used in rebellion against the Great Holy One, the skills and knowledge of the fallen angels served only to corrupt the earth, but the secrets of the creation, for example astronomy for Enoch to set up a calendar, were gifts from the angels. The angels taught Adam about agriculture and they taught Noah how to cure the ills brought by the fallen angels.[148] The Enoch tradition, and the biblical tradition as a whole, warned against claiming for oneself either knowledge or the way to use it. 'The fear of the LORD is the beginning of Wisdom' (Prov. 1.7). Deuteronomy, which had no place for angels,

---

145 Zeus punished Prometheus first by sending him first Pandora and her box of troubles. Prometheus resisted Pandora, but his brother married her and opened the box of troubles.

146 Written about 430 BCE.

147 A. McGrath 'Recovering the Creation' in *A Christian Approach to the Environment*, Transformation vol.16.3, 1999, pp. 19–27, p. 24, citing L. M. Lewis, *The Promethean Politics of Milton, Blake and Shelley*, London, University of Missouri Press, 1992.

148 *Jubilees* 3.15; 10.10–14.

taught that all knowledge and skill came from the LORD, and to forget
this was idolatry.

> Beware lest you say in your heart, "My power and the might of my hand have
> gotten me this wealth." You shall remember the LORD your God, for it is he who
> gives you the power to get wealth; that he may confirm his covenant . . . And if
> you forget the LORD your God and go after other gods and serve them and
> worship them, I solemnly warn you this day that you shall surely perish.
> (Deut .8.17–19)

For the Hebrew tradition, knowledge wrested from the LORD was not
liberation but disaster.

The counter-covenant of the rebel angels was the background to
Paul's teaching about the creation in Romans 8. He did not explain
why the evil was allowed to happen: just as the beast from the sea 'was
allowed to exercise authority' and the beast from the earth 'was allowed
to give breath to the image of the beast' (Rev. 13.5, 15), so too Paul
accepted that the subjugation of the creation was part of the divine
plan. He was explaining the role of the (new) sons of God. Those who
had received the Spirit were sons of God, and 'creation waits with eager
longing for the revealing of the sons of God' (Rom. 8.19). The creation
had been subjected to 'futility' and was in bondage to decay, the
counter-covenant. Instead of pattern and purpose there was 'futility',
a Greek word that shows what was in Paul's mind as he wrote. Its
equivalent in Hebrew was *hebel*, used for worthless idols and what they
brought: 'idols' (Deut. 32.21); worthless idols (Jer. 10.15); ill-gotten
money (Prov. 13.11); worthless help (Isa. 30.7); pointless worry
(Ps. 39.6); and, perhaps the most telling: a wasted life of 'nothing and
vanity', *tohu* and *hebel*, (Isa. 49.4).[149]

Martin Luther, in his lectures on Romans, understood 'creation',
ktisis, in this passage in a narrower way. For him, the word *ktisis* meant
a human being, and so it was the individual person who would be set
free from bondage to decay and obtain the glorious liberty of the
children of God. Since he put such great emphasis on the salvation of
the individual, it is understandable that he interpreted the word this
way, and his way of reading the verse has greatly influenced Protestant
thinking. The first Christians, however, understood *ktisis* to mean the
whole creation, and so the new 'sons of God' had to release the whole
creation from its bondage to decay. Irenaeus, writing on this passage at

---

149 The Greek word is used to translate the Hebrew *šw'*, 'You shall not take the
name of the LORD your God *in vain*' (Exod. 20.7).

end of the second century CE, said that creation would be restored to its original condition; there would be huge crops, and all the animals would live at peace with each other.[150]

For Paul, the first result of receiving the Spirit and becoming a son of God was releasing the creation from its bondage to the fallen angels, and, by implication, restoring the right use of knowledge. This was 'the glorious liberty of the children of God'. John expressed the same idea differently: establishing the Kingdom meant destroying the destroyers of the earth (Rev. 11.18). John knew the leader of the fallen angels as Satan, and described him as 'the deceiver of the whole world' (Rev. 12.9). The first Christians knew well that when trust had been destroyed, society would disintegrate. Commenting on the need for regulating a society that is to conserve the environment, biologists observed:

> In a hypothetical highly ordered society, consisting of honest people only, a liar suddenly appearing will become the most competitive individual, because all people, used to believing each other, are vulnerable to lies. However, such a liar will not contribute to the stability of the society, and will only lower the level of its organisation. In this sense the highly competitive liar contributes to the degradation of the society.[151]

The result of the fallen angels' teaching was that 'the world was changed', an enigmatic phrase sometimes translated 'alchemy', but whose traditional interpretation was 'changing a man into an animal'.[152] This does not mean literally changing people into animals; it was part of the literary code of these writers to describe heavenly beings as 'men' and mortals as 'animals'. Jesus used this code in the parable of the sheep and the goats, where the Son of Man and his angels separate the sheep from the goats (Mt. 25.31–3). The teaching of the fallen angels changed 'men' into 'animals', that is, it deprived people of their angel state and reduced them to mortality. This is the meaning of Genesis 2–3, and we shall return to this.[153] The *Gospel of Philip* described

---

150 Irenaeus, *Against Heresies* V.32–3.

151 V. G. Gorshkov, V. V. Gorshkov and A. M. Makarieva, *Biotic Regulation of the Environment*, p. 57.

152 *1 Enoch* 8.1. Some translations, for example R. H. Charles omit the words. 'alchemy' is found in E. Isaac, who notes too the traditional Ethiopian understanding. In OTP 1 p. 17.

153 See below, pp. 203–4, 221.

the same situation using different images. The text is damaged, but
the gist is clear:

> There are two trees in Paradise. The one bears [animals], the other bears men.
> Adam [ate] from the tree which bore animals. He became an animal and he
> brought forth animals. For this reason the children of Adam worship [animals]
> ... [If he] ate [the fruit of the other tree, that is to say the fruit of the tree of life],
> the one which bears men, [then the gods would] worship man.[154]

By eating from the tree of knowledge, Adam lost his angel state and
became mortal. The fruit of the other tree was wisdom, and the
distinction between wisdom and knowledge is fundamental to the
biblical vision for the creation.

The nature of human beings is closely bound up with their attitude
towards knowledge. The biblical picture says that human beings were
made as the image of God, but secular descriptions show how true is
the insight in the *Gospel of Philip*: we become what we believe ourselves
to be. Lynn Margulis concluded her account of symbiosis by reflecting
on the destructive role of human beings:

> We need to be freed from our species specific arrogance. No evidence exists that
> we are 'chosen', the unique species for which all the others were made. Nor are
> we the most important one because we are so numerous, powerful and danger-
> ous. Our tenacious illusion of special dispensation belies our true status as
> upright mammalian weeds.[155]

'Upright mammalian weeds' may be a deduction from reality but it is
not a vision to inspire. She had good reason to criticize the popular
but inaccurate picture of biblical teaching; we need to rediscover and
emphasize Paul's picture of Christians as the new angels who have to
heal the world and set it free.

154 *Gospel of Philip*, Coptic Gnostic Library II.3.71.

155 L. Margulis, *The Symbiotic Planet. A New Look at Evolution*, London: Weidenfeld
and Nicolson, 1998, p. 19.

Chapter 4

RESTORING CREATION

Restoring or perfecting the world, *tikkun ʿolam*,[1] is a fundamental Jewish teaching with roots deep in temple tradition. In their daily service, Jews still pray the ancient ʿAleinu[2] prayer:

> We therefore hope in thee, O LORD our God, that we may speedily behold the glory of thy might, when thou wilt remove the abominations from the earth, and the idols will be utterly cut off, when the *world will be perfected* under the kingdom of the Almighty . . .[3]

These lines were originally part of the prayers when the shofar was sounded in the autumn to mark the new year.[4]

The ancient calendar in Leviticus prescribes the observances for the first three weeks of the new year: blowing trumpets on the first day, observing the Day of Atonement on the tenth day, and observing the feast of Tabernacles for seven days beginning on the fifteenth day (Lev. 23.23–36). It was 'in the seventh month', but this reflects the different calendar in use when this text was written. One of the great changes in the time of King Josiah[5] had been moving the new year to the spring, for greater emphasis on the Passover, and this put the original new year into the seventh month. The Day of Atonement was the Day of Judgement when sins were either atoned or punished, and this is why images of harvest and vintage were associated with judgement. Amos saw a basket of summer fruit, *qyṣ*, and thought of the end, *qṣ*, two words

---

1 Sometimes spelled *tiqqun ʿolam*.

2 Meaning 'it is our duty.'

3 Translation in S. Singer, *The Authorised Daily Prayer Book*, London: Eyre and Spottiswoode, 1925, pp. 76–7.

4 R. Murray, *The Cosmic Covenant*, London: Sheed and Ward, 1992, p. 206 n.47.

5 Late seventh century BCE.

that sound similar (Amos 8.2). John the Baptist spoke of One who would gather the wheat and burn the chaff (Mt. 3.12), and John the Seer saw the harvest of the earth and the grapes of wrath (Rev. 14.14–20).

In biblical Hebrew the word *tikkun* is the opposite of iniquity/distortion, *'awon*. When Ben Sira in his pessimism was asking if human action could do anything about the world, he said that everything was *hebel*, vanity.[6] Nothing was new; nothing could be done. 'What is crooked cannot be made straight' 'Consider the work of God; who can make straight what he has made crooked?' (Eccl. 1.15; 7.13). Here, crooked is the root *'wn*, and made straight is *tqn*. Restoring the world, then, was the opposite of 'iniquity', and iniquity was the consequence of idolatry that affected future generations.[7] Isaiah said that the result of breaking the creation covenant was a crooked earth and scattered people (Isa. 24.1b), the opposite of the covenant process which was restoring and gathering into one. The crooked and scattered creation is what Paul called 'creation subjected to futility,'[8] but he knew that something new was possible. The creation could be set free and obtain the glorious liberty of the children of God' (Rom. 8.21).

When the later Kabbalists developed this idea, they used a new image. Instead of the covenant bonds being broken, they said that God poured light into vessels when he created the world, and they shattered. This world is the shattered urn that must be repaired, and the fragments of light must be gathered together. Rabbi Mark Winer described the shattered urn of his childhood in America – nuclear drills and racial segregation – but rejoiced at the growing relationship between Jews and Christians.

> Piece by piece, peace by peace, we have exemplified restoration of God's unity reflected in the world we share . . .
>
> We human beings become God's partners in making the world by completing the sacred work of creation, through personal dedication to righteousness, justice and compassion, which are the essence of *tikkun 'olam*.
>
> Each one of us is commanded by God to engage continually in *tikkun 'olam*. Only the 'shattered urn' repaired to wholeness, piece by piece, peace by peace, comprises ultimate peace.[9]

6 The Hebrew equivalent of 'futility' in Rom. 8.20.

7 See above pp. 54–7.

8 See above pp. 146–7.

9 M. L. Winer, 'Tikkun Olam: A Jewish Theology of "Repairing the World"', *Theology*, November/December 2008, vol. CXI, no 864, pp. 433–41.

This recent reflection on *tikkun 'olam* still uses the traditional words drawn from the biblical vision for restoring the world: completion, that is *šalom*, unity, righteousness, justice, compassion, and in the 'Aleinu prayer there is the Kingdom of the Almighty.

Such teaching is part of the common temple heritage of Jews and Christians, but Christians have different names for the same ideas. *Repairing the world was the original meaning of atonement, and atonement is at the heart of the biblical vision for the environment.* Peace, unity, righteousness, justification, justice, compassion and the Kingdom of God belong together in Christian teaching, as does the calling to become partners in the work of creation until it is complete. Paul used images from the Day of Atonement when he explained the meaning of the death and resurrection of Jesus. The Letter to the Romans is full of words such as justification, righteousness, reconciliation, peace, redemption, and none of these should be read apart from its original temple context of healing the whole creation, not just the individual sinner.

Sin was [and is] whatever breaks the original wholeness, and so the first part of restoration/atonement was acknowledging the sin, then repentance and putting right the wrong. This restored the creation or the social relationship, and above all, it restored relationship to God. Nobody who exploited the system was included: 'If a man said "I will sin and repent, and sin again and repent" he will be given no chance to repent. If he said "I will sin and the Day of Atonement will effect atonement," then the Day of Atonement effects no atonement.'[10] Rabbi 'Akiba, teaching early in the second century CE, also applied the idea of healing and renewal to the individual human life: 'As vessels of gold or glass, when broken, can be restored by undergoing the process of melting, thus does the disciple of the law, after having sinned, find the way of recovering his state of purity by repentance.'[11] Repentance – thinking and seeing things differently – was the key.

There were debates in the time of the early Church about what degrees of sin could be forgiven after repentance: according to the Scriptures, there were sins committed in error, and these could be atoned (Num. 15.22–28); but there were also sins committed deliberately 'with a high hand' and these could not be atoned. 'He shall be cut off from among his people . . . his iniquity shall be upon him.'

---

10 Mishnah *Yoma* 8.9.

11 Babylonian Talmud *Ḥagigah* 15a.

(Num. 15.30–31).[12] The Christians knew that the Day of Atonement offering was for the 'errors of the people' (Heb. 9.7), but they had a strict discipline for apostates, who could not be forgiven (Heb. 6.4–8). The rabbis eventually taught that true repentance would turn all but the most serious sins into errors that could be forgiven. Rabbi Ishmael, early in the second century CE, taught that most sins of omission and commission could be atoned on the Day of Atonement, but that graver sins required severe punishment, and desecrating Name or harming the whole people carried the death penalty.[13]

It is only recently that damaging the natural world has come to be regarded as a sin. John Zizioulas, addressing the first Symposium *Religion, Science and the Environment* in 1995 said: 'We are used to regarding sin mainly in social terms. But there is also sin against nature. Evil is not a matter for human beings but affects the entire creation. This morality still awaits to find its place in our Christian consciences.' Six years earlier, on 1 September 1989, the Ecumenical Patriarch Dimitrios had urged

> all the faithful in the world to admonish themselves and their children to respect and protect the natural environment . . . and all those who are entrusted with the responsibility of governing nations to act without delay in taking all necessary measures for the protecting and preserving of the natural creation.[14]

Many in the western churches have been slow to respond to the environment crisis, occupied instead with other matters they considered more urgent, such as gay rights.

In the time of Jesus, people were all too aware that sin caused the natural order to collapse. The prophets warned of the collapsing covenant; Haggai, for example, warned that neglect of the temple brought famine (Hag. 1.7–11). Attached to the calendar text in *1 Enoch* is a warning that, since sinners do not live in accordance with the correct calendar – a temple matter – human life is out of harmony with heaven, with all the seasons distorted and the crops failing.

---

12 Jesus prayed that his killers would be forgiven 'for they know not what they do' (Lk. 23.34).

13 Babylonian Talmud *Yoma* 86a.

14 John Zizioulas, 'Towards an Environmental Ethic' in *The Adriatic Sea*, Athens: Religion, Science and the Environment, 2003, pp. 93–101, p. 93. HAH Dimitrios, Encyclical, 1st September 1989.

Their seed shall be late on their lands and fields, and all things on earth shall alter . . . and the rain shall be kept back . . . and the fruits of the earth shall not grow in their time . . . the moon shall alter her order . . . and many chief stars shall alter their orbits and tasks . . .[15]

Jude used the same sequence of images when condemning the ungodly, which is unlikely to be a coincidence: 'waterless clouds . . . fruitless trees . . . wandering stars . . .' (Jude 12–13), and he quoted Enoch to warn of imminent judgement. These texts were known to the early Christians. There was a severe famine in Judea in 24–3 BCE, and Josephus left a vivid description that is very similar to the Enochic 'prediction'.[16] There was another great famine in the mid-40s CE, in the reign of Claudius,[17] which was predicted by Agabus (Acts 11.28). This was recorded as the opening of the third seal, the rider on the black horse with a balances to weigh the wheat and barley (Rev. 6.5). Jesus prophesied famines and pestilence, terrors and great signs in heaven as signs that the temple was to be destroyed (Lk. 21.11).

Philo thought in the same way and showed that disaster was due to idolatry, the contrast between 'restoration' and 'iniquity' that was his Jewish world view. He gave a contemporary understanding of the biblical curses on those who broke the covenant by abandoning the LORD's commandments, statutes and ordinances[18] (Lev. 26.14–15). He had explained at the beginning of his account of creation that the books of Moses show 'the world is in harmony with the Law and the Law with the world,' and so breaking the Law affected the creation. He drew his examples of environmental and economic disasters from Deuteronomy 28.15–27 and Leviticus 26, which is the culmination of the priestly holiness code (Lev. 19–25). Since the latter, with its four sevenfold curses, was the framework of the Book of Revelation, this is yet another indication of the thinking of the early Church.[19] Philo listed the disasters: poverty and death, the lack of necessaries and conditions of absolute destitution; crops ravaged while unripe or lost to enemies; locusts and pests; the earth sterile, the seasons out of order; cities devastated; violence among the desperate inhabitants; diseases and wars.

15 *1 Enoch* 80.2–3.

16 Josephus, *Antiquities* XV.299–316.

17 Josephus, *Antiquities* XX.51–3.

18 The latter literally 'engraved things' and 'justice', *mišpat*.

19 See my book *The Revelation of Jesus Christ*, Edinburgh: T&T Clark, 2000, p. 80.

He said that these were warnings, to prompt repentance.

> If they accept these chastisements as a warning rather than as intending their
> perdition, if shamed into a whole hearted conversion, they reproach themselves
> for going thus astray, and make a full confession and acknowledgement of all
> their sin, first within themselves with a mind so purged that their conscience is
> sincere and free from lurking taint, secondly with their tongues to bring their
> hearers to a better way, then they will find favour with God the Saviour, the mer-
> ciful, who has bestowed on mankind that peculiar and chiefest gift of kinship
> with his own Logos, from whom as its archetype, the human mind was
> created.[20]

Philo rooted the problem in ways of thinking; other Jews at that time
would have used the language of Wisdom, but the ideas are the same.
The only way to live and think was in accordance with the Logos, the
original Craftsman of the creation.

Day of Atonement

The Day of Atonement was part of the festival that marked the new
year and renewal of creation, and allusions to its rites and theology
are found throughout early Christian writings. The original prescriptions for the Day of Atonement are in Leviticus 16, and scholars now
recognize that this text is very old indeed. It is not easy to read because
there have been additions and rearrangements over the centuries,
but the complex ritual calls for two goats, one to be sent into the
wilderness bearing the sins of the people, and the other to be sacrificed. The high priest, purified and wearing special linen garments,
took the blood of the sacrificed goat and the blood of a bull into the
holy of holies and sprinkled it on the mercy seat. He did the same for
the tent of meeting and then emerged and sprinkled blood on the
altar 'to cleanse it and hallow it from the uncleanness of the people of
Israel' (Lev. 16.19). Thus he atoned the holy place and the tent of
meeting and the altar. *Atonement removed the effects of human sin.*

In the *Mishnah* there is a detailed account of how the Day of
Atonement was observed in the time of Jesus, but there is no explanation, no 'theology'. The high priest was washed and dressed in white
linen, then he drew lots over the two identical goats: one was 'for the
Lord' and the other was 'for Azazel', just as prescribed in Leviticus 16.

20 Philo, *On Rewards*, 163.

Throughout the ritual, the high priest confessed his sins and those of the people, and asked forgiveness. He took incense into the holy of holies, then the blood of a bull and then the blood of the goat, each time sprinkling blood first where the ark had stood and then on the temple veil. Then he mixed the two bowls of blood and sprinkled the golden incense altar inside the temple. Finally he sprinkled the altar of sacrifice in the temple court and poured the remaining blood under the altar so that it drained away. He put both his hands on the head of the second goat (the scapegoat), placed upon it all the iniquities of the people, and had it led into the desert where it was left to die.[21]

There is no explanation. There are only practical instructions such as to stir the blood lest it congeal, because congealed blood cannot be sprinkled.[22] What this meant has to be reconstructed from other texts. First, the temple was the creation, and only the priests were permitted to enter. This means that any uncleanness polluting the temple cannot have been literally brought there by the people. The polluted temple was the polluted creation, and to cleanse and consecrate the temple meant cleansing and consecrating the creation. This was the climax of the new year festivals, when the world was renewed. Second, since the high priest represented the LORD and wore the Name, this ritual was the LORD renewing the world. Third, the blood symbolized life, and so it was life that effected atonement (Lev. 17.11). Fourth, the life was brought out from the holy of holies, from the presence of the LORD, into the material creation. This was the theme of Peter's sermon in Solomon's porch: 'You denied the Holy and Righteous One ... and killed the Author of Life ... Repent therefore and turn again that your sins may be blotted out, that times of refreshing may come from the presence of the LORD' (Acts 3.14,15,19). This reconstruction of an early sermon in Jerusalem shows that Jesus' death was understood as the Day of Atonement sacrifice, and his ascension as the high priest entering the holy of holies (Heb. 9.11–14). The return of the high priest brought renewal, and so the earliest expectation of the second coming was the LORD emerging from heaven to restore the earth. Atonement in early Christian preaching implied the renewal that was ritualized every year on the Day of Atonement, except that this was 'once for all at the end of the age' (Heb. 9.26).

21 Mishnah *Yoma* 4–6.
22 Mishnah *Yoma* 4.3.

The two goats are frequently represented as 'for the LORD' and 'for Azazel' (Lev. 16.8), translations that raise the question: 'Why was an offering made to Azazel, the leader of the fallen angels who had brought the knowledge that corrupted the earth?' Origen, writing early in the third century and in contact with Jewish scholars in Caesarea, said that the goat sent into the desert *was* Azazel, that is, represented Azazel. This is one possible meaning of the Hebrew *lᵉ*, so *laᵃzaʾzel* could mean 'as Azazel'. Because it is described in the same way, the sacrificed goat would then be 'as the LORD', representing the LORD. The blood/life that came from heaven to renew the earth represented the life of the LORD. This is implied by the contrast in Hebrews: 'Neither by the blood of goats and calves but by his *own* blood he entered in once into the holy place, having obtained eternal redemption . . .' (Heb. 9.12, AV). The crucifixion fulfilled what the temple rites had foreshadowed. Hence Athanasius's introduction to his treatise on the Incarnation: 'The renewal of the creation has been the work of the self same Word that made it in the beginning.' This is the context for McGrath's important reminder about the distinctiveness of Christian belief.

> The Christian account of creation is set within the context of the economy of salvation. There is thus a presumption of interconnectedness between creation, redemption and consummation, which places a theological interdiction against seeing creation as an isolated action or event, complete in itself. In particular, the Christian concept of creation is linked to that of incarnation. Creation and redemption are affirmed to be the work of the same divine *Logos,* embedded in creation and embodied in Christ. There is thus a strong Christological hue to the Christian vision of creation, which distinguishes it from its deist alternatives.[23]

Placing the prophetic and ritual texts of the Old Testament side by side, it is clear that the high priest's actions in the temple represented the renewing work of the LORD, the Creator. In the ritual texts that give practical details, the priest atones a contaminated object – the high priest atones the holy place, the tent of meeting and the altar (Lev. 16.20) – but elsewhere, the LORD or his angel atones sin: 'Your sin is atoned.' (Isa. 6.7); 'O LORD . . . do not atone their iniquities . . .' (Jer. 18.23, translating literally); and, in the context of the LORD's establishing the creation covenant again with Jerusalem: '. . . when

---

23 A. McGrath, *The Open Secret: A New Vision for Natural Theology,* Oxford: Blackwell, 2008, p. 186.

I atone for you all that you have done' (Ezek. 16.63, translating literally). In the Psalms there are similar declarations: 'When our transgressions prevail over us*, you atone them' (Ps. 65.3 * the Hebrew is 'over me'). 'He was compassionate and atoned their iniquity' (Ps. 78.38, translating literally). This means that the high priest, representing the LORD, offering the goat's blood 'as the LORD', was symbolizing the self-offering of the LORD. The Creator was renewing the creation by self-sacrifice. This explains the emphasis in Hebrews, where Jesus took his *own* blood into the holy of holies (Heb. 9.12), and it explains Paul's exhortation to all who are 'in Christ': 'Present your bodies as a living sacrifice, holy and acceptable to God, which is your spiritual worship' (Rom. 12.1). The whole of the Christian's life had to be poured out as part of the great atonement. This is why John saw the souls of the martyrs under the great altar. The soul or life was represented by blood, and atonement blood was poured under the great altar. The martyrs were part of the great atonement (Rev. 6.9–11).

Atonement was renewing the bonds of the covenant with the blood/life of the LORD. Sin was carried away, and the breaches were repaired. The early Christians found this set out in the fourth of Isaiah's Servant songs (Isa. 52.13–53.12), which describes a high priestly figure who makes atonement by his own sufferings. Isaiah's original inspiration was the suffering of Hezekiah who recovered from plague, and the prophet interpreted his suffering and recovery in the light of current beliefs about the atoning role of the high priest. He intercepted wrath and took it onto himself, as did Aaron when he stopped the wrath and plague with his incense (Num. 16.46). Thus the Servant *intercepted* all the iniquity (Isa. 53.6) and stood between the transgressors and the wrath, the literal meaning of '*made intercession for* the transgressors' (Isa. 53.12). 'Intercepted' and 'made intercession for' are forms of the same Hebrew verb *pg'*. The Servant stood in the breach and protected his people. The atonement ritual is apparent in 'he makes himself an *'šm*, an offering for sin' (Isa. 53.10), the *'šm* being specifically for breach of the covenant;[24] and 'he poured out his soul to death' (Isa. 53.12) is the final blood pouring that completed the atonement offering. This Servant was to sprinkle many nations (Isa. 52.15, translating literally), another Day of Atonement motif, and as result, 'the Righteous One, my Servant shall make many righteous' (Isa. 53.11, translating literally). The pattern and purpose

24 J. Milgrom, *Leviticus 1–16*, New York: Doubleday, 1991, p. 347.

of atonement here is clear; the Righteous One makes many righteous by bringing them back into the covenant.[25] This passage was recognized by the early church as a key to understanding the person and work of Jesus, and it is another where the current Hebrew text differs from the one found at Qumran. The present text describes the Servant as disfigured, but the Qumran text has the anointed one (Isa. 52.14), a difference of one letter.[26]

Matthew's account of the last supper was written for Jewish Christians, and so he had to make clear which covenant Jesus meant in the words of institution. Jews knew of several covenants – with Noah, with Abraham, with Moses, with David – and the covenant at the last supper was specifically the covenant concerned with 'putting away' sins. None of the other covenants deals with sin: Noah's was the promise not to flood the earth; Abraham's was the promise of land and descendants; David's was the promise of heirs on the throne in Jerusalem. The Moses covenant at Sinai was the promise to keep the commandments. The only covenant for 'putting away' sins was the eternal covenant/creation covenant, renewed by atonement. Jeremiah's new covenant on the heart implies dealing with sin, but the context of this is also the creation covenant (Jer. 31.31–37). Jesus' words of institution at the last supper most likely referred to the creation covenant, as this was renewed by atonement: 'blood . . . poured out for many for the putting away, *aphesis*, of sins.' (Matt. 26.28).[27] *This must affect any understanding of the Eucharist.*

Another key text for Christians was Deuteronomy 32.43, which describes the LORD coming in judgement to avenge the blood of his servants and to atone the land of his people. The current Hebrew text here is only half the length of the Qumran text and the Old Greek text; half of it has disappeared, including the line that identifies it as important for Christians. 'Let all God's angels worship him' is one of the texts used in Hebrews to set out who Jesus was: the Son through whom God created the world, who upholds 'all things', who made purification for sins and has been exalted above the angels. 'When he brings the Firstborn into the world, he says, "Let all God's angels worship him"' (Heb. 1.6). Jesus here was identified as the LORD, the Firstborn of the sons of God, who came into the world to bring the judgement

25 See my article 'Hezekiah's Boil', *Journal for the Study of the Old Testament*, 95 (2001), pp. 31–42.

26 See my book *The Great High Priest*, London: T&T Clark, 2003, pp. 303–4.

27 For other translation possibilities, see above p. 136.

and atonement described in Deuteronomy 32.43, *but the identifying link line is not in the current Hebrew text.* This suggests two things: that Jesus the LORD bringing atonement for the land was an important element in early Christian teaching; and that this was so important and contentious an issue that the proof text did not survive in the Hebrew Bible as defined by the rabbis after the fall of Jerusalem in 70 CE, the Hebrew text from which the Old Testament of the Western churches is translated.[28] A text found at Qumran shows that the great high priest Melchizedek was expected to appear at exactly the time Jesus began his ministry. He would be a divine being, gathering his own and bringing the final Day of Atonement. Since Jesus was identified as Melchizedek (Heb. 7.1–28), this is another indication that renewing the creation by atonement was central to Christian belief.

Atonement was not just cleansing but also renewing. The 'iniquity' which had caused the damage had to be carried away,[29] so that the damage could be repaired. Thus Micah: 'Who is a God like you, *carrying iniquity*' (Mic. 7.18, translating literally); or Job: 'Why do you not *carry* my transgression and cause my iniquity to pass away?' (Job 7.21 translating literally). The high priests carried the iniquity of those for whom they atoned, because they ate their sin offering (Lev. 10.17), and they could do this with impunity because they wore the Name (Exod. 28.36–38). On the Day of Atonement it was the goat who carried the iniquities, having received them from the hands of the high priest who was himself carrying them during the rite of atonement. There is a clear description of atonement in Psalm 32.1, even though the word 'atonement' is not used: 'Blessed is the man carried in respect of his transgressions . . . to whom the LORD does not reckon iniquity' (translating literally). This was quoted by Paul to demonstrate how 'righteousness' was established by faith and not works (Rom. 4.7) – all within the framework of temple atonement.

Mary Douglas studied atonement texts with the eye of an anthropologist and concluded:

Terms derived from cleansing, washing and purging have imported into biblical scholarship distractions which have occluded Leviticus' own very specific and clear description of atonement. According to the illustrative cases from Leviticus, to atone means to cover or recover, to cover again, to repair a hole, cure a sickness, mend a rift, make good a torn or broken covering. As a noun, what is translated

28 The Qumran text that identified the LORD as one of the sons of God, Deut. 32.8, is also different in the current Hebrew.

29 The literal meaning of *ns'*, the Hebrew word for forgiveness, is 'carry'.

atonement, expiation or purgation means integument made good; conversely, the examples in the book indicate that defilement means integument torn. Atonement does not mean covering a sin so as to hide it from the sight of God; it means making good an outer layer which has rotted or been pierced.[30]

This outer layer was the protective bonds of the creation covenant, and Paul showed that Christians, restored to righteousness through faith, that is, re-integrated into the bond of the covenant, once again enjoyed its protection. Nothing in heaven or earth, he said 'will be able to separate us from the love of God in Christ Jesus our LORD' (Rom. 8.39).

Paul knew that all Christians were the body of Christ, which meant they were collectively the atoning high priesthood. When he exhorted them to the spiritual equivalent of the temple rite – self sacrifice – he followed the temple sequence in his exposition: 'Present your bodies as a living sacrifice . . . Do not be conformed to this world, but be transformed by the renewal of your mind . . .' (Rom. 12.1–2); in other words, he exhorted them to self-sacrifice and a new way of thinking. Those who had been restored were themselves to become restorers:

> Therefore, if anyone is in Christ he is a new creation; the old has passed away, the new has come. All this is from God, who through Christ reconciled us to himself and gave us the ministry of reconciliation; that is, in Christ God was reconciling the world to himself, not counting their trespasses against them, and entrusting to us the message of reconciliation. (2 Cor. 5.17–19)

Peter taught that the Christians were the royal priesthood (1 Pet. 2.9), and John heard this hymned in heaven: 'Thou hast made them a kingdom and priests to our God . . .' (Rev. 5.10). The high priest was the presence of the LORD on earth, and his unique role was to make the great atonement, to repair the covenant bonds and renew the creation.

Scientists have now discovered that sacrifice is a part of the natural order.

> What [cooperation] does show is that the whole evolutionary struggle has a sacrificial accompaniment, which in certain conditions creatively recurs and forms a vital part of the dynamics of evolutionary development. As this strategy is observed higher up the evolutionary scale, we start to find accompaniments to its manifestation that are truly intriguing – the widespread sacrificial activities of social insects, for instance, or the practice of a shoal of dolphins in surrounding a dying companion even at great risk to themselves . . . Ethical tendencies to self-sacrificial and forgiving behaviour, themselves productive and creative within

30 M. Douglas, 'Atonement in Leviticus', *Jewish Studies Quarterly* 1 (1993–4), pp. 109–30, p. 117.

populations, may have their preliminary roots in forms of life much lower than the human.[31]

Or maybe we could say that there is one pattern throughout the whole creation, and ponder the alternative ethic of mammon: 'It is the cardinal condition of corporate social responsibility that good works are constrained by profitability.'[32]

George Soros observed many years ago:

> The doctrine of laissez-faire capitalism holds that the common good is best served by the uninhibited pursuit of self interest. Unless it is tempered by the recognition of a common interest that ought to take precedence over particular interests, our present system . . . is liable to break down . . . Social Darwinism is one of the misconceptions driving human affairs today. The main point I want to make is that cooperation is as much a part of the [economic] system as competition, and the slogan 'survival of the fittest' distorts this fact . . . Our global, open society lacks the institutions and mechanisms necessary for its preservation, but there is no political will to bring them into existence. I blame the prevailing attitude, which holds that the unhampered pursuit of self-interest will bring about an eventual international equilibrium. I believe this confidence is misplaced.[33]

The Ecumenical Patriarch's words related atonement and healing through self-sacrifice to our current situation.

> There can be no salvation for the world, no healing, no hope for a better future, without the missing dimension of sacrifice. Without a sacrifice that is both costly and uncompromising, we shall never be able to act as priests of creation in order to reverse the descending spiral of ecological degradation.[34]

JUSTICE AND RIGHTEOUSNESS

Justice and righteousness, loving kindness, faithfulness and peace describe the atonement and covenant process. The words often appear

31 S. Coakley, in *The Church Times*, 21ˢᵗ November 2008, p. 17.

32 R. Patel, *Stuffed and Starved. Markets. Power and the Hidden Battle for the World Food System*, London: Portobello Books, 2007, p. 310.

33 G. Soros, 'The Capitalist Threat', The Atlantic Monthly, 279.2, 1997, pp. 45–58, pp. 53, 55.

34 HAH Bartholomew, Ecumenical Patriarch, 'Sacrifice: The Missing Dimension', in *The Adriatic Sea. A Sea at Risk, a Unity of Purpose*, Athens: Religion, Science and the Environment, 2003, pp. 217–20, p. 219.

together, but English translations are not consistent in their renderings, and so the recurring cluster of words is not so obvious (e.g. Ps. 36.5–6; 37.30; 85.10–12; 119.137; Jer. 9.24). The first step is 'justice', *mišpaṭ*, better translated 'judgement', which means recognizing what needs to be done to uphold the covenant. A judgement is a wise decision, and so when Solomon decided to give the baby to its natural mother: 'All Israel heard the *judgement* . . . they perceived that the wisdom of God was in him, to render *justice*' (1 Kgs 3.28). Thus the RSV, but both judgement and justice here are the same Hebrew word, *mišpaṭ*, which was a sign of divine wisdom. The LORD was a God of *mišpaṭ* (Isa. 30.18), which was manifested in the order of nature: 'Even the stork in the heavens knows her times; and the turtledove, swallow and crane keep the time of their coming; but my people know not the *ordinance* of the LORD' (Jer. 8.7), where ordinance translates *mišpaṭ*. It also meant the custom, right or entitlement; 'This shall be the priests' *due* from the people . . .' (Deut. 18.3). None of these covenant words is easy to translate, but *mišpaṭ*, represents whatever action is in harmony with the divine order: better far than sacrifice and offerings was to do justice *mišpaṭ*, to love kindness, *ḥesed*, and to walk humbly with God (Mic. 6.8).

Kindness/mercy/steadfast love, *ḥesed*, is another word with many different English translations. Compare '*Loyalty* and faithfulness preserve the king, and his throne is upheld by *righteousness*.' (Prov. 20.28 RSV, where both words translate *ḥesed*[35]); '*Mercy* and truth preserve the king: and his throne is upholden by *mercy*' (Prov. 20.28 AV, *ḥesed* again). Hosea knew that faithfulness and loving kindness upheld the covenant, and that without them society and the natural order began to collapse: 'There is no faithfulness nor *kindness*, and no knowledge of God in the land; there is swearing, lying, killing, stealing, committing adultery; they break all bounds and murder follows murder. Therefore the land mourns . . .' (Hos. 4.1–3). For the prophet, faithfulness and *ḥesed* were 'the knowledge of God', that is, recognition of God. When Isaiah was pleading for the refugees from Moab, he said:

> . . . be a refuge to them from the destroyer. When the oppressor is no more, and destruction has ceased . . . then a throne will be established in *steadfast love, ḥesed,* and on it will sit in faithfulness . . . one who judges and seeks justice, *mišpaṭ,* and is swift to do righteousness. (Isa. 16.4–5)

---

35 RSV takes 'righteousness' from the Old Greek.

The covenant is established by *ḥesed:* 'the LORD keeps covenant and *steadfast love* to those who love him and keep his commandments . . .' (Deut. 7.9); the covenant was established through the LORD's 'faithfulness to Jacob and *steadfast love* to Abraham' (Mic. 7.20). *Steadfast love* was the sign of the eternal covenant: 'For the mountains may depart and the hills be removed, but my *steadfast love* shall not depart from you, and my covenant of peace shall not be removed, says the LORD who has compassion on you' (Isa. 54.10).

People were *ḥasiyd,* often translated 'pious', but literally one who practises *ḥesed.* The LORD is *ḥasiyd,* so pious is not an appropriate translation. Merciful or kind is better, but the range of words chosen for English translations obscures the common thread of meaning: 'I am *ḥasiyd* says the LORD . . .' (Jer. 3.12). 'The LORD is just in all his ways, and *kind* in all his doings.' (Ps. 145.17) links together kindness and justice, which shows what covenant discourse meant by justice. The anointed one was the LORD's *ḥasiyd;* 'Of old thou didst speak to thy *ḥasiyd* and say . . .' (Ps. 89.20, RSV has 'faithful one'). People who practise *ḥesed* are 'the saints': 'Love the LORD all you his *saints* . . .' (Ps. 31.23; also 30.4; 37.28 and many other examples).[36] The LORD gives Wisdom to guard the paths of *mišpat* and preserve the way of his *ḥasiyd* (Prov. 2.8). Those who do not practice kindness are 'ungodly' (Ps. 43.1); and Micah saw society in his own time collapsing because 'The *godly* man has perished from the earth, and there is none upright among men' (Mic. 7.2).

The result of kindness and good judgement was righteousness, which meant both the state when the covenant was restored and also the actions that made this happen. The LORD is righteous (Jer. 21.1) and he acts to restore and uphold righteousness. 'The ordinances [*mišpatim*] the LORD are true and righteous altogether' (Ps. 19.9). Scholem described what this meant for the Kabbalah, which preserved so much temple tradition: 'God is the Righteous One insofar as he provides all living things with the vital energy which holds them to their own law.'[37] The LORD upholds his people with the 'right hand of my righteousness' (Isa. 41.10, AV). The atonement imagery is clear in Psalm 85. The LORD 'carried away' [i.e. atoned] his people's

36 The Old Greek here is *hosios.*

37 G. Scholem, *On the Kabbalah and its Symbolism,* London: Routledge, 1965, p. 105.

iniquity and he spoke peace to them. Then the effect of atonement is described:

> Surely his salvation is at hand for those who fear him,
> that [his] glory may dwell in our land.
> Steadfast love, *ḥesed,* and faithfulness will meet;
> righteousness and peace will kiss each other.
> Faithfulness will spring up from the land,
> and righteousness will look down from the heavens.
> The LORD will indeed give what is good,
> and our land will give her produce.
> (Ps. 85.2, 8–12, my translation)

Jonathan Porritt's definition of sustainability well describes both the process and the state of righteousness: 'Sustainable development is a process or journey which we must undertake in order to get to that destination, that is, sustainability.'[38] The frequently used phrase 'just and sustainable' is also quite at home in biblical discourse: no system can be just that destroys the earth, and so there can be no justice that is not sustainable. The biblical term is righteousness. A righteous person cannot be righteous in isolation, only in active relationship to God, to others and to the wider creation. The righteous person has been brought back into the covenant bond, and then works to maintain the covenant bonds. The Hebrew words for righteousness, *ṣdq,* and *ṣdqh* [usually pronounced zedek and zᵉdakah] appear throughout the Old Testament and underlie the New Testament terms 'righteous' and 'justification'. They are at the centre of Paul's teaching, and one of the earliest titles for Jesus was 'the Righteous One', meaning one who brings about the righteous state, that is, restores the covenant (Acts 3.14). In the parable of the sheep and the goats, Jesus described those who had fed the hungry and visited the sick as 'the righteous' who would inherit the Kingdom (Mt. 25.37). They had helped to create the state of righteousness.

Although 'righteousness' showed itself in actions, it was not achieved by actions. For Christians, 'justification' meant being made righteous, having the peace relationship restored within the covenant, like Micah's 'walking humbly with God'. The tax collector who prayed for forgiveness was justified, rather than the Pharisee who reminded God of all his good works (Lk. 18.14). The *Book of Jubilees,* known in

---

38 J. Porritt, *Capitalism as if the World Matters,* London: Earthscan 2005, p. 27.

the time of Jesus, described how the creation was restored after Noah's flood:

> The LORD made for all his works a new and righteous nature, so that they might not sin in all their nature for ever. And so that they might all be righteous, each in his kind, always . . . And for the children of Israel it has been written and ordained: "If they return to him in righteousness, he will forgive all of their sins and he will pardon all of their transgressions."[39]

Paul also emphasized justification by faith and trust, like the faith and trust of Abraham – one of the great themes of Romans, that is sometimes thought to be original to Paul – but James the Righteous had to balance this by reminding the Church that faith showed itself in works, in being what the LORD had prepared for each person to be within the covenant, the original understanding of righteousness. A person could not be 'righteous' other than in an active state of making righteous, healing broken situations (Jas 2.14–26).

Whenever justification and righteousness are mentioned in the New Testament, there are images from the Day of Atonement and the renewal of the creation covenant: the righteousness of God, that is, God's way of restoration, was effected by the atonement blood of Jesus (Rom. 3. 21–6). The result of justification was 'peace with God' (Rom. 5.1), meaning that the covenant of peace was restored. The implication of this covenant renewal has often been overlooked, due to emphasis on salvation for the individual person, for example by translating Romans 8 as salvation for the individual rather than as salvation for the whole creation. 'The creature itself shall be delivered from the bondage of corruption' (Rom. 8.21, AV) is very different from 'The creation itself will be set free from its bondage to decay' (Rom. 8.21, RSV). The word *ktisis* can mean either creature or creation, but the early Christians understood it here as creation. Irenaeus, describing the marvellous fertility of the Kingdom when all creation was restored to its original state, quoted these verses.[40] The covenant renewed in the New Testament was fundamentally *the creation covenant*. Paul, possibly quoting a well-known text, wrote: 'Through him to reconcile to himself all things, whether on earth or in heaven, making peace by the blood of his cross' (Col. 1.20). The two way nature of justification – the restored becoming the restorers, the

---

39 *Jubilees* 5.12, 17.

40 Irenaeus, *Against Heresies* V.28–33, see below, p. 190.

healed becoming the healers – is set in the context of the new creation: 'Therefore, if anyone is in Christ, he is a new creation; the old
has passed away, the new has come. All this is from God, who through
Christ reconciled himself to us and gave us the ministry of reconciliation' (2 Cor. 5.17–18). This is the great ministry of restoration.

In the time of Jesus there were people who sought to return to the
covenant they had neglected. The *Damascus Document* described such a
group who recognized that they lived in a time of wrath – lies, smooth
things and illusions. God sent them a Teacher of Righteousness, to
show them what it meant to keep the covenant.[41] They had to practise
'truth, righteousness and justice on the earth'.[42] The Teacher's
opponent was the Wicked Priest, who had been corrupted by money,
exploited the poor and defiled the temple.[43] Fragments of the *Damascus
Document* were found at Qumran among the Dead Sea Scrolls, along
with evidence for many copies of *1 Enoch*. Nobody knows who owned
them or who had access to them, or whether what has survived is a
representative sample of the original deposit. They are, however, the
only contemporary evidence, and show the importance of *1 Enoch* for
those who used the *Damascus Document*. It is estimated that there were
30 copies of Deuteronomy, 21 of Isaiah, 20 each of Genesis and *1 Enoch*,
and far fewer of the others. The evidence from *1 Enoch* is an important
factor in reconstructing the belief of the covenant community and
what the early Christians could have known.

Enoch was a 'righteous man whose eyes had been opened',[44] and
the whole Enoch tradition deals with the conflict between the faithful and the fallen angels, between righteousness and unrighteousness, between open eyes and closed eyes, between a restored and
flourishing earth and one that is corrupted. The fallen angels taught
unrighteousness on earth, and when the archangels saw the bloodshed and heard the cries, the Great Holy One sent them to bind the
fallen ones and heal the earth. The liberated earth was then 'tilled in
righteousness' in a time of truth and peace.[45] A short poem contrasts
Wisdom and unrighteousness: those who rejected Wisdom welcomed

---

41 *Damascus Document*, CD I.

42 *Community Rule*, 1QS I.5.

43 *Commentary on Habakkuk* 1QpHab VIII, XII.

44 *1 Enoch* 1.2.

45 *1 Enoch* 9–11.

unrighteousness in her place.[46] A brief history shows that righteousness had been lost long ago, but would be restored after the time of apostasy, and the chosen ones would receive 'sevenfold wisdom and knowledge', also described as the gift of Wisdom.[47] Even the material that has survived, full of dislocations and difficulties, shows that Enoch was concerned with the creation, its destruction and its restoration. When Paul was explaining the implications of the gift of the Spirit – that all who are lead by the Spirit are sons of God (Rom. 8.14) – his thought went immediately to Enoch's account of the rebel sons of God who had corrupted the earth, and so he taught that the first sign of the gift of the Spirit was releasing creation from bondage to decay, healing the earth. Thus Jesus said: 'Blessed are the peacemakers, for they shall be called sons of God' (Mt. 5.9), meaning that the sons of God restore the covenant of peace.[48]

Righteousness was the main focus of the temple cult: teaching what it was, and ritualizing its restoration and protection. Like Micah in the sixth century BCE, Amos in the eighth century denounced the shallow temple worship of his time and the people who were waiting for the day of the Lord, reminding them that the day of the Lord and temple worship were about justice and righteousness: 'I hate, I despise your feasts . . . Let justice, *mišpaṭ*, roll down like waters, and righteousness, *ṣdqh*, like an ever-flowing stream'(Amos 5.18–24). In temple imagery, Amos' stream of righteousness flowed from the heavenly throne of the Lord; Enoch called it the fountain of righteousness and the fountains of Wisdom;[49] and John saw the river of the water of life flowing from the throne (Rev. 22.1). Justice, *mišpaṭ* and righteousness, *ṣdqh*, appear together with Wisdom, especially in Isaiah and the Psalms, and they ensured *šlm*, peace: 'Righteousness and justice are the foundations of [his] throne' (Ps. 89.14; also 97.2); and when the Lord was enthroned, all creation rejoiced: 'He will judge the world with righteousness . . .' (Ps. 96.13). 'Judge' here is the same root as *mišpaṭ*, and so the line means: 'He will make decisions that lead to *ṣdq*.' Isaiah proclaimed: 'The Lord of Hosts is exalted in justice, and the Holy God shows himself holy in righteousness' (Isa. 5.16); 'The Lord is exalted, for he dwells on high; he will fill Zion with justice and righteousness; and

46 *1 Enoch* 42.2–3.

47 *1 Enoch* 93.10; 91.10.

48 The Greek has sons, *huioi*, and translations such as AV, GNB, NRSV that have 'children of God' lose this vital link to the angels.

49 *1 Enoch* 48.1.

he will be the stability of your times, abundance of salvation, wisdom
and knowledge; for the fear of the L ORD is his* treasure' (Isa. 33.5–6,
*or her). Wisdom and knowledge were part of the stability of the
L ORD's justice and righteousness.

Isaiah saw his land under the influence of the fallen angels,[50] and
condemned the result: 'Jerusalem the faithful city has become a harlot, she that was full of justice! Righteousness lodged in her, but now
murderers' (Isa. 1.21). He told the parable of the L ORD's vineyard that
produced sour grapes. Expecting a harvest of justice and righteousness, he found only bloodshed and a cry of despair. Righteousness,
ṣdqh, sounds like cry, *ṣʿqh,* and justice, *mšpṭ* like bloodshed, *mśpḥ.*
Bloodshed and cries became signs of the broken covenant: when the
fallen angels were corrupting the earth there were bloodshed and
cries[51]; and the martyrs under the altar cried out for their blood to be
avenged (Rev. 6.9–10). Isaiah also condemned the inversion of covenant values, people who call evil righteousness for the sake of a bribe,
and 'turn away the righteousness of the righteous' (Isa. 5.23). On the
day of the L ORD, warned Malachi centuries later, the distinctions would
be established again: 'Then once more you shall distinguish between
the righteous and the wicked, between the one who serves God and
the one who does not serve him' (Mal. 3.18). On that day, the Sun of
righteousness would rise with healing in her wings (Mal. 4.2),[52] her son
would be enthroned, and Satan, the deceiver of the whole world,
would be thrown down (Rev. 12.9).

'The Righteous One' was a name or title in the temple. There was
an ancient priest king called Melchi*zedek,* king of Salem, whose name
meant king of righteousness and king of peace (Gen. 14.18; Heb. 7.1–2);
Zadok the priest anointed Solomon (1 Kgs 1.39); and there were high
priests called *Zadok*ites. The high priest Simeon the Righteous – a title
that indicates his function – was remembered for teaching that the
whole world was maintained by three things: the Law, the Temple
service and deeds of loving kindness, *ḥesed.*[53] Human conduct as well
as temple ritual were required. The first bishop of the Jerusalem
church was called 'James the Righteous One' and remembered as a
high priest who wore linen garments and prayed in the sanctuary for

50 See above, p. 143.

51 *1 Enoch* 9.1–2.

52 See below, p. 264.

53 Mishnah *Aboth* 1.2, see above p. 48.

forgiveness of the people's sins.[54] He exhorted his people using covenant language: 'Pray for one another, that you may be healed. The prayer of a righteous man has great power in its effects' (Jas 5.16). He was also known as the 'bulwark', a curious title whose meaning can only be deduced from his role. After he had been martyred by a mob in Jerusalem in 62 CE, people said that the city had no more defence against enemies, and a prophet appeared, uttering oracles of woe against the city until he was killed in the siege seven years later.[55] James the Righteous One was a high priest,[56] and he protected the city by his presence just as Aaron and the Servant had protected the people by their priestly presence, maintaining the endangered covenant.[57] The role of the Righteous One was fundamental to the belief of the early Church in Jerusalem.

The Righteous One was the Servant who made the atonement, a figure glimpsed in Isaiah's mysterious Servant songs.[58] The early Church used both these titles for Jesus (Acts 3.13–21), and Isaiah's Servant songs were important prophecies. The setting of the poems is the royal high priest on the Day of Atonement, bringing forth *mišpaṭ*; presumably from the holy of holies. He received the Spirit, was called in righteousness and appointed as the [eternal] covenant (Isa. 42.1, 6). Then he brought forth justice, *mišpaṭ*. At his birth the angels sang of establishing his kingdom with justice and righteousness, and one of his throne titles would be 'Prince of Peace' (Isa. 9.6–7). He would judge with righteousness, and under his rule the whole creation would be at peace, the wolf dwelling with the lamb: 'They shall not hurt or destroy in all my holy mountain, for the earth shall be full of the knowledge of the LORD as the waters cover the sea' (Isa. 11.4–9). This ideal was not forgotten: Zechariah hoped for a King, a Righteous One and Saviour, who would come to Jerusalem in humility, riding an ass (Zech. 9.9, translating literally). Unfortunately, the key Servant text that describes atonement and righteousness (Isa. 53.11) has survived in several different versions. The Qumran text is: 'After the suffering of his soul *he will see light,* and be satisfied, and through his knowledge, his Servant,

---

54 'Righteous One' in *Gospel of Thomas* 12; Eusebius, *Church History* 2.23 quoting earlier sources; 'high priest' Epiphanius, *Against Heresies* 29 quoting Hegesippus.

55 Eusebius, *Church History* 2.23; 3.7; Josephus, *Jewish War,* VI.300–309.

56 Too little is known of this early period; presumably he functioned only for the Christian community.

57 See below, pp. 124–5.

58 Isa. 42.1–4; 49.1–4; 50.4–9; 52.13–53.12.

the Righteous One, will make many righteous and bear their iniquities.'[59]

Righteousness was the role of both priests and people alike. The high priest restored the covenant, realizing in ritual the work of the Lord,[60] and it became the responsibility of each Christian – 'Present your bodies as a living sacrifice . . .' (Rom. 12.1) – to transform the ritual into their way of life, since the Christians were 'in Christ' and so collectively the atoning high priesthood. They were also the new temple: 'living stones, a spiritual temple, a holy priesthood offering spiritual sacrifices' (1 Pet. 2.5).[61] They emphasized their high priestly role in the world: they were the covenant that held all things together, the righteous who held back the wrath. Aristides, explaining his faith to the Emperor Hadrian in 125 CE, said that the Christians knew the loving-kindness of God and so lived lives of loving-kindness themselves. This made the world a better place: '. . . the glorious things which are in the world flow forth to view . . . They strive to be righteous . . .' The prayers of the Christians sustained the world.[62] A generation later, Justin declared that the presence of the Christians preserved the world and prevented it collapsing under the influence of the fallen angels: 'God delays causing the confusion and destruction of the whole world, by which the wicked angels and demons and men shall cease to exist, because of the seed of the Christians, who know they are the cause of the preservation in nature.'[63] The *Letter to Diognetus*, written about the same time, compared the Christians to the soul of the world: 'The soul, shut up inside the body, nevertheless holds the body together . . . and it is the Christians who hold the world

59 'See the light' is not in the MT. MT also has 'my Servant'.

60 There is more of Isaiah's wordplay in this poem: 'Upon him was the chastisement that made us whole, and with his stripes we are healed' could also be 'The bond of our peace was his responsibility, and by his joining us together we are healed' (Isa. 53.5).

61 The Christmas stories suggest that 'the righteous' may even have been a distinct group into which Jesus was born: Gabriel said that John the Baptist would turn the hearts of the disobedient 'to the wisdom/discernment of the righteous ones' (Lk. 1.17); Zechariah hoped for the time when his people would be delivered from their enemies, and 'serve the Lord with holiness and righteousness . . .' (Lk. 1.75). Joseph was unwilling to put Mary to public shame because he was a righteous man, presumably meaning a man who did what was necessary for peace, and not, in this case, what public opinion expected (Mt. 1.19).

62 Aristides *Apology* 16.

63 Justin *Apology* II.7.

together.'[64] In our own time, an Orthodox theologian has described the transformed world in a similar way: 'This is not an "other" world, different from the one God has created and given to us. It is our same world, already perfected in Christ, but not yet in us. It is our same world redeemed and restored, in which Christ "fills all things with himself."'[65]

It had originally been the duty of the Davidic king to realize the ideal (Isa. 9.7). Throughout the Old Testament, establishing and maintaining righteousness was the criterion of good government and the precondition for prosperity, and so it was the rulers who were condemned for unrighteous trading practice. Jeremiah condemned the king who neglected his duties of *mišpat* and *ṣdqh*:

> Woe to him who builds his house by unrighteousness, and his upper rooms by injustice; who makes his neighbour serve him for nothing, and does not give him his wages . . . Do you think you are a king because you can compete in cedar? Did not your father eat and drink and do justice and righteousness? Then it was well. "Is not this to know me?" says the Lord. But you have eyes and heart only for dishonest gain, *beṣa'*, for shedding innocent blood and for practising oppression and violence. (Jer. 22.13, 15–7)

He looked for a future king 'a righteous Branch . . . to execute justice and righteousness in the land . . .' (Jer. 23.5–6; 33.15–16). Dishonest profit made through violence is condemned throughout the Bible: corrupt rulers are dogs who do not know when they have enough, 'they have all turned to their own way, each to his own violent gain, *beṣa'*' (Isa. 56.11, my translation). Israel was punished for 'the iniquity of his covetousness', literally 'the distortion of his violent gain' (Isa. 57.17). Ezekiel condemned dishonest rulers in the same way: profits made through violence and bloodshed 'destroying lives to get dishonest gain' (Ezek. 22.13, 27). '"Enough, O Princes of Israel! Put away violence and oppression, and execute justice and righteousness; cease your evictions of my people", says the Lord God. You shall have just, *ṣdq*, balances and a just, *ṣdq*, ephah and a just, *ṣdq*, bath . . .' (Ezek. 45.9–10). Righteousness included trade – weights and measures.

Righteous trade is a recurring theme in the Bible, but as with the 'What would Jesus drive?' question, so too the biblical principles have

---

64 *Letter to Diognetus*, 6.

65 A. Schmemann, *The World as Sacrament*, London: Darton, Longman & Todd, 1974, p. 51, in A. McGrath, *The Open Secret*, p. 207.

to be applied to the global trade issues of the twenty-first century. First, what is 'righteous' trade? 'Righteousness' is not an element in economic theory, and so the biblical injunction means there should be more to any economic system than money and profits. A good system is one that works, but not at any price. Amos condemned those who sold the righteous for silver and trampled the head of the poor into the dust (Amos 2.6); he warned of the LORD's judgement on those who falsified their weights and measures, and sold adulterated food (Amos 8.5–6). These were doubtless profitable activities, but the prophet reminded traders that there were other considerations. Ezekiel condemned the elite of his time for their trading practices: 'iniquity was found in you' (Ezek. 28.15). Abundance of trade brought corrupted wisdom and violence: 'By the multitude of your iniquities in the unrighteousness of your trade, you profaned your holy places . . . All who know you among the peoples are appalled at you; you have come to a dreadful end . . .' (Ezek. 28.18–19). Isaiah had prophesied great wealth and glory for Jerusalem (Isa. 60.4–9), but John the Seer saw how wealth had corrupted the city with alien ways: violence, sorcery and fornication, and a confidence built upon its wealth. 'Alas! Alas, thou great city . . . for thy merchants were the great men of the earth, and all nations were deceived by thy sorcery. And in her was found the blood of the prophets and saints . . .' (Rev. 18.10, 23–4).

'Trade justice' is the name adopted by non-governmental organizations who have been pressing for changes in the current rules and practices of world trade. Trade cannot exist only on its own terms. Even those who do not adopt a faith standpoint recognize this: 'The reconciliation of environment and trade regimes in a fair and equitable manner still remains a major challenge.'[66] In biblical terms, trade justice would mean trade that results in 'righteousness' – sustaining the creation covenant. Biblical concepts would come into the picture: is the result of the proposed system *shalom* – peace and integrity for the creation and human society? Was the system devised in a spirit of wise judgement, *mišpat*, and maintained by loving kindness, *ḥesed*? Fair wages, decent conditions of employment, social justice and care of the environment have to be balanced with sound money management and an awareness of corruption presented as local custom or respect for autonomy. Whether this is achieved by free markets or by intervention in markets is a matter for experts with wisdom, the biblical term for

66 UNEP *Global Environment Outlook Report 1*, Geneva: UNEP, 1997.

knowledge that holds all things together.[67] The conflict so often reduces to a clash between God and mammon, morality and money. Re-examining his belief in the open society – the problem of several simultaneous sets of ideals – George Soros wrote this:

> There has been an ongoing conflict between market values and other, more traditional value systems, which has aroused strong passions and antagonisms. As the Market mechanism has extended its sway, the fiction that people act on a given set of non-Market values has become progressively more difficult to maintain . . . Unsure of what they stand for, people increasingly rely on money as the criterion of value . . . What used to be a medium of exchange has usurped the place of fundamental values, reversing the relationship postulated by economic theory. What used to be professions have turned into businesses. The cult of success has replaced belief in principles. Society has lost its anchor . . .[68]

In the biblical vision, human society and the whole creation flourish together if there is a righteous ruler. Traditional wisdom exhorted the king to 'Open your mouth, give a judgement [a verb linked to *mišpat*] of righteousness, *ṣedeq*, and uphold the cause of the poor and needy' (Prov. 31.9, my translation). Psalm 72 is a prayer for the king, asking that he would bring the justice and righteousness of the LORD:

> Give the king thy justice, O God, and thy righteousness to the royal son!
> May he judge thy people with righteousness, and thy poor with justice.
> Let the mountains bear prosperity for the people, and the hills, in righteousness . . .
> In his days may righteousness flourish, and peace abound . . .
>
> (Ps. 72.1–3,7).

Isaiah too, hoped for the righteous rulers: 'A king will reign in righteousness, and princes rule in justice . . .' (Isa. 32.1), and this passage shows better than any other the link between the righteous ruler and the well-being of creation. The Spirit would be poured from in high, and then

> Justice will dwell in the wilderness
> And righteousness abide in the fruitful field.
> And the effect of righteousness will be peace,
> And the result of righteousness, quietness and trust for ever
>
> (Isa. 32.16–17).

67 See below, p. 247.
68 G. Soros, 'The Capitalist Threat', pp. 45–58, p. 52.

Jared Diamond, in his book *Collapse,* sets side by side two maps: one is 'Political Trouble Spots of the Modern World' and the other is 'Environmental Trouble Spots of the Modern World'. They are identical.[69]

The Earth Charter ['Values and Principles for a Sustainable Future'] was a UN World Commission on Environment and Development initiative, proposed in 1987 that became part of the unfinished business of the 1992 Rio Earth Summit. It was finally launched in 2000, and set out 'fundamental principles for building a just, sustainable and peaceful global society in the 21st century'. 'The earth Charter's inclusive ethical vision recognizes that environmental protection, human rights, equitable human development and peace are interdependent and indivisible. It provides a new framework for thinking about and addressing these issues.' A new framework? New to whom? *The earth Charter sounds very like the 'eternal covenant', and there is little in it that is not also in the Bible.* 'The mission of the Initiative is to establish a sound ethical foundation for the emerging global society and to help build a sustainable world based on respect for nature, universal human rights, economic justice and a culture of peace.'

- 'We must realise that when basic needs have been met, human development is primarily about being more, not having more.'
- 'We urgently need a shared vision of basic values to provide an ethical foundation for the emerging world community.'
- 'Recognize the importance of moral and spiritual education for sustainable living.'
- 'Recognize that peace is the wholeness created by right relationships within oneself, other person, other cultures, other life, Earth, and the larger whole of which we are all a part.'
- 'This requires a change of mind and heart. It requires a new sense of global interdependence and universal responsibility.'
- 'We must find ways to harmonize diversity with unity, the exercise of freedom with the common good, short term objectives with long term goals.'[70]

What is missing from the Earth Charter is God. All the other biblical concepts are there, except that the call to self-sacrifice is reduced to

---

69 J. Diamond, *Collapse. How Societies Choose to Fail or Survive*, London: Penguin, 2005, p. 497.

70 The Earth Charter: preamble, 14d, 16f, post script.

'act with restraint'. As McGrath observed: 'The idea that human morality might ultimately be grounded in something built into the fabric of the universe itself has obstinately refused to die out.'[71] The Venice Declaration, signed in 2002 by the Pope and the Ecumenical Patriarch, affirmed: 'It is on the basis of our recognition that the world is created by God that we can discern an objective moral order within which to articulate a code of environmental ethics.'[72]

The biblical principle of righteousness is very similar to the 'restorative justice'[73] that is now being explored and developed in some youth and community programmes, the best known example being the Truth and Reconciliation Commission in South Africa. Peace and healing are the keys to this system rather than retribution, and the emphasis is on the effect of wrongdoing on the individual or the community, and what needs to be done to heal the hurt and make good the damage. The offender meets the victim[s], hears about the effect of what she/he has done, takes responsibility for it and makes some amends. This is very different from a process where lawyers dispute over points of law and do everything possible to secure their clients' acquittal – even on a technicality – and the victim may not even be informed of the process. Any process of restorative justice for the environment, which cannot speak for itself, must recognize first that the environment needs protection – one cannot really speak of 'rights' – and then make sure that extraction industries, for example, make good their sites, that polluters pay for full restoration, not just the immediate cleaning up of their mess, and are forbidden similar action or processes in the future. Otherwise, the cost of pollution would simply be included in the cost of production, and there would be no restoration and healing.

The biblical perspective emphasizes the responsibility of the offender, that she/he is free to repent and make restoration, the earthly aspect of atonement. Retribution was also part of atonement, but it was the LORD who brought retribution. Peace, *shalom*, and recompense, *shillem*, are both written *šlm,* and were two aspects of the same process. Thus 'Vengeance is mine, and recompense' (Deut. 32.35), and Isaiah's picture of the warrior coming to bring judgement: there was no justice, and so the LORD armed himself with righteousness and

71 McGrath, *The Open Secret,* p. 295.

72 The Venice Declaration, signed by Pope John Paul II and Patriarch Bartholomew, 10th June 2002.

73 Pioneered by Howard Zehr.

appeared to *repay* and *requite* his enemies (Isa. 59.15–18, *šlm* each time).
Paul set this into the Christian covenant context:

> Live in harmony with one another . . . if possible live peaceably with all . . . never
> avenge yourselves, but leave it to the wrath of God; for it is written, 'Vengeance
> is mine, I will repay, say the LORD.' No, 'if your enemy is hungry, feed him, if
> he is thirsty, give him drink; for by so doing you will heap burning coals upon his
> head. (Rom. 12.16–20)

The latter is Paul's own, but the rest is covenant theology, upholding
shalom.

THE JUBILEE

'Economically and socially, this dream of *shalom* found expression in
what I call a theology of enough.' Thus John Taylor in his 1975 book
Enough is Enough, which set out the biblical perspective on the culture
of ever increasing consumption and excess. He continued:

> We shall not find in scripture the blueprint of an economic system relevant to
> our own day. What we do find is a number of independent enactments, moral
> judgements and traditions . . . all of them utterly different in detail from what we
> know today, and yet together revealing a consistent attitude and style diametri-
> cally opposed to the excess . . . [that characterizes our present way of life][74]

'Enough' certainly sums up the biblical attitude to the material things
of life – knowing when to stop; and the 'consistent attitude' was the
expression of the covenant ethos. Underlying all the various rules and
customs was recognition that the LORD was the Creator and Provider,
and that everything was to be received and used within the bonds and
patterns of the covenant.

The ancient body of law known as the Holiness Code (Lev. 19–26)
commanded the people to be holy because the LORD was holy
(Lev. 19.2). Whatever they believed about the LORD had to be the
rule for their own lives, and this included righteousness and generos-
ity. They could not reap all their harvest or gather all their grapes:
some had to be left for the poor, the stranger, and, presumably, for
wild life. Enough was enough (Lev. 19.9–10). In the time of Jesus the
corners of the field left unharvested had to be at least one sixtieth of

74 J. V. Taylor, *Enough is Enough*, London: SCM Press, 1975, p. 42.

the crop, or more if there were many poor people in the district. Crops included vegetables, not just grain, and the harvest of trees included vines, nuts and palms, as well as orchards.[75] Wages had to be fair and paid promptly (Lev. 19.13). Judgements had to be honest and righteous (Lev. 19.15). There was to be no cross breeding of animals or crops (Lev. 19.19). Fruit trees had to grow to maturity before their fruit could be taken (Lev. 19.23–5). All weights and measures had to be honest (Lev. 19.35–6). If the people observed the Laws of the LORD, the land would give them enough food and they would be secure (Lev. 25.18–19; 26.3–6). If they ignored the laws of the LORD and broke the covenant, then the land would not support them: they would sow seed in vain (Lev. 26.16); there would be no harvest from field or orchard (Lev. 26.20); wild animals would destroy their cattle (Lev. 26.22); and their bread would not satisfy them (Lev. 26.26). The land would become desolate and then enjoy all the Sabbaths it had been denied while lawless people were living there (Lev. 26.34–5).

In the time of Jesus, there were complex laws for tithing, developed from the original biblical rule that one tenth of the seeds, fruit and animals were holy to the LORD (Lev. 27.30). They offered the first fruits in recognition that they had been set in a good land (Deut. 26.5–11). In addition, there was a tithe paid every third year for the poor: the landless Levites, the aliens, the orphans and the widows (Deut. 26.13). Jesus condemned those who were meticulous about tithing but had lost touch with the underlying principles: 'You tithe mint and dill and cumin, and have neglected the weightier matters of the law, justice and mercy and faith; these you ought to have done, without neglecting the others' (Mt. 23.23). Jesus and his followers paid the temple tax (Mt. 17.24–7); presumably those who were eligible paid their tithes. They observed the real meaning of the Sabbath, attending the synagogue, but not refusing to do works of mercy (Mk 1.21–6; Luke 6 1–11; Jn 5.1–17).

Lending money at interest was forbidden in the oldest law code in the Bible (Exod. 22.25–7), and the prohibition was expanded in Deuteronomy: 'You shall not lend upon interest, *nešek*, to your brother, interest on money, interest on victuals, interest on anything that is lent for interest. To a foreigner you may lend upon interest . . .' (Deut. 23.19–20). Leviticus emphasized loans to the poor: 'If your brother becomes poor . . . take no interest from him or increase, but

75 Mishnah *Peah* 1.2; 3.3.

fear your God; that your brother may live beside you. You shall not lend your money at interest, *nešek*, nor give your food for profit, *marbiyt* (Lev. 25.35–7). When Ezekiel defined the righteous man, he was one who did *mišpat* and *ṣ'daqah*, who shunned idolatry and sexual immorality, who

> does not oppress anyone, but restores to the debtor his pledge, gives his bread to the hungry and covers the naked with a garment, does not lend at interest or take any increase, who withholds his hand from iniquity, executes true justice between man and man, walks in [my] statutes and is careful to observe my ordinances . . . (Ezek. 18.5–9).

When he denounced the corruption in Jerusalem, it was in similar terms: '"In you people have taken bribes to shed blood, you have taken interest, *nešek*, and profit, *marbiyt*, and you have made unjust gain from your neighbours by extortion, and you have forgotten me", says the LORD God' (Ezek. 2.12, my translation).

These fundamental injunctions were elaborated in many ways to apply to specific circumstances. The rules in the time of Jesus were later set down in the *Mishnah*:

> It is usury when a man lends four *denars* for five *denars*, or two *seahs* of wheat for three. It is profit/increase when a man increases in produce. If he bought wheat at 25 denars a *kor* when that was the market price, and then the wheat price rose to thirty and he said, 'Deliver me my wheat since I would sell it to buy wine with the price,' and the other said 'Let thy wheat be reckoned to me at thirty *denars*, and thus thou now hast a claim on me for wine' – although he has no wine . . . No bargain may be made over produce before its market price is known.

To give a gift in hope of a loan or in gratitude for a loan was regarded as usury, and all those involved in lending at interest were equally responsible: 'the lender, the borrower, the guarantor and the witnesses'.[76] There were many more. The idea of shared responsibility for loans has recently been taken up by the Jubilee debt campaign.[77]

Money dealing with interest barred the parties from the temple: 'LORD, who shall dwell on thy holy hill? . . . [He who] does not put out his money at interest and does not take a bribe . . .' (Ps. 15.1,5). In the time of Jesus, however, even the high priests were lending at interest: 'Will not those who pay you interest suddenly arise . . . then you will be booty for them' (Hab. 2.7, my translation) was applied to the priests in

76 Mishnah *Baba Metzia* 5.1, 7, 10, 11.
77 See below, p. 187.

Jerusalem, as the Qumran *Habakkuk Commentary* shows. The beast in
Revelation was the anti-Christ, who operated through the business
practices of the time, possibly a reference to the temple establishment.
The faithful were those who resisted the beast and all his ways
(Rev. 15.2). The mark of the beast was worn by all his followers in the
places where observant Jews wore their phylacteries: on the forehead
and on the right hand (Deut. 6.8). The mark, *charagma,* of the beast
was literally the mark left by a snake bite, and in Hebrew the word for
a snake bite is *nešek,* which also means interest. The description of the
beast and his followers meant that commitment to commerce had
replaced the usual texts in the phylacteries,[78] and this is why nobody
could buy or sell without the mark (Rev. 13.16–17). The mark is mentioned six times in Revelation (13.17; 14.9,11; 16.2; 19.20; 20.4), and
always in conjunction with worshipping the image. Money dealing
without interest barred people from the markets (Rev. 13.17). The
beast was an alternative religion, the market his temple, and the mark
his sign. This is why Jesus said: 'You cannot serve God and Mammon.'
All the evidence shows that lending at interest epitomised the rejection of the LORD, and yet one of the inexplicable texts in the New
Testament is that Jesus recommended investing a talent at interest
(Mt. 25.27).

The covenant ethos determined all aspects of life, and the covenant
was described as the LORD's oath; the two words appear in parallel:
'I have made a covenant . . . I have sworn to David . . . (Ps. 89.3, also
89.34–5); 'the covenant with Abraham . . . the oath to Isaac . . .' to give
them the Canaan (Ps. 105.9,11, my translation); 'to remember his holy
covenant, the oath which he swore to our father Abraham' (Lk. 1.72–3).
There are many examples: Enoch described the creation covenant as
the great oath that kept all things in their appointed place.[79] The oath
was linked especially to the promise of the land. The LORD swore to
[the patriarchs] to give their descendents the land (Deut. 1.8, and
often in Deut.). 'I will give you all these lands, and I will fulfil the
oath which I swore to Abraham your father . . .' (Gen. 26.3); 'the land
which I swore to their fathers I will give them' (Josh. 1.6); 'the oath
which I swore to your fathers to give them a land flowing with milk and
honey' (Jer. 11.5, also Exod. 13.5).

The system was expressed in the intricate word play that characterized temple discourse. The Hebrew root for words meaning swear or

78 Exod. 12.43–13.16 and Deut. 5.1–6.9.
79 See above, pp. 119–20.

oath is *šb'*, giving *šaba'*, swear, and *šᵉbuʿah,* oath; but the same letters are also the root for 'seven', *šebaʿ*, the sacred number. There was a strong link between the two. Isaac dug a well, *be'er,* and called it Beer-sheba, the place where he sacrificed seven lambs and swore an oath (Gen. 21.30–31). The covenant/oath that bound the creation was also linked to 'seven', and so time was divided into sevens, each marked by remembering the creation and the covenant, and by satisfaction, *šabaʿ* – an almost identical word – and rest *šabbat.* There was the weekly Sabbath, and there was the Feast of Weeks, 7 × 7 days after Passover when the first wheat was offered on the fiftieth day. In the time of Jesus two other festivals were known: 7 × 7 days after the Feast of Weeks on the fiftieth day there was a Feast of New Wine, and 7 × 7 days after that, on the fiftieth day there was the Feast of New Oil.[80] Every seventh year was a Sabbath Year, and after 7 × 7 years there was the Jubilee. The end of history was described as the great Sabbath.

'Seven' was the key to understanding the creation. Aristobulus[81] the Egyptian Jewish philosopher, explained to King Ptolemy: 'The whole world of living creatures, and of all plants that grow, revolve in sevens.'[82] The seventh day, he said, was kept holy 'as a symbol of our sevenfold Logos, to which we owe our knowledge of human and divine things'.[83] The sevenfold Spirit gave true knowledge of the creation, such that it was well ordered, and the earth was full of the knowledge of God (Isa. 11.1–9). When Enoch ascended through the heavens, he saw the seven great angels who controlled the creation, all identical and acting as one:

> I saw there seven angels, grouped together . . . and there was no difference between their faces or in their dimensions or in the mode of their being . . . they make all celestial life peaceful, and they preserve the commandments and instructions and sweet voices and singing, every kind of praise and glory.[84]

80 According to the Temple Scroll found at Qumran, IIQTXIX–XXIII, see J. Maier, *The Temple Scroll,* Sheffield: *Journal for the Study of the Old Testament Supplement* 34, 1985, pp. 71–6. These extra festivals explain the pattern of the Book of Revelation, see my book *The Revelation of Jesus Christ*, pp. 242–3.

81 Lived in Alexandria early in the second century BCE, was of the high priestly family and tutor to King Ptolemy (2 Macc. 1.10), for whom he wrote a book.

82 Quoted in Eusebius, *Preparation of the Gospel*, XIII.12.

83 Translation by M. Hengel, *Judaism and Hellenism,* London: SCM Press, 1974, vol.1, p. 167.

84 *2 Enoch* 19.1–3.

These seven appear in Revelation as the sevenfold presence of the high priest, dressed in the white linen and golden girdle of a high priest (Rev. 15.5–8). Sevenfold wisdom and knowledge would be restored to the chosen ones at the end of the seventh week of history, in a scheme that saw all history as 'weeks'.[85] Daniel prophesied seventy times seven years until everlasting righteousness was restored (Dan. 9.24).

The most familiar and yet mysterious of the sevens is John's vision of the Lamb 'standing as though it had been slain, with seven horns and with seven eyes which are the seven spirits of God sent out into all the earth' (Rev. 5.6). This is temple theology at its most complex. The Lamb was the Servant: in Aramaic both are *talya*'. In the literary code of the visionaries, 'men' represent angels, and animals represent humans, and so the Lamb was the human Servant who had been slain and was resurrected, standing. He was enthroned and received the homage of all creation, before opening the seven seals and inaugurating the judgement. His seven horns were seven beams of light, meaning that he radiated the complete light. Isaiah had used this image: when right teaching was restored and idolatry rejected, the creation would flourish again, and the sun would shine with a sevenfold light (Isa. 30.19–26). Philo described it as the invisible complete light known only to the mind and made known by the divine Logos.[86] One of the Qumran hymns thanked God: 'I shall shine in a sevenfold light in [the council appointed by] Thee for Thy glory; for Thou art an everlasting light to me . . .'[87] The Lamb's seven eyes were the seven spirits given to the anointed one (Isa. 11.1–3), which Zechariah saw as the seven lamps of the menorah (Zech. 4.10). The vision of the Lamb enthroned described the human with sevenfold wisdom who had offered himself, and then been set to rule and judge the creation. Isaiah expressed this too in his fourth Servant Song, a key prophecy for the early Church: 'Out of the suffering of his soul he will see light and find satisfaction, and through his knowledge his Servant the righteous one will make many righteous' (Isa. 53.11, as in the Qumran Isaiah Scroll).

---

85 *1 Enoch* 93.10.

86 Philo, *Creation*, 31. The horns derive from the story of Moses coming down from Sinai, when the skin of his face beamed because he had been talking with the LORD (Exod. 34.29). The Hebrew 'beamed' *qrn*, derived from 'horn', also *qrn*, and so some translations, for example the Vulgate, gave Moses horns: 'quod cornuta esset facies sua'.

87 *Thanksgiving Hymns*, 1 QH XV.24.

The system of sevens represented completeness, that is restored righteousness, satisfaction and rest, and so time itself was measured in
sevens. The first division of time was the weekly Sabbath when every
person and animal rested (Exod. 20.8–11). It was the sign of the creation
covenant (Exod. 31.12–17), and was observed every seventh day,
because God finished the work of creation in six days and rested on the
seventh (Exod. 20.8–11). The Sabbath celebrated enough. There was
no striving for maximum production, and a recent Church of England
report on the environment devoted a section to 'the Sabbath feast of
enoughness.'[88] The Sabbath gave rest to all people and animals, in
gratitude for release from slavery in Egypt (Deut. 5.12–15). The injunction was addressed to employers: servants and animals were entitled to
rest. Adam, created on the sixth day, became the co-creator, and at the
end of the sixth day God looked at everything and saw it was very good.
There have been problems with this idea that God completed everything
and then rested, as though the task had been completed, but it is clear
that in the time of Jesus, the days of creation were seen as a pattern for
the whole of history, with the sixth day representing the human era,
and Adam as the co-creator.[89]

Today this could be seen as achieving a sustainable state, 'meeting
the needs of the present without compromising the ability of future
generations to meet their own needs.'[90] Since there is only one earth,
the 'needs' of many will have to be reassessed:

> But no one in First World governments is willing to acknowledge the dream's
> impossibility: the unsustainability of a world [if] the Third World's large popula-
> tion were to reach and maintain current First World living standards . . . What
> will happen when it finally dawns on all those people in the Third World that
> current First World standards are unreachable for them, and the First World
> refuses to abandon those standards for itself?[91]

The biblical picture of creation recognizes the limit and the right to
rest, for people and all creatures. The beast, the religion of the Market

---

88 Church of England's Mission and Public Affairs Council, *Sharing God's Planet,
A Christian Vision for a Sustainable Future*, London: Church House Publishing 2005,
pp. 27–8.

89 See below, p. 216.

90 *Our Common Future* (World Commission on Environment and Development: the
Brundtland report), Oxford: Oxford University Press, 1987.

91 Diamond, Collapse, p. 496.

with its non-stop sweat shop labour and battery farms, does not, as Harvey Cox observed ten years ago:

> There is one contradiction between the religion of the Market and the tradi-
> tional religions that seems to be insurmountable. All of the traditional religions
> teach that human beings are finite creatures, and that there are limits to any
> earthly enterprise . . . For the Market, however, there is never enough, and so the
> Market that never stops expanding dies.[92]

Then there was the Feast of Weeks, 7×7 days after Passover, on the fiftieth day, when the covenants were celebrated with harvest offerings. Covenant is not linked with harvest in the way the Old Testament is usually read. In the second century CE, the rabbis began to associate the Feast of Weeks with Sinai and the Moses covenant, but in the time of Jesus, it was linked to the covenants with Noah and Abraham, accord-ing to the *Book of Jubilees* which tells the story from creation to Exodus using this pattern of sevens. Adam was seven years in Eden. Noah celebrated the Feast of Weeks – or was it Oaths? the text could mean either[93] – to mark the LORD's everlasting covenant and oath to pre-serve the creation. Noah had atoned the land to remove all the effects of sin and vowed never to consume blood. Abraham offered his first fruits at the Feast of Weeks, when the LORD changed his name to Abraham and commanded circumcision. He promised him descen-dents who would possess the land.[94] The Church celebrated the Feast of Weeks as Pentecost, when the Spirit was given, and Peter interpreted this as the outpouring prophesied by Joel (Acts 2.17–21; Joel 2.28–32). The original context of Joel passage, however, was the renewal of the creation: green pastures and rain, fruit, grain and oil, 'You shall eat in plenty and be satisfied' (Joel 2.26). Peter preached next about fulfill-ing the Day of Atonement, repentance, blotting out sins ' that times of refreshing may come from the presence of the LORD' (Acts 3.19). The covenant renewal on the Christian Feast of Weeks was the creation covenant.

Then there was the Sabbath year, every seventh year when the land was left to rest (Lev. 25.2–7), and debts were cancelled (Deut. 15.1–11). Every Hebrew had to cancel the outstanding debts of fellow Hebrews to ensure that there were no poor people within the covenant com-munity, but this remission did not extend to foreigners (Deut. 15.3).

92 H. Cox, 'The Market as God', *The Atlantic Monthly*, 283.3 (1999), pp. 18–23, p. 23.

93 See O. S. Wintermute, *Jubilees*, in OTP2, p. 67.

94 *Jubilees* 3.17; 6.1–19; 15.1–16.

Since some people paid their debts by labour and became slaves, all Hebrew slaves had to be released in the seventh year.[95] Breaking this law was such a serious matter that it caused the exile. According to Jeremiah, certain slave owners had gone through the process of releasing their slaves, only to re-enslave them (Jer. 34.8–22), and this brought the exile. In the Sabbath year, the land was not cultivated, vineyards were not pruned, nor was their produce harvested. People lived on what grew naturally (Lev. 25.1–7). These commitments were solemnly reaffirmed when Nehemiah re-established Jerusalem after the exile: there would be no marriage outside the community, no buying from people outside the community on the Sabbath and 'we will forgo the crops of the seventh year and the exaction of every debt' (Neh. 10. 30–31). However difficult this may seem, the Sabbath for the land was observed. There were detailed laws in the time of Jesus for observing the fallow year: how late one could plant trees or prune them or protect saplings.[96] In the second century BCE, during the war against Syria, the town of Beth Zur was not able to withstand a siege 'because they had no provisions . . . since it was the sabbatical year for the land.' In Jerusalem too 'they had no food in storage because it was the seventh year . . .' (1 Macc. 6.49, 53). The land had, in effect, the right to rest. The desolation in Judah when so many people were in exile in Babylon for 70 years (Jer. 25.12) was seen as a time of Sabbath rest, to allow the land to recover from the years when the Sabbath had not been observed (2 Chron. 36.21; Jer. 17.19–27).

Finally, there was the Sabbath of Sabbaths, the Jubilee year, observed after seven Sabbath years. It was proclaimed on the Day of Atonement (Lev. 25.9) and prompted the people's practical response to the atonement ritual in the temple. It signified the renewal of society, the year of release, *d'ror*. The land was left fallow, people returned to their family and their ancestral property. Family land could not be sold, but only rented out for the period up to the next Jubilee year, the rate being calculated by the number of crops that could be expected from it (Lev. 25.13–17). So important were these years of rest that they were described as laws from Sinai, equal in importance to the ten

95 *Jewish Encyclopedia*, 'Sabbatical Year', p. 605. 'The law of the Sabbatical year acts as a statute of limitation, or a bankruptcy law for the poor debtor, in discharging his liability for debts contracted and enabling him to start life anew on an equal footing with his neighbour, without the fear that his future earnings will be seized by his creditors.'

96 Mishnah *Shebiith* 1.1; 2.1–4.

commandments (Lev. 25.1). The biblical regulations are complex and some of the detail is no longer clear. What they show is that rest from labour and freedom from debt were part of the divine order for the world, as were family ties and a place to call home, but that this only applied within the covenant community, where all recognized the same obligations as well as the same rights.

The Jubilee and Sabbath years were a return to Eden. Just as the weekly services in the temple remembered the days of creation, so too did the cycles of seven years. At the end of the sixth day, when the creation was completed, God saw that everything was 'very good' (Gen. 1.31), and this was the state that the Sabbath and Jubilee years recreated. Adam had been given food that grew naturally – every plant yielding seed and every tree with seed in its fruit (Gen. 1.29) – and so people did not cultivate the land. The toil of cultivating difficult soil was part of Adam's punishment (Gen. 3.17–19). In Eden there were no debts, no slaves, and no landless exiles; Sabbath and Jubilee years made a new beginning possible.

It was the Servant who brought the Jubilee; it was the purpose of the high priestly atonement. He had to release prisoners and open eyes (Isa. 42.7); he had to bring Israel back and re-establish the land (Isa. 49.5, 9); and he was anointed to bring good tidings to the poor and liberty to the captives (Isa. 61.1), this latter being the passage read by Jesus in the synagogue at Nazareth (Lk. 4.16–21). The key word is release/liberty, *d'ror*, the word that identifies Jubilee thinking (Lev. 25.10; Isa. 61.1; Jer. 34.15; Ezek. 46.17). In the Old Greek translation of the Old Testament, this became *aphesis*, the word used by Jesus over the cup at the last supper: 'This is my blood of the covenant, poured out for many for the *aphesis* of sins' (Mt. 26.28). For the Jewish Christians of Matthew's community, this identified the Eucharist as part of the Jubilee, another indication that the covenant at the last supper was the creation covenant renewed on the Day of Atonement.

It is not clear how literally the Jubilee was interpreted in the time of Jesus. The almost contemporary Melchizedek text from Qumran[97] suggests that the Sabbath year and Jubilee concepts had been spiritualized, or had received an additional spiritual interpretation. The text is broken, but it does seem to present the Jubilee release from slavery as releasing captives from the power of Belial; cancelling debt as releasing from iniquities, the benefit of atonement; and causing people to return

---

97 *11Q Melchizedek.*

to their family roots. The text links Jubilee passages to Isaiah 52.7 – the messenger of good news who announces peace and proclaims the Kingdom. In the Old Greek, the messenger of good news is the *evangelizomenos*, the gospel bearer. The Melchizedek text, then, links the Jubilee and all its benefits to the gospel and the Kingdom.

Knowing this, the Jubilee pattern in the New Testament becomes clear: Jesus' first miracle was an exorcism, setting someone free from the power of evil (Mk 1.21–26); he released a woman bound by Satan (Lk. 13.16); he spoke of slaves to sin whom the Son could set free (Jn 8.31–38). He forgave sins, and illustrated this with a story about two debtors whose debts were cancelled (Lk. 7.41–8). The healing miracles dealt with conditions that made people ritually unclean and so excluded them: the disabled, lepers, a bleeding woman. This was the ingathering of the scattered, and Jesus said the meek would inherit the land. Jubilee and atonement themes are the framework of the beatitudes: the Kingdom, comfort, inheritance restored, mercy, true purity, peace making, righteousness (Mt. 5.3–10). Paul has similar themes: atonement, freedom from slavery to sin, cancelling the debt of sin, gathering in the Gentiles.

Jubilee issues were not just spiritualized. A Jubilee was due in the autumn of 66 CE, and that was when the liberation struggle began against Rome. The first act of the insurgents in August 66 CE was to set fire to the buildings in Jerusalem where the money lenders held their bonds, in other words, to destroy all records of debt. Economic issues were closely bound up with the final struggle against evil, and there is contemporary evidence that religious leaders were part of the corrupt system that exploited the poor. The Wicked Priest in Jerusalem 'forsook God for the sake of riches . . . The last priests in Jerusalem shall amass money and wealth by plundering the people . . .'[98] The Christian community had been plundered (Heb. 10.34); James, their bishop in Jerusalem, condemned the rich who had not paid their workers while themselves living in luxury (Jas 5.1–6). Josephus, reflecting on the causes of the war, concluded it was due to 'the men of power oppressing the multitude and the multitude earnestly labouring to destroy the men of power'.[99] This was the socio-economic situation of the early Church, the context of the parable of the rich fool, the anxieties about food and clothing, and the warning against treasure on earth (Lk. 12.13–34). Jesus said: 'Seek ye first the kingdom of God and his

98 *Habakkuk Commentary*, 1QpHab VIII, IX.

99 Josephus, *Jewish War*, VII.261.

righteousness, and all these things shall be yours as well' (Mt. 6.33); 'You cannot serve God and money' (Mt. 6.24); and 'It is easier for a camel to go through the eye of a needle than for a rich man to enter the kingdom of God' (Mk 10.25).

The Jubilee release raises the same question as does 'righteous trade': how might it be possible to apply biblical principles to the contemporary situation? The Jubilee restored the harmony and balance in society, and there is no doubt that this is needed in the twenty-first century. Originally, the benefits of the Jubilee were for those who had repented of their sin, and had done what they could to make restitution before receiving the benefits of atonement and confirmation in the covenant community. In the contemporary global community, this raises many questions: should Jubilee benefits be conditional on accepting the Jubilee premises? Or on accepting conditions from the money lenders, for example the privatization of basic services, or the cutting of government spending?[100] Should debt be forgiven to a country that tolerates slavery in any form?

The fundamental of the biblical Jubilee was hope. Since no financial hardship could last for more than six years, release and a new start were always possible. Those who benefited from the Jubilee were also obliged to extend those benefits to others, should the situation change. The Bible gives few details of how it worked in practice, but later texts show, for example, that debt owed to an orphan could not be cancelled, and that there were sophisticated rules for running Jubilee compliant enterprises that limited the scope of Jewish business. It would not have been prudent to lend – as opposed to give – money where there was no hope of its return in six years.[101] This sense of shared responsibility for the debt was emphasized by the Jubilee 2000 campaign for debt relief.

> One of the central messages of the Jubilee 2000 campaign was that creditors should take some responsibility for the debt crisis. Creditors have lent money irresponsibly to corrupt governments, or imposed conditions on their lending that in many cases have worsened rather than improved the economic situation of the countries they were supposed to be helping. Providing debt relief should amount to an acknowledgement by creditors that they need to take their share of the costs of past mistakes.[102]

100 'Fool's Gold. The Case for 100% Multilateral Debt Cancellation for the Poorest Countries,' report published jointly by ActionAid, Cafod and Oxfam, 2004.

101 For detail, see *The Jewish Encyclopedia*, 'Sabbatical Year.'

102 'Fool's Gold' report.

'Few in the Global North have not profited from the exploitation of rural people in the Global South . . . Today, many of those economies send tribute to the Global North in terms of debt repayment. It is time those debts were cancelled . . .'[103] Most of the debt of poor countries is from the 1970s, when the rich elite in the world were keen to lend money, sometimes to ensure allegiance in the Cold War, and those who still suffer from the consequences of debt repayment are so often people who did not benefit from the original loan. The same situation is developing with the financial crisis affecting the world in 2009. People were lent money they could not possibly repay, and so the 'rich' world now has a debt crisis too, which will mean less money to help the poor.

Cancelling debt was one sign of the Jubilee. Another was leaving the land fallow for a year, so that it could rest. In contemporary terms, this would mean caring for the soil and not cultivating it to the point of exhaustion, in other words, changing practices of land management. There are many examples of desertification where human activity – over grazing, deforestation, over-cultivation – has been an important factor: the damage to the prairie lands of North America in the 1930s due to intensive farming without crop rotation and then drought; the deforestation in the Amazon region for the short-term gain of soya; cultivation and grazing of marginal lands due to population increase in parts of Africa. It would also mean reserves: land areas set aside to allow their own ecosystems to recover from the effects of industrialized farming; and marine reservations so that the seas can recover from the devastation caused by industrialized fishing.

The other Jubilee signs, however, would be difficult if not impossible to realize. Returning to live in the family home after 50 years would mean a massive movement of migrant people back to the country of their family's origin. Making all land and property transactions valid for only a limited period presupposed that nobody in fact owned anything. Everything belonged to the LORD; people held land and property as a family trust and nothing could be sold. This could mean more equitable distribution of land in situations where people have been dispossessed, and it would prevent the unrealistic rise in property prices that has distorted the economy for a generation.

The last of the 'sevens' was the final Sabbath, 'a Sabbath rest for the people of God' (Heb. 4.9). The seven days did not only represent

---

103 R. Patel, *Stuffed and Starved*, p. 315.

the process of creation as represented by the temple; they were also the plan for history. Barnabas explained to the first Christians:

> The significance of "he finished them in six days" is this, that he is going to bring the world to an end in six thousand years, since with him one day means a thousand years (Ps. 90.4). . . . After that, he rested on the seventh day indicates that when his Son returns, he will put an end to the years of the Lawless One, pass sentence on the godless, transform the sun, moon and stars and then, on the seventh day, enter into his true rest.[104]

The current era was seen as the sixth day of creation, the state before creation was completed, and so before the Creator could say that everything was very good. Jesus saw himself as living on the sixth day; when he healed a paralysed man on the Sabbath, he reminded his critics that it was not the Sabbath, if God still had work to be done (Jn 5.17).

The final Sabbath was the Kingdom, the reign of Christ. John saw 'the priests of God and of Christ reigning for a thousand years' (Rev. 20.6), an earthly kingdom, since a heavenly kingdom would not have been measured in time. Before the Kingdom was set up, Satan was bound for a thousand years (Rev. 20.1–3). The parable of the sheep and the goats describes setting up the Kingdom: there is no place in it for the devil and his angels, those who do not help to bring righteousness.[105] The oldest material in *1 Enoch* knew that the earth would not be fruitful while the evil angels were upon it, but once their leaders had been bound, 'the whole earth [would be] tilled in righteousness, and all planted with trees and be full of blessing.'[106] Paul knew that the gift of the Spirit at Pentecost meant the Jubilee for the creation, release from bondage (Rom. 8.18–23), that the new sons of God had replaced the fallen angels.[107] Justin said that the Kingdom would be the return to Eden, fulfilling the prophecy in Isaiah 65.17–25: no more weeping or early death, no fruitless toil, but prosperity and peace. These ideas were not unique to the Christians; they drew them from their contemporary Jewish culture which said that in the time of the Messiah, the earth would give huge harvests, and there would be no more hunger.[108]

104 *Letter of Barnabas* 15.

105 See above, pp. 142–4.

106 *1 Enoch* 10.18.

107 Anselm, *Cur Deus Homo* 1.16 later said that the depleted number of the angels had to be made up by humans.

108 *2 Baruch* 29.5–6.

Irenaeus spelled out the detail of the fertile Kingdom, including some sayings of Jesus which he had found in the writings of Papias, who had learned them from John.

> For in as many days as this world was made, in so many thousand years shall it be concluded . . . For the Day of the LORD is as a thousand years; and in six days created things were completed . . . After the reign of the antichrist, then the LORD will come from heaven in the clouds . . . bringing in for the righteous the times of the Kingdom, that is, the rest of the hallowed seventh day . . .

He then linked the fertile Kingdom to Romans 8, and explained:

> The predicted blessing, therefore, belongs unquestionably to the times of the Kingdom, when the righteous shall bear rule upon their rising from the dead; when also the creation, having been renewed and set free, shall bear fruit with abundance in all kinds of food . . .

Then he quoted Jesus as recorded by Papias:

> The days will come when vineyards will grow, each having ten thousand shoots, and in one shoot ten thousand branches . . . and upon every sprig ten thousand clusters, and in every cluster ten thousand grapes, and every grape when pressed shall yield twenty five measures of wine.
>   Every grain of wheat would yield huge quantities of flour, fruit trees and pasture would flourish and all animals live at peace with each other.[109]

What might the first Christians have believed about the creation? It is clear that Sabbath, Feast of Weeks, Jubilee and Kingdom were important elements in their world view, and all of them concerned the place of the human being in the creation and the hope of the restoration of Eden: the Sabbath rest to mark the completion of creation, the Feast of Weeks to celebrate the covenant by offering the first fruits, the Jubilee to restore hope and remit debt, and the final Sabbath of the Kingdom when evil – characterized as deception and the religion of money – would be banished so that the earth could enjoy rest and fertility. When the Christians prayed 'Thy Kingdom come, thy will be done', this is how they envisaged the Kingdom.

---

109 Irenaeus, *Against Heresies* V.28–33. The words attributed to Jesus are very similar to those in *2 Baruch*. Jesus also promised ample restitution of anything sacrificed for the Kingdom, Lk. 18.29–30.

The biblical vision is that we work together with the Creator until everything is very good, and, although there is room for disagreement as to what is meant by 'the good', there is a remarkable correspondence between the ideals of the Kingdom and the Millennium Development Goals adopted by the United Nations Millennium Summit in September 2000. The eight goals, to be achieved by 2015, are:

1. *Eradication of extreme poverty and hunger, by halving the number of people who live on less than one dollar a day and those who suffer from hunger, and to achieve full and decent employment for all including women.*
'To preach good news to the poor, to proclaim release to the captives, the recovering of sight to the blind, to set at liberty those who are oppressed' (Lk. 4.18).
'They shall hunger no more, neither shall they thirst any more; the sun shall not strike them, nor any scorching heat' (Rev. 7.16).

2. *Provision of universal primary education for boys and girls*, and,

3. *Promotion of gender equality especially in education.*
'God created the human in his own image . . . male and female he created them' (Gen. 1.27).
'In Christ there is neither Jew nor Greek, neither slave nor free, neither male nor female, for you are all one in Christ Jesus' (Gal. 3.28).

4. *Reduction by two thirds of the mortality rate for children under five.*
'No more shall there be in it an infant that lives but a few days, or an old man who does not fill out his years' (Isa. 65.20).

5. *Improvement in reproductive health and maternity care, thus reducing the maternal mortality rate*, and,

6. *Combating disease.*
'He will swallow up death for ever, and the LORD God will wipe away tears from all faces' (Isa. 25.8).
'Sorrow and sighing shall flee away' (Isa .35.10).

7. *Ensuring environmental stability by sustainable development and by reversing the loss of natural resources and biodiversity, halving the proportion of people without access to safe drinking water and sanitation.*
'The earth is the LORD's and the fullness thereof' (Ps. 24.1).
'Let everything that breathes praise the LORD' (Ps. 150.6).
'When the poor and needy seek water and there is none . . . I the LORD will answer them . . .' (Isa. 41.17).

8. *Developing a global partnership for development, that includes an open and fair financial system, special consideration for less developed countries, debt relief, provision of affordable medicines and access to new technology especially in information and communication.*

'You shall not steal nor deal falsely nor lie to one another . . . You shall not oppress your neighbour or rob him . . . You shall do no wrong in measurement, in measures of length or weight or quantity' (Lev. 19.11,13, 35).

'If your brother becomes poor and cannot maintain himself with you, you shall maintain him . . .' (Lev. 25.35).

'At the end of every seven years you shall grant a release from debt' (Deut. 15.1).

The environmental and economic crisis shows that the covenant is collapsing; environmental degradation is a sign that the world is not living in accordance with the Creator's law. Repentance, the precondition for atonement, means seeing things differently, working with different models, for which the older religious language has to be recovered and re-established in contemporary discourse. The biblical vision for restoring the world is atonement: self-sacrifice by humanity who recognize that they are the high priests of creation.

Chapter 5

HIGH PRIEST OF CREATION

The first Christians knew that the original Adam was a glorious figure. According to the Qumran texts, some of their contemporaries were people whom 'God has chosen for an everlasting covenant'; they hoped they would regain 'all the glory of Adam', and so learn 'the knowledge of the Most High . . . the wisdom of the sons of heaven'.[1] The everlasting covenant, heavenly knowledge and angelic wisdom must have been aspects of the lost glory of Adam. These people claimed to be the priests in Ezekiel's vision of the new temple, 'the sons of Zadok who had not gone astray' (Ezek. 44.15), and God had revealed to this faithful remnant how others had strayed from the ancient faith: 'Those who hold fast to it are destined to live for ever and all the glory of Adam shall be theirs.'[2] They sang that 'God would cause them to inherit all the glory of Adam and abundance of days.'[3] They knew that Psalm 37.18 – 'The LORD knows the days of the blameless and their heritage will abide for ever' – was a prophecy of their community: 'the penitents of the desert who, saved, shall live for a thousand generations and to whom all the glory of Adam shall belong, as also to their seed for ever.'[4] And they prayed: 'Thou has fashioned A[dam] our [F]ather in the likeness of [Thy] glory . . .'[5] – suggesting that for them, the glory of Adam was the likeness of the glory of the LORD. *Adam was the original high priest, his temple was the creation, and he was the glorious image of the Creator.*

---

1 *Community Rule*, 1QS IV.

2 *Damascus Document* III.

3 *Thanksgiving Hymns*, 1QH IV.15.

4 *Commentary on Psalms*, 4Q171.III.

5 4Q504.8.

Nobody knows for certain who put the scrolls in the Qumran caves: they could have been the writings of a small sect, or they could have been the temple library, hidden away when war with Rome was imminent. What is certain is that some people in the time of Jesus knew more about Adam than the Genesis story as we now read it – the man of dust who brought disaster because his wife persuaded him to eat forbidden fruit. Since it was faithful priests who hoped for the lost glory of Adam, this was priestly tradition, but Adam as a glorious priest is not how the Old Testament is usually read today. Nor does the Old Testament say that Adam was the son of God, but this is how Luke described him (Lk. 3.38). Paul contrasted the first Adam and the last Adam (1 Cor. 15.17), the man of dust and the glorious future figure, which suggests that Christians shared the hope of the Qumran community: 'Just as we have borne the image, *eikōn*, of the man of dust, we shall also bear the image, *eikōn*, of the man of heaven.' (1 Cor. 15.49), wrote Paul, and: 'We are being changed into [the LORD's] likeness, *eikōn*, from one degree of glory to another . . .' (2 Cor. 3.18). If Paul was consistent in his use of language, he said in one place that Christians were being changed into the *eikōn* of the LORD, and in another that they would have the *eikōn* of the man of heaven – exactly what the Qumran text implied: that the glory of the original Adam was the likeness of the glory of the LORD.[6] Paul also knew that the Christians, led by the Spirit of God, were 'sons of God' (Rom. 8.14). Since they were also a high priestly community – being 'in Christ', the great high priest – it seems that the Christians shared the hope of the Qumran texts, that they would inherit all the glory of Adam. John saw all the servants of the LORD in the holy of holies, marked with the Name and standing before the throne (Rev. 22.3–4), meaning they were all high priests. And they had access to the tree of life (Rev. 22.14), that is, they were restored to their original and intended Adamhood in Eden.

The Adam stories, as they were told in the time of Jesus, are a key element in recovering what the first Christians believed about human beings and their role in the creation. The biblical story says that the creation was entrusted to Adam *before he sinned* and lost his glory, and Adam losing his glory was reflected in the degradation of the earth. This is the key to the biblical story: the degradation of the earth is the direct result of the status of human beings; what they are/believe

6 The AV translates *eikōn* consistently as image, but the RSV uses both image and likeness as though they were synonyms. They are not.

themselves to be, determines what the earth becomes. Everything that was intended for Adam, the words usually translated 'be fruitful and multiply, fill the earth and subdue it, and have dominion . . .' (Gen. 1.28) – applied to the original state. When sinful Adams did such things, the result was disaster, but the Christians were restored Adams, with access again to the tree of life (Rev. 2.7). They resumed the task of tilling and keeping the garden (Gen. 2.15) insofar as they released creation from its bondage to decay (Rom. 8.19–21). The restoration of Adam was expected in the time of the Messiah, and all these themes are woven through the early Christian writings, as we shall see. The Eden story begins with Adam – male-and-female – formed from the ground, *'adamah*, which is the feminine form of Adam. The Eden story ends with the soil being cursed because Adam chose the forbidden tree (Gen. 3.17–19). *Whatever Adam did to lose his glorious state also destroyed his relationship with the soil.* When John saw the Kingdom established on earth, he saw that the destroyers of the earth were destroyed (Rev. 11.18). This aspect of the Kingdom has been much neglected, but a key prophecy to describe the work of Jesus shows its importance. Deuteronomy 32.43 was included in a collection of proof texts (Heb. 1.5–14), identified by a single line about the angels worshipping the Firstborn (Heb. 1.6). The full form of the text, however, describes the LORD coming to heal the land - literally to heal the soil, *'adamah* – of his people.[7]

'God said, "Let us make man in our image, after our likeness . . ."' (Gen. 1.26). This is one of the most enigmatic lines in the Bible, and yet also one of the most important. It means that the human has to be like God in caring for the creation. One of Israel's ancient law codes, the Holiness Code (Lev. 19–26), set out a complete pattern for life based on the injunction: 'You shall be holy, for I the LORD your God am holy' (Lev. 19.2). There follow, in addition to the laws familiar as the ten commandments and the rules for worship, laws about leaving some of the harvest for the poor, paying fair wages and paying promptly, caring for fruit trees, having just weights and measures, observing the Sabbath year and the Jubilee; and promising prosperity to those who imitate the holiness of the LORD (Lev. 26.1–13). Jesus, when exhorting his followers to trust God, reminded them that the Creator cared for the lilies of the field and the birds of the air (Mt. 6. 25–33; 10.29). This is how they thought of the Creator; not as a figure in the past who had completed the work and then left it; it was a picture of constant loving care. Adam, as the image of God, was expected to do this too.

7 Deut. 32.43 in the Qumran text, 4Q Deut[q].

Adam was the last to be created, and God set him in the world that was prepared for him. Recent interpretation of the Genesis story has suggested that the Sabbath was the crown of creation rather than Adam,[8] but this was not how the story was read in the time of Jesus. Adam, the image, was the crown of creation, and the earth was a feast prepared for him. Philo wrote: 'Man was the last whom the Father and Maker fashioned . . . partaker of kinship with God himself in mind and reason, the best of gifts. But God did not begrudge him other gifts and made ready for him beforehand all things in the world.' Thus the Creator provided both the means of living – the material world – and also the means of living well – the knowledge of the invisible divine world. The former made him mortal, the latter immortal. Losing sight of the divine world, however, caused problems in the material world. People had all they needed, said Philo, 'if irrational pleasures do not get control of the soul, making their assaults upon it through greediness and lust, nor the desires for glory or wealth or power arrogate to themselves the control of life . . .'[9] This passed into Jewish interpretation: teachers in the second century CE taught:

> God first created [Adam's] food requirements, and only then did he create him . . . "What is man that thou art mindful of him, and the son of man that thou thinkest of him?" (Ps. 8.4). A tower full of good things and no guests – what pleasure has its owner in having filled it?.[10]

The early Christians explained this to the contemporary world. Addressing the Emperor Antoninus Pius, Justin said: 'We have received by tradition . . . that [God] in the beginning did of his goodness, and for Man's sake, create all things out of unformed matter . . .'[11] His older contemporary Rabbi 'Akiba taught: 'Beloved is Man, for he was created in the image of God; still greater was the love in that it was made known to him that he was created in the image of God . . .'[12] The human being, then, was unique, with unique status, privilege and responsibility. This is in stark contrast to more recent estimates of the role of Man: that he is no more than the product of an evolutionary

---

8 Thus J. Moltmann, *God in Creation. An Ecological Doctrine of Creation*, London: SCM, 1985, p. 188.

9 Philo, *Creation*, 77–80.

10 *Genesis Rabbah* VIII.6.

11 Justin, *Apology* I.10, and similar in *Clementine Recognitions* I.28.

12 Mishnah *Aboth* 3.15.

process, that any claim to be special is a 'species specific arrogance' derived from a 'tenacious illusion of special dispensation [which] belies our true status as mammalian weeds'[13]; that 'the human race is just a chemical scum on a moderate sized planet, orbiting a very average star in the outer suburb of one among a hundred million galaxies.'[14] 'Science, it appeared, could change man's entire perspective of himself and his relation to the universe.'[15] The question has now become: has this change been for the good? Why, given the knowledge that is available, has so very little been done in the current situation? Which self-image is more likely to inspire people to care for the creation: the mammalian weed and mere chemical scum, or the image and likeness of the Creator? Is the reduced image of man the cause of the current crisis, the internal deserts of human life being expressed in the external deserts of the world, as Pope Benedict said, 'the emptiness of souls no longer aware of their dignity or the goal of human life'.[16] There is no obvious link between mammalian weeds and chemical scum or the current explorations into the ultimate physical origins of the universe, and, for example, the current cry for human rights and environment justice, whereas the biblical ideal is the ultimate origin of both, and sets them in its vision of the origin and purpose of all creation. It is the ethos that gives rise to the ethics.

The status of 'Adam' has received attention recently in the form of the Anthropic Principle, a name first used by Brandon Carter in 1973, when he noted that 'our location in the universe is necessarily privileged to the extent of being compatible with our existence as observers.'[17] As modern scientific cosmology has developed, the role of the human in the universe has become less important, and human existence just one more coincidence. Simultaneously, however, environmentalists have been warning the world that human behaviour could well lead to the destruction of ourselves and the earth as we know it. There would then be nobody to observe the processes of

13 L. Margulis, *The Symbiotic Planet. A New Look at Evolution*, London: Weidenfeld and Nicolson, 1998, p. 119.

14 Attributed to Stephen Hawking, but no source given, in D. Deutsch, *The Fabric of Reality*, London: Penguin, 1997, pp. 177–8.

15 P. Davies, *God and the New Physics*, London: Penguin, 1983, p. 58.

16 See above, p. 148.

17 B. Carter, 'Large Number Coincidences and the Anthropic Principle in Cosmology' in *Confrontation of Cosmological Theories with Observation* [Copernicus Symposium II, Kraków, 1973], ed. M. S. Langair and Dordrecht: Reidel, 1974, pp. 291–8, p. 291.

cosmology and formulate theories about the ultimate origin of matter.
So much scientific speculation, fascinating though it may be, is of less
use in our current crisis than the traditional vision offered by the Bible.
The 'Weak Anthropic Principle' explains why certain conditions
happen to be right for the existence of life on earth, and why people
are able to observe this. There could be other universes – the multi-
verse – where conditions are very different and so there would be no
human life to observe them. The 'Strong Anthropic Principle' asks a
deeper question: given the universe in which we exist, why are its laws
so finely tuned as to sustain life and especially human life? A. R. Wallace,
who drew such very different conclusions about evolution from those
of Darwin, namely 'that this vast and wonderful universe . . . has ever
required and still requires, the continuous co-ordinated agency of
myriads of such intelligences,'[18] had earlier concluded: 'Such a vast
and complex universe as that which we know exists around us, may
have been absolutely required . . . in order to produce a world that
should be precisely adapted in every detail for the orderly development of life culminating in man.'[19] Creation was a directed process,
and human life was the high point in the process so far.

There is now talk about the 'fine tuning' of the universe such that
life, and human life, can exist, but a certain reluctance to draw any
theological conclusions from these 'anthropic' phenomena which
introduce the idea of purpose – the 'why' of creation, rather then just
the 'how' – possibly because 'the observation of anthropic phenomena
resonates with the core themes of the Christian vision of reality.'[20]
Or, as Paul Davies observed: 'Teleology, or final causation, is taboo in
orthodox science. The concept of a universe destined to bring forth
life and observers is clearly teleological.'[21] There are unmistakable
echoes here of George Orwell's *Nineteen Eighty-four:* some things are
not available for discussion, and *Newspeak* has excluded the words and
concepts from public discourse. Trying to imagine another physical
world is known as counterfactual thinking, and results in such questions as: What if the world was such that we could not live in it? What if
we could not begin to understand the physical world? What if we were
not here to make the observations? But do these questions have any

18 See above p. 35. He was talking about angels, but did not use that word.

19 A. R. Wallace, *Man's Place in the Universe: A Study of the Results of Scientific Research in Relation to the Unity or Plurality of Worlds*, London: George Bell, 1904, pp. 256–7.

20 A. McGrath, *The Open Secret*, Oxford: Blackwell, 2008, p. 243.

21 P. Davies, *The Goldilocks Enigma*, London: Penguin, 2007, p. 293.

point? We can and do live in the world, people have begun to understand some of its wonders, and we are here to make observations. If
things were different there would be different questions, but they are
not, and so

> many would argue that the finely tuned fruitfulness of the world and the
> intelligibility of the world, though both insights that arise from science,
> nevertheless call for some explanation and understanding which, by its very
> nature, is likely to go beyond what science itself can provide.[22]

The original 'anthropic principle' was set out in Genesis, and so we
have to ask: what did (and does) it mean to be the image and likeness
of God? 'God said, "Let us make man in our image, *b'ṣalmenu*, after our
likeness, *kidmutenu*,"'[23] but 'image' and 'likeness' are complementary
terms, not synonyms.

The modern debate about Adam began with a much reprinted
article, originally published in 1967,[24] which claimed that the biblical
picture of Adam was a major factor in the ecological crisis. 'Our
science and technology have grown out of Christian attitudes towards
man's relation to nature which are almost universally held not only
by Christian and neo-Christians, but also by those who fondly regard
themselves as post-Christian.' Technology was not the answer, said
Lynn White, but rather to 'find a new religion or rethink our old
one.' Some of his examples show that he did indeed need to rethink
the old one: 'No item in the physical creation has any purpose but to
serve man's purposes' – presumably he did not know the psalms that
exhort all creation to praise the LORD (e.g. Ps. 150); 'Christianity is
the most anthropocentric religion the world has seen.' '[It] insisted
that it is God's will that man exploit nature for his proper ends' –
presumably he had not heard that 'the earth is the LORD's . . .'
(Ps. 24), and that the image of God meant the image of a caring and
creating God.

Another description of Adam often heard is that he was appointed
the steward of creation. *This has no basis in the Bible*, nor does it appear
in any tradition in the time of Jesus. It does have the merit, however, of

22 McGrath, *The Open Secret*, p. 244.

23 Not the words used in the commandment against idolatry, where graven Image
is *pesel*, and likeness is *t'munah* , Exodus 20.4; Deuteronomy 5.8.

24 Lynn White, 'The Historical Roots of our Ecologic Crisis', *Science* 155.3767
(1967), pp. 1203–7, criticized by J. Barr, 'Man and Nature – the Ecological Controversy
and the Old Testament', *Bulletin of the John Rylands Library* 55.1 (1972), pp. 1–27.

limiting any claim that Adam was created as the lord of creation.

> The replacement of the model of proprietor and possessor with that of steward
> of creation may be useful to exclude the undoubtedly unacceptable view that the
> human being is the lord of creation, or may behave as such a lord. Ecologists
> recognised this and adopted the model of stewardship.[25]

Stewardship implies a business relationship, but the biblical model is
very different. Adam, as we shall see, was the high priest of the creation, with all that that implied in the time of the first Christians. He
was responsible for 'atonement' in the sense of the sacrificial self-giving
that promotes healing, and he was responsible for maintaining the
covenant of creation. In that sense, and in that sense only, was Adam
the lord of the creation and the image of God.

THE IMAGE

'God said, "Let us make man in our image, after our likeness"' (Gen. 1.26).
The verb is plural – 'Let us make' – and so who was involved in the
creation of Adam? Jewish tradition said that 'Let us make' meant that
God took counsel with himself, or that he took counsel with the works
of heaven and earth that were already created, or that he took counsel
with the angels. Some taught that the angels could not agree about the
wisdom of creating Adam, but God said the Adam had already been
created.[26] The letters *n'ṣh* can be read as 'Let us make' or 'He is made',
and so it is possible to read the line as 'God said "Adam is made in our
image, after our likeness."'[27] The plural 'Let us make' was seen by some
Jews as 'an excuse for heretics',[28] meaning that it was significant for
Christians, since it showed more than one involved in the creation of
Adam. Some said that when the Hebrew Scriptures were translated
into Greek, thirteen changes were made in passages open to such
misunderstanding, and one of these was Genesis 1.26, which became:
'Let me make man in an image, in a likeness . . .'[29] Jerome knew that

---

25 John Zizioulas, 'Proprietors or Priests of Creation?' www.rsesymposia.org.

26 All these interpretations are in *Genesis Rabbah* VIII.3–9; the angel helpers are
also in Philo, *Creation* 75.

27 'He is made', the niph'al participle, as in Neh. 5.18 'was made'.

28 *Genesis Rabbah* III.8.

29 Jerusalem Talmud *Megillah* 71a. The King of Egypt was Ptolemy II (308–246 BCE)
for whom, according to the tradition, the first Greek translation of the Torah was made.

'certain mystical elements and prophecies of the Messiah had been sup-
pressed, lest they give the king of Egypt the impression that the Jews
worshipped a second God.'[30] None of this survives in any Greek version,
but there must have been great sensitivity about the plural forms in
Genesis 1.26 and the creation of Adam.

For the Christians, 'Let us make' sometimes indicated the Father
and the Son. Justin, in the mid-second century, was emphatic in his
debate with Trypho the Jew that when God said 'Let us make . . .' God
was not speaking to himself nor was he addressing the elements of
creation already in existence, the interpretations found in the *Genesis
Rabbah*: he was speaking to a being other than himself.[31] Barnabas, in
the first generation, had written of Jesus: 'He is LORD of all the earth,
to whom at the foundation of the world God had addressed these
words, "Let us make man, in our own image and likeness."'[32] God the
Father was speaking to God the Son. Others said it was God speaking
to Wisdom. Thus *2 Enoch*, echoing Proverbs 8.22–31, had: 'On the
sixth day I commanded my Wisdom to create man . . . And on the
earth I assigned him to be a second angel, honoured and great and
glorious. I assigned him to be a king and to reign on earth and to have
my Wisdom.'[33] Although the date of *2 Enoch* is uncertain, it does
include material known in earlier texts, such as the explanation that
Adam's name represented the four points of the compass. This is also
found in the Sibylline oracles of the second century BCE,[34] and similar
ideas are found in the early Christian *Apostolic Constitutions*:

> Having given order by your Wisdom you created, saying: "Let us make man
> according to our image and likeness", having declared him a cosmos of the
> cosmos, having formed for him the body out of four elements, and having pre-
> pared for him the soul out of non-being . . .[35]

30 Jerome, Preface to *Hebrew Questions on Genesis,* text and translation
C. T. R. Hayward, *Jerome's Hebrew Questions on Genesis*, Oxford: Oxford University Press,
1995.

31 Justin, *Trypho* 62.

32 *Letter of Barnabas* 5.

33 *2 Enoch* 30.8, 11–12.

34 See below, p. 224.

35 *Apostolic Constitutions* 7.34.6. Cosmos can mean both ornament and ordered
universe, so here perhaps Adam is the ornament of creation.

One generation later, Theophilus of Antioch said that the image was double: 'To no one else but his own Word and Wisdom did he say 'Let us make . . .'[36] Adam, then, was the image of the Word and of the Wisdom, just as the original image had been male and female. Philo knew this too. First, he said that the human was made as the image, *eikōn*, not of the Father, but of the 'second God, who is his Logos',[37] and this image was found in the human mind. He also said that the second place was occupied by Wisdom, but she was described as feminine because she was subordinate to the Father.[38] Thus Word and Wisdom were two ways of describing the 'second God', as is clear throughout Philo's work: Wisdom was the image of God's goodness, Logos was the image of God; Wisdom was the firstborn, Logos was the firstborn; Wisdom penetrated all things, Logos was the bond of creation; Wisdom was given Israel for her inheritance, Logos was depicted as Israel's guardian angel.[39] When Philo described the 'image of the Word', and other writers described Adam's robe of Wisdom, they were saying the same thing. Paul also knew this 'double' image: 'Christ the Power of God and the Wisdom of God' (1 Cor. 1.24), the position implicit in Genesis, where the image is male and female.

Image, *ṣelem* (in Greek *eikōn*) was used elsewhere of forbidden religious objects: 'your images which you made for yourselves' (Amos 5.26); 'their abominable images' (Ezek. 7.20); images in the temple of Baal (2 Kgs 11.18). These images were offered food and often dressed in golden, jewelled garments, which may explain why the high priest wore such elaborate vestments: he functioned as the image of the LORD.

> In the priestly tabernacle, it is Aaron who bears God's image . . . and it is Aaron who plays God's part in the drama of creation . . . When, in Genesis 1.26, man is made in God's *image* and likeness . . . the priestly author of Genesis seems to be saying that only humanity is truly God's idol.[40]

'Idol' is perhaps not the best word to choose, but Adam was the original image, and this was later represented by the sons of Aaron. The

---

36 Theophilus, *To Autolycus*, II.18.

37 Philo, *Questions on Genesis* II.62.

38 Philo, *Flight*, 51.

39 For detail, see my book *The Great Angel. A Study of Israel's Second God*, London: SPCK, 1992, pp. 130–2.

40 C. H. T. Fletcher-Louis, *All the Glory of Adam. Liturgical Anthropology in the Dead Sea Scrolls*, Leiden: Brill, 2002, p. 71.

final act in Genesis 1 was the creation of Adam, and the final act in Exodus 40 was the purification of Moses, Aaron and the sons of Aaron, in other words, preparing the high priests for their service in the tabernacle. Since assembling the tabernacle corresponded to the days of creation, as we have seen, the creation of Adam corresponded to the installation of the high priest. Adam – the male-and-female – was the original high priest, the image of the LORD set on earth to preserve it. The LORD set Adam in Eden 'to till it and keep it' (Gen. 2.15), both these being 'temple' words: till, *'abad,* also means to serve a liturgy, and keep*, šamar,* also means to preserve the law or tradition. Adam the high priest was the Servant of the LORD, whose service in the temple was to preserve the creation, as Simeon the high priest taught: 'By three things is the world sustained: by the Law, by the temple service and by deeds of loving kindness.'[41]

Adam the image wore as his vestment the garment of God's glory, but he lost it through sin. In the time of Jesus, the master copy of the sacred texts kept in the temple said that God originally made for Adam and Eve 'garments of light', rather than garments of skin (Gen. 3.21).[42] In Hebrew, light is *'or* and skin is *'or,* making the two words similar both in appearance and in sound. Isaiah had seen the garment of God's glory filling the temple which represented the creation, and he heard the heavenly voices proclaiming that the whole world was full of his glory (Isa. 6.1–3). Only when Adam lost the garment did the earth become a place of dust, thorns and thistles. All the Targums mention the garments of light: *Neofiti,* for example, says the human pair had 'garments of glory for the skin of their flesh'. The tradition was long remembered by both Jews and Christians, and there are many examples: 'In Rabbi Meir's Torah it was found written "Garments of light"; this refers to Adam's garments'[43]; and '[Adam] wept and said, "Why have you done this to me, that I have been estranged from my glory with which I was clothed."'[44] In the Syriac speaking Church, Ephrem taught that 'God clothed Adam in glory,' and a collection of legendary material said that 'Adam and Eve were in Paradise, clothed in glory and shining with praise for three hours . . .'[45] A Jewish text adopted by

41 Mishnah *Aboth* 1.2.

42 See J. P. Siegel, *The Severus Scroll,* Missoula: SBL, 1974.

43 *Genesis Rabbah* XX.12.

44 *Apocalypse of Moses* 20.2.

45 Ephrem, *Commentary on Genesis* 2; *The Book of the Cave of Treasures,* I.

Christians knew that 'Through this tree – the knowledge of good and evil – Adam was condemned and stripped of the glory of God.'[46]

Adam, *while he was still wearing the robe of glory and everything it represented*, was told 'be fruitful and multiply, and fill the earth' – the usual translation – which should also be read in the temple context: Adam was to fill the earth with glory. Since the Hebrew words for 'be fruitful', *parah*, and 'be beautiful/glorified', *pa'ar*, are similar,[47] and 'multiply', *rabah*, can also mean 'be great', the wordplay that characterizes temple teaching showed the original Adam created to be beautiful and great, and to fill the earth with glory. 'Adam's wisdom makes his face shine,' wrote one of the wise teachers (Eccl. 8.1, translating literally), and so Adam was described in the time of Jesus as very tall and beautiful, the 'other' meaning of the description in Genesis. A Jewish text written just after the destruction of the temple in 70 CE recounted Abraham's vision of the history of his people. It began with Eden, where Abraham saw 'a man very great in height, and terrible in breadth, incomparable in aspect, entwined with a woman who was also equal to the man in aspect and size . . .'. This was remembered by Jewish teachers well into the Christian era. Adam filled the world.[48] A Jewish oracle text from the late second temple period described his beauty: Adam was a 'youthful man, beautiful, wonderful'.[49] In the time of the Messiah, said a rabbi in the late third century CE, everything Adam had lost and had caused the earth to lose would be restored: his lustre, his life, his height, the fruit of the earth, the fruit of the trees and the bright light of the heavenly luminaries.[50]

The vestment of any high priest was described as a garment of glory. When Enoch was vested, he stood before the heavenly throne and was given garments of God's glory,[51] and this too was long remembered. Centuries later, it was said that Aaron's vestments were a copy of the garments of God,[52] and that the garments of the high priest had been

46 *3 Baruch* (Greek text) 4.16.

47 With a derived word *p'er* meaning the turban of the high priest which was his glory.

48 *Apocalypse of Abraham* 23.5; *Genesis Rabbah* VIII.1.

49 *Sibylline Oracles* 1.23–4. He was a youth because some people read Gen. 2.7 with different vowels: the LORD formed Adam as *'oper*, a young man, rather than *'apar*, dust,. *Genesis Rabbah* XIV.7.

50 Rabbi Samuel b. Nahman, *Genesis Rabbah* XII.6; also Philo, *Creation* 145.

51 *2 Enoch* 22.6–10.

52 *Exodus Rabbah* XXXVIII.8.

cut from the fabric of the divine mystery.[53] There are hints of this in the Old Testament: Moses had to make garments for Aaron and his sons so that they could serve as priests, 'holy garments . . . for glory and for beauty' (Exod. 28 2). Since they wore the Name on their foreheads, the glorious garment and the Name indicated that they were the presence of the LORD (Exod. 28.36–8). Thus the presence of the priests was the glory: 'Moses and Aaron went into the tent of meeting; and when they came out they blessed the people, and the glory of the LORD appeared to all the people' (Lev. 9.23). Similarly, the high priest Simon made the temple court glorious with his presence when he put on the garment of glory and the perfection of beauty, presumably the turban;[54] and a Jewish visitor to Jerusalem said the vested high priest was like someone from another world.[55] A Greek writing early in the third century BCE described the high priest as an angel who brought God's commandments to his people. The Jews, he said, used to fall down before him in worship.[56] When Alexander the Great went to Jerusalem, he was met by a crowd of priests in white linen, and at their head the high priest wearing his glorious vestment and turban on which was the golden Name. Alexander paid homage to this figure whom he had seen in a dream.[57]

The glorious vestment symbolized Wisdom, and so losing the garment meant losing Wisdom, or, as the Genesis story says, rejecting the tree of life in favour of the forbidden tree. Those who wore the garment of glory were children of Wisdom, as we shall see. Philo described the Logos as 'the Son of Wisdom his Mother, through whom (fem.) the universe came into being',[58] and an early Christian Wisdom text found in Egypt had Wisdom speaking to her children:

> I am giving you a high-priestly garment woven from every [kind of] wisdom . . . Do not become desirous of gold and silver, which are profitless, clothe yourself with wisdom like a robe, put knowledge upon you like a crown, and be seated upon a throne of perception . . . Return to your divine nature . . . return to your first father, God, and Wisdom your mother, from whom you came into being.

---

53 Zohar *Exodus* 229b.

54 Ben Sira 50.11, were *doxa* translates *kabod*, glory, and *kauchēma*, translates *tiperet*, beauty.

55 *Letter of Aristeas* 99. See also Ben Sira 45.6–13.

56 Hecataeus of Abdera quoted in Diodorus Siculus XL.3.5–6.

57 Josephus, *Antiquities* XI.331.

58 *Philo, Flight*, 109.

From the very first, in order that you might fight against all your enemies, the powers of the Adversary . . . keep the holy commandments of Jesus Christ, and you will reign over every place on earth and will be honoured by the angels and archangels . . .[59]

The vestment of wisdom symbolized the original human nature that was intended to rule the earth and be honoured by the angels. Wisdom as the high priest's vestments was proverbial by the time of Jesus: Ben Sira had advised his son to accept the restriction that Wisdom's discipline imposed: 'There is a golden ornament upon her, and her bonds are a blue cord. You will wear her as a garment of glory and put her on as a crown of gladness' (Ben Sira 6.30–31, my translation), the golden ornament and blue cord being the golden seal of the Name worn by the high priest on his crown (Exod. 28.36–7).

The high priest's vestment was a complex symbol remembered in later Christian tradition as a symbol of incarnation.[60] It represented the material world insofar as it was woven from gold – the divine – and the four colours that represented matter: red for fire, white for earth, blue for air and purple for water. The design and colours represented different parts of the creation: 'On [Aaron's] long robe the whole world was depicted' (Wis. 18.24).[61] The high priest thus 'was' the whole creation offering worship, and in this respect he differed from Gentile priests, who offered prayers and sacrifices only for people: 'The high priest of the Jews makes prayers and gives thanks not only on behalf of the whole human race, but also for the parts of nature: earth, water, air, fire.'[62] The vestment was made from the same fabric as the veil showing that it veiled the glory of God from human eyes (Exod. 26.31; 28.5–6),[63] and therefore also symbolized the LORD in the creation. According to the Gospel of James,[64] when Mary was pregnant with her Child, she was weaving a new veil for the temple; the early Christians were well aware of this symbolism. The veil both concealed and revealed the glory, and was a sign of the LORD incarnate.

59 *The Teaching of Silvanus*, C G VII.4.89, 91. Parts of this text were later incorporated into the teaching attributed to St Anthony.

60 Symeon of Thessalonike, died 1429, taught that the vestment signified incarnation, *On Prayer*, 41:

61 For more details, Philo, *Special Laws* I.84–7.

62 Philo, *Special Laws* 1.96.

63 Josephus, *Antiquities* III.184 explains the colours of the veil. See also p. 64.

64 *Gospel of James* 11.

The logic of the symbolism would suggest that the coloured outer vestment represented the creation and incarnation, and that the linen garments worn in the holy of holies were the garments of glory (Lev. 16.3–4). Philo said linen symbolized the life of the holy of holies: 'Fine linen is not, like wool, the product of creatures subject to death'; and he distinguished these garments from the elaborate outer vestment which was the ' likeness and copy of the universe.'[65] Angels wore white linen (Ezek. 9.2; Dan. 10.5; Mt. 28.2; Rev. 15.6), as did the transfigured Jesus (Lk. 9.29). The Peshitta[66] says the angel who appeared to Daniel wore a robe of glory; the original Hebrew just says he wore linen (Dan. 10.5; 12.7). Enoch described the archangels as men in white garments,[67] and when he received his garments of glory, he said he looked just like an angel, presumably dressed in white.[68] That is how John saw the redeemed in heaven (Rev. 7.9,13). There is, however, insufficient evidence for certainty.

The Christians knew that they had received this robe of glory. Early hymns describe the Christian experience at baptism using imagery that originally described the Adam high priest: Wisdom, the garment of God's glory that was lost, contrasted with the earthly garment of folly.

> I rejected the folly cast upon the earth
> and stripped it off and cast it from me.
> And the LORD renewed me with his garment
> and possessed me by his light
> And from above he gave me immortal rest . . .
> And he took me to his Paradise . . .[69]
> I was covered with the covering of thy Spirit
> and I removed from me my garments of skin.[70]

Most enigmatic is a passage where 'the perfect Virgin', said to be the Church but more likely Wisdom, assures her children:

> They who have put me on shall not be falsely accused
> But they shall possess incorruption in the new world.[71]

65 Philo, *Special Laws* I.84.

66 The most important Syriac translation of the Bible, probably from the early second century CE.

67 *1 Enoch* 87.2; 90.21–2.

68 *2 Enoch* 22, 8,10.

69 *Odes of Solomon* 11.10–12, 16. Translation in J. H. Charlesworth, *The Odes of Solomon*, Oxford: Clarendon Press, 1973.

70 *Odes* 25.8.

71 *Odes* 33.12.

An early Christian text found at Nag Hammadi observes: 'In this world, those who put on garments are better than the garments. In the Kingdom of heaven, the garments are better than those who have put them on.'[72] The Christians were confident that they would wear, or were already wearing, the glorious robe of Adam, the image.

THE LIKENESS

The oldest translation of Genesis used in Palestine, and probably known in the time of Jesus, avoided the word 'image', presumably because of its pagan associations. Instead, it used 'likeness': 'And the LORD said: "Let us create man in our likeness, similar to ourselves." And the Memra of the LORD created him in his own likeness, in a likeness from before the LORD he created him.'[73] The later Palestinian rendering also avoided the 'image of God', implying that Adam was the likeness of the angels who were the co-creators: 'And God said to the angels who minister before him . . . "Let us make man as our image, as our likeness."'[74] Symmachus, who made a new Greek translation in the late second century CE, chose: 'God created man in different/excellent image, *diaphoros*, . . . He created him upright.' The original cultural context of the Genesis story – the aftermath of the exile and the experience of Babylonian idolatry – probably did mean that Adam as the image was presented as the only legitimate representation of the LORD. Jesus' teaching that the LORD was worshipped by offering food or garments to anyone in need – 'as you did it to one of the least of these my brethren, you did it to me' (Mt. 25.40) – is an echo of the older custom of feeding and clothing the pagan statues. Paul argued that worshipping a false image led to an impure lifestyle: 'Claiming to be wise, they became fools, and exchanged the glory of the immortal God for images resembling mortal man or birds or animals or reptiles. Therefore God gave them up in the lusts of their hearts to impurity . . .' (Rom. 1.22–4).

Adam was the image of the 'likeness', *d'mut*, (in Greek *homoiōsis*), a word also used by Ezekiel to describe Adam, but the English translations do not make this clear. In his vision, the prophet saw a figure

72 *Gospel of Philip*, CG II.3.57.

73 Targum *Neofiti* Gen.1.26–7.

74 Targum *PseudoJonathan* Gen. 1.26.

seated on a sapphire throne, 'the likeness, *d^emut,* as the appearance of Adam' (Ezek. 1.26b, my translation), which was 'the appearance of the likeness, *d^emut,* of the glory of the LORD' (Ezek. 1.28b). Ezekiel's consistent use of the two words *d^emut* and *mar'eh,* likeness and appearance, shows that 'appearance' was what Ezekiel saw in his vision, and 'likeness' was the heavenly reality it represented.[75] The 'likeness as the appearance of Adam' meant the heavenly reality visible as Adam, and 'the appearance of the likeness of the glory of the LORD' meant that this was how the reality of the LORD's glory was manifested. For Ezekiel, then, the glory of the LORD showed itself as the glory of the original Adam, enthroned.

In Genesis Adam was created 'in our image, after our likeness' – the usual translation – but Ezekiel's words may indicate more about that parallelism. Adam was '*as* our image', this being another meaning for the Hebrew *b^e,* as in: 'I appeared to them *as* El Shaddai (Exod. 6.3) and Adam was 'the equivalent of our likeness' (translating Gen. 1.26 literally).[76] When Isaiah scorned those who made idols, he used the verbal form of 'likeness': 'To whom then will you *liken* God, or to what *likeness* compare him?' (Isa. 40.18, also v.25). The craftsman made an idol, but it did not move. Another passage scorning idols asked: 'To whom will you *liken* me . . . and compare me that we may be *alike?*' (Isa. 46.5). These are examples of the exilic polemic against idols that underlies the Genesis description of Adam. Translating *d^emut* by 'likeness', though, obscures an important element in its meaning, since *d^emut* and its related verb imply a thought or a concept preceding an action: 'As I have *planned,* so shall it be' (Isa. 14.24). The *d^emut* was the original, the invisible divine reality represented by Adam as its 'image'. Isaiah's polemic against idols was asking what statue could represent the invisible divine reality. A statue that could not even move?

Sin, however, prevented man from seeing the *d^emut* and all that it represented. Sin prevented Adam seeing what he was created to be: Adam could not know the true nature of the human being, the full potential. 'Because of sin, it was not given for man to know the *d^emut* on high; were it not for this sin, all the keys would be given to him, and he would know how the heavens and the earth were created . . .'[77] Knowing and being the 'likeness' resulted in a certain knowledge.

---

75 See my book *The Great High Priest,* London: T&T Clark, 2003, pp. 178–84.

76 In Gen. 5.1, Adam was created 'as the *likeness* of God'.

77 *Abot de Rabbi Nathan* A 39, see above p. 87.

Satan had promised that when they ate the forbidden fruit their eyes would be opened, and they would see as God sees. That was the great deception, making the fruit of the forbidden tree seem exactly like the fruit of the tree of life. As we shall see, it was eating from the tree of life that opened human eyes, that is, gave spiritual vision, and this is why, when they had taken the forbidden fruit, they knew they were naked; they had lost the garment of Wisdom.

We are back in the world of the 'engraved things' described in the Qumran texts.[78] There was a distinction between the *d^{e}mut*, better translated as 'the form', and various other engraved things. The process of creation seems to be the form, *d^{e}mut*, then the visionary appearance, *mar'eh*, then the material creation, *şelem*.[79] Ezekiel identified the invisible form that he saw as the visionary appearance, but it was not a material object. Adam, however, was the form of God and its material state, its *şelem*. The intermediate state, *mar'eh*, is not mentioned in Genesis, but it was probably represented in the Targums by the Memra, often translated 'word', and represented in Greek by Logos. Philo, however, knew the Logos as the aspect of God that was *seen*, and so Logos=Word is not the best translation.[80] When he explained Genesis 9.6, 'God made man in his own image,' he said, as we have seen: 'Nothing mortal can be made in the likeness (the verb is from *eikōn*) of the Most High One and Father of the Universe, but only in that of the second God who is his Logos,' a passage important for Christians since it was quoted by Eusebius.[81] Philo also tried to explain this in terms of geometry: 1 was a point, 2 was a line, 3 was a surface, and 4 was a solid object. Thus, he said, the number 4 brought us from the realm of the invisible into 'the conception of a body of three dimensions, which by its nature first comes within the range of our senses.'[82]

The three stages of creation – the invisible, then the vision and then the material – were described as stages of 'sonship': the Father, whom no man has ever seen (Jn 1.18); the Son, who has made him known (Jn 1.18); and finally the human manifestation of the Son, originally Jesus, but then the status of all Christians:

---

78 See above, p. 84.

79 See Barker, *The Great High Priest.* pp. 182–3.

80 See my book *Temple Themes in Christian Worship*, London: T&T Clark, 2007, pp. 149–54.

81 Philo, *Questions on Genesis* II.62; Greek text extant in Eusebius, *Preparation of the Gospel* VII.13.

82 Philo, *Creation* 49.

All who are led by the Spirit of God are sons of God . . . Those whom [God] foreknew he also predestined to be conformed to the image, *eikōn*, of his Son, in order that he might be the first-born among many brethren. (Rom. 8.11,29)

The original Adam was created as the image of the invisible *dᵉmut*, and Jesus, the second Adam, was 'the *image* of the invisible God' (Col. 1.15), the Greek *eikōn* corresponding to the Hebrew *ṣelem* in Genesis. The words *dᵉmut*, and *ṣelem* were carefully distinguished in Genesis. The *dᵉmut* was the pattern for Adam (Gen. 1.26; 5.1), but the three dimensional *ṣelem* was created as male and female, both equally expressions of the divine *dᵉmut*. The male and female nature of the physical image is important: it is the basis for Jesus' teaching that marriage is a monogamous life long union of male and female (Mt. 19.3–4; Mk 10.6–9). It was also the rule of the Qumran Community: marrying a second wife while the first was still alive was contrary to the Law, 'the principle of creation is "Male and female he created them."'[83]

The broken prayer text from Qumran, quoted at the beginning of this chapter, says more about the glorious Adam as the likeness.

Thou hast fashioned A[dam] our [f]ather in the likeness, *dᵉmut*, of [thy] glory; Thou didst breathe [a breath of life] into his nostrils and, with understanding, knowledge . . . Thou didst make [him] to rule [over the gar]den of Eden which thou didst plant . . . and to walk in the land of glory . . . he guarded . . .[84]

Adam was the likeness, *dᵉmut*, of the glory, endowed with understanding and knowledge as the ruler [from the verb *mašal*], walking in the glorious Garden of Eden, and guarding something. This is very similar to Ezekiel's account of the glorious guardian cherub who was expelled from Eden. In its current form, the text describes the ruler of Tyre, *ṣwr*, first as a prince and then as a king (Ezek. 28.2, 12), but Tyre is another interesting word. In its present position in Ezekiel's oracles against foreign nations, the passage obviously refers to the city of Tyre, and is followed by an oracle against Sidon. The Hebrew letters *ṣwr*, however, also mean one of the 'forms/engravings' of the invisible creation, as can be seen in the Qumran *Songs of the Sabbath Sacrifice*, where the words likeness, *dᵉmut*, and 'engraving', *ṣwr*, are distinguished, but both

83 *Damascus Document* IV.
84 *The Words of the Heavenly Lights*, 4Q 504.8.

describe the *'elohim* of the holy of holies. In mediaeval Jewish texts, *ṣwr* meant an angel form.[85]

It is likely that the glorious guardian cherub was originally a heavenly 'engraving' of a ruler. The Greek translation of this text, probably made in the mid second century BCE, shows that the cherub was the high priest. Its twelve jewels are exactly those the high priest, listed in the same order (Lxx Ezek. 28.13; Exod. 28.17–20). This is an oracle about a glorious cherub high priest being driven from Eden. The text is full of problems: there is a mixture of masculine and feminine forms to describe the figure, and several words are ambiguous; but it is clear that the figure had walked in Eden, the garden of God, dressed as a high priest. This male-and-female high priest in Eden, whatever the current context in the Old Testament, was how Ezekiel knew Adam. He described a guardian cherub[86] who walked among the stones of fire in the holy mountain garden of God, as the Qumran text says of Adam.

The Qumran Adam had understanding, *biynah*, and knowledge, *da'at*. Contemporary with the Qumran text was Philo's explanation of the word cherub; it meant, he said, recognition, *epignōsis*, as in recognizing and acknowledging God (Prov. 2.5; Rom. 1.28); and *epistēmē pollē*, full knowledge. There is nothing in the form of the Hebrew word to suggest this meaning, and so Philo probably had Ezekiel's cherub in mind. Here there is a complex pattern of wordplay. Ezekiel's mysterious cherub had been created as the *seal* of proportion/pattern,[87] *filled* with wisdom and perfected in beauty (Ezek. 28.12). It was driven from Eden because it corrupted its great wisdom and splendour through pride, greed and violence. 'Your greatness in trading *filled* your midst with violence and you sinned, and I profaned/loosened you from the mountain of God and caused you to perish, guardian cherub, from the midst of the stones of fire' (Ezek. 28.16 translating the opaque Hebrew very literally). This is fallen Adam: his greatness – but in trade; his filling [the earth] – but with violence; and then being destroyed, *'bd*, instead of being the servant, *'bd*. The cherub's heart became proud/ exalted through its beauty, its wisdom was corrupted for the sake of its splendour/shining beams of light. Adam again: the beautiful, exalted

85 See M. Fishbane, 'The Measures of God's Glory in the Ancient Midrash', in *Messiah and Christos. Studies . . . presented to David Flussner*, ed. I Gruenwald, S. Shaked and G. G. Stroumsa, Tübingen: Möhr, 1992, pp. 53–74, p. 65.

86 Ezek. 28.14 is better read: 'You, anointed cherub, I appointed as the guardian . . .'

87 Proportion is *toknit*, pattern is *tabnit*, which look very similar in Hebrew.

figure, the wisdom, the shining light, and then the corruption. The punishment hints at another story of Adam, not in the Old Testament, but known in the time of Jesus. Adam was presented to the angels as their ruler, but Satan refused to worship him and so was thrown from heaven. He vowed revenge – and the familiar story of the fall was the result.[88] Ezekiel's cherub too was thrown to the earth, in the presence of the kings, a word that is very similar to angels, so that they could gloat. The cherub was turned into ash, *'eper*, whereas Adam had been formed from dust, *'apar* (Ezek. 28. 17–18).

Ezekiel saw the cherub 'seal' profaned/loosened as it was thrown down. The double meaning of the verb shows an important aspect of holiness: just as sin was anything that destroyed the covenant bonds, so too, whoever did not seal the bonds was no longer holy. The cherub had abused its wisdom and was cut loose. Here there is a whole web of words linking wisdom and the stability of creation: the high priest's garments, as we have seen, were proverbially likened to the yoke, fetters and bonds of Wisdom (Ben Sira 6.23–31), and Psalm 2 depicted the LORD's Anointed facing rebel powers who wanted to break their bonds, *moser*, (Ps. 2.3). The discipline, *musar*, of Wisdom was described in the same way, but the word has been classified differently. The consonants for both words are, however, identical: *mwsr*, and they are part of a complex wordplay. The guardian cherub had been full of wisdom and was the seal of the covenant. Adam was given understanding and knowledge, according to the Qumran text, and it seems he had the same role as the cherub. When he sinned, he lost the garment of glory that was described as his righteousness,[89] in other words, he lost his power to uphold the 'righteous' state of the covenant.

The Book of Proverbs begins with a description of the different aspects of wisdom, showing how these words relate to each other (Prov. 1.2–3). They are 'proverbs', an important word related to the word for 'rule',[90] and they are given so that people may know wisdom and discipline/bond *mwsr*, may discern the words of discernment, *biynah*, and receive the discipline, *mwsr*, of insight: righteousness, *ṣedek*, and justice, *mišpat*, and straight ways [the word is the opposite of *'awon*, distortion, iniquity]. It is almost impossible to translate these words, but they are all integral to upholding the creation covenant. Wisdom was imagined as bonds and discernment that produced the covenant

88 See below, p. 216–218.

89 *Ap. Moses* 20.1.

90 Proverb, *mašal*, ruler *mošel*.

virtues of justice, righteousness and harmony. Bond/discipline is of particular interest. Jeremiah spoke of his people 'breaking out of bonds', because they had deserted the LORD (Jer. 2.20; 5.5). When Ezekiel gave the LORD's promise of restoration he said: 'I will bring you into the bond/discipline, *mswrt*, of the covenant' (Ezek. 20.37, translating literally). The Servant of the LORD, who was given insight [Isa. 52.13: RSV 'shall prosper'] became the seal of the covenant by his self-giving. 'The discipline/bond of our peace/wholeness was his responsibility, and by his joining us together we are healed' is the literal, and more likely, translation of Isaiah 53.5b, usually given as: 'Upon him was the chastisement that made us whole, and with his stripes we are healed.' And so, as we have seen, by his righteousness, the Servant made many righteous (Isa. 53.11).

Adam's robe of glory represented righteousness, the wisdom to uphold the creation covenant. Thus clad, the image was commanded 'to be fruitful and multiply, and fill the earth and subdue it; and have dominion' over other living creatures' (Gen. 1.28). These words have caused many problems, and read out of context have seriously misrepresented what people believed in the time of Jesus. The words should be read in the light of Adam's status: as the image of the Creator, robed in glory and righteousness, what might those words have meant? We have seen that 'Be fruitful and multiply and fill the earth' were given additional meanings in the time of Jesus: Adam was beautiful and tall and his glory filled the earth. So too with 'subdue' the earth and 'have dominion' over other living creatures. 'Subdue', *kabaš*, usually means to enslave or subdue (e.g. Num. 32.22; Jer. 34.11), but Micah 7.18–9 suggests another context too: atonement, although that word does not appear. 'Who is a God like you, carrying i.e. forgiving, iniquity? . . . He does not retain his anger for ever, because he delights in steadfast love, *hesed*. He will again have compassion on us and will *kabaš*, our iniquities' (my translation). The atonement process was one of renewing the damaged bonds of the covenant, and so 'binding up' our iniquities, in the sense of restoring the creation, seems to be the meaning here, in a context of forgiveness, *hesed* and compassion. This was one aspect of the work of the Servant – 'the bond of our peace was his responsibility, and by his joining us together we are healed', and is part of what *kabaš* meant for the original Adam, in his role as the 'seal' of the covenant. The other aspect was 'binding' the rebel powers that threatened the creation, the role of the king in Psalm 2 and of the LORD when he sealed the powers with his Name.[91]

'Have dominion' did not imply violence, as is often suggested. Adam was to have dominion, *radah*, the word used to describe Solomon's reign: he ruled, he had dominion, *radah*, and there was peace all around (1 Kgs 4.21,24). Adam's dominion over the animals did not extend to killing them for food; Adam was only given plants and trees for food (Gen. 1.29). In the Dead Sea Scrolls,[92] there was a different verb: Adam ruled, *mašal*, the word used in Psalm 8.6: 'Thou hast given him dominion . . .' Now *mašal* has a web of associations: it meant 'rule' in the sense of determining how things shall be, and it implies maintaining the correspondence of heaven and earth. Isaiah put *d^emut* and *mašal* together: 'To whom will you *liken* me [the verbal form of *d^emut*] and make me equal, to whom will you compare, *mašal*, me that we may be *alike* [the verbal form of *d^emut*]? (Isa. 46.5). The shepherd ruler, *mošel*, would come forth from eternity, that is, from the holy of holies (Mic. 5.2). The faithful servant prayed that sins would not 'rule' him (Ps. 19.13), and it was a great punishment to have no 'ruler' and be reduced to the state of a 'crawling thing' (Hab. 1.14). Philo, explaining the significance of Adam being created after the other creatures, wrote:

> [He was created last] so that suddenly appearing to the other animals he might produce consternation in them; for they were sure, as soon as they saw him, to be amazed and do homage to him as to a born ruler or master . . . For all things mortal in the three elements of land and water and air did he make subject to men, but exempted the heavenly beings as having obtained a portion more divine.[93]

He went on to explain that man was created 'to drive and steer the things on earth', to care for animals and plants 'like a governor subordinate to the chief and great King'.[94] A proverb or parable was the same word, *mašal*, and it imparted wisdom, which Solomon famously derived from observing the creation:

> He uttered three thousand proverbs; and his songs were a thousand and five. He spoke of trees, from the cedar that is in Lebanon to the hyssop that grows out of

91 See above, pp. 120–21.

92 In 1QS III.17 and 4Q 504.8 the word is clear: 'you made him rule'; but elsewhere for example, 4Q381, the word might refer to the heavenly lights 'ruling' as in Gen. 1.16–8.

93 Philo, *Creation*, 83–4.

94 Philo, *Creation*, 88.

the wall; he spoke also of beasts and of birds, and of reptiles and of fish. And men
came from all peoples to hear the wisdom of Solomon. (1 Kgs 4.32–4)

The wise ruler learned from the creation, recognized the patterns and
upheld them.

Thus the two commands to Adam – *kabaš*, 'subdue' and *radah*, 'have
dominion' – in their original context agree with Philo's observation
that the human was created as the image of the Logos, and was thus
able to discern the Logos in the creation. *The Logos was the seal of the
bonds.* It was far more than just the human capacity to reason, as is
often said: '[There is a] long standing view that the *imago Dei*
designates the human capacity to reason – or, more accurately, to
conform mentally to the patterns established by the divine Logos
within creation – and hence to discern God albeit partially and
imperfectly.'[95] The image had the capacity to maintain the covenant in
accordance with the divine pattern, not simply to observe it. Or, as
John Zizioulas said of later developments in the Church Fathers:

> *Logos* or rationality had a particular meaning at that time, and it had mainly to
> do with the capacity of the human being to collect what is diversified and even
> fragmented in this world and make a beautiful and harmonious world (*cosmos*)
> out of that. Rationality was not, as it came to be understood later, simply a capac-
> ity to reason with one's mind. Instead, as the ancient Greeks thought of *logos*, it
> is man's capacity to achieve the unity of the world and to make a *cosmos* out of it.
> Man has the capacity to unite the world.[96]

The biblical equivalent would be Wisdom, who joins all things together
(Prov. 8.30 Lxx). This was the original Adam: created on the sixth day
as the co-creator, and at the end of the sixth day, the creation was 'very
good'. Our present era is this sixth day, and humans work together
with the Creator to complete the creation.

THE RULER OF ANGELS

One part of Adam's story is not told in the Bible, the part that shows
what was meant by subduing the powers or upholding the bonds.
Adam was created as the divine image, and the Lord God summoned
all the angels – the powers of creation – to worship his image. Adam

---

95 A. McGrath, *The Open Secret*, p. 190.

96 Zizioulas, see n.25 above.

was the image of the Lord of Hosts, and so the hosts should serve him. Satan refused and was driven from heaven together with his angels. He vowed revenge. The story is the source of many later Adam legends: it was translated into several languages, and was widely known in mediaeval Europe. There are two main ancient sources: a Greek text known as the *Apocalypse of Moses*, and a Latin text known as the *Life of Adam and Eve*, which overlap, but are not identical. The style suggests they had a Hebrew original. Milton's *Paradise Lost* is the best known retelling of the story, and a version appears in several places in the Qur'an.

The *Life of Adam and Eve* tells how Satan met Adam and Eve by the river Tigris, and they asked why he was so hostile to them: 'What have we done to you, that you should pursue us with deceit? Have we stolen your glory and made you to be without honour?' Satan then told his story. When Adam was created, God breathed into him the breath of life and so his 'countenance and likeness' became the image of God. Michael presented Adam to the angels, and the Lord God declared him to be his image. Michael instructed the angels to worship the image, but Satan refused, saying that he was created before Adam, and so Adam should worship him. Satan's angels also refused to worship Adam, and so the Lord God expelled them all from their glorious state in heaven. In revenge, Satan tempted Eve, and thus both Adam and Eve were also expelled from their state of bliss.[97] The Qur'an mentions this story many times. God commanded the angels to bow down to Adam but Iblis [Satan] refused because Adam was created from clay and he, Iblis, from fire.[98] Iblis took revenge by tempting Adam and his wife with the tree.[99]

Some of the story in the *Life of Adam and Eve* is like Genesis: Adam was formed from clay as the image of the Lord God;[100] but there are other details, such as that Adam was originally clothed in glory and righteousness,[101] or that access to the tree of life would be restored at time of resurrection: 'At the time of the resurrection, [the Lord] will raise you again, and then there shall be given to you from the tree of life and you shall be immortal for ever.'[102] This was Jesus' promise to

97 *Life* 12–16.

98 Qur'an 7.11–25; 15.26–44; 18.50–53; 38.71–88.

99 Qur'an 20.116–128.

100 *Life* 27.2; 14.1.

101 *Ap. Moses* 20.1–2.

102 *Ap. Moses* 28.4.

the faithful Christian: 'To him who conquers, I will grant to eat from the tree of life, which is in the Paradise of God' (Rev. 2.7). There is other evidence that Jesus knew this story. When he described his time in the wilderness (Mt. 4.1–11; Mk 1.12–13; Lk. 4.1–12) he said the devil questioned his status: 'If *you* are the Son of God . . .' turn stones into bread and summon the angels to help you. In other words, the angels would serve the Son, and he would be able to undo the ancient curse on the ground, that it would only bring forth bread with toil and pain. These temptations have a specific context, and Jesus refused Satan's challenges. Then the devil showed him all the kingdoms of the world and said: 'All these I will give to you, if you will fall down and worship me.' This was the ancient rivalry that had caused Satan's expulsion from heaven, but Jesus refused to worship Satan. Mark's brief summary of Jesus' time in the wilderness also assumes knowledge of this story: '[He was] tempted by Satan . . . and the angels ministered to him' (Mk. 1.13). The angels served him, just as they had been commanded to serve Adam the image. Thus too Hebrews: 'Are they not all minister- ing spirits sent forth to serve, for the sake of those who are to obtain salvation?' (Heb. 1.14). The familiar New Testament texts have been shaped by the story of Adam in Genesis but also by the story the fall of Satan. Jesus saw himself as the new Adam, just as Paul and later Irenaeus taught,[103] but he did not succumb to Satan.

Two key proof texts used by the early Christians were also based on this story. 'For to what angel did God ever say, "Thou art my Son, today I have begotten thee"?' (Heb. 1.5) quotes Psalm 2.7, which describes how the LORD set his human king on Zion, and established him as his son. The text at the end of this psalm is difficult, and the Authorized Version is closest to the Hebrew: 'Be wise now, therefore, O ye kings: be instructed, ye judges of the earth. Serve the LORD with fear and rejoice with trembling. Kiss the Son lest he be angry, and ye perish from the way when his wrath is kindled but a little' (Ps. 2.10–12). This is the warning to the angels to pay homage to the Son, here transferred to the earth where the rulers have to acknowledge the LORD's king in Zion. The second proof text is in the same collection in Hebrews: 'And again, when he brings the Firstborn into the world, he says, "Let all God's angels worship him"' (Heb. 1.6, quoting Deut. 32.43). 'Firstborn' was a title for the Davidic king who called the

103 Irenaeus, in a pattern known as recapitulation, contrasted Adam with the new Adam, Jesus, Eve with the new Eve, Mary, and the forbidden tree with the cross, *Demonstration of the Apostolic Preaching* 32–4

LORD his father (Ps. 89. 27), meaning that he was the human presence of the LORD. He, like Adam was the image. Jesus was 'the image of the invisible God, the Firstborn of all creation' (Col. 1.15), in other words, he was the second Adam. The proof text in Hebrews 1.6, however, has been found at Qumran in a significantly longer form than has survived in the current Hebrew,[104] but very similar to the Old Greek translation. The shorter form lacks the lines used as the proof text, and so has nothing about the angels being called to worship. The longer [original] form in the Greek reads: 'Rejoice with him, heavens, bow down to him, sons of God, rejoice with his people, nations, confirm him all you angels of God' (Deut. 32.43 LXX). The rest of the verse follows the gist of the current Hebrew: the LORD comes to bring the judgement and to atone the land/soil of his people. In Hebrews, summoning the angels to worship the Firstborn was a proof text to identify Jesus; he was the image, the human presence of the LORD coming to make atonement. The detail of angel worship, however, is drawn from the story of the fall of Satan, and it was these lines that did not survive in the Hebrew text.

There are also two instances of the story in Revelation. When Kingdom of the LORD and his Anointed One was established on earth, John heard the heavenly voices declaring that the reign of the LORD God Almighty had begun, the time for 'rewarding thy servants, the prophets and saints, and all who fear thy name both small and great, and for destroying the destroyers of the earth' (Rev. 11.15–18). This was the renewal of the creation with the new regime. Then John saw a woman giving birth to the boy child who would fulfil Psalm 2,[105] and the dragon, 'who is called the devil and Satan' trying to destroy the child as he was set on the throne of God. Michael and his angels then drove Satan and his angels from heaven (Rev. 12.1–12). This is the fall of Satan after his challenge to the image enthroned. Then, in the description of the beasts, John described how their 'image' was made. John's style – presumably the tradition of his community – was to present the evil as the exact counterpart to the good. Sometimes wordplay was involved, as in the description of the great harlot, the mother of harlots and abominations (Rev. 17.5). In the underlying Hebrew, harlots would have been *qᵉdešim*, which was identical in its written from to *qᵉdošim*, holy ones; and abomination is *mšḥyt*, very similar in written form to anointed one, *mšyḥ*. The harlot city was the

104 The Masoretic Text.
105 See below, p. 250.

counterpart of the true Jerusalem who was the mother of holy one and anointed ones. In the case of the beasts, the dragon gave his authority to the beast from the sea who had died and come to life again (Rev. 13.3–4), and the beast's agent made an image of the beast (Rev. 13.14). 'It was allowed to give breath to the image of the beast so that the image of the beast should even speak, and to cause those who would not worship the image of the beast to be slain' (Rev. 13.15). This was the beast's Adam. The contemporary interpretations of Genesis 2.7 – 'the LORD God . . . breathed into his nostrils the breath of life' – all say that this gave Adam the power of speech,[106] and the command to worship the image of the beast exactly parallels the command to worship Adam. The beast and his image were the counterpart of the LORD and his image, and Revelation describes the conflict between them.

The beast, as we have seen, had made commerce and deceit his hallmark, and this has also been the reason for the cherub's fall from Eden: abundance of trade, violence, pride, corrupted wisdom. 'By the multitude of your distortions, in the unrighteousness of your commerce, you made your holy places unholy; I brought forth fire from you midst and it consumed you, and I turned you to ashes on the earth . . .' (Ezek. 28.18, my translation). When Jesus came as the LORD to his temple and cleansed it, he used a 'whip of cords' (Jn 2.15), an interesting detail, because the instructions for cleansing the temple on the day of atonement were that the high priest sprinkled the blood 'as though wielding a whip'.[107] Jesus drove out the traders – a conflict that persists:

> Consumerism was the triumphant winner of the ideological wars of the 20th century, beating out both religion and politics as the path millions of Americans follow to find purpose, meaning, order and transcendent exaltation in their lives. Liberty in this market democracy has, for many, come to mean freedom to buy as much as you can of whatever you wish, endlessly reinventing and telegraphing your sense of self with each new purchase.[108]

The image of the beast.

There are other possible allusions to the story in the New Testament, especially in Paul: 'Satan was angry and transformed himself into the

---

106 All the Targums to Genesis 2.7.

107 Mishnah *Yoma* 5.4.

108 April Witt, 'Acquiring Minds: Inside America's All Consuming Passion', Washington Post Magazine Dec 14th 2003, quoted in P. Stiles, *Is the American Dream Killing You?*, New York: HarperCollins, 2006, p. 110.

brightness of angels'[109] is very similar to 'For even Satan disguises himself as an angel of light' (2 Cor. 11.14); and '[The LORD said] "Take him up into Paradise, into the third heaven"'[110] is what Paul described: 'I was caught up to the third heaven . . . Caught up into Paradise' (2 Cor. 12.2–3). Maybe Paul was alluding to the story when he said that covetousness was the origin of sin: '[Satan] sprinkled his evil poison on the fruit which he gave me to eat, which is his covetousness. For covetousness is the origin of every sin'[111] could have prompted 'But sin, finding opportunity in the commandment, wrought in me all kinds of covetousness . . .' (Rom. 7.8; and also Jas 1.13–15). The angels worshipping Adam the image is also clear in the vision of the enthroned Lamb who was worshipped by the host of heaven and all creation (Rev. 5.11–14), and the Name-bearing Jesus who was acknowledged by all in heaven and earth, and recognized as the LORD (Phil. 2.9–11). Philo, however, seems to deny the story of ruling the angels; Adam was to rule all living things but not the heavenly beings.[112]

The end of this story appears in the Church's understanding of the Ascension. When Jesus was taken up, this was understood as Adam restored to his intended place, enthroned again above the angels. Early representations of the Ascension show Jesus in the chariot that Ezekiel saw, the figure he described as the likeness of the glory of the LORD (Ezek. 1.28).[113] Much earlier, it was the theme of John Chrysostom's sermon for Ascension Day: the human who had been driven from Paradise 'and condemned to so great a curse' was now exalted to the height of heaven and enthroned, 'made capable through Christ of being exalted to so great a degree of happiness and glory'. The angels had guarded Paradise from human nature, and now it was restored to the highest place. Psalm 24 was fulfilled: 'Lift up your heads, O gates . . . that the King of Glory may come in' (Ps. 24.7, 9). 'Now the angels have received what they used to long for, the archangels have seen what they have long desired. Today they have seen our

---

109 *Life* 9.1

110 *Ap. Moses* 37.5.

111 *Ap. Moses* 19.3.

112 Philo, *Creation*, 83–4.

113 For example, the illustration in the 6th century Rabula Gospels reproduced in my book *An Extraordinary Gathering of Angels*, London: MQP, 2004, p. 111.

nature on the throne of royal splendour, shining with glory and immortal beauty.'[114]

The image of God worshipped by the angels, and that image restored to its intended place with the ascension of Jesus, describes in the vivid imagery of angels and cosmic worship the intended nature of Adam. The human was to be the seal of creation and uphold the bonds, and was to harness and master the powers of the creation. This was the command to Adam: *kabaš*, 'subdue'. It was the image in John's vision and Paul's hymn; all the powers of heaven and earth acknowledging that Jesus Christ is Lord.

The Man of Dust

Paul contrasted the man of dust and the man of heaven. Since he was explaining to the Corinthians what Christians understood by resurrection, the contrast between the man of dust and the man of heaven was central to the belief of the original church: 'The first man was from the earth, a man of dust; the second man is from heaven . . . Just as we have borne the image of the man of dust, we shall [or let us] also bear the image of the man of heaven' (1 Cor. 15.47, 49). The man of heaven was the original Adam. The Qumran community thought in the same way.

> I know there is hope for him whom Thou hast shaped from dust for the everlasting council. Thou hast cleansed a perverse spirit of great sin that it may stand with the host of the Holy Ones, and that it may enter into community with the congregation of the sons of heaven. Thou hast allotted to man an everlasting destiny amidst the spirits of knowledge, that he may praise thy name in a common rejoicing, and recount your marvels before all your works.[115]

Here, the restored Adam is one of the angels, praising the Creator and telling of his works. Another hymn declares: 'I shall shine like a sevenfold l[ight which] you prepared for your glory; for you are my everlasting light . . .'[116] Another contrasts the man of dust and the promised glory: 'He is a structure of dust, fashioned with water . . . Only by your goodness is man declared righteous. You will make him beautiful with your splendour, and cause him to reign [*mašal*] over [ma]ny delights

---

114 *Patrologia Graeca-Latina*, vol L, col. 448ff. The only English version I know is W. Scott, *The Fourth Panegyric*, London: Crowder, 1775.

115 *Thanksgiving Hymns*, 1QH XI 22–24.

116 1QH XV.24.

["Edens"] with everlasting peace and length of days.'[117] This Qumran hymn seems to allude to the temple ritual described in Psalm 110, when the human king is seated on a divine throne – as Adam the image? – to rule over his foes as the image was to rule the angels. He is declared Melchi-zedek, the king who upholds righteousness, he was 'born',[118] as was the king in Psalm 2, and oil is part of the ritual, described as 'dew', the sacrament of Wisdom and the symbol of resurrection. This, then, was the original Adam as known in the time of Jesus. The people of dust who were, collectively, the high priesthood, hoped to return to this state of Adamic high priesthood: robed in glory, ruling in Eden, enjoying a long life and the peace of eternity. The Qumran community and the early Christians, 'accepted as a fundamental axiom of their theology the belief that as originally created and as restored within the community of the righteous, the true Israel, humanity belongs firmly within the divine world'.[119] The true human is an angel.

The creation of one Adam was the basis for important rules in the Sanhedrin in the time of Jesus. 'A single man was created in the world, to teach that if any man has caused a single soul to perish, Scripture imputes it to him as though he had caused a whole world to perish.' Similarly, if anyone saved a single person, it was like saving the whole world. A single man was created to promote peace on earth, so that nobody could claim a more noble family line. Each person was stamped with the image:

> For man stamps many coins with the one seal and they are all like one another, but the King of kings, the Holy One, blessed is he, has stamped every man with the seal of the first man, yet not one of them is like his fellow. Therefore everyone must say, 'For my sake was the world created.[120]

Jesus used this example to answer the Pharisees' question about paying taxes (Mk 12.13–17), but the point of his teaching was different: each person stamped with the image of the Creator was not Caesar's currency and had another loyalty. The seal was sometimes said to join the bonds of creation; at other times, to imprint the divine image. Philo

---

117 1 QH V.21, 22–4.

118 'I have begotten you' is how the Greek understood 'your youth will come to you.'

119 Fletcher-Louis, *All the Glory of Adam*, p. 135.

120 Mishnah *Sanhedrin* 4.5.

explained 'The Logos of him who makes [the world] is himself the seal
by which each thing that exists has received its shape . . .'[121] 'When [the
substance of the universe] had no definite character, God moulded it
into definiteness, and, when he had perfected it, stamped the entire
universe with him image, *eikōn*, and an ideal form, *idea*, even his own
Logos.'[122]

Adam was a man of dust (Gen. 2.7), a creature of clay – exactly as
other cultures explained the origin of the human race – but the
Mesopotamian Adam, as we have seen, was formed from dust and
the blood of a defeated God.[123] The storytellers of Israel, probably
knowing that blood and dust story, said Adam was formed from the
earth, and then the Lord God breathed life into him. The breath of
life was a gift from God. This is a very different answer to the question: what is man? This question is still the great mystery at the heart
of creation: living beings are made from non-living constituent parts,
so what is it that brings the dust to life? 'The divine nature of life,
especially human life, continues to be a central feature of contemporary religious doctrine.' 'Life cannot be reduced to a property of
an organism's constituent parts. How can a collection of inanimate
atoms be animate?'[124] The characteristic of so much western scientific thinking has been reductionist, with a corresponding diminu-
tion of what it means to be a human being. 'Dust thou art and to
dust thou shalt return' (Gen. 3.19) has become not a curse but a
realistic assessment of the human state, and this in turn has become
a self-fulfilling prophecy. The destructive ethos that characterizes
our current situation derives from this new estimate of human worth:
consumer rather than image of God and co-creator.

In the time of Jesus, scholars scrutinized every detail of the text, to
discover what the Scripture revealed about human nature. Adam was
universal: the four letters of the name Adam, according to a Greek
Jewish text of the second century BCE, represented the four points of
the compass: *Anatolē*, east, *Dusis*, west, *Arktos*, north and *Mesēmbria*,
south.[125] Later they said he was created from the dust of the future
temple site, the place of his future atonement – thus R Samuel who was

121 Philo, *Flight*, 12.

122 Philo, *On Dreams* II.45.

123 See above, p. 35.

124 Davies, *God and the New Physics*, p. 59, 60.

125 *Sibylline Oracles* 3.24.

teaching in Palestine at the end of the third century CE.[126] Adam was formed from the earth as were the animals, but the two verbs were spelled differently: the LORD God formed, *yiṣer*, animals and birds from the earth (Gen. 2.19), but he formed, *yyiṣer*, the Adam from the earth. Why the double 'y'? It was a sign, they said, that human beings had two natures: the creature was under two influences, a good *yeṣer* and an evil *yeṣer*; or it was destined to live in this world and the next, a creature of heaven and of earth; or the creature of dust was Adam and Eve.[127]

First, the two influences. The Qumran community described them as two spirits that vied for the soul:

> The God of Knowledge . . . has created man to govern, *mašal*, the world, and has appointed for him two spirits in which to walk . . . the spirits of truth and of wrong. All the children of righteousness are ruled by the Prince of Light and walk in the ways of light, but all the children of injustice are ruled by the Angel of Darkness and walk in the ways of darkness.[128]

The works of the two spirits are made clear, and those who follow the Prince of Light will receive the spirit of truth and be chosen for the everlasting covenant, where 'all the glory of Adam shall be theirs.'[129] This was a commonplace of early Christian teaching: Jesus contrasted the wide and narrow gates (Mt. 7.13–4), John contrasted those who live in the light and those who live in darkness (1 Jn 1 5–7), and Paul contrasted the way of the Spirit and the way of the flesh (Gal. 5.16–23). The early manual of Christian teaching, the *Didache*, set out the Two Ways: most of the 'way of life' is an expansion of the Sermon on the Mount,[130] but the way of death concludes:

> Gentleness and patience are beyond their conception; they care for nothing good or useful, and are bent only on their own advantage, without pity for the poor or feeling for the distressed. Knowledge of their Creator is not in them: they make away with their infants and deface God's image; they turn away the needy and oppress the afflicted; they aid and abet the rich but arbitrarily condemn the poor; they are utterly and altogether sunk in iniquity.[131]

---

126 *Genesis Rabbah* XIV.8. Thus too Targum *Pseudo-Jonathan*; Adam was created from the dust of the sanctuary.

127 *Genesis Rabbah* XII.8; XIV.2–5.

128 *Community Rule* 1QS III.19.

129 1QS III.23.

130 Or the Sermon on the Mount could be a summary of the Two Ways.

131 *Didache* 5.

Working out what it meant to be the image of God was fundamental to the early Christian lifestyle.

Second, the one who belonged in two worlds. The human was formed from the earth and the breath of the Creator, and so belonged to earth and heaven. The breath/life of human beings was different from that of the animals, and this gave them special privileges as well as special responsibilities. Human life was sacred, because it was in the image of God (Gen. 9.5–6). Ecclesiastes, in his pessimism, questioned this:

> Man has no advantage over the beasts; for all is vanity. All go to one place; all are from the dust and all turn to dust again. Who knows whether the spirit of man goes upward and the spirit of the beast goes down to the earth? (Eccl. 3.19–21)

He was presumably questioning the commonly held view. Philo explained Genesis 2.7 thus:

> The man who was moulded as by a potter was formed out of dust and earth, in respect of his body. And he obtained a spirit when God breathed life into his face. The mixture of his nature was a mixture of the corruptible and the incorruptible.

The invisible part of man was 'a copy of the original seal . . . the Logos of God.'[132]

> Every man, in respect of his mind, is kinsman of the divine Logos, having come into being as a copy or fragment or ray of that blessed divine nature, but in the structure of his body, he is kin to the whole creation, formed of the same things: earth, water, air and fire, each of the elements having contributed its allotted part, to complete a material sufficient in itself for the Creator to take and fashion this visible image.[133]
>
> In man [that which is holy] is the mind, a fragment of the Deity, as the words of Moses in particular bear witness, 'He breathed into his face a breath of life and man became a living soul.'[134]

All the Targums say that the divine breath gave Adam the power of speech to praise God: 'Let everything that breathes praise the LORD' (Ps. 150.6); 'It is Thou who hast created breath for the tongue . . . [to]

---

132 Philo, *Questions on Genesis* I.4.

133 Philo, *Creation*, 146. The Qumran hymn writer thought he had been created from just clay and water: 'I, a shape of clay, kneaded in water . . .' 'I, a creature of clay, what am I? Kneaded with water, what is my worth . . .?', 1QH IX.21, 27; XI.23.

134 Philo, *On Dreams* I.35.

tell of Thy glory and recount Thy wonders . . .'[135] Adam's breath as the gift of God distinguished him from the animals.

Third, the male and female nature of the original Adam. There was speculation about what this actually meant: was Adam hermaphrodite or did Adam have two heads, perhaps? And was it a rib that was taken to make Eve, or was it one of Adam's sides? Was he in fact split into two, such that Eve was literally his other half? The Hebrew can mean either.[136] And should the letters of the Hebrew word 'female' be read differently? Since 'female', *n'qebah*, is similar in form and sound to *n'qubaw*, 'his apertures', did God create the male and his apertures as his image? This, they said, is how the text was altered for Ptolemy, so that he should not think that the Jewish God was in any way female.[137] The male and female has always been a problem! One possible way to read Ezekiel's description of the cherubs in the temple is that they had two heads (Ezek. 41.19), and the male and female union was later used to describe Christ and the Church, a development of the older idea that Jerusalem/Israel was the bride of the LORD. Many stories were told about the wedding in Eden: they said the cherub Ezekiel described in Eden, decked with every precious stone and under a glorious canopy, was Eve on her wedding day,[138] but soon afterwards she was thrown out for abusing wisdom. The detail is beyond us, but the ideal not: the original glorious Adam, restored in Christ, was neither male nor female, as Paul noted: 'For as many of you as were baptised into Christ have put in Christ. There is neither Jew nor Greek, there is neither slave nor free, there is neither male nor female; for you are all one in Christ Jesus' (Gal. 3.27–8). The absolute equality of male and female – distinct but equal – is fundamental to the biblical vision for the creation.

Before being separated into distinct male and female forms, Adam was taken to Eden and set in the garden to 'till it and to keep it' (Gen. 2.15). *Jubilees* tells a slightly different story at this point, to emphasize that Eden was the temple: the impurity laws after childbirth, that a woman may not enter the holy place for forty days after the birth of a son or eighty after the birth of a daughter (Lev. 12, 2–5), were applied to Adam and Eve after their 'birth'. Adam was set in Eden after forty days and Eve after eighty, showing that Adam was divided

135 1QH IX.27.

136 *Genesis Rabbah* VIII.1.

137 *Genesis Rabbah* VIII.11, and see above p. ***.

138 *Genesis Rabbah* XVIII.1, attributed to R. Hama b. Haninah, third century CE.

before he was set in Eden.[139] The temple 'was' Eden, and the high
priest in the temple was the Adam, which explains another detail in
Genesis: why was Adam set in the garden 'to till it and to keep it'?.
Those particular Hebrew words have a temple context, and are literally
to serve, *'abad*, and to preserve, *šamar*: to serve as a priest and to keep
the tradition/commandments. Neither of the traditional interpretations thought the command was literally about gardening, and so
'Adam the earthkeeper', which is often heard nowadays, would not
have been familiar to the early Church. The debate was: did it mean
serve/work, (the same verb) for six days and then preserve/keep (the
same verb) the Sabbath (Deut. 5. 12–3); or did it mean serve God and
perform the sacred duties, as in 'You shall serve God' (Exod. 3.12) and
keep the festivals (e.g. Passover, Exod. 12.17) and the words of the
covenant (Deut. 29.9)?[140]

Adam then had to name the animals and birds, which had also been
formed from the earth, although the story does not say they received
the breath of God (Gen. 2.19). Animal life was different from human
life in this respect. Philo said that when the LORD formed the animals
and birds from the soil, he was making the material reality that corresponded to the archetypes created on the fifth day in the invisible
world, just as Adam the man of dust was the material reality of the
image created on the sixth day.[141] The angels had asked the LORD what
human nature would be like, and the LORD said: 'Wiser than the
angels'. To demonstrate this, the LORD asked the angels to name
the animals, but they could not do it. The LORD then asked Adam, and
he was able to name every living creature. Naming the creatures implies
knowing their natures. Tradition said that Adam also named himself,
knowing he was formed from the soil, and he also named his Creator
'Yahweh', the LORD – 'the One who causes to be'– the name by which
people addressed the LORD.[142] Contemplating the meaning of the
Name was contemplating the deepest mystery of creation. To see the
raz nihyeh, the mystery of existence, was the aspiration of the wise ones,
and they glimpsed this as they contemplated the LORD enthroned in

139 *Jubilees* 3.8–14.

140 *Genesis Rabbah* XVI.5.

141 Philo, *Questions on Genesis* I.19.

142 *Genesis Rabbah* XVII.4, attributed to R. Aha, late third century CE. The verse
quoted is Isa. 42.8. Yahweh, meaning 'he who causes to be' was the human recognition
of the nature of the Lord, whereas Exod. 3.14 shows the different name by which the
Lord called himself; 'I cause to be.'

the holy of holies. A section of *1 Enoch* tells how the leader of the evil angels tried to learn the secret of the Name and thus the secret of life itself, in order to gain power over the creation,[143] and there have been many tales of people who have tried to create a human being by bringing a man-made form to life.[144] This, and so much more, is the context for the Christian claim that Jesus is the LORD, the source of Life, and the reason why Christians view with concern some recent developments in cloning and related areas.

Adam's wisdom, represented by the garment of glory, showed itself in naming the animals, that is, in recognizing their role in creation. 'Wisdom protected the first formed father of the world, when he alone had been created; she delivered him from his transgression and gave him strength to rule all things' (Wis. 10.1). Philo also knew that giving names was a sign of Adam's authority: 'Names exist by being given and not by nature . . . [Adam] was the first to be worthy of being Lord over all, and the first introducer and author of the giving of names . . .'[145] Adam's wisdom is another aspect of his nature that is not explicit in Genesis, but is mentioned elsewhere in the Hebrew Bible. When Eliphaz questioned Job's judgement, he asked: 'Are you the first Adam that was born? Or were you brought forth before the hills? Have you listened in the council/to the counsel, *sod*, of God? And do you limit wisdom to yourself?' (Job 15.7–8, my translation). Others who listened in the council of God were called prophets: Amos knew that the LORD God did nothing without revealing his *sod* to his prophets (Amos 3.7). Adam, too, was remembered as a prophet: the Hebrew text implies this with the word 'the deep sleep', *tardemah*, which fell upon Adam (Gen. 2.21),[146] which the Old Greek version translated as 'ecstasy'. It was given to Adam as a divine revelation that humanity was male and female, the first revelation in the Bible. Islam also describes Adam as the first prophet, and a version of this story of Adam being wiser than the angels appears in the Qur'an. When God proposed to create a vicegerent on earth, the angels said he would make mischief. God taught Adam, but not the angels, the names of things. Then he asked the angels to tell him the names but they could not, and this is why all the angels, except Iblis, bowed down to Adam.

---

143 *1 Enoch* 69.13–16; one possible meaning of a very obscure text.

144 For example, the Golem of Prague.

145 *Questions on Genesis* I.20.

146 This was the deep sleep of Daniel 12.9, and Luke 9.32.

Satan then tempted Adam with the forbidden tree, and Adam had to leave the garden.[147]

There were two trees in the garden; the story was that Satan planted the second tree as part of his revenge. The tree of life which was the symbol of Wisdom (Prov. 3.18), was intended as Adam's food; the other tree, so similar in many ways, symbolized the opposite of Wisdom. The Eden story does not say that all knowledge was forbidden; it was not the Prometheus legend, with a courageous man snatching forbidden knowledge from the gods. Adam was intended to have Wisdom but was deceived into choosing 'the knowledge of good and evil', a mysterious term that means knowledge that can be used for good or evil. Once evil was a possibility, it soon became reality. Adam was deceived by the possibility of real choice and power, but both were an illusion. Adam was created with free will – it was *possible* to chose the forbidden tree; but Adam was not created free, he did not create the system within which he exercised his free will. He did not chose what choices were available to him, but he did know the outcome of the choice: 'In the day that you eat of it you shall die' (Gen. 2.17). Satan's voice persuaded him that the system was different: 'You shall not die' (Gen. 3.4). This is the key to the Eden story: Adam was created with free will, but not freedom. Familiar phrases such as 'Man is born free' or 'Liberty and the pursuit of happiness' are not biblical; in fact, the very opposite. The illusion of freedom was offered by Satan. 'Then the eyes of both were opened and they knew that they were naked' (Gen. 3.7). They had lost their garments of glory. Biblical freedom is found within the security of the covenant bonds. The glorious liberty of the children of God was knowing that nothing could separate them from the love of God in Christ Jesus (Rom. 8.21,39). Or, as Augustine later said: 'To know God is to live, and to serve him is to reign as a king.'[148]

Adam's dignity and high status depended on his being part of the divine plan for creation. Adam was created as the image, and this in itself limited what was available to him. He was created as the Servant, and by choosing the forbidden tree, he disobeyed. Adam as the Seal of the covenant secured the very bonds that limited him. He was not outside the system, but at its centre. The creature of earth and heaven upheld within his own being the bond that joined the material world to its source of life. As with the angels, so too Adam enjoyed his special

---

147 Qur'an 2.30–39.

148 Deus, quem nosse vivere est, cui servire, regnare est, Augustine, *Meditation* 22.

status only as long as he remained within the system. Milton's Raphael later said to the human pair in Eden:

> Myself and all the Angelic host that stand
> In sight of God enthroned, our happy state
> Hold, as you yours, while our obedience holds . . .[149]

Ben Sira wrote: 'It was he who created man in the beginning, and he left him in the power of his inclination. If you will, you can keep the commandments, and to act faithfully is a matter of your own choice' (Ben Sira 15.14). Justin showed the implication of the original system: 'Since God in the beginning made the race of men and angels with free will, they will justly suffer in eternal fire the punishment of whatever sins they commit.'[150]

Rowan Williams, speaking in the context of the financial crisis that began in 2008, made some observations about the human state that well describe Adam standing before the forbidden tree:

> Acquisitiveness is . . . associated with pride, the root of all human error and failure; pride, which is most clearly evident in the refusal to acknowledge my lack of control over my environment, my illusion that I can shape the world according to my will.
>
> Maximised choice is a form of maximised control. And it presupposes and encourages a basic model of the ideal human agent as an isolated subject confronting a range of options, each of which they are equally free to adopt for their own self-defined purposes.
>
> The only way of "maximising choice" is to make sure that it is still possible to choose and to use something, and to secure the possibilities of reasonable choice for our children and grandchildren, even at the price of restricting some options. Without that restriction, nothing is solid: we should face a world in which everything flows, melts, dissolves, in a world of constantly shifting and spectral valuations.[151]

This is the biblical picture: the Satanic lure of complete choice, without the restraint of Wisdom, the fruit of the intended tree, the Wisdom that binds all things together in harmony.[152] By opting for the free use of knowledge, Adam abandoned his role as Seal of the covenant. By

---

149 Milton, *Paradise Lost*, 5.535–7.

150 Justin, *Apology* II.7.

151 R. D. Williams, 'Ethics, Economics and Global Justice', lecture given in Cardiff, 7 March 2009, www.archbishopofcanterbury.org/2323

152 The Greek version of Prov. 8.30.

opting for idolatry, as the commandment warned, the chosen distortion affected the third and fourth generations, and without the bonds of the covenant in place, the whole system collapsed.[153]

There was considerable debate in the time of Jesus over whose fault it was, and this has left a bitter legacy. Some said Eve was to blame: 'From a woman sin had its beginning, and because of her we all die' (Ben Sira 25.24); 'Adam was not deceived, but the woman was deceived and became a transgressor' (1 Tim. 2.13–14). A version of the biblical story known in Palestine in the time of Jesus said:

> I taught the first man, saying, 'If you do not transgress what I have commanded you, all things will be subject to you.' But that man transgressed my ways, and was persuaded by his wife, and she was deceived by the serpent. And then death was ordained for the generations of men. And the LORD continued to show him [Moses] the ways of paradise and said to him, 'These are the ways that men have lost by not walking in them, because they have sinned against me.'[154]

Others, who also scrutinized every letter of the text, drew a different conclusion: they said that Adam had not passed on God's command accurately, and this is how Satan managed to deceive Eve. Adam was commanded not to eat the fruit, but he told Eve not to eat the fruit or even to touch it, on pain of death. When she saw that Satan could touch the fruit safely, she decided that Adam had not told her the truth, and so ate the fruit.[155]

Then came the questions: 'Where are you?' and 'What have you done?' (Gen. 3.9,13), questions that could form the basis of any environmental audit. This is how Philo understood the text, not as an indication that the LORD did not know what had happened. 'The things said appear not to be a question but a kind of threat and reproach: "Where art thou now, from what good hast thou removed thyself, O man . . ."'[156] And then the curses: first on the serpent; then on Eve, who would be afflicted with the pain of childbirth and the need for a husband; and finally on Adam who would have to work

---

153 It has been remarkable to read how much 'secular' comment too has used the biblical covenant imagery without being aware of it. It seems as though it is a natural way to think.

154 Pseudo-Philo, *Biblical Antiquities* 13.10.

155 *Abot de Rabbi Nathan* A.1, quoted in J. L. Kugel, *Traditions of the Bible. A Guide to the Bible as it was at the Start of the Common Era*, Cambridge, MA: Harvard University Press, 1998, p. 103.

156 Philo, *Questions on Genesis* I.45.

difficult soil to bring food from the earth. (Gen. 3.14–19). Adam would rule Eve, the sign of the fallen state, and so, in the time of Jesus, Philo could explain: 'Woman is not equal in honour with man.'[157] Finally, the pair were driven from Eden, and cherubim prevented their access to the tree of life. Too late they realized that they could not eat from both trees: the fruit of the tree of life – wisdom that joins all things together – was incompatible with the knowledge of good and evil. Later storytellers said it was the archangel Uriel who blocked their way to the tree of life, Uriel, whose name means the one who brings divine light and inspiration to the human mind.

As the human pair left Eden, the angels took pity on them and gave them gifts to remember the lost garden. There are many versions of this story. Pre-Christian Jewish texts link leaving Eden and leaving the temple: *Jubilees* says that Adam burned temple incense as he was leaving the garden.[158] The *Apocalypse of Moses* says Adam begged the angels to let him take some seeds of the perfumes of Eden, so that he could continue to make offerings to God.[159] Perfumed smoke offered to God is a powerful symbol, and it is all too easy to see the polluting smoke clouds of industry as the incense of the beast: blocking out the light and poisoning the air that is essential for life. The often-quoted words of a nineteenth century Chicago business man are chilling in their naivete: 'Smoke is the incense burning on the altars of industry. It is beautiful to me. It shows that men are changing the merely potential forces of nature into articles of comfort for humanity.'[160] The Christians preserved these stories of Adam taking gifts from Eden in, for example, *The Testament of Adam*, a collection of Jewish and Christian material known by the early third century CE. When Adam died, the gifts he had brought from Eden were buried with him: gold, frankincense and myrrh. These were symbols of the lost Paradise, and also of the lost temple: the gold of the sacred vessels, the incense for the offerings and prayers, and the myrrh for anointing oil. 'And the sons of kings, the magi, will come and take the treasures to the son of god, to Bethlehem of Judea . . .'[161] The wise ones gave Jesus the tokens of Eden and recognized him as the new Adam, but to set this claim in

---

157 *Questions on Genesis* I.27.

158 *Jubilees* 3.27.

159 *Ap. Moses* 29.6.

160 W. P. Rend, quoted in C. M. Rosen, 'Businessmen against pollution in 19th Century Chicago', *Business History Review* 69, 1995, pp. 351–97, p. 385.

161 *Testament of Adam* 3.6.

context, it is necessary to look at Adam's role in contemporary theological debate.

There was, as we have seen, a ruling in the Sanhedrin: a single person was created by God to teach that if anyone killed a single person it was as though she/he had killed the whole world, and if anyone saved a single person, it was as though she/he had saved the whole world.[162] For some, the single disobedience in Eden was also the disobedience of all people, resulting in mortality for all: thus Adam reproached Eve: 'What have you done? You have brought upon us a great wound, transgression and sin in all our generations.'[163] For others, death became a possibility and people made their own choices. 'God . . . does not delight in the death of the living . . .' 'God created man for incorruption, and made him in the image of his own eternity/nature, but through the devil's envy death entered the world, and those who belong to his party experience it' (Wis. 1.13; 2.23–4). Those who choose Satan experience death. Thus Paul wrote: 'As sin came into the world through one man and death through sin, and so death spread to all men *because all men sinned . . .*' (a possible translation of Rom. 5.12). This is one of the most debated texts in the New Testament. How did the sin of Adam affect future generations? Were people born as sinners, or only as human beings with free will? Paul's subsequent reasoning was 'as by one man's disobedience, many were made sinners, so by one man's obedience, many will be made righteous' (Rom. 5.19). Since the obedience that made righteousness possible had to be received by a personal act of faith, this implies that the disobedience of Adam had also to be appropriated by a personal choice, and this was the position in near contemporary Jewish texts.

The political situation in Palestine in the early years of the Church, and especially the tragedy of the destruction of Jerusalem in 70 CE, gave rise to much reflection on the nature of evil and the cause of suffering. What was the role of role of Adam and Eve? Two Jewish texts in particular record the debate, both preserved by Christians and both written about 100 CE: *2 Baruch*,[164] and *2 Esdras*,[165] which was expanded by a Christian introduction and appendix. Individual responsibility is

162 Mishnah *Sanhedrin* 4.5.

163 *Life of Adam and Eve* 44.2

164 Originally in Hebrew, but the extant Syriac was translated from a Greek text.

165 Also known as 4 Ezra and even 5 Esdras, originally in Hebrew, but the extant Latin was translated from a Greek text.

clearly set out in *2 Baruch*, which was known to the early Christians.[166] 'Baruch' asked the Creator about the current disaster, and the LORD said that only the wicked would be destroyed.[167] Then he prayed:

> Although Adam sinned first and has brought death on all who were not of his own time, yet each of them who has been born from him has prepared for himself the coming torment . . . Adam is not the cause, except only for himself, but each of us has become our own Adam.[168]

When 'Esdras' pondered the destruction of his city, he too thought of Adam, who was given only one commandment yet disobeyed: 'and immediately [God] appointed death for him and his descendents' (2 Esd. 3.7). 'Esdras' spoke of the evil heart of Adam, and it is important to remember that at that time, the heart was the seat of thought rather than emotion. This is why the Greek gospels add a word to Jesus' quotation of the second great commandment, to love the LORD with all your heart, soul and strength (Deut. 6.5). To convey the meaning, they had to add 'mind' and so Jesus taught: 'You shall love the LORD your God with all your heart and with all your soul and with *all your mind* and with all your strength.' (Mk 12.29–30), and 'For from within, from the heart of man, come evil thoughts . . . (Mk 7.21). 'Esdras' concluded:

> For the first Adam, burdened with an evil heart, transgressed and was overcome, as were all who were descended from him. Thus the disease became permanent; the law was in the people's heart, along with the evil root, but what was good departed and the evil remained.

Over the years, people chose to repeat Adam's action, Adam's way of thinking, and so eventually Jerusalem was destroyed. (2 Esd. 3.21–7).

The archangel Uriel spoke to Esdras: the evil seed sown in Adam's heart/mind was ripening to a great harvest of evil that would soon be fully grown for harvest (2 Esd. 4.30). The evil heart/mind had alienated people from God and brought them to ways of corruption and death (2 Esd. 7.48). It seemed to Esdras that even the human mind was made from dust and not just the body: 'O earth what have you brought forth, if the mind is made out of dust like other created things' (2 Esd. 7.62). Uriel explained that the Creator had not

---

166 *2 Baruch* 61.7 is quoted in *Letter of Barnabas* 11.

167 *2 Baruch* 48.29.

168 *2 Baruch* 54.15, 19.

intended human beings for death, but they had defiled the holy Name and been ungrateful to the One who gave them life (2 Esd. 8.60). Questioning this, Esdras said it would have been better if Adam had never been created: 'For what good is it to all that they live in sorrow now and expect punishment after death?' Uriel replied that all could choose: there was a battle to wage against evil and the victorious would receive the promised world (2 Esd. 7.127–8). This is the picture in the Book of Revelation: the heavenly warrior with a sword in his mouth that represents his teaching, overcoming evil so that the creation could be renewed.

The picture, though fragmented, is consistent. Adam was created glorious, to be the image of the Creator, his likeness made visible. His garment of glory was Wisdom, and thus clad, Adam was set to uphold the creation and fill the earth with glory. But Adam was deceived by the promise of power and choice, the freedom to use knowledge for good or evil. As a result, Adam lost the garment of glory, and lost the Wisdom to uphold the creation, which became a place of thorns, thistles and dust. *Adam's punishment was to live with the consequence of that choice: to be no more than the dust from which she/he had been formed.* Martin Luther said that righteousness had been part of Adam's original nature, part of what it meant to be the image of God. But Adam lost righteousness when he sinned.[169] In other words, by choosing the forbidden tree, Adam lost the ability to maintain the bonds of creation and hold all things together. 'This eucharistic or priestly function of man reconnects created nature to infinite existence, and thus liberates it from slavery to necessity by letting it develop its potentialities to the maximum.'[170] What Adam lost was restored in Christ, the second Adam. 'In him all things hold together' (Col. 1.17). When Paul exhorted the Christians in Rome to live as their high priestly status required – 'present your bodies as a living sacrifice' – he made clear what this meant: 'Do not be conformed to this world, but be transformed by the renewal of your mind' (Rom. 12.1–2). We must now consider how the human mind was transformed and renewed.

169 *Lectures on Genesis*, on Gen. 2.17, in *Luther's Works*, ed. J Pelikan, St Louis: Concordia Publishing House, 1958, vol.1.

170 John Zizioulas, *Being as Communion: Studies in Personhood and the Church*, London: Darton, Longman and Todd, 1985, p. 119.

Chapter 6

EMBRACING CREATION

Creation began to degrade when Adam and Eve disobeyed. That is how the biblical story is usually told, with the emphasis on Eve's disobedience and Adam's folly. The detail rarely mentioned is the precise nature of that disobedience: *their attitude to knowledge.* The human pair chose the forbidden tree and thereby rejected the tree intended for their food. They rejected Wisdom, defined as 'a tree of life to those who lay hold of her; those who hold her fast are called happy' (Prov. 3.18). Wearing garments of glory, they were appointed as the image of the Creator to maintain the covenant. As high priests of the creation, they were to be nourished by Wisdom, but when they chose the other food – the knowledge of good and evil – they lost the garments of glory and found that they lived in a very different world. Some of the other symbols of Wisdom were the water of life, the bread of the presence, the song of the angels, the anointing oil and the menorah, probably her stylized tree. Jewish tradition remembered that the true menorah, the Spirit, and the anointing oil were missing from the second temple, but would be restored in the true temple of the Messiah.[1] In other words, some Jews continued to think that Wisdom was missing from the second temple.

The distinction between Wisdom and knowledge is fundamental in the Eden story, *and in our current situation.* Wisdom is the God-given way of knowing the world, but knowledge is secular, wrenched from its source.

> The knowledge that comes from the second tree is partial. It is knowledge only of a god-forsaken world in which human beings have themselves assumed the

---

1 *Numbers Rabbah* XV.10; Babylonian Talmud *Horayoth* 21a.

237

role of gods. In the process, of course, they have discovered that abstracted from the Creator and Source of Life, they are doomed to die.[2]

The 'god forsaken' world means a world view that has abandoned or marginalized God, where the mighty angels of the creation have become the ornamental putti of elaborate plasterwork, or have been removed because someone finds them offensive. In the Genesis story, the second tree offered knowledge from the serpent, whom John described as 'that ancient serpent, who is called the Devil and Satan, the deceiver of the whole world' (Rev. 12.9).[3] Adam and Eve knew immediately that they were naked; they had eaten the forbidden fruit and lost their garment of glory. The battle was then between the snake and the Woman: 'I will put enmity between you and the woman, and between your seed and her seed . . .' (Gen. 3.15). When John saw the Woman [again] in heaven, and her son set on the throne of God, then the snake and his angels were thrown from heaven.

The quest for Wisdom involves many aspects of temple theology: not only its content but also its methods. The Wisdom tradition has been neglected, and so methods developed for other aspects of biblical study are not necessarily the most useful for this task. It is important to remember that those who compiled the books of Moses were telling two stories: the history of their people and the history of the troubled era of the second temple. Adam and Eve leaving Eden was, as we have seen, also an account of the ancient priesthood leaving the original temple. The story of Amram's children – Miriam, Aaron and Moses – was also describing that troubled era. People remembered, centuries later, that Aaron represented the priesthood, Moses the Law, and that Miriam was Wisdom. Miriam/Wisdom was banished and died. She was buried in Kadesh, *qadeš*, which means 'the holy place' (Num. 20.1), and after her death, 'there was no water for the congregation.' There were stories of her miraculous well that had followed the Israelites in the desert, but the lost water was eventually restored to them because of the merits of Moses and Aaron.[4] Water was one of the symbols of Wisdom, and it cannot have been coincidence that the early Christians, when they told the story of the annunciation in more detail, said that

---

2 R. C. Chartres, 'Wisdom, Knowledge and Information' in *The Adriatic Sea*, Athens: Religion, Science and the Environment, 2003, pp. 153–8, p. 153. Also at www.rsesymposia.org

3 Devil, *diabolos*, literally means 'deceiver'.

4 Babylonian Talmud *Ta'anit* 9a.

Mary/Miriam, the mother of the Son of God, first heard Gabriel's message when she was at the well.[5]

When Enoch described the heavenly throne in the holy of holies, he said there were fountains of righteousness and wisdom by the throne, where the thirsty could drink and be filled with Wisdom, that Wisdom was poured out like water.[6] This is probably what the first Christians understood when Jesus taught: 'Blessed are those who hunger and thirst for righteousness, for they shall be satisfied' (Mt. 5.6), and when John described the river of the water of life flowing from the tree of life (Rev. 22.1–2). Wisdom would be given to the chosen ones after the great judgement,[7] according to the opening passage of *1 Enoch* from which Jude quoted (Jude 14–15). This sequence is described in more detail later in *1 Enoch*: the holy LORD would come forth to judge the earth; iniquity and all its strongholds would be burned and disappear from the earth – presumably the judgement described in 2 Peter 3.11–13; and then the righteous would arise from their sleep and be given the promised Wisdom.[8] This is also the sequence in the Book of Revelation: the LORD comes forth with his angels; the beast and his allies are thrown into the lake of fire (Rev. 19.11–21); the earth is renewed and the bride of the Lamb appears (Rev. 21.1, 9). John then sees the tree of life and the water of life – two symbols of Wisdom – and hears the Spirit and the Bride summoning the thirsty to drink (Rev. 22.1–2, 17).

Miriam was also associated with the design and construction of the temple: 'It was from her that Bezalel descended, from whom, in turn, David who was king.'[9] Miriam, then, was the mother of the tabernacle builder, who was 'filled with the Spirit of the *'elohim*, with wisdom, intelligence, knowledge and all craftsmanship' (Exod. 35.31), and the ancestor of David to whom the plan for the temple was revealed (1 Chron. 28.18–9). Here, in addition to the familiar gifts of wisdom, intelligence and knowledge, Bezalel received 'craftsmanship', practical skills. The children of Miriam/Wisdom were able to realize the heavenly vision in practical ways. Craftsmanship, *m^ela'kah*, is an interesting word as it is the feminine form of the word for an angel,

5 *Infancy Gospel of James* 11.

6 *1 Enoch* 48.1; 49.1.

7 *1 Enoch* 5.9.

8 *1 Enoch* 91.10.

9 *Exodus Rabbah* XLVIII.4.

and seems to indicate creative work. 'God finished his craftsmanship which he had done' (Gen. 2.2, my translation). The word appears many times in the Exodus 35, describing the construction of the tabernacle, but is variously translated: 'any *use* in the work', v. 24; 'anything for *the work . . .*', v. 29; 'every skilled *craft*', v. 33; 'every sort of *work . . .* any sort of *work*man', v. 35. The children of Wisdom are co-creators, taking the raw materials and transforming them.

Wisdom and her works were well known in the time of Jesus, something that seems strange to anyone who uses only the Hebrew Bible that became the Protestant Old Testament. The *Wisdom of Jesus ben Sira*, included in the Greek Old Testament[10] and therefore in the Bible of the earliest Christians in the Mediterranean world, is an extensive exploration of the nature of Wisdom, her role in the creation, and her teaching for the conduct of daily life. The images used point to her ancient self: a mother who fed her children, the tree of life, and water to irrigate her garden with teaching and prophecy. She was also a mighty angel who spoke in the council of the Most High; her throne was in a pillar of cloud; she was a servant in the temple on Zion, in other words, a high priest; she was the incense and anointing oil in the temple; and she fed those who loved her with herself: 'those who eat me will hunger for more, and those who drink me will thirst for more' (Ben Sira 24.1–30).

The *Wisdom of Solomon*, also part of the Greek Old Testament, was composed in Alexandria just before Jesus was born. It tells Israel's history as under the protection of Wisdom, which means she was deemed the equivalent of the LORD. She protected Adam, strengthened Abraham, guided Jacob, protected Joseph, empowered Moses, and then led her people through the Red Sea (Wis. 10.1–21). Wisdom in Egyptian Judaism is often said to be the goddess Isis absorbed by the Jews from the religion of Egypt, but Wisdom – under various names – was part of the ancient faith of those Jews. She came with them when they fled as refugees from Jerusalem in 586 BCE, but she appears in the Hebrew Bible as the rejected 'Queen of Heaven' (Jer. 44.18). Her people had worshipped her with incense, libations and '*kawwanim*, loaves, to represent her' (Jer. 44.19, translating literally).[11] The Queen was represented by bread, presumably the bread that Wisdom fed her devotees. The people for whom Jeremiah spoke blamed the worship of

---

10 The Hebrew text is now known too.

11 Also Jer. 7.18, where the women knead dough to make the *kawwanim*.

the Queen for the destruction of the city; others who fled to Egypt said it was neglecting her that had caused the disaster.[12]

The people from Jerusalem who honoured the Queen told their history differently, using a pattern of sevens or 'weeks': they knew about Noah and Abraham, about the Law given on Sinai and building the temple and then, they said, there had been a great disaster. The temple was burned and the people scattered because the priests lost their vision and abandoned Wisdom.[13] *Wisdom, then, opened eyes and gave spiritual vision.* When the temple was built again, there was an impure and apostate generation; the temple bread was not pure, and the eyes of the sheep were not open.[14] The Christians knew this temple as the harlot in Revelation, who had usurped the place of the Bride. At the end of the seventh 'week', however, chosen witnesses to righteousness would arise and receive sevenfold wisdom and knowledge.[15] Wisdom would return, but not to all Israel. As we have seen, those who hoped for all the glory of Adam knew they would be given the wisdom of the sons of heaven. The Enoch tradition claimed that when Wisdom was rejected and went back to heaven, her place was taken by unrighteousness, who was received 'like rain in the desert, and dew on a thirsty land'.[16] 'Unrighteousness' was the usurper who then watered the thirsty land instead of Wisdom. 'Baruch', written in the second century BCE, knew that Israel's problems were caused by deserting Wisdom: 'You have forsaken the fountain of Wisdom. If you had walked in the way of God, you would be dwelling in peace for ever' (Bar. 3.12–13).

Rediscovering Wisdom, the Queen that Jeremiah and some of his contemporaries rejected, is not easy. Reading with familiar eyes, often called the traditional reading, one can miss what is actually there, and so the study of 'Wisdom', more often written 'wisdom', was neglected by biblical scholars for many years, in favour of the 'history of Israel' approach. This imbalance, as we have seen, had serious consequences for the general perception of biblical teaching, and left many Bible-based communities with a much reduced basis for teaching

---

12 For detail, see my book *The Great High Priest*, London: T&T Clark, 2003, pp. 229–61.

13 *1 Enoch* 93.8.

14 *1 Enoch* 89.73–4.

15 *1 Enoch* 93.3–10.

16 *1 Enoch* 42.2–3.

about the care of the creation.[17] Wisdom was viewed with suspicion, and texts that mentioned Wisdom were 'translated' in ways that concealed her importance. She was rarely written with a capital letter, and her pronoun was often 'it' rather than 'she',[18] as in 'the Sun of righteousness shall arise with healing in *its* wings' (Mal. 4.2), where the Hebrew has 'her wings'. She has been deemed a late personification of an aspect of the LORD, even though anthropomorphism, when it refers to the LORD, is said to be a sign of early texts, for example when the LORD shut the door of Noah's ark (Gen. 7.16). Consistency requires that Wisdom also be deemed early.

Biblical scholars did not wish to find Wisdom, and devised ways of avoiding wisdom. Even when she was before their eyes, they did not recognize her. An outstanding example of this is Michelangelo's 'creation of Adam' on the ceiling of the Sistine Chapel (1508–12). Wisdom is the woman beside the Creator, just as she is described in Proverbs. The two hover above Adam in what is usually assumed to be a dark cloud, but is in fact a picture of the human brain in which are God, Wisdom and the angels. It is clear from his other work that Michelangelo had studied anatomy, and in this fresco he depicts Wisdom at the centre of the brain.[19] He does not show Adam coming to life – Adam's eyes are already open; he shows Adam receiving something more than life itself. The divine-and-human fingers do not quite touch, but something is passing between them. 'Michelangelo portrays that what God is giving to Adam is the intellect.'[20] Or maybe Michelangelo was depicting the gift of Wisdom, which he experienced as the craftmanship that was given to Bezalel, the craftsmanship that was the partner of angelic inspiration. Sculpting, he wrote in one of his poems, giving life to stone, was not achieved by human skill.

> In painting too, this is perceived:
> Only after the intellect has planned
> The best and highest, can the ready hand
> Take up the brush and try all things received.[21]

17 See above, pp. 9–11.

18 There is no word for 'it' in Hebrew.

19 Not Eve, as is sometimes suggested.

20 F. L. Meshberger, 'An Interpretation of Michelangelo's Creation of Adam based on Neuroanatomy', *Journal of the American Medical Association*, 264 (1990) pp. 1837–41, p. 1841. I am grateful to Dr G. M. Cooper for telling me about this article.

21 Quoted in Meshberger, 'An Interpretation of Michelangelo's Creation of Adam based on Neuroanatomy', p. 1837.

The practical creativity that Wisdom inspires is very similar to the creative process portrayed and thus realized by the world view and liturgies of the temple, the temple that Wisdom had planned and enabled her children to build.

The loss of Wisdom is not a recent phenomenon: Wisdom was obscured in each of the stages that marked the development of the Hebrew Scriptures. First, the scribes of the second temple period looked back with hostility on the Lady, and described her as Asherah, a Canaanite goddess, when all the surviving Hebrew inscriptions[22] show that she was called Ashratah.[23] Uncritical readers of the works of these scribes have accepted that the Lady was imported from Canaanite religion, and so those who expelled her from the temple could be called reformers. Cutting down and burning her symbol – the tree – was a purification. Such a judgement creates huge problems for reading Revelation; if removing the Lady and her tree from the temple was a reform, why did the early Christians celebrate her return? John saw the woman who appeared in heaven, the mother of the one enthroned, and the tree of life restored by the throne in the midst of the new city.

The Hebrew text of 2 Kgs 23 as now read says that her cult involved prostitution, and that her female devotees wove hangings for her tree (2 Kgs 23.4–14). Thus Josiah's temple purge in 623 BCE is described as his 'reform' of the temple. The word for 'prostitutes', however, can also be read as 'holy ones',[24] and this 'double reading' underlies the implied contrast between the two women figures in Revelation: the harlot who was the mother of harlots and abominations, and the Bride of the Lamb who was the mother of holy ones and anointed ones (Rev. 17.5).[25] Josiah's younger contemporary Ezekiel described the Lady's throne in the temple precincts as 'the seat of the image of jealousy that provokes to jealousy' (Ezek. 8.3) – an unlikely title, unless it was another scribal alteration to avoid mentioning the unmentionable. Removing one silent letter from the Hebrew gives 'the image of the *creatrix* who creates' the feminine counterpart of Melchizedek's title for God: 'the *Father* of heaven and earth'.

---

22 That is, evidence that has not passed through the hands of editors, see G. I. Davies, *Ancient Hebrew Inscriptions*, Cambridge: Cambridge University Press, 1991, 8.017, 8.021.

23 See my book *The Great High Priest*, pp. 229–61.

24 The unpointed Hebrew text can be read two ways.

25 There would have been wordplay in a Hebrew version of this text, see below, p. 250.

(Gen. 14.19).[26] Philo, an Egyptian Jew, still knew this Lady in the time of Jesus: the Logos, he said, was the 'Son of Wisdom his Mother, through whom (fem.) the universe came into being.'[27] An early Christian Wisdom text, also found in Egypt, had Wisdom speaking to her children: 'I am giving you a high priestly garment woven from every [kind of] Wisdom . . . return to your first Father, God, and Wisdom your Mother . . .'[28]

Second, when the Jewish canon was defined at the end of the first century CE, overtly Wisdom texts were not included, even though there was a Hebrew text of *The Wisdom of Jesus ben Sira*. It was not simply a matter of rejecting Greek texts. A story from this time says that when 'Ezra' received the lost Scriptures from the Most High, he dictated 94 books to his scribes, 24 to become the Hebrew Scriptures for public reading, and the remaining 70 to be reserved for the wise: 'For in them is the spring of understanding, the fountain of wisdom and the river of knowledge.'[29] It is generally acknowledged that this story is not about the biblical Ezra, but a thinly veiled account of how the Hebrew Scriptures were preserved and the Hebrew canon defined at the end of the first century CE. This text, 2 Esdras, was preserved only by the Christians, as were the other ancient Jewish books from this period that were not included in the Hebrew canon.[30] It was the Church that preserved the books reserved for 'the wise' which were the source of understanding, wisdom and knowledge, presumably because Wisdom was important for the early Christians. The Christians also kept the Wisdom texts in the Greek Old Testament, that is, until the new translations were made in Europe as part of the reformation. The English versions were based on the Hebrew text and canon, and the Church of England's Thirty Nine Articles of Religion made clear that the Wisdom of Solomon and Ben Sira could be read, but that 'the Church doth not apply them to establish any doctrine.'[31]

26 There was a Lady in Ugarit, too, the Mother of the gods, whose title was concealed by that extra letter in Ezekiel. See my book *The Great Angel*, London: SPCK. 1997, p. 54.

27 Philo, *Flight* 109; also *Questions on Genesis* IV.97.

28 *The Teaching of Silvanus*, CG VII.4.89, 91. A Christianized early Gnostic text, *The Wisdom of Jesus Christ*, uses this title for Wisdom, 'the begettress Sophia', CG III.4.83.

29 *2 Esdras* 14.37–47.

30 The so-called apocrypha and pseudepigrapha of the Old Testament.

31 Article 6.

The role of the Lady was still controversial in the early years of Christianity, and the rules against idolatry seem to have had her in mind: any object with a picture of the sun, the moon or a dragon was to be thrown into the Dead Sea; and any tree pruned into a special shape for worship was to be shunned. It was forbidden to sit in its shade, or even to grow crops in its shade, and it was forbidden to use its wood to heat an oven as it made the bread unclean, or to make a weaver's shuttle.[32] All such items had to be thrown into the Dead Sea. Branches from a shaped tree could not be used in a Tabernacles procession – presumably some Jews who celebrated Tabernacles had been using branches from such a tree.[33] This is an interesting list of prohibitions: the Mother of the Messiah was a woman clothed with the sun and standing on the moon, and she was threatened by a dragon (Rev. 12.1–6); and aspects of her cult were baking bread (Jer. 44.19) and weaving (2 Kgs. 23.7).

The early Church had a 'branches' ceremony, according to a vision of the Christian prophet Hermas who lived in Rome early in the second century CE. The archangel Michael cut pieces of wood from a huge willow tree and gave them to the Christians. The pieces took on the character of each recipient, and their state determined who should enter the 'tower' that represented the Kingdom.[34] This may have been a ceremony performed by the Roman Christians; it was certainly modelled on the prescriptions for Tabernacles, and a temple ceremony in a community with many Hebrew members is not unlikely.[35] Perhaps it was the Christians who used branches from the Lady's trees for Tabernacles. Juvenal, the Roman satirist contemporary with Hermas, used what must have been a recognizable stereotype when he mocked a poor Jewish woman: she was a fortune-teller, 'a high priestess of the tree, a reliable mediator with highest heaven'.[36] Why was a tree the most obvious symbol of Judaism? Later still, in the sixth century CE, when the Christians were a major group in Palestine, the Jews described the Christian cross as the *asherah*, the forbidden tree, the symbol of the Lady. Christian churches were dedicated to Mary, and hymns composed

---

32 Mishnah *Aboda Zarah* 3.3, 7–9.

33 Mishnah *Sukkah* 3.2.

34 *Hermas*, Parable 8.1–2.

35 Paul's letter to the Romans shows he was writing to a community with many Jewish members. For detail of this ceremony, see my book *Temple Themes in Christian Worship*, London: T&T Clark, 2007, pp. 42–4.

36 Juvenal *Satires* 6.543–5.

to her using the ancient imagery of the Lady: 'It is easy to see how the Jews could identify Mary with the Canaanite goddess Asherah and execrate the idolatrous worship of Christians.'[37] When Jewish memories were recalling that Miriam/Mary represented Wisdom, the Christians were dedicating great cathedrals and churches to the Holy Wisdom, and when the Emperor Justinian built a great church in Jerusalem that was clearly a new temple,[38] it was dedicated to Mary. Maximos the Confessor (died 662 CE), taught:

> God, who in his mercy for us has desired that the grace of divine virtue be sent down from heaven to those on earth, has symbolically built the sacred tent and everything in it as a representation, figure, and imitation of Wisdom.[39]

Jesus spoke of Wisdom: 'Wisdom is justified by all her children/ deeds'[40] (Lk. 7.35); 'The Wisdom of God said "I will send them prophets and apostles . . ." Woe to you lawyers, for you have taken away the key of knowledge . . .' (Lk. 11.49, 52). Jesus assured his followers that, in a time of crisis, they would be given wisdom to know what to say (Lk. 21.15). After teaching in a synagogue, the congregation asked: 'Where did [Jesus] get this wisdom and these mighty works?' (Mt. 13.54; Mk 6.2). Luke noted twice that the child Jesus was blessed with wisdom and God's favour (Lk. 2.40, 52), and Gabriel announced to Zechariah that his son John would prepare the people for the Lord by turning the disobedient to the wisdom of the righteous ones (Lk. 1.17). James, the leader of the church in Jerusalem, wrote to his scattered flock about wisdom, contrasting the heavenly wisdom with its earthly counterpart, at the same time as John was contrasting the image of the beast and the image of God, the mother of harlots and abominations and the mother of the holy and anointed ones. The words James chose to describe Wisdom reveal where she fitted into the earliest Christian world view. They were words drawn from creation covenant discourse, as we should expect: pure, peaceable, gentle, obeying rules, full of mercy and good fruits, not separated out, sincere. 'The fruit of righteousness is sown in peace by those who make peace.' (Jas 3.17–18) alludes to her tree of life and its fruit,

---

37 R. L. Wilken, *The Land Called Holy*, New Haven: Yale University Press, 1992, p. 211.

38 Consecrated in 543 CE, see my book *Temple Themes in Christian Worship*, pp. 70–2.

39 Maximos, *Chapters on Knowledge*, 1.88.

40 The Sinaiticus text has 'deeds', as does Matt. 11.19.

as does Paul's description of the fruit of the Spirit: 'Love, joy, peace, patience, kindness, goodness, faithfulness, gentleness, self control' (Gal. 5.22–3).

Wisdom was at the LORD's side before there was a material creation. Before the mountains and hills were shaped, before the sea was confined within its limits, 'I was beside him, joining all things together in harmony' (Prov. 8.30 Lxx). The creation covenant, the original 'binding' that gives the covenant its name, was Wisdom/the work of Wisdom. Since she was with the LORD before the material world was made, she belonged, in temple terms, in the holy of holies. Wisdom was described as the breath of the power of God, and it was the breath of God that transformed Adam from a creature of clay into a living being (Wis. 7.25; Gen. 2.7). When the human couple rejected Wisdom, the curse on them was to live with what they had chosen – to return to the dust because they had rejected the Wisdom that transformed the dust. The breath of God gave Adam the power of speech, and words themselves were a form of Wisdom. Since she joined all things together in harmony, the literary forms for expressing Wisdom were parables and proverbs – noting similarities, comparing opposites, the basis for natural science. Since she was also a mighty angel, one of the assembly of God Most High (Ben Sira 24.2), she revealed herself as did the angels. To know Wisdom was to know her role in the creation.

The *Wisdom of Solomon* described Wisdom in great detail.

> Wisdom is radiant and unfading, and she is easily discerned by those who love her, and is found by those who seek her. (Wis. 6.12).
> For both we and our works are in [God's] hand, as are all understanding and skill in crafts.
> For it is he that gave me unerring knowledge of what exists,
> to know the structure of the world and the activity of the elements;
> the beginning and end and middle of times, the alternation of the solstices and the changes of the seasons,
> the cycles of the year and the constellations of the stars,
> the natures of animals and the tempers of wild beasts,
> the powers of spirits and the reasonings of men,
> the varieties of plants and the virtues of roots;
> I learned both what is secret and what is manifest,
> For Wisdom the fashioner of all things taught me.
>
> (Wis. 7.16–22)

These are the secrets of creation revealed in the holy of holies, the angel lore that was the natural science of the time, and here it is

Wisdom who has the role of the revealing angels.[41] The Qumran community, living in Judea in the time of Jesus, called this 'wisdom concealed from men, knowledge and wise design', a fountain of righteousness, a storehouse of power, a spring of glory, all hidden from mortals but revealed to those who had joined the assembly of angels.[42] *The earliest claim of the Christians was that Jesus had revealed the secrets of the holy of holies to his disciples.*

Wisdom also joins together all the aspects of creation theology in this book:

- She appears again in the temple as the Kingdom is proclaimed.
- She opens eyes so that people see differently.
- She is enthroned on the foundation stone of the creation.[43]
- She is concealed in the Holy of Holies.
- She enables the vision at the heart of the covenant system.
- She binds all things together.
- She enables justice and righteousness.
- She is the co-Creator.
- She is the Mother of the Logos/Messiah.

Two observations now from speakers at a *Religion, Science and the Environment* symposium.

> Some of the concepts of modern science actually seem to me to enhance the plausibility of this work of entry into the divine wisdom. There are a number of concepts that make the recovery of an authentically biblical and spiritual awareness of living wisdom more than a possibility.[44]
>
> Most of [the unsolved and outstanding problems of science] are precisely to do with what makes things wholes. How do ecosystems or societies or organisms function as wholes?. . . The reductionist approach . . . doesn't add up to understanding how the whole organism works. In fact it leads to an increasing fragmentation of research . . . A science of interconnectedness could have beneficial effects for our understanding of the environmental crisis.[45]

---

41 See above pp. 114–6.

42 *Qumran Community Rule*, 1QS XI. 6–7.

43 See above p. 50.

44 Chartres, 'Wisdom, Knowledge and Information', pp. 153–8, p. 157, see above n.2.

45 R. Sheldrake, 'Need Science and Wisdom be Separate' in *The Adriatic Sea, A Sea at Risk, a Unity of Purpose*, Athens: Religion, Science and the Environment, 2003, pp. 109–15, 112, 115.

This is, of course, how all knowledge was understood in the culture of the West before the so-called Enlightenment, and, as Zizioulas observed, science and theology have for a long time gone their separate ways as though there were different sorts of truth, 'making truth subject to the dichotomy between the transcendent and the imminent'.[46]

The rejection/corruption of Wisdom begins the biblical story in Genesis, and her restoration is the climax of the Revelation to John. She is at the heart of the vision of the Kingdom and in fact makes it possible. But there can be no Kingdom realized on earth while human beings think they own knowledge. 'Intellectual property' has commercial value, and in a knowledge based economy, knowledge cannot be shared, only traded. There is little sign of Wisdom's influence in the way information and knowledge are used today, or in the way that, for example, natural life processes are patented and used for profit. Creation is being destroyed, not through ignorance, but through knowledge, often very great knowledge, divorced from Wisdom. Well might we ask, in the words of T S Eliot:

> Where is the Wisdom we have lost in knowledge?
> Where is the knowledge that we have lost in information?[47]

THE MOTHER

Philo, implying that everyone would agree with him, asked: 'And who is considered to be the daughter of God but Wisdom who is the first-born mother of all things?'[48] The *Gospel of Philip*, an early Christian text said: 'The soul of Adam came into being by means of a breath . . . The spirit given him is his mother.'[49] The next section of the text is fragmented, but compares the two trees in Eden: the fruit of the tree of knowledge made Adam an animal [i.e. mortal] and he worshipped what he created; whereas the fruit of the tree of life nourished men [i.e. angels] whom the gods would worship. 'It would be fitting for the gods to worship men.' In other words, those fed by Wisdom and her tree became angels, the Adams whom the angels had to honour. These early Christians also knew, as we have reconstructed from Revelation,

---

46 See above, p. 66.

47 T. S. Eliot, *The Rock*, chorus 1.

48 Philo, *Questions on Genesis* IV.97.

49 *The Gospel of Philip* CG II.3.70.

that: 'Wisdom is the Mother of the angels.' This was the title of the Lady whom Ezekiel knew in the temple.[50]

There are many texts and images to describe Wisdom: she was the mother who fed her children with bread and water; she was the tree of life whose fruit gave wisdom, whose leaves were for healing, and whose oil was used for anointing, to open eyes and restore Adams to their original state; and she was the bond who held all things in harmony. She was, in effect, the creation covenant, described sometimes as the Spirit and sometimes as righteousness. She came forth from the mouth of the Most High and covered the earth like a mist (Ben Sira 24.3). All the images are interrelated, and so it is not easy to enter the system. There is word play characteristic of temple discourse, often indicating the good and its evil opposite, and there are memories rooted deep in the world of the first temple. Allusions to Wisdom are found in many early Christian writings, even in familiar texts that do not mention her by name.

Jesus spoke of Wisdom as the mother of many children: 'Wisdom is justified by all her children' (Lk. 7.35), although it is not clear what was meant by 'justified.' The woman clothed with the sun also had other children, and when the dragon failed to destroy her son, he 'went off to make war on the rest of her offspring' (Rev. 12.17). Since her other offspring kept the commandments of God and bore testimony to Jesus, she was regarded from the earliest period as the mother of Christians. Now the Christians described themselves as saints, *hagioi*, literally 'holy ones' (e.g. Rom. 1.7; 1 Cor. 1.2; Phil. 1.1), and the name Christian means 'anointed'. We conclude that the woman clothed with the sun was the mother of the holy and anointed ones. Behind the Greek text of Revelation lies the Hebrew text of the Jerusalem Christians, in which holy ones would have been *qᵉdošim*, also meaning angels, and anointed ones *mᵉšihim*. The woman who had replaced Wisdom, according the Enoch, was unrighteousness,[51] and she is the one who appears in John's vision as 'the mother of harlots and the abominations of the earth.' (Rev. 17.5). In Hebrew these words are similar to holy and anointed ones: harlots are *qᵉdišim* (e.g. 2 Kgs 23.7), corrupted ones are *mašhitim* (e.g. Isa. 1.7). The two women in Revelation were Wisdom and her evil opposite, described in some Qumran texts as 'Folly', and they were mothers of angels and anointed ones, or of harlots and abominations.

---

50 *The Gospel of Philip* CG II.3.63.

51 *1 Enoch* 42.2–3.

One such Qumran text,[52] copied about 50 BCE but not necessarily composed at that time, shows how closely John's vision of the two contrasted women reflected the cultural context of the early Christians. It warned against Folly: she was clothed in the shadows of twilight, whereas Wisdom was clothed with the sun. Her disciples would have an inheritance 'amid everlasting fire, and not among those who shine brightly'. Jesus warned that the devil and his angels would go to everlasting fire (Mt. 25.41), whereas the wise were destined to 'shine like the brightness of the firmament, and those who turn many to righteousness, like the stars for ever and ever' (Dan. 12.3). Folly was the beginning of all the ways of iniquity, in contrast to Wisdom who was the beginning of the ways of the LORD (Prov. 8.22). Folly waited by the city gates and in the squares to entice the righteous and upright, so that they would turn away from the commandments and statutes and lead other people astray, whereas Wisdom called out in the gates and markets of the city to turn the fools and scoffers from their complacency, warning that they would eat the fruits of their own ways (Prov. 1.30–33). Folly 'sets up her dwelling in the foundations of gloom, and inhabits the tents of silence', whereas Wisdom lived in the light of glory where the heavenly hosts sang praises to the Creator. When Enoch was taken on a journey through the heavens, he was guided by shining men with golden wings, who were 'clothed in singing'.[53] In the second heaven he saw some fallen angels imprisoned in darkness,[54] and in the fifth heaven he saw the Watchers standing in silence, unable to sing the liturgy because they had rebelled against the LORD.[55] This is what the Qumran Wisdom text was describing: the disciples of Folly destined for her dark and silent places. The ways of Wisdom and their opposite were an important issue in the time of the early Christians.

Wisdom clothed, fed and gave water to her children, and each of these symbolized herself. Adam, as we have seen, wore the garment of Wisdom. An early Christian Wisdom text says: 'Wisdom summons you in her goodness, saying . . . I am giving you a high priestly garment, which is woven from every wisdom . . . Clothe yourself with Wisdom like a robe, put knowledge upon you like a crown, and be seated upon a throne of

---

52 4Q 184, in D. J. Harrington, *Wisdom Texts from Qumran*, London: Routledge, 1996, pp. 31–5.

53 *2 Enoch* 1.5.

54 *2 Enoch* 7.1–2.

55 *2 Enoch* 18.2.

perception.'[56] The *Gospel of Thomas* has a longer version of Jesus' teaching about John the Baptist (Mt.11.2–15; Lk. 7.18–27): 'Jesus said "Why have you come out into the desert? To see a reed shaken by the wind? And to see a man clothed in fine garments like your kings and your great men?"' Upon them are the fine garments, and they are unable to discern the truth.'[57] This suggests that the Jesus' saying was an observation that the ones wearing fine garments lacked the finest garment of all: Wisdom. Thus Matthew and Luke report that Jesus gave the signs of Wisdom restored: healing the plagues brought by the fallen angels, sight and hearing restored, and the dead raised. And then the warning that only Wisdom's children understand these things: 'He who has ears to hear, let him hear' (Mt. 11.15). Perhaps there was a double meaning in Jesus' saying about anxiety: 'Do not be anxious about your life, what you shall eat or what you shall drink, nor about your body, what you shall put on.' The heavenly Father would feed them, and they would wear clothes more glorious than the robes of Solomon, the proverbially wise king. All these would be given to those who sought the Kingdom (Mt. 6.25–33).

'[Wisdom] will meet him like a mother, and like the wife of his youth she will welcome him. She will feed him with the bread of understanding, and give him the water of Wisdom to drink' (Ben Sira 15.2–3); and Wisdom promised those who loved her: 'Those who eat me will hunger for more, and those who drink me will thirst for more' (Ben Sira 24.21). Centuries earlier, the devotees of the Queen had baked loaves to represent her (Jer. 44.19), and Wisdom had invited people to her table: 'Come, eat of my bread and drink of the wine I have mixed. Leave those who lack wisdom, and live, and walk straight/ happily, in the way of insight' (Prov. 9.5–6), (my translation). Centuries after the time of Jesus, Jewish tradition still remembered: 'The house of Wisdom is the tabernacle, and Wisdom's table is the Bread of the Presence and the wine.'[58] Although the table for bread and wine in the tabernacle/temple (Exod. 25.23–30) was remembered as Wisdom's table, nothing was said about it in the Hebrew Scriptures except that the high priests ate the bread of the presence[59] each Sabbath as their most holy food. Their most holy food had to be eaten in the holy place (Lev. 24.9), and was remembered as the most holy of all the

---

56 *The Teaching of Silvanus*, CG VII.4.89.

57 *The Gospel of Thomas*, 78.

58 *Leviticus Rabbah* XI.9.

59 Often translated into English as the 'shewbread'.

offerings.[60] Since 'most holy' meant 'actively holy, imparting holiness', the bread of the presence nourished the priests with holiness, and this was remembered as eating from Wisdom's table.[61] *These were memories and showed how the text was understood.*

Then Wisdom was rejected, and Malachi said that the bread in the second temple was polluted; he looked for the day when the cereal offering would again be pure (Mal. 1.7, 11).[62] The Church understood this as a prophecy of the Eucharist,[63] and even though only few texts survive from the earliest period, several link the eucharistic bread to Wisdom. The *Didache*,[64] a description of Church practices in the second or even the first generation, has the earliest account of the Eucharist outside the New Testament. Over the bread they prayed: 'We give thanks to thee our Father, for the life and knowledge thou hast made known to us through they servant Jesus.' After the distribution they prayed: 'Thanks be to thee Holy Father, for thy sacred Name which thou hast caused to dwell in our hearts, and for the knowledge and faith and immortality which thou hast revealed to us through thy servant Jesus.'[65] There was more to the origin of the Eucharist than the last supper described in the New Testament. Thanks for 'life and knowledge' and for 'knowledge and faith and immortality' suggest an important place for Wisdom, and the Orthodox Church still reads Wisdom's invitation to her table on Maundy Thursday (Prov. 9.1–6).

Other early references may imply the bread of Wisdom. The writer of Hebrews described the Christians of the first generation as 'those who have been enlightened, who have tasted the heavenly gift, and have become partakers of the Holy Spirit, and have tasted the goodness of the Word of God and the powers of the age to come . . .' (Heb. 6.4–5). Clement of Rome, writing to Corinth at the end of the first century, said:

60 Targum *Onqelos* Lev. 24.9.

61 By the end of the second temple period, the bread was eaten by all the priests, Mishnah *Menahoth* 11.7. *Genesis Rabbah* XLIII.6 said the bread and wine were the offerings of Melchizedek.

62 Malachi means 'my angel' and the collection of material under this name may be from several sources.

63 *Didache* 14; Justin, *Trypho* 41.

64 Also known as the *Teaching of the Twelve Apostles.*

65 *Didache* 9.

> Through [Jesus Christ the high priest] . . . the eyes of our hearts are opened,
> through him our dim and clouded understanding unfolds like a flower to the
> light; for through him the Lord permits us to taste the wisdom of eternity.[66]

Opening the eyes of the heart is Wisdom discourse: the heart at that time was deemed the seat of the intellect, and opening its eyes meant 'the renewal of your mind' (Rom. 12.2). 'To taste the wisdom of eternity' or 'to taste the heavenly gift' described Wisdom feeding her children. Christian ritual involved tasting wine and bread, and, in the light of the temple symbolism of the most holy bread that nourished the priests with holiness and wisdom, the most likely meaning of the allusions in Hebrews and *1 Clement* is that the Christians too were fed with Wisdom. Bishop Serapion's people, in early fourth century Egypt, were still using this 'wisdom' form of the Eucharist. At the fraction they prayed:

> Count us worthy of this communion also, O God of truth, and make our bodies
> contain purity and our souls prudence and knowledge. And make us wise,
> O God of compassions, by the participation of the body and the blood . . .

In the offertory prayer, Bishop Serapion had prayed: 'Make us living [i.e. resurrected] men . . . that we may be able to tell forth thy unspeakable mysteries . . .'

Wisdom also quenched her children's thirst, and a whole complex of images was used to convey this. The *Gospel of Thomas* has words of Jesus not found in the New Testament. When Jesus was in the world, he said:

> I found all of them intoxicated but I found none of them thirsty. My soul was
> afflicted for the sons of men, because they are blind in their hearts and do not
> have sight . . . For the moment they are intoxicated; when they shake off their
> wine, then they will repent . . . There are many around the drinking trough, but
> there is nothing in the cistern.[67]

Enoch described the fountains of righteousness and wisdom that flowed from the heavenly throne.[68] In the original temple the psalmist sang of the children of men taking refuge

> in the shadow of thy wings.
> They feast on the abundance of thy house,
> and thou givest them drink from the river of thy delights [literally your Edens].
> For with thee is the fountain of life;

66 *1 Clement* 36.

67 *The Gospel of Thomas* 28, 74.

68 *1 Enoch* 48.1; 49.1.

and in thy light do we see light.

(Ps. 36.7–9)[69]

The Qumran hymns echoed this: the fountain flowed with light for those who would receive it, and with the fire of judgement for others. 'A source of light shall become an ever flowing fountain, and in its bright flames all the [ ] shall be consumed . . .'[70] Wisdom's living water was a temple image that passed into Christian usage. Water flowing from the holy of holies became an important part of the Christian vision. When Justinian built his great restored temple in Jerusalem, in every respect like the temple of Ezekiel's vision, there was a water cistern under its eastern end, presumably to provide a fountain in the holy of holies,[71] and, according to the mediaeval Muslim travel writer Ibn Battuta, water flowed out of the church of the Holy Wisdom in Constantinople. '[The water flows] between two walls about a cubit high, constructed in marble inlaid with different colours and cut in the most skilful art, and trees are planted in rows on both sides of this channel.'[72]

Wisdom herself said she would water her garden and drench her plot, pouring out teaching like prophecy (Ben Sira 25.31–3). Water was the symbol of wise teaching, and so the familiar images of sweet water[73] in the Hebrew Bible can be read with their two meanings: water flowed out of Eden (Gen. 2.10). In his vision, Ezekiel saw water flowing from the restored temple, to transform the salt water of the Dead Sea,[74] and along the banks of this river was a grove of trees of life (Ezek. 47.1–12). On the day when the LORD became king, living waters would flow from Jerusalem (Zech. 14.8–9); a fountain would come forth from the house of the LORD (Joel 3.18). John saw the river of life flowing from the holy of holies, watering the roots of the tree of life, or perhaps issuing from it (Rev. 22.1–2),[75] and the

69 The wings refer to the giant cherubim that formed the throne in the holy of holies.

70 1 QH XIV 17–18.

71 This was the Nea Church, consecrated in 543 CE; for detail, see my book *Temple Themes in Christian Worship*, pp. 70–2.

72 *Travels of Ibn Battuta, AD 1325–1354*, tr. H. A. R. Gibb, London: Hakluyt Society, 1959, vol.2, p. 509. No other source mentions this.

73 The sea meant something different; salt water and sweet water were distinguished for example Rev. 14.7.

74 With certain exceptions that recognized the value of the salt industry!

75 The text is not clear.

Spirit and the Bride invited anyone who was thirsty to drink the water of life without price (Rev. 22.17). This was a sign of the new creation, and God promised 'To the thirsty I will give from the fountain of the water of life without payment' (Rev. 21.6). Jesus himself, teaching in the temple on the last day of the feast of Tabernacles, also invited people to drink from him: 'If anyone thirst, let him come to me and drink . . .' John explained that this was the gift of the Spirit. Those who drank became conduits of the living water, which would flow from their hearts (Jn 7.37–8). Now the heart, as we have seen, was the seat of the intellect: Jesus warned that evil thoughts that lead to evil behaviour come from the human heart (Mk 7.21–3), and so the gift of living water from the LORD had the effect of changing how people think and act. The same way of thinking is found in the Qumran hymns. Someone 'into whose heart Thou hast put teaching and understanding, that he might open a fountain of knowledge to all men of insight'[76] had become a traitor.

John saw those who had come through the great tribulation, and they were serving in the temple; God sheltered them with his presence, they had neither hunger nor thirst, for the Lamb guided them to the springs of living water (Rev. 7.15–17). Isaiah assured the righteous man that he would see the king [in the holy of holies] and his bread and water would be assured (Isa. 33.16–7). In this temple context, lamenting the broken covenant, the prophet did not mean simply bread and water. They symbolized good teaching, Wisdom. Through his prophet, the LORD had warned Jerusalem and Judah that the regime of the fallen angels would bring disaster, and so Jerusalem losing its bread and water was not simply a prediction of food shortages (Isa. 3.1, reading in the context of the preceding chapter). This 'famine', due to ignoring the prophet's warning, would cause people to curse God as they looked on the distress and darkness all around them (Isa. 8.16–22). And the familiar words follow: 'The people who walked in darkness, have seen a great light . . . For to us a Child is born . . .' (Isa. 9.2,6). John saw this as Wisdom giving birth to her Son, and, according to the *Gospel of the Hebrews,* Jesus himself referred 'my mother the Holy Spirit.'[77] This gospel, now lost apart from quotations in other writers, said it was the Holy Spirit who spoke to Jesus at his baptism and called him 'My son.'[78]

---

76 1QH X.16–17.

77 Origen *On Jeremiah*, Homily 15, quoting the *Gospel of the Hebrews*.

78 Jerome, *On Isaiah* 11.

Jeremiah also linked the throne and the fountain: 'A throne set on high from the beginning is the place of our sanctuary . . . They have forsaken the LORD, the fountain of living water' (Jer. 17.12–13). He warned that the people had exchanged their glory for something worthless, they had changed their gods and forsaken the LORD, the fountain of living waters (Jer. 2.12–13). When Ezekiel saw the holy of holies leaving the temple and appearing in Babylon, he described the glory as the throne and the likeness upon it, and the fiery beings beneath. Their sound was like many waters (Ezek. 1.24), and he heard many waters as the glory returned (Ezek. 43.1–2). John also heard the sound of the host on Mount Zion and the sound of the great multitude in heaven as 'the sound of many waters' (Rev. 14.2; 19.6). He also said, enigmatically, that he heard the waters in the voice of the risen LORD (Rev.1.15).[79]

Water symbolized wise teaching and the words of the LORD. The LORD spoke through Isaiah: 'For as the rain and snow come down from heaven, and return not thither but water the earth . . . so shall my word be that goes forth from my mouth' (Isa. 55.10–11; Hos. 6.3 is similar). When the Spirit of the LORD comes to rest on the branch from Jesse, 'the earth shall be full of the knowledge of the LORD, as the waters cover the sea' (Isa. 11.9, also Hab. 2.14). The song of Moses began: 'May my teaching drop as the rain. . . my speech distil as the dew . . . as the gentle rain . . . and as the showers'(Deut. 32.2). There are various forms of the same wise saying about the fountain of life: Proverbs 13.14 'The teaching of the wise / the fear of the LORD is a fountain of life, that one may avoid the snares of death' (Prov. 13.14/14.27). There was wordplay too: the same Hebrew verb *yarah*, literally to throw or to shoot, came to mean either to give water/ rain, or to give instruction/teaching. Several passages are, as a result, ambiguous. Rain and teacher are the same word, *moreh.* Joel called for repentance, and then rejoiced that the LORD had given 'rain for righteousness' or was it 'a teacher for righteousness' such as we find in the Qumran texts? Maybe it meant both. And there was the mysterious Teacher who would no longer be hidden. After a time of 'the bread of adversity and the water of affliction', the people would abandon their unclean images and they would enjoy rain and running water to bring prosperity (Isa. 30.19–25).

The wise are trees planted by this water. The Psalter begins: 'Blessed is the man who walks not in the counsel of the wicked', who shuns

---

79 'Ezra' too heard the heavenly voice as 'many waters', 2 Esdras 6.17.

sinners and scoffers, and loves the Law of the LORD. 'He is like a tree planted by streams of water, that yields its fruit in season and its leaf does not wither' (Ps. 1.1–3, and something very similar in Jer. 17.7–8). Sinners are like an oak that withers, like a garden without water (Isa. 1.30). The LORD leads the faithful by the waters of rest, along the paths of righteousness (Ps. 23.2–3), and searching for the LORD is like the quest for water (Ps. 63.1). One of the Qumran hymns is a long description of the community of trees in their watered garden, similar to the grove of trees of life that Ezekiel saw growing by the water from the temple: 'Thou hast placed me beside a fountain of streams in an arid land, and close to a spring of waters in a dry land . . .' By this source of water was a plantation of trees – the community – whose roots were joined to the everlasting spring. The well spring of life and the waters of holiness were only for the community, and not for anyone who 'seeing has not discerned, and considering has not believed in the fountain of life . . .'[80]

In contrast, a parched land was without Wisdom or Spirit. When a king reigned in righteousness and princes ruled in justice – the signs that the creation covenant was maintained – these rulers were like streams of water in a dry place (Isa. 32.2). The signs of Wisdom follow: eyes see, ears hear, the human mind has good judgement. Fools with their folly and iniquity are recognized for what they are: people who leave the hungry unsatisfied and deprive the thirsty of drink. (Isa. 32.3–6). Then the Spirit is poured out, and the wilderness becomes fruitful field. There is justice and righteousness and peace for the creation. In other words, justice for the environment follows the gift of the Spirit/Wisdom to rulers (Isa. 32.15–20; 44.3–4 is similar). When waters break forth in the wilderness and streams in the desert, the dry land blossoms. This is not just a statement about irrigation, because again, the signs of Wisdom follow: those who did not see, do see; those who did not hear, do hear; those who were unable to walk can jump; and those who did not speak sing for joy (Isa. 35.1–7). The *Psalms of Solomon*, composed in the mid first century BCE, still used the image of drought: 'The heavens withheld rain from falling on the earth. Springs were stopped: the perennial far underground and those on the high mountains. For there was no one among them who practised justice and righteousness . . .'[81]

80 1QH XVI 3–14.
81 *Psalms of Solomon* 17.18–9.

There was also polluted water, which was false teaching. 'Like a muddied spring or a polluted fountain is a righteous man who gives way before the wicked' (Prov. 25.26). Jeremiah described how his people had turned to deceit, how those who called themselves wise had rejected the word of the LORD and committed abomination without shame. There was no hope, he said, 'the LORD our God has given us poisoned water to drink, because we have sinned against [him]' (Jer. 8.8–15). There was neither peace nor healing. It was a theme of the Wisdom writings that those who rejected Wisdom received as punishment exactly what they had chosen. The LORD twists the surface of the earth, said Isaiah, because its inhabitants have chosen a twisted lifestyle (Isa. 24.1, 6).[82] Who, said Jeremiah, was wise enough to understand what was happening. The land was ruined because the people had forsaken the law of the LORD and gone after other gods: 'Behold I will feed them with wormwood, and give them poisoned water to drink, for from the prophets of Jerusalem ungodliness has gone forth into all the land' (Jer. 23.15; also Jer. 9.15). Wormwood and poison were proverbial as signs of the broken covenant: 'You who turn justice to wormwood, and cast righteousness down to earth'; 'You have turned justice into poison, and the fruit of righteousness into wormwood' (Amos 5.7; 6.12). The Qumran community told of opposition from 'the Scoffer who shed over Israel the waters of lies, causing them to wander in a pathless wilderness . . . abolishing the ways of righteousness . . .' People had not understood the true meaning of prophecy because someone who rained down lies had preached to them,[83] and the early Christians knew of a star who fell from heaven like the king of Babylon (Isa. 14.12) and turned the rivers and fountains into wormwood so that 'many men died of the water.' (Rev. 8.10–11). These were all pictures of false teaching.

The images of Wisdom and her opposite transfer all too easily to our present situation. Wisdom feeds her children, her opposite brings famine. Wisdom bound all things together in harmony, but reports about future food and environment security reveal a very different set of relationships. Increased population necessitates more food, which necessitates intensive management of land, which necessitates dependence on fuel for machinery and transport and the input of fertilizers and pesticides, which run off into water courses and pollute them, so that fish are no longer available as food. Water tables are

---

82 The wordplay on iniquity, *'awon*, distortion.

83 *Damascus Document*, CD I.15–16; VIII.13.

falling in many countries, and this reduces the harvest. Exhausted soil becomes unproductive; a recent report estimates that if the present rate of soil degradation continues, Africa will be able to feed only 25 per cent of its people by 2025.[84] Increased population and a diet that includes more animal products mean that grain has to be imported from countries with a surplus, but as their population grows, they have less surplus to export. This has all the signs of the counter-covenant, what Paul called creation subjected to futility and in bondage to corruption, *phthora* (Rom. 8.20–21), waiting to be set free by those who are led by the Spirit of God. This contrast was probably in his mind when he wrote:

> Do not be deceived; God is not mocked, for whatever a man sows that will he also reap. He who sows to his own flesh will from the flesh reap corruption, *phthora*; but he who sows to the Spirit will from the Spirit reap eternal life. (Gal. 6.7–8)

But how often have food shortages been exacerbated or even caused by selfish or misguided human choices? Overpopulation is a major factor, as is desertification of land, and disease that reduces the workforce. Too often it is the ordinary people, all made as the image of God, who become the victims of economic policies, political strife and ambition, or suffer even when food is available because there is no efficient storage and distribution. Starvation can itself be used as a weapon by those who control food distribution. Money, often aid money, 'disappears', or has been spent on other things considered more important, such as weapons, palaces and luxury cars. And 'the Market' is a major factor: world trade systems and accumulated debt; merchants who stockpile food to get higher prices which the poor cannot afford and which reduce the purchasing power of aid money. Food is even taken away from stricken regions because it can command higher prices elsewhere.[85] 'Food insecurity' leads to riots and war and migration. '[A] formidable risk in the global struggle for survival is that the ecological limits as they affect the long term sustainability of agroecosystems will be easily forgotten to cope with emergencies of

---

84 United Nations University Institute for National Resources in Africa, report December 2006.

85 During the great famine in Ireland, food was taken from Ireland to England, where it sold for a higher price. During the famine in Ethiopia, food was taken from the stricken area to be sold in the capital.

the moment.'[86] Poor people kill their animals for food and eat their seed corn, and then migrate to the cities, where crime grows from desperation.

Where there is food, the Market has contrived to deliver health-destroying obesity even to the very poor. Hunger and obesity have a common root. There is, apparently 'choice' – the snake's original deception – but most people have to buy their food from the nearest outlet. Transport costs are high – even when there is transport – and the 'choice' in the food shop is determined by what is on the shelves, and this in turn is determined by the power of the food corporations. Fruit has to look right, and is chosen because it travels well or keeps well, but people are increasingly alarmed by the residues on their fruits and vegetables. Farmers have to sell to the big buyers, who in turn set out their requirements, and even though there are now strict rules about labelling food products in many countries, writing a label has become a skill worthy of the snake and his deception. Junk food means far more than the sugar and fat laden goods that have caused so many problems: a loaf of bread or a mass produced chicken will not be what our grandparents knew. Robert Kenner's film *Food, Inc*, released in mid-2009, highlighted the huge power of the food production companies, showing the lesser known and less palatable aspects of meat production and the growing of vegetables and grains. The contamination of the whole process of food and feeding is symbolic of the curse on Adam when he rejected Wisdom: 'Cursed is the ground because of you' (Gen. 3.17).

So too with water: Wisdom offers her children the water of Wisdom, the water of life, but we live in a world where one eighth of the population does not have access to water that is safe to drink and two-fifths lack basic sanitation. This unsafe water leads to illness and death, especially among children. At any one time, half the population of the developing world is suffering from a disease associated with poor water or sanitation. To reach the UN millennium development goal of halving the proportion of people without access to safe drinking water and sanitation by 2015, would cost half as much as the rich world spends on mineral water each year. The knowledge and the means to improve the situation are there, but the will is lacking. There are still many places where the provision of water is women's work. They carry a weight of about 20 kg on their heads, and this occupies 26 per cent

---

86 D. Pimentel and M. Giampietro, *Food, Land, Population and the US Economy*, 1994, Washington: Carrying Capacity Network, 1994, IV.

of their time. Governments, however, choose to spend their money on armaments: Pakistan, one example among many, spends 47 times more on the military than on water provision, and as a result some 118,000 people die each year of diarrhoea.[87]

Pollution can take many forms. Even the rain, the symbol of wise teaching coming to water the earth, is now falling through polluted air and watering the earth with acid. Rivers are polluted with industrial waste, with agricultural waste and with human waste which eventually flows into the sea. Run-off from chemical fertilizers can find its way into sources for drinking water. Winds and ocean currents carry pollutants far from their source, and affect communities who had no part in producing them. Arctic peoples as well as wildlife are threatened by a mixture of polychlorinated biphenyls carried from the industrialized world, and passed up the food chain from plankton to fish, seals and polar bears. The greatest health dangers, especially for women, come from eating contaminated blubber: earlier births, reduced birth weights and fewer baby boys. Pregnant women are now advised to avoid traditional Inuit food.

> In the north of Greenland, near the Thule American airbase, only girl babies are born to Inuit families. This has become a critical question of people's survival, but few governments want to talk about the problem of hormone mimickers, because it means thinking about the chemicals you use.[88]

The Baltic Sea is but one example of how various human activities can pollute water and destroy life. Military waste such as World War II munitions and reactor equipment from Russian nuclear submarines has been dumped in the sea, and there is the threat of oil spills from increased tanker traffic to Russia. Chemical fertilizers have been used to grow more food, and most rivers carry agricultural run-off water, whose fertilizer nutrients cause eutrophication, reducing oxygen in the water and thus threatening other organisms. In addition, there has been damage to the sea floor and to fish stocks due to industrialized fishing, and the natural balance has been destroyed. As a result of the Baltic Symposium in 2003, when a group of religious leaders, scientists and fishermen shared their concerns, the Bread and Fish movement was created to encourage co-operation in protection of the local envi-

---

87 Statistics from Water Aid 2009.

88 Aqqaluk Lynge, President of the Inuit Circumpolar Council, addressing the RSE Symposium in Greenland, 2007, quoted in *The Tablet*, 22 September 2007, p. 7.

ronment.[89] This is Wisdom at work, passing into holy souls and making them friends of God and prophets (Wis. 7.27).

THE TREE OF LIFE

The Bible story begins with Adam and Eve barred from the tree of life and ends with the faithful servants of the LORD returning to eat from the tree. The tree of life represented Wisdom, and there is ample evidence that the tree – fruit, leaves, branches and oil – was a key symbol for the early Christians. The story in the New Testament in effect reverses the story in Genesis. The risen LORD promised his faithful servants; 'To him who conquers, I will grant to eat of the tree of life, which is in the Paradise of God' (Rev. 2.7). 'Conquers' is a word with many meanings: the faithful Christian 'conquers', the Lion of Judah 'conquered' to open the scroll and the faithful in heaven were 'conquering from' the beast and its image and the number of its name (Rev. 2.7; 5.5; 15.2, translating literally). 'Conquers' probably represents the Aramaic *zk'*, which can mean conquering, worthy or pure, but the richness of the wordplay does not transfer to the Greek. For the early Christians, the conquering/worthy/pure Lion of Judah opens the scroll; and the conquering/worthy/pure Christian eats again from the tree of life and is conquering the beast. The Book of Revelation closes with John's vision of the tree of life and the river of the water of life flowing through the new Jerusalem. The tree bears fruit all through the year, and its leaves are to heal the nations (Rev. 22.1–2). 'Blessed are those who have washed their robes/keep the commandments,[90] that they may have the right to the tree of life and that they may enter the city by the gates' (Rev. 22.14). Eating from the tree of life was a sign that they had regained the glory of Adam, and were nourishing themselves with the Wisdom that Adam rejected. They no longer bore the image of the man of dust (1 Cor. 15.49). This was a glimpse of the Kingdom, when the earth was no longer a place of dust, death and degradation.

The Book of Proverbs defined Wisdom, and the nuances of the Hebrew words reveal more than is apparent in the English translations.

---

89 I am grateful to J. Thulin for help with this information.

90 Some ancient versions have 'washing their robes', *plunontes tas stolas autōn*, others have 'doing his commandments', *poiountes tas entolas autou*. The Greek looks remarkably similar.

'She is a tree of life to those who grasp/support, *ḥzq*, her; those who grasp/support, *tmk*, her are happy/blessed/led in straight paths, *mᵉ'ušar*.' (Prov. 3.18, my translation). The tree of life supported those who grasped it, and they too supported the tree. Then there is *mᵉ'ušar*, one of the several forms and meanings derived from the word *'ašar*, (pronounced ashar). These are often associated with Wisdom, and are wordplay on her ancient name Ashratah. They mean happy or blessed, but also walking in the straight path or the path of discernment. The blessed ones are walking in the right path. 'Blessed are those who . . .' – as in the Beatitudes – is the style of Wisdom teaching. Elsewhere in Proverbs, Wisdom invites her guests to desert the simple/deceived people and live, and *to be happy/blessed/walk straight in the path of discernment* (Prov. 9.6, my translation). In Malachi, there was the promise that this state of Wisdom would be restored after the LORD's judgement on temple corruption, when tithes were paid and the land was again fertile, 'then all nations will call you *blessed* . . .' (Mal. 3.12). After the judgement, people would once again distinguish between the righteous, *ṣadiyq*, and the wicked, between the servants of God and those who did not serve (Mal. 3.18). The arrogant and the evil doers would be burned like stubble, [presumably what Peter envisaged 2 Pet. 3.12–13], and then: 'for you who fear my name, the Sun of righteousness shall rise with healing in her wings' (Mal. 4.2, translating literally).[91]

This is the Sun who reappeared in the same setting in Revelation. As the Kingdom was proclaimed, with punishment for the destroyers and reward for the servants of the LORD, the heavenly temple opened to reveal the ark, and then a winged woman clothed with the sun (Rev. 11.17–12.1, 14). John knew who she was: he said her son was caught up to the throne of God where he ruled the nations with a rod of iron. She was the mother of the Messiah, described in Psalm 2, the one whom the angels had to worship. Then John saw war in heaven and Satan 'the deceiver of the whole world' and his angels were thrown down (Rev. 12.9). This was a vision of the fall of Satan, where the Son of the woman was the image of the LORD set on the heavenly throne. The vision ended with the beast that controlled the markets and his image (Rev. 13.13–8). The winged woman was crowned with stars (Rev. 12.1, 14). She was the Queen of heaven, Wisdom the rejected

---

91 Sun can be a masculine or feminine noun in Hebrew. Here it is feminine, *her* wings.

one who had returned to her place among the angels[92] was restored to her temple. As she appeared, the Kingdom was established on earth.

The tree of life, from which Adam and Eve had been barred, also reappeared in the holy of holies, and the servants of God-and-the-Lamb stood before it. John saw them there, together with the throne of God-and-the-Lamb, the temple way of describing the single figure who was both divine-and-human. The tree was bearing fruit each month and its leaves were to heal the nations (Rev. 22.1–2). The Genesis story of the rejection of the tree reflected the actual events of temple upheavals in the eighth and seventh centuries BCE, and just as the events of the reformation in Europe are still a factor in Church life five centuries later, so too the effects of the temple purges were still apparent in the time of Jesus. When John saw the woman and the tree in the holy of holies, he showed that the Christians were faithful to the older ways. Their temple was the ancient temple, and so the woman and her tree and everything they represented, shaped their way of thinking. Wisdom/Miriam was the mother of the Messiah, and that is how the Christians told the story of the birth of Jesus.

In the books of the prophets, the earliest reference to the tree was in Isaiah. When he stood before the heavenly throne, he heard the voices of the seraphim: 'Holy, Holy, Holy is the LORD of hosts; the whole earth is full of his glory.' Then he was overcome with a sense of guilt: 'Woe is me, for I kept silent,[93] for I am a man of unclean lips and I dwell in the midst of a people of unclean lips' (Isa. 6.5, my translation). He was conscious of wrong teaching that he had done nothing to correct. A man standing before the throne was a high priest; that was his privilege. His duty was to teach, and in this Isaiah had failed. The evidence for Isaiah's attitude to the Lady is that he condemned and prophesied the death of Hezekiah, who had cut down the Asherah (Isa. 38.10; 2 Kgs 18.4). If there had been a conflict over the status of the Lady, this would explain Isaiah's response to the throne vision. He warned that people would hear but not understand, see but not perceive, (Isa. 6.9). Now understanding, *biynah*, and perception/knowledge, *da'at*, were the fundamentals of Wisdom teaching (Prov. 1.2), and losing them was the punishment for whatever Isaiah regretted. This was the Wisdom pattern; those who rejected her lived with what they had chosen, and so Isaiah warned of the consequences

---

92 *1 Enoch* 42.2.

93 The Hebrew can mean either 'am lost' or 'kept silent'. The Latin and some Greek versions understood it to mean 'kept silent'.

of rejecting Wisdom: they would not see with their eyes nor hear with their ears, nor understand with their hearts [i.e. minds], and so they would not 'turn and be healed.' Cities would lie waste, the land desolate, and the people would be removed – 'until great is the forsaken One in the midst of the land', the other way to read v.12b.[94] The next verse is almost opaque,[95] but seems to describe Ashratah returned to the land and then burned again, like a terebinth or an oak tree, Ashratah who spreads her branches/sheds her leaves, and the holy seed is in her trunk. The tree shedding her leaves was a sign of healing (Rev. 22.2).

The fate of the tree was the fate of Wisdom. On his heavenly journey with the archangels, Enoch saw a fragrant tree, set among other trees but surpassing them all.[96] Its fragrance was the sweetest, its leaves, wood and blossoms did not wither, and its fruit hung in clusters like the fruit of a palm. The fragrant tree stood by a mountain on which was the throne of the great Holy One, and the fruit of the tree would one day give life to the chosen ones. After the great judgement, said the archangel Michael, the tree of life would be transplanted northwards to a holy place by the house of the LORD.[97] In another vision, when he was in the third heaven, Enoch saw the tree of life at the centre of Paradise and it was the most fragrant and beautiful of all the trees, red and gold, looking like fire. Under its wide spreading branches, the LORD used to set his throne when he came to Paradise,[98] and the tree had 'something of every orchard tree and every fruit'.[99] Paul had a similar experience, 'caught up to the third heaven . . . to Paradise . . . and heard things that cannot be told' (2 Cor. 12.2–4). Presumably he saw what Enoch saw. For John, this was the climax of his vision: the tree of life by the throne, with twelve kinds of fruit as food for the faithful (Rev. 22.1–2; 2.7). John did not mention the perfume, but 'Ezra', writing around 100 CE, knew that the fragrant tree was promised to the Christians: 'The tree of life shall give them fragrant perfume, and

---

94 For detail see my book *The Great High Priest*, p. 239.

95 It has many words that sound like Ashratah: 'tenth', *'aśryh*, and 'which', *'aśer*, which could have been wordplay.

96 *1 Enoch* 24.1–25.7.

97 *1 Enoch* 25.5.

98 This detail is also in the *Apocalypse of Moses* 22.4.

99 *2 Enoch* 8.1–4.

they shall neither toil nor become weary.'[100] One of the books in a fourth century Christian library described the tree of life: 'The colour is like the sun, and its branches are beautiful. Its leaves are like those of a cypress, its fruit like clusters of white grapes, and its height rises up to heaven.'[101] The tree of many types is an important detail; the tree of life was not any known tree. Wisdom compared herself to a cedar, a cypress, a palm, a rose plant, a beautiful olive tree, a plane tree (Ben Sira 24.13–4).

Then Enoch was taken to see a place where there were living branches sprouting from a felled tree, and from this place he could look across to see the Gihon spring.[102] The community of living branches appears in the Qumran hymns, apparently a group who were guarding the true teaching. The singer of one hymn rejoices that he has been set among these branches of the council of holiness.[103] Another voice, as we have seen, gives thanks that he has been set beside a fountain of streams, a watered garden where the LORD has established a plantation of trees. The shoot of the everlasting plant was there, 'protected by spirits of holiness.' The speaker seems to be the teacher who irrigates the garden with his teaching: 'Thou, O my God, hast put into my mouth as it were rain for all [those who thirst], and a fount of living waters which shall not fail.'[104] The early Christians would have found the same image in the *Psalms of Solomon*: '[In] the LORD's Paradise, the trees of life are his devout ones.'[105] Isaiah described Jerusalem as the LORD's carefully tended vineyard, which he expected to bear fruit (Isa. 5.1–7), and Jesus retold this parable to condemn the temple authorities of his time (Mk 12.12). He also described himself as the true vine and his disciples as the branches (Jn 15.1,5). Isaiah described the Messiah and Davidic king as a shoot, *ḥoter*, from the stump of Jesse and a branch *neṣer*, from his roots (Isa. 11.1), the stump here being the royal house, but the tree imagery is common to both. Ezekiel described the great mother vine, planted by water and full of branches. Her strongest stem was the ruler's sceptre, but she had been

100 2 Esdras 2.12, part of the Christian preface added to the Jewish original.

101 The Nag Hammadi library: *On the Origin of the World*, Coptic Gnostic Library II.5.110.

102 *1 Enoch* 26.1–6: he was looking from the Mount of Olives.

103 1QH XV.9–10.

104 1QH XVI.4–15.

105 *Psalms of Solomon* 14.2. The *Psalms of Solomon* were listed in the fifth-century Codex Alexandrinus, after the Old and New Testaments.

stripped of her fruit, and left with no strong branch to be the ruler (Ezek. 19.10–14). Isaiah foresaw the day when the branch, *şemah*, of Yahweh would be beautiful and glorious in Zion (Isa. 4.2); Jeremiah prophesied a righteous branch, *şemah* (Jer. 23.5; 33.15); Zechariah looked for the branch, *şemah*, the Servant of the LORD who would rebuild the temple (Zech. 3.8; 6.12).[106]

The branches of the tree appeared in Isaiah 61, immediately after the lines Jesus read in the synagogue at Nazareth at the start of his ministry. He proclaimed the year of the LORD's favour, and said: 'Today this scripture has been fulfilled in your hearing' (Lk. 4.16–21). In the year of the LORD's favour, said Isaiah's prophecy, those who were mourning in Zion would rejoice and be called the oaks of righteousness, the planting of the LORD. They would build up the ancient ruins and repair the ruined cities; they would be restored to their glorious state and receive the oil of gladness; they would be recognized as priests of the LORD. The prophecy in Isaiah 6 about the fallen tree said that the cities would be waste and the land desolate until the Lady and her way of seeing were restored. The passage Jesus read seems to describe its fulfilment: the oaks of righteousness were Enoch's community of branches from the fallen tree; people were restored to all the glory of Adam and anointed; and they were recognized as the ancient priesthood. This set of images passed into the early Church; the first Christians hoped to join the blessed company of trees and branches and receive the anointing oil. In one of the *Odes of Solomon*, the singer told how his eyes were enlightened and his face received the dew, that is the anointing oil, how his breath/soul was refreshed with the fragrance of the LORD. Then he was taken to Paradise where he saw wonderful fruitful trees watered by a river of gladness. 'Blessed are they who are planted in thy land.'[107]

Oil from the tree was the symbol of opening eyes to receive wisdom, and its leaves were the symbol of healing; Paul described healing as one of the gifts of the Spirit (1 Cor. 12.9, 28). It was an aspect of heavenly knowledge that the fallen angels corrupted. They taught people about metal working to make weapons, about astronomy, magic and 'the cutting of roots' – medicine and exorcism were both used for healing and for evil ends. Another list says they taught how to kill an unborn child.[108] Christians rejected magic, abortion and

---

106 Thus too in *Damascus Document* I.7 and *Testament of Judah* 24.4.

107 *Odes of Solomon* 11.18.

108 *1 Enoch* 8.1–3; 69.12.

infanticide, even though their cultural environment accepted them: 'Practise no magic, sorcery, abortion or infanticide.'[109] The corrupted knowledge of the fallen angels brought bloodshed, lawlessness and cries to heaven,[110] and so the archangels were sent to 'heal the earth which the angels have corrupted'.[111] The faithful angels taught Noah about herbs to cure the illnesses brought by the offspring of the fallen angels,[112] and there had been a temple guild of Levites led by Asaph, 'expert in music, incantation and divination' to avert demonic powers that caused illness. Asaph and his family were appointed by David to invoke, thank and praise the LORD (1 Chron. 16.4), and the psalms of Asaph (Pss 50, 73–83) suggest that they repelled the evil forces that threatened the LORD's good order, the covenant.[113] Psalm 80, for example, calls on the LORD to shine forth and save his people, Psalm 82 describes the judgement on the fallen angels. Jesus' healing ministry included exorcism.

The Essenes studied texts about the healing of body and soul, and 'made investigations into the medicinal roots and the properties of stones' so that they could treat diseases.[114] There was a similar group,[115] the Therapeuts, whose name can mean either healer or worshipper. Philo, who recognized the double meaning of their name, said they practised the art of healing both body and soul. They were philosophers [a name that means, literally, lovers of Wisdom] who studied the ancient texts of their group. Other ways of life, he argued, were folly, and incurable because their adherents had lost their spiritual vision, 'which alone gives a knowledge of truth and falsehood'. The Therapeuts were 'a people taught from the beginning to see and desire the vision of the One Who Is', the name of the LORD in the Greek Old Testament (Exod. 3.14). They already lived the life of heaven, and so gave away their earthly goods; they were living all over the world, but had a major settlement west of Alexandria. At dawn they prayed, as did the Essenes, towards the sunrise, 'praying for the heavenly light to fill their minds.'[116]

---

109 *Didache* 2; *Letter of Barnabas* 19.

110 *1 Enoch* 9.1–2, conditions that indicate the broken covenant, see p. **.

111 *1 Enoch* 10.7.

112 *Jubilees* 10.12–14.

113 R. Murray, *The Cosmic Covenant*, London: Sheed and Ward. 1992, pp. 75–81.

114 Josephus, *Jewish War* II.136.

115 Or even identical.

116 Using a different image, the Sun rose with healing in her wings (Mal. 4.2).

They were a priestly group, fasting for long periods and only eating at night, preferring Wisdom's banquet. Their leaders ate shewbread.[117] Although many modern scholars say he was wrong, Eusebius said they were Christian communities.[118]

Healing was one of the gifts of Wisdom, a sign of her triumph over evil. The *Wisdom of Solomon*, a text the Therapeuts could have known, had 'Solomon' claim: 'For [God] gave me unerring knowledge of what exists . . . the varieties of plants and the virtues of roots; I learned both what is secret and what is manifest, for Wisdom the fashioner of all things taught me' (Wis. 7.17, 20–22). Deep in temple tradition, the leaves of the tree of life had been the symbol of healing. Ezekiel saw trees planted on the banks of the stream that flowed from the temple; their leaves did not wither, and were for healing (Ezek. 47.12). John saw the tree restored to the holy of holies, watered by the river of life, 'and the leaves of the tree were for the healing of the nations' (Rev. 22.2). But before he saw the tree of life restored, he saw the other woman thrown down, the harlot who was 'the great city' (Rev. 17.18). Her merchants had been the great men of the earth, dealing in luxury goods and human traffic, 'and all nations were deceived by your drugs/sorcery, *pharmakia*' (Rev. 18.11–12, 23). Such was the world without Wisdom.

The sacrament of Wisdom was oil from the fragrant tree of life, and from the beginning, anointing – which gives Christians their name – gave knowledge. John wrote: 'You have the chrism of the Holy One, and you all have knowledge/know all things' (1 Jn 2.20, also v.27).[119] The early Christians sang:

> My eyes were enlightened,
> and my face received the dew,
> and my life/soul/breath was refreshed
> with the pleasant fragrance of the LORD.
> He anointed me with his perfection and I became as one of those near him.[120]

Oil transformed the anointed one into an angel, and so wisdom's children were the holy and anointed ones. The early Christians said the fragrance of the oil from the tree had been replicated in the

---

117 Philo, *On the Contemplative Life*, 2, 21–2, 27, 35–6, 81, 89.

118 Eusebius, *Church History*, 2.17.

119 There are two ancient versions of this text, you all know, *pantes,* and you know all things, *panta.*

120 *Odes of Solomon* 11.14–15; 36.6.

perfumed anointing oil. In the *Clementine Recognitions*,[121] Peter taught Clement:

> Among the Jews a king is called Christ. And the reason for the name is this: although he was the son of God and the beginning of all things, He became man. God anointed him with oil taken from the wood of the tree of life, and from that anointing he is called the Christ. He himself also, as appointed by the Father, anoints with similar oil every one of the pious when they come to his Kingdom . . . so that their light may shine, and, being filled with the holy Spirit, they may be endowed with immortality . . . In the present life, Aaron, the first high priest, was anointed with a blended oil that was made as an exact copy of the spiritual oil of which we have spoken . . . If this temporal grace blended by men, was so powerful, consider how potent was the oil extracted by God from a branch of the tree of life.[122]

The age of this belief is not known, but it seems to be as old as the tradition about the tree of life. Anointing conferred the gifts of Wisdom, and the anointed one was Wisdom's child. The branch from the root of Jesse was given the manifold spirit of the LORD: wisdom, understanding, counsel, might, knowledge, and the fear of the LORD. This was the gift of Wisdom to her child and was described as his 'perfume': 'His perfume shall be the fear of the LORD' (Isa. 11.3).[123] *Wisdom changed how people thought.* The anointed one gave forth the fragrance of the tree of life. Paul wrote of the fragrance of the knowledge of Christ, spread by Christians who were themselves his fragrance (2 Cor. 2.14–16). In the tree and Wisdom context, the knowledge of Christ would have meant knowing in the same way as Christ knew, having the anointed knowledge, not, as is often said, knowing Christ. Thus Dionysius[124] wrote: 'We learn that the transcendent fragrance of the divine Jesus distributes its conceptual gifts over our own intellectual powers, filling these with a divine pleasure.'[125] The sign of anointed knowledge was described by Isaiah, not judging on the basis of human perception, but rather with anointed eyes and ears: 'With righteous-

---

121 Attributed to Clement, bishop of Rome at the end of the first century, but now thought to be later.

122 *Clementine Recognitions* 1.45–6.

123 RSV translates as delight, AV as pleasure, Jerusalem Bible as breath. The Hebrew word is *reyah*, whose primary meaning is perfume.

124 Originally thought to be Paul's convert, Acts 17.34, and the first bishop of Athens, Eusebius, *Church History*, 3.4, but now thought to be a fourth/fifth century writer.

125 Dionysius, *Ecclesiastical Hierarchy* 477 C.

ness shall he judge the poor' – the covenant task of upholding righteousness; 'the wolf shall lie down with the lamb' – the restoration of the covenant of peace; and the earth shall be full of the knowledge of the LORD, as the waters cover the sea (Isa. 11.4–9). Dionysius explained how this symbolism of the oil passed into the Church:

> The unction with ointment gives a sweet odour to the one who has been initiated for the perfect divine birth joins the initiates together with the Spirit of the Deity. This outpouring is not something describable, for it is in the domain of the mind that it does its work of sweetening and making perfect.[126]

There was a Jewish tradition that the oil had been kept in the holy of holies,[127] but was hidden away in the time of Josiah.[128] This is consistent with the tree/*asherah* disappearing at that time, if the tree was the source of the oil. The anointing oil was perfumed with spices, predominantly myrrh (Exod. 30.22–33), and Ben Sira described Wisdom as the anointing oil, that is the myrrh oil, that sent forth its perfume (Ben Sira 24.15). The ancient high priests were anointed with this oil on their forehead and on their eyelids, to open their eyes and their minds. They received Wisdom herself, together with her gifts of life, vision and wisdom. When the oil was gone, Enoch said that Wisdom was abandoned, those in the temple lost their vision.[129] Jesus, in the *Gospel of Philip*, taught: 'When the light comes, then he who sees will see the light, but he who does not see will remain in darkness.'[130] The return of the oil became an important element in Christian tradition. 'For the ray of the most holy sacred things enlightens the men of God, as kin of the light, purely and directly; it spreads its sweet fragrance into their mental reception openly.'[131] The Armenian church tells how the apostle St Thaddeus brought some oil blessed by Christ, with he which healed King Agbar. He then hid the oil, and it was rediscovered by St Gregory,[132] the first bishop of the

---

126 Dionysius *Ecclesiastical Hierarchy* 404D.

127 Tosefta *Kippurim* 2.15.

128 Babylonian Talmud *Horayoth*12a.

129 *1 Enoch* 93.8.

130 *The Gospel of Philip*, CG II.3.64.

131 Dionysius, *Ecclestiastical Hierarchy* 476B.

132 Late third century CE.

Armenians. The holy myrrh oil, the *muron,* is still central to the life of the Armenian church.[133]

The tree and its water, ancient symbols of Wisdom joining all things together and giving the breath of life to Adam, are apt indeed in our present situation. Trees are the lungs of the planet, and more than 20 per cent of the world's oxygen is produced in the Amazon rainforest. The earth has a climate thermostat controlled by plants, and so Amazonia, for example, is a powerful system to change climate, functioning as a great green ocean that creates rain for all South America.[134] Research is now showing the vital role of trees in the global hydrological cycle, so that felling tress affects not only the immediate region, but the global atmosphere. Experiments in the interaction of atmosphere and biosphere have shown that losing the trees of the Amazon forest not only affects the hydrological cycle, but disrupts the plant–animal balance such that once the tropical forests are destroyed, they might not be able to re-establish themselves.[135]

> To obtain [the Brazil nut] the most important wild harvested crop of the Amazon extractivists, one needs the action of the bee in the canopy, the presence of the epiphytic orchids perched on the trees of the nearby forest, and the work of the agouti on the forest floor to plant the seeds.[136]

The leaves of Wisdom's tree are for the healing of the nations, but the Amazon forest, which has the largest collection of living plant and animal species in the world, is losing some 50,000 species each year, and with them, the possibility of finding new cures for diseases. Some 25 per cent of today's medicines have rainforest sources, and research programmes are using forest plants to discover new possibilities for medicines. It is, however, a race against other competing monetary interests, even though harvesting forest produce and medicinal plants has more long-term and sustainable economic value than cutting timber and using the land for cattle grazing or soya for immediate profits. Rainforest timber is sometimes burned just to make charcoal to power local industry. Even the voices of the Market must realize that

133 For detail about the oil, see my books *The Great High Priest,* pp. 127–36, and *Temple Themes in Christian Worship,* pp. 125–34.

134 A. D. Nobre, addressing the Amazon Symposium 2006.

135 J. Shukla, C. Nobre and P. Sellers, 'Amazon Deforestation and Climate Change', *Science* 247 (1990), pp. 1322–25.

136 A vivid example, given by G. T. Prance, addressing the Amazon Symposium, 2006.

managed forest is, in the long term, more profitable that felled trees
and devastated land. Much of the destruction is the result of unplanned
and unco-ordinated use of natural resources – thinking that has not
joined all things together in harmony. As a result, one century
of human activity with no vision but profit has wrought great
destruction in the creation, failing to recognize: 'LORD, how manifold
are they works! *With Wisdom thou hast made them all'* (Ps. 104.24, my
translation.).

THE KINGDOM

Jesus taught that the Kingdom of God was in the midst (Lk. 17.21), an
allusion to the old temple pattern where the LORD was enthroned at
the heart of creation, and so the Kingdom was the holy of holies. The
Christian gospel, *evangelion,* expressed this vision, as can be seen from
the bitter wordplay attributed to two rabbis in the second century CE:
not *evangelion,* they said, but *awen gilyon* or *awon gilyon,* the worthless or
wicked revelation.[137] For Jewish scholars in the early years of Christianity, an important feature of Christianity must have been the vision of
the Kingdom. The Targums understood the Kingdom as a vision/
revelation of salvation or of judgement: 'The LORD of Hosts will reign
on Mount Zion . . . and before his elders he will manifest his glory.'
(Isa. 24.23) in the Targum became 'The Kingdom of the LORD of Hosts
shall be revealed in the mountain of Zion . . . and before the elders of
his people in glory'; 'Your God reigns' (Isa. 52.7) became 'The
Kingdom of your God has been revealed'; 'Your doom has come'
(Ezek. 7.7) became 'The Kingdom has been revealed to you.'[138] Jesus
promised his disciples that they would see the Kingdom 'come with
power' before they died, and then he was transfigured before them
(Mk 9.1–8). They saw him in the glorious light of the holy of holies.
Jesus told Nicodemus that only those born again or born from above[139]
could *see* the Kingdom, and only those born of water and Spirit could
enter. Flesh and Spirit were different ways of being (Jn 3.1–6).

---

137 Thus Rabbi Meir and Rabbi Joḥanan ben Zakkai , Babylonian Talmud *Shabbat*
116a, a line censored from some editions.

138 See my book *The Secret Tradition of the Kingdom of God,* London: SPCK, 2007,
pp. 78–82.

139 Greek *anōthen* means either 'again' or 'from above'.

Entering the Kingdom meant seeing as the visionaries saw, knowing the ways of Day One, the biblical vision of the creation. When the disciples asked Jesus 'tell us how our end will be?'– that question that modern cosmology has not yet answered – Thomas' Jesus said: 'Have you discovered the beginning that you look for the end? For where the beginning is, there the end will be. Blessed is he who will take his place in the beginning: he will know the end and not experience death.'[140] This is temple discourse: seeing *from* the beginning, the vision *from* the Kingdom was Wisdom, as Job's detractors reminded him: 'Are you the first man that was born?' Are you Adam? 'Or were you brought forth before the hills?' Are you Wisdom or her son? 'Have you listened in the council of God?' Have you learned the secrets of Day One? 'And do you limit Wisdom to yourself?' (Job 15.7–8).

Jesus taught about the Kingdom in parables – a form of Wisdom teaching – so that those without Wisdom would not understand the secret of the Kingdom: 'To you has been given the secret of the Kingdom of God, but for those outside, everything is in parables; so that they may indeed see but not perceive, and may indeed hear but not understand; lest they should turn again and be forgiven' (Mk 4.11–12). This was the LORD's ancient warning to those who had rejected Wisdom and her gifts (Isa. 6.9–13); they lost the ability to 'see'. Speaking of Wisdom and her children, Jesus rejoiced that his teaching as hidden from the 'wise and understanding' but was revealed to infants (Mt. 11.25). The Kingdom parables described how people became aware of the vision of the Kingdom, as implied by Jesus' saying in the *Gospel of Thomas*: 'The Kingdom of the Father is spread out upon the earth and men do not see it.'[141] Some received the vision gradually – the parables of the sower or the mustard seed or the yeast (Mt.13.18–33); some received a single moment of revelation – the man who found treasure or the merchant who found the pearl (Mt. 13.44–46); and some discovered the Kingdom as their moment of judgement – the net of fish or the separation of the sheep from the goats or the return of the master to ask about his talents (Mt. 13.47–50; 25.14–46). The parables about the wedding feast and the Bridegroom (Mt. 22.1–14; 23.1–13) allude to the marriage of the Lamb and the Bride (Rev. 19.7–8), and the Bride was Wisdom.

Christians prayed for the coming of the Kingdom on earth, and understood this to mean the state when heaven and earth were united in obedience to God: 'Thy Kingdom come, thy will be done on earth as it is in heaven . . .' 'Give us this day our daily bread' according to Jerome, who was reading the Hebrew version of Matthew's gospel, meant 'Give us today the bread of tomorrow, *maḥar*.'[142] Since the early Christians thought of themselves as living in the sixth day of history, 'tomorrow' was the great Sabbath, the Kingdom. They were praying for the Sabbath bread of the Kingdom, and the Sabbath bread, as we have seen, was the shewbread, Wisdom's food for her children.[143] When the Kingdom was established on earth, the elders worshipped because the time had come to reward the servants of the LORD and destroy the destroyers of the earth (Rev. 11.18). This echoed the role of Adam, set in Eden to serve, *'bd*, and preserve, *šmr* two Hebrew words that sound very like their opposites: *'bd*, destroy and *šmd*, exterminate.[144] This is yet another indication that the early Christians knew the old temple teaching, and so when the Kingdom was established on earth, the servants were rewarded and the destroyers were destroyed. Immediately, Wisdom appeared in heaven giving birth to her son, and Satan, the deceiver was thrown down.

John is the only New Testament writer who actually described the Kingdom. He saw the throne surrounded by the heavenly host, and he heard them singing praises to the enthroned Creator (Rev. 4.8–11; 5.8–14); he saw the host who followed the Lamb and heard their music (Rev. 14.1–5); he saw the host beside the sea of glass and heard their music. They were singing a 'new song' (Rev. 5.9; 14.3). John saw the heavenly city as a huge golden cube which in temple tradition had only one meaning: the holy of holies (Rev. 21.16). This too was the Kingdom 'in the midst', which he also described as 'the Bride of the Lamb', introducing another complex of Wisdom images which we assume the early Church also knew. The holy of holies/Bride is described exactly as 'Solomon' described Wisdom, and so we conclude that the Kingdom was/is the state of Wisdom returned from heaven to earth. Her golden city was a place of light and purity (Rev. 21.22–7). The tree of life was there, the river of life, the throne and, we assume, the heavenly music John had heard.

142 The Greek for 'daily', *epiousios*, Mt. 6.11; Lk. 11.3, is a rare word of uncertain meaning.

143 For detail, see my book *The Hidden Tradition of the Kingdom of God*, London: SPCK, 2007, pp. 123–6.

144 The comparison is with the hiph'il form.

- The city was huge, a cube of 12,000 *stadia* (Rev. 21.16); '[Wisdom] reaches mightily from one end of the earth to the other and she orders all things well' (Wis. 8.1).
- It was radiant with the glory of God (Rev. 21.11); '[Wisdom] is a pure emanation of the glory of the Almighty' (Wis. 7.25a).
- It was a place of perpetual light (Rev. 21.25); [Wisdom] is 'a reflection of eternal light, a spotless mirror of the working of God' (Wisd.7.26).
- Nothing unclean could enter (Rev. 21.27); 'Nothing defiled gains entrance to [Wisdom]' (Wis. 7.25b).
- The citizens were the resurrected (Rev.20.4); 'Because of [Wisdom] I shall have immortality' (Wis. 8.13).

There are many more examples[145] in this kaleidoscope of images – holy of holies, city, mother, Wisdom – and all represented the Kingdom of resurrected angel priests reigning in their city which had become the holy of holies on earth (Rev. 5.14; 22.3–5), and the visible creation rejoined to the invisible, that is, the eternal covenant restored: 'that God may be all in all' (1 Cor. 15.28 AV).

The heavenly city had long been described as a woman, even as an abandoned woman. The Second Isaiah, speaking to the generation of the exile, foresaw a glorious future for the stricken city, who was an abandoned Queen. Her restoration would be the sign that the covenant of peace stood firm (Isa. 54.10). She would put on her beautiful robes again and be rebuilt with precious stones (Isa. 52.1; 54.11–12). The barren woman would have many more children (Isa.54.1; 66.7–14). Paul applied this prophecy to the Christians; the heavenly Jerusalem, he said, is our mother: 'Rejoice, O barren one who does not bear . . . For the children of the desolate one are many more than the children of her who is married' (Gal. 4.26–7). The early *Gospel of Philip* knew she was Wisdom: 'Wisdom, who is called barren, is the mother of the angels.'[146] 'Ezra', writing about 100 CE, saw her as a mourning woman, whose only son had died on his wedding night. Then she changed; her face began to shine and she turned into a great city, just as John described Jerusalem as both the Bride and the heavenly city. The archangel Uriel explained to 'Ezra' that the city and the woman were indeed Jerusalem, who had been barren until Solomon built the

145 For details see my book *The Revelation of Jesus Christ*, Edinburgh: T&T Clark, 2000, pp. 319–27.

146 *Gospel of Philip*, CG II.3.63.

temple. Then her only son was born, and the destruction of the temple signified his death (2 Esd. 9.38–10.54). The explanation is brief and enigmatic, but it seems that the woman's only son was born in the temple.

John saw Wisdom's son born in the temple (Rev. 12.1–6). The liturgical reality of the vision was the ritual in the holy of holies when the human king became the divine Son. He was anointed with her oil and became the priest like Melchizedek. Psalm 110, much quoted in the New Testament, describes how the Son was born, but all that remains of the key verse is confused. '. . . on the day you lead your host upon the holy mountains. From the womb of the morning, like dew your youth will come to you' (Ps. 110.3). The Greek understood 'your youth' as 'I have begotten you'; dew was a symbol of the oil and the resurrection it bestowed; and 'upon the holy mountains' could also be 'in the glory of the holy ones' or 'in the glorious ornaments/robes of holiness.' The human king became the divine Son when he was anointed in the holy of holies, or anointed and received the robe of holiness. This is exactly how Philo understood the transformation of the high priest, who was the Logos, the LORD.

> He is the child of parents incorruptible and wholly free from stain, his Father being God who is likewise Father of all, and his Mother Wisdom, through whom (fem.) the universe came into existence; because, moreover, his head has been anointed with oil, and by this I mean that his ruling faculty is illumined with a brilliant light, in such wise that he is deemed worthy to put on the garments.[147]

Wisdom had other children, the holy and anointed ones. The Christians had received Wisdom's gift of sight, and so Paul exhorted the Christians in Rome: 'Do not be conformed to this world, but be transformed by the renewal of your mind' (Rom. 12.2). Theophilus, a Christian teacher in Antioch about 180 CE, described the vision in terms of Wisdom without actually mentioning her name:

> For God is seen by those who are enabled to see him, when they have the eyes of their souls opened. For all have eyes, but in some they are overspread, and they do not see the light of the sun. Yet it does not follow that the light of the sun does not shine.[148]

---

147 Philo, *On Flight* 108–10.
148 Theophilus *To Autolycus* I.2.

The Christians had seen the glory, not in the holy of holies but incarnate in their midst – the other meaning of 'the Kingdom of God is in your midst'. 'The Logos became flesh and *tabernacled* among us, full of grace and truth, and we have beheld his glory . . .' (Jn 1.14, translating literally) confirms that John was thinking in temple terms.

'Where there is no vision, the people unravel' (Prov. 29.18, literal translation), has to be read alongside Wisdom's description of herself, that she was the first of all things and beside the Creator as he made the material world: 'When he established the heavens I was there . . . when he made firm the foundations of the earth, then I was beside him, joining all things together in harmony' (Prov. 8.27, 29, 30, Greek text, translating literally). This was Wisdom in the holy of holies, and so 'Solomon' prayed: 'Give me the Wisdom that sits by thy throne.' (Wis. 9.4). Psalm 104.24 also described her role in creation: 'With Wisdom thou hast made them all,' and so the Targumist rendered the first line of Genesis: 'In the beginning, with Wisdom, the Memra of the LORD created and perfected the heavens and the earth'; and the community at Qumran were singing 'When all his angels saw [the creation] they sang, for he showed them that which they had not known . . . / Blessed is he who created the earth with his power, who established the world with his wisdom.'[149] Her role in creation was to hold all things together in harmony, and so Philo described the powers, her angel children, as a choir: 'a most holy chorus of bodiless souls in the air, accompanying the heavenly powers, and commonly called angels . . .'[150]

When Enoch passed into the sixth heaven he saw seven clustered angels [or seven clusters of angels] 'brilliant and very glorious' and all identical. They studied and controlled the movements of the stars, sun and moon, and the well-being of the whole cosmos. 'They are the leaders of the angels of celestial speech, and they make all celestial life peaceful; and they preserve the commandments and instructions, and sweet voices and singing, every kind of praise and glory.' There were angels of times, seasons, rivers, oceans, in fact, angels of all aspects of creation. Their song could not be described – either because it was beyond words, or because it was forbidden to speak of it.[151] The bonds of the eternal covenant and the harmony of all creation are like the images now used by physicists in their quest for a comprehensive theory to describe the creation: they suggest strings or superstrings, as

149 *Targum Neofiti* Gen. 1.1; 11Q5. XXVI.

150 Philo, *Tongues* 174.

151 *2 Enoch* 19.1–6.

the fundamental of the creation, with the strings vibrating according to their function. Some are also predicting that there are more than the four dimensions of natural human experience, dimensions beyond our normal experience. This is very similar to temple view of the harmony of creation and the many heavens.

From the beginning, the bonds, the angels and their music were part of the temple and its world view.[152] David appointed musicians to play before the ark even before the temple was built, 'to invoke, to thank and to praise the LORD' (1 Chron. 16.4). The word 'praise' can also mean 'shine', showing it was music that called on the LORD 'to make his face shine and be gracious . . . and give peace' (Num. 6.24–6). Vision and music were inseparable and the key to the eternal covenant, the state of peace. The translator of the Greek Scriptures assumed that seeing the LORD meant singing in harmony: the Hebrew of Exodus 24.11 says that the men who ascended Sinai saw the angels, *'elohim*, in a vision, but the Greek says that none sang in discord. The vision and the song were equivalents, inseparable. In the time of Jesus, Philo was linking this passage to the harmony of the powers of creation:

> He is everywhere because he has made his powers extend through earth and water, air and heaven, and left no part of the universe without his presence, and uniting all with all has bound them fast with invisible bonds that they should never be loosed, *on account of which I will celebrate it in song* . . .

Commentators are puzzled by this link and assume the text is disordered,[153] yet even in the biblical accounts, music usually accompanied the vision of the Creator enthroned, the *raz nihyeh*, the mystery of the origin of creation. Isaiah saw the LORD and heard the seraphim, John saw the Lamb enthroned and heard the praises of all creation. Only the vision of the Man ascending (Dan. 7.9–14) does not mention music. Nor are there many references to angel song, but there may be far more singing angels in the Old Testament than is immediately obvious. The Targums understood the heavens rejoicing to mean that the angels were singing. 'Let the heavens be glad and let the earth rejoice' (1 Chron. 16.31) became 'Let the angels on high rejoice and let the inhabitants of the earth rejoice.'[154] Psalm 19 describes the silent

---

152 Amos implied that music was no substitute for what it represented: justice and righteousness flowing like water, Amos 5.23.

153 Philo, *Tongues*, 136.

154 Targum to 1 Chron. 16.31.

praise of the angels throughout the creation, and Psalm 148 shows that the praises of the angels are part of establishing the fixed order of creation.

The song of the angels accompanied, or maybe enabled, the process of creation, whence the Lord's question to Job: 'Where were you when I laid the foundation of the earth . . . when the morning stars sang, *rnn*, together, and all the sons of God shouted for joy, *rw'*?' (Job 38.4, 7). This particular word for 'sing', *rnn*, is translated in various ways and so the pattern is not always clear: 'The nations are glad and *sing for joy*' when the Lord shines forth with his righteous judgement – a covenant context (Ps. 67.5, my translation); '*Sing aloud with gladness*' . . . as the Lord restores his people (Jer. 31.7, 12; Zeph. 3.14); the people *sing for joy* as the Lord appears to establish his kingdom (Isa. 24.14); the resurrected *sing for joy* (Isa. 26.19); the desert will *sing* and the tongue of the dumb *sing for joy* (Isa. 35.2, 5) as the people return to re-establish their land.[155] 'Shout for joy', *rw'*, has similar associations, and is also translated in several ways: 'Sing [to the Lord] a new song . . . with *shouts for joy*' (Ps. 33.3 my translation); as the Lord goes up to his throne in triumph 'God has ascended with *a shout of joy*, the Lord with the sound of a shofar . . .' (Ps. 47.5, my translation); 'Blessed are those who know *the shouting for joy*, who walk, O Lord, in the light of your face . . .' (Ps. 89.15, my translation). Each of these has a temple context, marking a new beginning, a moment of new creation. This is clear in: 'All Israel brought up the ark of the covenant of the Lord with *shouts of joy*, the sound of the shofar . . .' (1 Chron. 15.28); 'They swore an oath to the Lord with a loud voice and *with shouts of joy* and with trumpets and shofars . . .' (2 Chron. 15.14); and when the foundation of the restored temple was laid, the people *shouted for joy* (Ezra 3.11, 12,13).

At new year there was a memorial of the shout of joy (Lev. 23.24, translating literally), perhaps because they were re-enacting the creation, or perhaps because the description in Job was naturally given in terms of the temple creation rite. The Levites made atonement with their song, according to Rabbi Benaiah, teaching early in the third century CE;[156] and singing also part of the Jubilee, which marked a new beginning, proclaimed by the shofar of the shout of joy on the day of atonement (Lev. 25.9). The 'new song' (Pss. 33, 96, 98, 144, 149),

---

155 Thus too Isa. 42.11; 44.23; 49.13; 54.1; 65.14.

156 Jerusalem Talmud *Ta'anit* 4.2.

should probably be understood as 'the renewing song',[157] as too the new song in John's vision, (Rev. 5.9–10; 14.3) and in the description of the King in the *Hekhalot Zutarti*: 'Your servants crown you with crowns, and sing a new song to you. They install you as King for ever, and you shall be called One for ever and ever.'[158] When heaven and earth praise the Creator together, the earth is renewed and the unity of all creation is restored.

Those who were granted the vision learned the song that renewed and sustained the creation. Isaiah, as we have seen, saw the LORD and the powers of heaven, then saw the glory of the LORD filling the whole earth, and then learned the consequences of rejecting Wisdom. Aristobulus, writing in the mid second century BCE, described the experience of the holy of holies, Day One, as 'the first [day], the one in which the light was born by which all things are seen together'.[159] The *Apocalypse of Abraham*, a Jewish text from the first or second century CE, describes Abraham's ascent to the heavenly throne. His angel guide told him that the Eternal One would come to him in the many voices of the 'Holy, Holy, Holy', and then there was a sound like many waters. Abraham and the angel both bowed in worship, and Abraham recited the song the angel had taught him.[160] Caught up in the fiery light, Abraham saw the living creatures under the throne, and heard his angel guide teaching them 'the song of peace . . . and I heard the sound of their sanctification like the voice of a single man'.[161] Then he looked down, and was able to see the angels who had formerly been invisible to him, 'and the hosts of the stars and the orders they were commanded to carry out, and the elements of the earth obeying them'.[162]

Philo described the ascent in his characteristic way. The human mind, he said, made in the image of God, explored first the arts and sciences and then 'when on soaring wing it has contemplated the atmosphere and all its phases, it is borne yet higher to the ether and

157 The Hebrew letters would be the same.

158 A much later text, *Hekhalot Zutarti* #418, can be found in P. Schäfer, *The Hidden and Manifest God*, New York: State University of NY Press, 1992, p. 61.

159 Aristobulus was a Jewish scholar working in Alexandria and known to Eusebius who quoted this passage in *Preparation of the Gospel* XIII.12.

160 *Apocalypse of Abraham* 16.3–17.7, according to one possible reconstruction of a difficult text.

161 *Apocalypse of Abraham* 18.11.

162 *Apocalypse of Abraham* 19.9.

the circuit of heaven, and is whirled round with the dances of planets and fixed stars in accordance with the laws of perfect music, following that love of Wisdom that guides its steps.' The mind then reaches the invisible world [corresponding in temple terms to the holy of holies] and longing to see the King, is dazzled by 'pure and untempered rays of concentrated light that stream forth like a torrent'.[163] We cannot, he said, express our gratitude to the Creator by buildings and ceremony: 'No, it must be expressed in hymns of praise, not such as the audible voice shall sing but strains raised and re-echoed by the mind too pure for eye to discern.'[164]

The *Ascension of Isaiah* is a Christian text from the late first century, built around older Jewish material. Isaiah ascended with an angel guide, and heard the two choirs of angels, on the right and on the left, but was forbidden to join them. When he reached the sixth heaven, however, there was a choir 'of one appearance', and he was able to sing with them, praising the Father, the Christ and the Holy Spirit 'with one voice.' In the seventh heaven he stood before the throne, and again sang with the angels 'with one voice'.[165] Ignatius, bishop of Antioch at about this time, had a similar vision. Socrates, the Church historian in the mid fifth century, wrote of him:

> Ignatius, who had conversed with the apostles themselves, saw a vision of angels hymning in alternate chants the Holy Trinity; after which he introduced the mode of singing he had observed into the Antiochian church, whence it was transmitted by tradition to all the other churches. Such is the account we have received in relation to these responsive hymns.[166]

Angel song was important for the Christians and their vision, but it seems there were two opinions about how the angels sang: with one voice, or as two choirs. The Therapeuts, whom Philo knew, used both styles and sang as they danced: 'They sing hymns to God . . . sometimes chanting together, sometimes taking up the harmony antiphonally . . . and rapt with enthusiasm, reproduce sometimes the lyrics of the procession, sometimes the halt and the wheeling and counter wheeling of a choric dance.'[167] Eusebius said they were the early Christians, and so,

---

163 Philo, *Creation* 70–71.

164 Philo, *On Planting* 126.

165 *Ascension of Isaiah* 9.16–18; 27–8.

166 Eusebius, *Church History* 6.8.

167 Philo, *Contemplative Life*, 84.

writing early in the fourth century CE, cannot have found anything
strange in this description of their worship.

Thus the song of heaven was taught on earth, and the sustaining
praise had to begin with human beings. Although their worship
joined that of the angels, the angels responded to the praises of
Israel, what the psalmist described as the Lord enthroned on the
praises of Israel (Ps. 22.3). John and the early Christians knew this
pattern: all creatures praised the Lamb and then the living creatures
and elders replied (Rev. 5.12–14). Christians in Egypt in the third
century were singing: 'all [noble] creatures of God together . . . shall
not be silent, nor shall the light bearing stars lag behind . . . all the
rushing rivers shall praise our Father and Son and Holy Spirit, *all the
powers shall join in* saying Amen and Amen, power and praise . . .'[168]
Enoch, after a time of contemplation before the throne, said that the
Holy One illuminated his eyes and his heart [that is, his mind] so that
he could sing psalms, praise, jubilation, thanksgiving, song, glory,
majesty and strength: 'And when I opened my mouth and sang praises
before the throne of glory, the holy creatures below the throne of glory
and above the throne of glory responded after me saying "Holy Holy
Holy" and "Blessed be the glory of God in his dwelling place."'[169] The
later Jewish mystical texts knew that 'all the ministering angels, . . .
when they hear the sound of the hymns and praises which Israel speaks
from below, begin from above with "Holy, Holy. Holy."'[170]

When heaven and earth were singing to each other,[171] the earth was
fruitful. Hosea described the future restoration of the creation
covenant:

> I will make a covenant or them on that day, with the beast of the field and the
> bird of the heavens, and with the creeping thing of the soil; and I will break the
> bow and the sword and war from the land and I will make you lie down in safety.
> And I will betroth you to me for ever, I will betroth you to me in/with righteous-
> ness, justice, steadfast love and mercy. I will betroth you to me in/with faithful-
> ness, and you will know that I am the Lord. And on that day I will make the
> heavens sing, and they will make the earth sing, and the earth shall sing with

168 Oxyrhynchus Papyrus XV 1786, quoted in J. Quasten, *Music and Worship in
Pagan and Christian Antiquity*, Washington DC: National Association of Pastoral
Musicians, 1983, p. 71.

169 *3 Enoch* 1.12.

170 *Hekhalot Rabbati* # 179, in P. Schäfer, *The Hidden and Manifest God*, p. 47.

171 The Hebrew verb *'anah* has several meanings: answer, sing, be busy, be afflicted.
There is probably temple wordplay here, responsive singing and its opposite,
affliction.

corn and wine and oil, and they will sing that God sows . . . (Hos. 4.18–22 in literal paraphrase).

The praise was unceasing. The ancient temple had Levites to serve continually before the LORD (1 Chron. 16.37), and the rule for the Qumran community describes the continuous cycle of prayer and praise at dawn and dusk, and at the beginning of each new month.[172] Simeon the high priest, as we have seen, said the world was upheld by the Law, the temple service and deeds of loving kindness.[173] The Benedicite, as we have seen,[174] was exhorting all the powers of creation to praise the one seated on the throne of his Kingdom, and a text from the time of Jesus describes how the various groups in creation praised in turn throughout day and night: in the fourth hour of the night, for example, Adam used to hear the praise of the seraphim but once he had sinned, he heard it no more. In the third hour of the day the birds praise, and in the fourth the beasts.[175] This text was incorporated into the *Testament of Adam* and was preserved by the Christians.

'Thy Kingdom come' meant the constant prayer and praise to make the Kingdom present by restoring the bonds between earth and heaven. Thus Thomas's Jesus taught: 'When you make the two one, and you make the inside like the outside, and the outside like the inside, and the above like the below and when you make the male and the female one and the same . . . then you will enter [the Kingdom].'[176] Entering the Kingdom meant seeing from a Kingdom perspective, seeing from the throne as did Isaiah. A different perspective literally means a different world, because the way the world is 'seen' determines how it is treated. 'The world is, to a degree at least, the way we imagine it . . .'[177] The Kabbalah retained the ancient Wisdom that the visible and invisible worlds were one and acted on each other, and that prayer and praise healed the wounds in the creation:

172 *The Community Rule* 1 QS X, also 1 QH XXI.

173 Mishnah *Aboth 1.*2 see above p. 48.

174 See above, p. 76.

175 *Testament of Adam* 1–2.

176 *Gospel of Thomas* 22.

177 W. Wink, *The Powers that Be*, New York and London: Doubleday, 1988, p. 14, see above p. 20.

> The one who prays rises from the depths to the world of the Godhead, and in every world he accomplishes something with his words of praise and veneration. He not only acknowledges the greatness of creation and the Creator; he also puts order in creation and brings about something which is necessary to perfect its unity and which without his act would remain latent.[178]

From the beginning, Christians have worshipped with music: 'Be filled with the Spirit, addressing one another in psalms and hymns and spiritual songs, singing and making melody to the LORD with all your heart ...' (Eph. 5.19), and their vision of heaven was all creation worshipping the Lamb on the throne (Rev. 5.11–14). Music was a symbol of harmony, and the harmony of the church was expressed in music. Clement of Rome at the end of the first century, exhorted the divided church in Corinth to think of the harmony of creation that the church should reflect:

> The sun, moon and starry choirs roll on in harmony at his command ... Upon all of these the great Architect and LORD of the universe has enjoined peace and harmony ... Think of the vast company of angels who all wait on him to serve his wishes ... In the same way, we ought ourselves, gathered together in a conscious unity, to cry to him as it were with one voice ...[179]

They knew that seeing the Kingdom and hearing the song were one experience, and so, in the late fourth century, Gregory of Nyssa could preach a Christmas sermon that the LORD had appeared to restore the original unity of all creation, which was 'the temple of the LORD of creation'. The mouths of those who had once offered praise had been closed by sin, and the symphony of celebration had ceased because the human creation did not join with the praises of heaven. The work of Christ meant that sinners could join again in the liturgy of earth and heaven.[180] Cyril of Jerusalem, a few years earlier, taught that in the liturgy, the worshippers joined themselves with the whole creation, visible and invisible, 'to mingle our voices in the hymns of the heavenly hosts'. Then they consecrated the bread and wine, and prayed for peace and healing. This was temple atonement in a Christian setting: the LORD emerges – but here in the bread and wine – to heal and

---

178 G. Scholem, *On the Kabbalah and its Symbolism*, New York: Schocken Books, 1965, p. 127.

179 *I Clement* 20, 34.

180 *Patrologia Graeca* XLVI 1127–8; I do not know of an English version. For more detail, see my book *Temple Themes in Christian Worship*, pp. 221.38.

restore creation.[181] 'It came upon the midnight clear' is still a popular Christmas carol, and yet how many of those who sing pay heed to its angel lore? The earthly noise that has drowned the angel song, the heavenly music contrasted with earthly wars and wrongs, the ancient belief that the anointed one enables the world to join again in the song of the angels.

> O hush the noise, ye men of strife,
> And hear the angels sing!

Adam and Eve lost their garments of glory when they left Eden and they lost the sound of the divine harmony, but they never forgot what they had lost. Thus the Hebrew storytellers expressed a profound truth and explained the human longing for a better world than the one we have made for ourselves.

> They heard the sound of the LORD God walking in the garden in the cool of the day, and the man and his wife hid themselves from the presence of the LORD among the trees of the garden. But the LORD God called to the man, and said to him, 'Where are you?' And he said, 'I heard the sound of thee in the garden, and I was afraid, because I was naked; and I hid myself' (Gen. 3.8–10).

The aggressive secularism that characterizes our time is just such a hiding, but there is nowhere to hide. 'Adam where are you?' is the most pressing question we face today.

Some will speak of tipping points: in changes to the environment, or in perceptions of those changes. Others will speak of paradigm shifts: seeing within a new framework to give a new perspective, new significance to details that could not be fitted into the old system. The Bible speaks of opening eyes with the oil of Wisdom, or restoring vision: the vision at the heart of creation, and the ability to see that vision. The Bible exhorts all creation to praise the Creator, and yet our life noise has drowned the praises of creation. Birds sing louder near motorways, so that they can communicate with each other, even if they no longer speak to us. The noise of shipping and seabed industry has made it impossible for sea creatures to communicate with each other. Living creatures lost their power of speech, said the ancient storyteller, when Adam sinned.[182] Outside Eden was a world of noise, not only from industry but also from the constant 'music' of shopping malls

---

181 Cyril of Jerusalem, *Catecheses* 23.6–10.

182 *Jubilees* 3.28.

and other temples of Mammon. Even our churches have forgotten why there are angel figures in the choir, praising the LORD in the holy of holies, and allowing the human voice to echo with the form of the building that represents the creation. Instead there is amplified noise in the nave. Both are symbolic.

Many Christians have been searching for a comprehensive and characteristically Christian theology for the environment crisis because the knowledge of the angels and the vision of Wisdom have been lost. Both were central to the Church's original faith, with all that this implies for Christian teaching today. The tendency has been to take up positions formulated by secular environmentalists, lightly baptise them, and deck them with decently with a few lines of Scripture. In the time of the Hebrew storytellers, creation was the domain of Wisdom, who,

> . . . being but one, can do all things,
> and while remaining in herself, she renews all things;
> in every generation she passes into holy souls
> and makes them friends of God and prophets; for God loves nothing so much as
> the man who lives with Wisdom
>
> (Wis. 7.27–8).

The snake was always subtle: the English translation says he was *'arum*, subtle, but in Hebrew, this word looks exactly like the word *'erum*, naked (Gen. 3.1). Similar looking words mean blindness, *'iwwaron*, and destitute, *'ar'ar*. The subtle snake promised sight, but left Adam and Eve without sight, promised them they would be like the *'elohim*, (Gen. 3.4–5) but they were left naked, destitute and mortal. The risen LORD promised faithful Christians the gifts they had lost to the snake: true riches, white garments of glory, and ointment for their eyes so that they could see again (Rev. 3.18).

Ecumenical Patriarch Bartholomew concluded his Greenland Symposium in 2007 by saying:
'If there is one single message it is this: time is short. Humanity does not have the luxury of quarrelling over racial or economic or political matters. *May God grant us the wisdom to act in time.*'

BIBLIOGRAPHY

PRIMARY SOURCES

Pseudepigrapha, English versions of these texts can be found in J. H. Charlesworth, ed., *The Old Testament Pseudepigrapha*, 2 vols, [OTP], London: Darton, Longman and Todd, 1983, 1985.

Life of Adam and Eve [OTP 2] is a Latin text, which overlaps to a great extent with the *Apocalypse of Moses* [OTP 2], a Greek text. Both seem to derive from a Hebrew original that was known in the time of Jesus.

Apocalypse of Abraham [OTP 1] is extant only in Slavonic, but certain words and phrases suggest it had a Hebrew original, written about the end of the first century CE.

Letter of Aristeas [OTP 2] was written in Greek by an Alexandrian Jew, probably in the early second century BCE, but the work cannot be accurately dated.

Ascension of Isaiah [OTP 2] is fully extant only in Ethiopic, but parts of the text exist in Greek, Latin, Slavonic and Coptic. It is a Christian expansion, originally in Hebrew, of a Jewish text about the martyrdom of Isaiah, and was compiled at the end of the first century CE.

2 Baruch [OTP 1], also known as *Syriac Baruch*, was translated from Greek into Syriac but probably had a Hebrew original. Since it reacts to the fall of Jerusalem in 70 CE, it was probably written at the end of the first century CE.

3 Baruch [OTP 1] was written in Greek, and there is a Slavonic translation. It is a Jewish text expanded by Christians, and was known to Origen early in the third century CE.

1 Enoch [OTP 1] is extant in Ethiopic and some of it in Greek. Aramaic fragments were found at Qumran. The Enoch material must be older than the earliest fragments, dated to the third century BCE. Isaiah presupposes knowledge of something very similar. Text and tr. in M. A. Knibb, *The Ethiopic Book of Enoch. A New Edition in the Light of the Aramaic Dead Sea Fragments*, Oxford: Oxford University Press, 1978.

2 Enoch [OTP 1], also known as the *Book of the Secrets of Enoch*, is extant in Slavonic and was probably translated from Greek. Similar ideas are known in first century CE, but the book is impossible to date. It could be very old.

3 Enoch [OTP 1], also known as the *Hebrew Enoch*, contains material of Palestinian origin attributed to Rabbi Ishmael, who taught in the second century CE. It probably reached its present form in the fifth or sixth century CE.

Jubilees [OTP 2], also known as the *Little Genesis*, is extant in Ethiopic, and parts in Greek, Syriac and Latin. Fragments of the original Hebrew text have been found at Qumran and at Masada. It is mentioned in the Damascus Document (CD XVI) found at Qumran, and was known early in the second century BCE.

Testament of Adam [OTP 1] is a Syriac Christian text that expands earlier Jewish material. There are many ancient versions: Greek, Arabic, Ethiopic, Georgian, Armenian. The final compilation dates from the mid-third century CE.

Testament of Judah [OTP 1] is part of the *Testaments of the Twelve Patriarchs*, written in Greek by an Egyptian Jew at the end of the second temple period, but preserved and expanded by Christians. This was a popular genre, and the last words of the twelve sons of Jacob exist in many forms: there were fragments of a Hebrew *Testament of Naphtali* and an Aramaic *Testament of Levi* at Qumran.

Pseudo-Philo Biblical Antiquities [OTP 2] is a Latin text, translated from a Hebrew original via a Greek version. It retells the Old Testament story from Adam to King Saul, and was known in the time of Jesus. It was transmitted together with the works of Philo, hence its name.

Sibylline Oracles [OTP 1] were widely known in the ancient Mediterranean world, and claimed to be the oracles of ten female seers, the Sibyls. Books 1 and 2 are Jewish oracles from the end of the second temple period, expanded by Christians in the mid second century CE. Book 3 is Jewish text written in Egypt in the mid second century BCE.

Psalms of Solomon [OTP 2] are extant in Greek and Syriac, but originally in Hebrew, composed in response to the capture of Jerusalem by Pompey in 63 BCE.

Philo [about 20 BCE–50 CE] was from a priestly family and lived in Alexandria. He headed that community's embassy to Caligula in

40 CE. Many of his writings survive. The Greek texts and English translations can be found in Colson, F. H., and Whittaker, G. H., *Philo*,12 vols, Loeb Classical Library, Cambridge MA: Harvard University Press, 1929–63.

Flavius *Josephus* [about 35–100 CE] was the Roman name of Joseph ben Matthias, who came from a royal and high priestly family. Greek texts and English translations of his writings can be found in Marcus, R., and Thackeray, H. St J., *Josephus*, 12 vols, Loeb Classical Library, Cambridge MA: Harvard University Press, 1927 onwards.

Qumran Texts. Translations of most of the non-biblical texts are in Vermes, G., *The Complete Dead Sea Scrolls in English*, London: Penguin, 1997. Translations of the biblical texts are in Abegg, M., Flint, P. and Ulrich, E., *The Dead Sea Scrolls Bible*, Edinburgh: T&T Clark, 1999.

The *Mishnah* is a collection of religious law from the end of the second temple period, compiled about 200 CE by R. Judah ha Nasi. Tr. Danby, H., *The Mishnah*, Oxford: Oxford University Press, reprinted 1989.

The *Talmud* is an expansion of the *Mishnah*. The Palestinian Talmud in English: Neusner, J., ed., *The Talmud of the Land of Israel*, Chicago and London: 1989 onwards. The Babylonian Talmud in English: *The Babylonian Talmud*, 35 vols, London: Soncino Press, 1935–52.

Abot de Rabbi Nathan, tr. Cohen, A., is in *Minor Tractates of the Talmud*, vol.1, London: Soncino Press, 1965.

The *Targums* are Aramaic translations and expansions of biblical texts.

T. Neofiti Genesis, tr. McNamara, M., Edinburgh: T&T Clark, 1992.

T. Neofiti Exodus, tr. Hayward, C. T. R. and McNamara, M., Edinburgh: T&T Clark, 1994.

T. Pseudo Jonathan Genesis, tr. Maher, M., Edinburgh: T&T Clark, 1992.

T. Pseudo Jonathan Exodus, tr. Maher, M., Edinburgh: T&T Clark, 1994.

T Neofiti 1 Numbers and T. Pseudo Jonathan Numbers, tr. McNamara, M. and Clarke, E. G., Edinburgh: T&T Clark, 1995.

T. Onqelos Genesis, tr. Grossfeld, B., Edinburgh: T&T Clark, 1988.

T. Onqelos Leviticus and Numbers, tr. Grossfeld, B., Edinburgh: T&T Clark, 1988.

T. Ruth and Chronicles, tr. Beattie, D. R. G. and McIvor, J. S., Edinburgh: T&T Clark, 1994.

T. Psalms, tr. Stec, D. M., Edinburgh: T&T Clark, 2004.

T. Isaiah, tr. Chilton, B., Edinburgh: T&T Clark, 1987.

Midrash Rabbah, the Great Midrash, is the work of the scribes, explaining and expounding the biblical texts. It was assembled over many centuries, and contains material from many periods. *Genesis Rabbah*, tr. Freedman, H.; *Exodus Rabbah*, tr. Lehrman, S. M.; *Leviticus Rabbah*, tr. Israelstam, J. and Slotki, J. J.; *Numbers Rabbah*, tr. Slotki, J. J.: all London, Soncino Press, reprinted 1961.

Merkavah Texts are collections of writings attributed to Jewish temple mystics. The original texts of *Hekhalot Rabbati* [The Greater Palaces], *Hekhalot Zutarti* [the Lesser Palaces] and *Merkavah Rabbah* [The Great Chariot] are in Schäfer, P., *Synopse zur Hekhalot Literatur.*

The *Zohar* claims to be R. Simeon ben Yohai's commentary on the Pentateuch, but the earliest known text is from Spain in the thirteenth century. *Zohar*, tr. Sperling, H. and Simon, M., London: Soncino Press, 1949.

CHRISTIAN TEXTS [IN ALPHABETICAL ORDER]

Many can be found in the Ante-Nicene Fathers [ANF] and most online.

Anselm [died 1109] was Archbishop of Canterbury. His writings are in Hopkins, J. and Richardson, H., *Anselm of Canterbury*, London: SCM Press, 1974.

The *Apostolic Constitutions* is a collection of material on Church order, compiled about the end of the fourth century. The prayers cited in this volume can be found in OTP 2.

Aristides was a teacher in Athens in the second century CE. *Apology* is in ANF 9.

Athanasius [died 373 CE], was Bishop of Alexandria. Against the Heathen and On the Incarnation in Nicene and Post Nicene Fathers II.4.

Barnabas, Letter of, attributed to Barnabas the Levite (Acts 4.36), was written after 70 CE. Tr. in Staniforth, M., *Early Christian Writings, the Apostolic Fathers*, London: Penguin, 1968.

Chalcidius translated part of Plato's Timaeus into Latin in the early fourth century CE. *Timaeus a Calcidio Translatus Commentarioque Instructus*, ed. Waszink, J. H., London: Warburg Institute, 1962.

Clement of Alexandria [died about 214 CE] was head of the Catechetical School in Alexandria and taught Origen. *Miscellanies* is in ANF 2; *Excerpts* is in Casey, R. P., *Excerpts from Theodotus*, Studies and Documents 1, London 1934.

Clement of Rome was bishop there at the end of the first century. Tr. of *1 Clement* in Staniforth, M., *Early Christian Writings, the Apostolic Fathers*, London: Penguin, 1968.

Cosmas was a sixth century Egyptian Christian. *A Christian Topography*, tr. McCrindle, J. W., London: the Hakluyt Society, 1897.

Cyril was bishop of Jerusalem 349–387 CE. Catecheses in *Catecheses 13–18 and Mystagogical Lectures* [i.e. Catecheses 19–23], tr. McCauley, L. P., and Stephenson, A. A., Fathers of the Church vol. 64, Washington, DC: Catholic University of America Press, 1970.

The Didache, 'The teaching of the Lord through the twelve Apostles to the Nations' is a manual for church life, possibly from the first century. Tr. in Staniforth, M., *Early Christian Writings, the Apostolic Fathers*, London: Penguin, 1968.

Letter to *Diognetus*, is anonymous, possibly from the second century. Tr. in Staniforth, M., *Early Christian Writings, the Apostolic Fathers*, London: Penguin, 1968.

Dionysius was once thought to be Dionysius the Areopagite (Acts 17.34) and thus a first generation Christian. Most now think he lived in Syria about 500 CE. *Celestial Hierarchy* and *Ecclesiastical Hierarchy* in *Pseudo-Dionysius. The Complete Works*, tr. Luibheid, C., Mahwah NJ: Paulist Press, 1987.

Ephrem the Syrian [died 373 CE] founded the theological school in Edessa. *Commentary on Genesis* in *Selected Prose Works. Ephrem the Syrian*, tr. Matthews, E. G. and Amar, J. P., ed. Mcvey, K., The Fathers of the Church vol. 91, Washington DC: Catholic University of America Press, 1994.

Epiphanius was bishop of Salamis on Cyprus in the mid fourth century. *Panarion* [meaning 'medicine chest' against heresies], tr. Williams, F., Leiden: Brill, 1987.

Eusebius [died 340 CE] was bishop of Caesarea in Palestine. *The History of the Church*, tr. Williamson, G. A., London: Penguin, 1965; *Preparation of the Gospel*, tr. Gifford, E. H., Oxford: Oxford University Press, 1903.

Hermas was a Christian prophet in Rome at the end of the first century. *The Shepherd*, tr. Lake, K., in *The Apostolic Fathers*, vol.2, Loeb Classical Library, Cambridge MA: Harvard University Press, reprinted 1948.

Ignatius [martyred about 107 CE] was bishop of Antioch from about 69 CE. *Letters*, tr. in Staniforth, M., *Early Christian Writings, the Apostolic Fathers*, London: Penguin, 1968.

Infancy Gospel of James, also known as the *Protevangelium*, is an early Christian text that tells a fuller version of the Christmas story. Tr. in Barker, M, *Christmas. The Original Story*, London: SPCK, 2008.

Irenaeus [died about 202 CE] was born in Smyrna and became bishop of Lyons. *St Irenaeus. The Demonstration of the Apostolic Preaching*, tr. Robinson, J. A., London: SPCK, 1920; *Against Heresies*, 5 vols, in ANF 1.

Jerome [died 420 CE] prepared a Latin translation of the Bible for Pope Damasus. *Hebrew Questions on Genesis* in Hayward, C. T. R., *Jerome's*

Hebrew Questions on Genesis, Oxford: Oxford University Press, 1995.
On Isaiah in Patrologiae Latinae vol. 24.17.
Justin [martyred 165 CE], was born near Samaria, lived for a time in
  Ephesus and became a Christian teacher in Rome. Tr. of *Exhortation
  to the Greeks, Dialogue with Trypho,* and *Apology* all in ANF 1.
Maximus the Confessor [died 662], was the great interpreter of Dionysius.
  Chapters on Knowledge tr. Berthold, G. C., *Maximus Confessor. Selected
  Writings*, Mahwah NJ: Paulist Press, 1985.
The Odes of Solomon are Christian baptismal hymns from the late first
  century CE. Tr. in OTP 2.
Origen [died 253 CE] was the greatest biblical scholar in the early
  Church. *Homilies on Numbers* Patrologiae Graecae 12. 583; *Homilies
  on Jeremiah* Patrologiae Graecae 13.256.
Symeon of Thessalonike [died 1429]. *Treatise on Prayer,* tr. Simmons,
  H. L. N., Brookline MA: Hellenic College Press, 1984.
Theophilus, [died about 185 CE], was patriarch of Antioch. *To Autolycus*
  is in ANF 2.

SECONDARY SOURCES

ActionAid, Cafod and Oxfam, 'Fool's Gold. The Case for 100%
  Multilateral Debt Cancellation for the Poorest Countries', 2004.
Anderson, B. W., *The Living World of the Old Testament,* 4th edn., Harlow:
  Longman, 1988.
Barker, M., *The Great Angel. A Study of Israel's Second God,* London: SPCK,
  1992.
  The Revelation of Jesus Christ, Edinburgh: T&T Clark, 2000.
  The Great High Priest, London: T&T Clark, 2003.
  An Extraordinary Gathering of Angels, London: MQP, 2004.
  Temple Themes in Christian Worship, London: T&T Clark, 2007.
  The Secret Tradition of the Kingdom of God, London: SPCK, 2007.
  'Hezekiah's Boil', *Journal for the Study of the Old Testament,* 95 (2001),
    pp.31–42.
Barr, J., *Man and Nature – the Ecological Controversy and the Old Testament,*
  Bulletin of the John Rylands Library 55.1 (1972).
Bartholomew, Ecumenical Patriarch, 'Sacrifice. The Missing Dimen-
  sion', in RSE, *The Adriatic Sea, 2003.*
  The Venice Declaration, in RSE, *The Adriatic Sea, 2003.*
Barton, J., *Reading the Old Testament. Method in Biblical Study,* London:
  Darton, Longman and Todd, 1996.
Bauckham, R., *Jude, 2 Peter,* Waco: Word Books, 1983.

Bernhardt, K-H., *Theological Dictionary of the Old Testament*, Grand Rapids, MI: Eerdmans, 1974–

Berry, R. J., ed., *Care of Creation*, Leicester: InterVarsity Press, 2000.

Boccaccini, G., *Roots of Rabbinic Judaism*, Grand Rapids, MI: Eerdmans, 2002.

Brownlee, W. H., 'The Ineffable Name of God', *Bulletin of the American Schools of Oriental Research*, 226 (1977), pp.39–46.

Brundtland, G. H., 'The Test of our Civilisation', *New Perspectives Quarterly*, 6.1 (1989).

Burkert, W., *Lore and Science in Ancient Pythagoreanism*, tr. E. L. Minar, Cambridge, MA: Harvard University Press, 1972.

Carling, R. C. J., and Carling, M. A., *A Christian Approach to the Environment*, Transformation, 16.3 (1999) reprinted The John Ray Initiative, 2005.

Carson, R., *Silent Spring*, London: Hamilton, 1963.

Carter, B., 'Large Number Coincidences and the Anthropic Principle in Cosmology', in Langair, ed., *Confrontation*, 1974.

Casey, M., 'The Original Aramaic Form of Jesus' Interpretation of the Cup', *Journal of Theological Studies*, 41 (1990), pp.1–11.

Charles, R. H., *The Book of Enoch*, Oxford: Clarendon Press, 1912.

Charlesworth, J. H., *The Odes of Solomon*, Oxford: Clarendon Press, 1973.

Chartres, R. C., 'Wisdom, Knowledge and Information', in RSE, *Adriatic Sea*, 2003, pp.153–8.

Coakley, S., Nowak, M. A., *Evolution, Games and God. The Principle of Co-operation*, Cambridge, MA: Harvard University Press, 2009.

Coles, P., *Cosmology. A Very Short Introduction*, Oxford: University Press, 2001.

Cornford, F. M., *Plato's Cosmology*, London: Routledge and Kegan Paul, 1937.

Cox, H., 'The Market as God', *Atlantic Monthly*, 283.3 (1999), pp.18–23.

Cross, F. M., ed., *Magnalia Dei: The Mighty Acts of God*, Garden City, NY: Doubleday, 1976.

Daley-Denton, M., 'Singing Hymns to Christ as to a God' in Newman, C., ed., *Jewish Roots*, 1999, pp.277–92.

Darwin, C., *The Origin of Species*, London: Dent, Everyman edition, 1959.

Davies, G. I., *Ancient Hebrew Inscriptions*, Cambridge: Cambridge University Press, 1991.

Davies, P., *God and the New Physics*, London: Penguin, 1983, reprinted 1990.
The Mind of God. Science and the Search for Ultimate Meaning, London: Penguin, 1993.
The Goldilocks Enigma, London: Penguin, 2007.

Davila, J. R., Lewis, G. S., and Newman, C. C., *The Jewish Roots of Christological Monotheism*, Leiden: Brill, 1999.

Deutsch, D., *The Fabric of Reality*, London: Penguin, 1997.

Diamond, J., *Collapse. How Societies Choose to Fail or Survive*, London: Penguin, 2005.

Dillistone, F. W., *The Christian Understanding of Atonement*, Philadelphia: Westminster Press, 1968.

Douglas, M., 'Atonement in Leviticus', *Jewish Studies Quarterly*, 1 (1993–4), pp.109–30.

Fishbane, M., 'The Measures of God's Glory in the Ancient Midrash', in *Messiah and Christos. Studies in the Jewish Origins of Christianity Presented to David Flussner*, ed. I. Gruenwald, Tübingen: Mohr, 1992.

Fletcher-Louis, C. H. T., *All the Glory of Adam. Liturgical Anthropology in the Dead Sea Scrolls*, Leiden: Brill, 2002.

Fox, M., and Sheldrake, R., *The Physics of Angels. Exploring the Realm where Science and Spirit Meet*, San Francisco: HarperSanFransisco, 1996.

Fretheim, T. E., *God and World in the Old Testament*, Nashville: Abingdon Press, 2005.

Giampietro, M., and Pimentel, D., *Food, Land, Population and the US Economy*, Washington, DC: Carrying Capacity Network, 1994.

Gibb, H. A. R., tr., *Travels of Ibn Battuta*, London: Hakluyt Society, 1959.

Ginzberg, L., *Legends of the Jews*, 6 vols, Philadelphia: Jewish Publication Society of America, 1913–.

Gore, A., *Earth in Balance. Ecology and the Human Spirit*, Boston: Houghton Mifflin, 1992.

Gorshkov, V. G., Gorshkov, V. V., and Makarieva, A. M., *Biotic Regulation of the Environment. Key Issue of Global Change*, Chichester: Praxis, 2000.

Gruenwald, I., ed., *Messiah and Christos. Studies in the Jewish Origins of Christianity Presented to David Flussner*, Tübingen: Mohr, 1992.

Hardin, G., 'The Tragedy of the Commons', *Science*, 162.13, pp.1243–8.

Harrington, D. J., *Wisdom Texts from Qumran*, London: Routledge, 1996.

Harris, P., 'A New Look at Old Passages' in Berry, ed., *Care of Creation*, 2000, pp.132–9.

Hawken, P., *The Ecology of Commerce*, London: Phoenix, 1995.

Hawking, S., *A Brief History of Time. From the Big Bang to Black Holes*, London: Bantam, 1988.

Hayward, C. T. R., *Jerome's Hebrew Questions on Genesis*, Oxford: Oxford University Press, 1995.

The Jewish Temple: A Non-biblical Sourcebook, London: Routledge, 1996.

Hedges, C., 'Path to Riches (But No Coveting): Seeking, After Rough Stretch, to Unlock the Inner Tycoon', *New York Times*, December 12th 2002.

Hengel, M., *Judaism and Hellenism*, 2 vols, London: SCM Press, 1974.

Hoyle, F., *The Nature of the Universe*, Oxford: Basil Blackwell, 1960.
   'The Universe: Past and Present Reflections', *Engineering and Science* (November 1981), pp.8–12.

Huxley, T. H., *Evolution and Ethics*, New York: Appleton and Co., 1896.

Jacobson, H., 'Origen's Version of Genesis 1.2', *Journal of Theological Studies* 59.1 (2008), pp.181–2.

Jaubert, A., *Clément de Rome, Épître aux Corinthiens*, Sources Chrétiennes 167, Paris: Editions du Cerf, 1971.

Jewish Encyclopedia, New York: Funk and Wagnalls, 1901.

Kingsley, P., *Ancient Philosophy, Mystery and Magic. Empedocles and the Pythagorean Tradition*, Oxford: Clarendon, 1995.

Klinkenborg, V., 'Chronicle Environment: Be Afraid, Be Very Afraid', *New York Times*, section 7.19, May 30th 2004.

Kugel, J. L., *Traditions of the Bible. A Guide to the Bible as it was at the Start of the Common Era*, Cambridge, MA: Harvard University Press, 1998.

Langair, M. S., ed., *Confrontation of Cosmological Theories with Observation* [Copernicus Symposium II, Kraków, 1973], Dordrecht: Reidel, 1974.

Lethaby, W. R., *Architecture, Mysticism and Myth*, (1891) reprinted Bath: Solos Press, 1994.

Lewis, L. M., *The Promethean Politics of Milton, Blake and Shelley*, London: University of Missouri Press, 1992.

Lovelock, J. E., and Margulis, L., 'Gaia and Geognosy' in Rambler, *Global Ecology*, 1989.

Lyell, C., *Principles of Geology*, London: John Murray, 1835.

Maier, J., *The Temple Scroll*, Sheffield: Journal for the Study of the Old Testament Supplement 34, 1985.

Margulis, L., *The Symbiotic Planet. A New Look at Evolution*, London: Weidenfeld and Nicolson, 1998.

Margulis, L., and Lovelock, J. E., 'Gaia and Geognosy' in Rambler, *Global Ecology*, 1989.

Margulis, L., and Rambler, M. B., 'Global Ecological Research and Public Response', in Rambler, *Global Ecology*, 1989.

May, G., *Creatio Ex Nihilo*, tr. Worrell, A. S., Edinburgh: T&T Clark, 1994.

McGrath, A. E., *Glimpsing the Face of God*, Oxford: Lion, 2002.
   The Open Secret. A New Vision for Natural Theology, Oxford: Blackwell, 2008.

'Recovering the Creation', in Carling, ed., *A Christian Approach . . .* 1999, pp.19–27.

Meshberger, F. L., 'An Interpretation of Michelangelo's Creation of Adam Based on Neuroanatomy', *Journal of the American Medical Association,* 264 (1990), pp.1837–41.

Milik, J. T., *The Books of Enoch. Aramaic Fragments of Qumran Cave 4,* Oxford: Clarendon Press, 1976.

Milgrom, J., *Leviticus 1–16,* New York: Doubleday, 1991, p. 347.

Moltmann, J., *God in Creation. An Ecological Doctrine of Creation,* London: SCM Press, 1985.

Montefiore, H. W., *The Question Mark . The End of Homo Sapiens?,* London: Collins, 1969.
'Why Aren't more Church people interest in the Environment', in Carling, ed., *A Christian Approach . . .,* 1999, pp.5–18.

Moore, G. F., *Judaism in the First Centuries of the Christian Era,* vol.1, *The Age of the Tannaim,* reprinted Peabody, MA: Hendrickson, 1997.

Murray, R., *The Cosmic Covenant,* London: Sheed and Ward, 1992.

Nesteruk, A. V., *Light from the East. Theology, Science and the Eastern Orthodox Tradition,* Minneapolis: Fortress, 2003.

Newman, C. C., Davila, J. R., and Lewis, G. S., eds., *The Jewish Roots of Christological Monotheism,* Leiden: Brill, 1999.

Newman, J. H., *An Essay in Aid of a Grammar of Assent,* 2nd edn., London: Burns and Oates, 1870.
Parochial and Plain Sermons, 8 vols, Cambridge: Rivingtons, 1868, reprinted Bibliobazaar, 2009.

Nobre, A., Sellers, P., and Shukla, J., 'Amazon Deforestation and Climate Change', *Science* 247 (1990), pp.1322–25.

Northcott, M., 'Christians, Environment and Society', in Carling, ed., *A Christian Approach . . .,* 1999, pp.105–32.

Nowak, M. A., and Coakley, S., *Evolution, Games and God. The Principle of Co-operation,* Cambridge MA: Harvard University Press, 2009.

Olson, D., *Enoch. A New Translation,* North Richland Hills: Bibal Press, 2004.

Orwell, G., *Nineteen Eighty-Four,* London: Secker and Warburg,,1949.

Patel, R., *Stuffed and Starved. Markets. Power and the Hidden Battle for the World Food System,* London: Portobello Books, 2007.

Penrose, R., *The Emperor's New Mind. Concerning Computers, Minds and the Laws of Physics,* Oxford: Oxford University Press, 1999.

Pimentel, D., and Giampietro, M., *Food, Land, Population and the US Economy,* Washington, DC: Carrying Capacity Network, 1994.

Polkinghorne, J., *Science and Creation. The Search for Understanding,* London: SPCK, 1988.

Porritt, J., *Capitalism as if the World Matters*, London: Earthscan, 2005.

Pullman, P., *The Subtle Knife*, London: Scholastic, 1998.

Quasten, J., *Music and Worship in Pagan and Christian Antiquity*, Washington DC: National Association of Pastoral Musicians, 1983.

Rambler, M. B., Margulis, L., and Fester, R., *Global Ecology. Towards a Science of the Biosphere*, London and San Diego: Academic Press, Inc., 1989.

and Margulis, L., 'Global Ecological Research and Public Response', in Rambler, *Global Ecology*, 1989.

Rasmussen, L. L., *Earth Community, Earth Ethics*, Geneva: World Council of Churches Publications, 1996.

Reiser, A., *Albert Einstein. A Biographical Portrait*, London: Butterworth, 1931.

Religion, Science and the Environment, *The Adriatic Sea. A Sea at Risk, a Unity of Purpose*, Athens: Religion, Science and the Environment, 2003.

Rosen, C. M., 'Businessmen against pollution in 19th century Chicago', *Business History Review* 69.1995, pp.351–97.

Rowland, C. C., *The Open Heaven*, London: SPCK, 1982.

Runia, D. T., *Philo of Alexandria and the Timaeus of Plato*, Leiden: Brill, 1986.

Philo of Alexandria: On the Creation of the Cosmos According to Moses, Leiden: Brill, 2001.

Sadruddin Aga Khan, 'Is Sustainable Sustainable?' in RSE, *The Adriatic Sea*, 2003.

Schäfer, P., *Synopse zur Hekhalot Literatur*, Tübingen: Mohr, 1981.

The Hidden and Manifest God, New York: State University of New York Press, 1992.

Schmemann, A., *The World as Sacrament*, London: Darton, Longman and Todd, 1974.

Scholem, G. G., *On the Kabbalah and its Symbolism*, London: Routledge, 1965.

Sellers, P., Shukla, J., and Nobre, A., 'Amazon Deforestation and Climate Change', *Science* 247 (1990), pp.1322–25.

Sheldrake, R., 'Need Science and Wisdom be Separate?', in RSE, Adriatic Sea, 2003, pp.109–15.

Sheldrake, R., and Fox, M., *The Physics of Angels. Exploring the Realm Where Science and Spirit Meet*, San Francisco: HarperSanFrancisco, 1996.

Shukla, J., Nobre, A., and Sellers, P., 'Amazon Deforestation and Climate Change', *Science*, 247 (1990), pp.1322–25.

Siegel, J. P., *The Severus Scroll*, Missoula, Society of Biblical Literature, 1975.

Singer, S., *The Authorised Daily Prayer Book*, London: Eyre and Spottiswoode, 1925.

Skidelsky, R., 'Where do we go from here?', *Prospect Magazine*, 154, January 2009.

Soros, G., 'The Capitalist Threat', *Atlantic Monthly* 279.2 (1997), pp.45–58.

Stiles, P., *Is the American Dream Killing You?*, New York: HarperCollins, 2006.

Stone, M. E., 'Lists of Things Revealed in the Apocalyptic Literature', in *Magnalia Dei* ed. Cross, 1976.

Taylor, J. V., *Enough is Enough*, London: SCM Press, 1975.

United Nations Environment Programme, *Global Environment Outlook Report 1*, Geneva: UNEP, 1997.

Vawter, B., 'Prov.8.22: Wisdom and Creation', *Journal of Biblical Literature*, 99 (1980), pp.205–16.

Wallace, A. R., *Man's Place in Nature. A Study of the Results of Scientific Research in Relation to the Unity or Plurality of Worlds*, London: George Bell, 1904.
The World of Life, London: Chapman and Hall, 1910.

Wellesz, E., *A History of Byzantine Music and Hymnography*, Oxford: Clarendon Press, 1980.

World Council of Churches, 'Moving beyond Kyoto with Equity, Justice, and Solidarity', Geneva: WCC, 2004.

Westermann, C., *Genesis 1–11, A Commentary*, tr. J. J. Scullion, London: SPCK, 1984.

White, L., 'The Historical Roots of our Ecologic Crisis', *Science*, 155.3767 (1967), pp.1203–7.

Wilken, R. L., *The Land Called Holy*, New Haven: Yale University Press, 1992.

Wilkinson, J., *Egeria's Travels*, Warminster: Aris and Phillips, 2002.

Williams, R. D., 'Ethics, Economics and Global Justice', lecture on March 7th, 2009, www.archbishopofcanterbury.org/2323.

Winer, M. L., 'Tikkun Olam. A Jewish Theology of Repairing the World', Theology CXI.864 (November/December 2008), pp.433–41.

Wink, W., *The Powers that Be*, New York and London: Doubleday, 1998.

Witt, A., 'Acquiring Minds. Inside America's All Consuming Passion', *Washington Post Magazine*, p.W14, December 14th 2003.

World Commission on Environment and Development, *Our Common Future* [The Brundtland Report], Oxford: Oxford University Press, 1987.

Worster, D., *Nature's Economy: A History of Ecological Ideas*, Cambridge: Cambridge University Press, 2ⁿᵈ edn. 1994.

Wright, G. E., *Biblical Archaeology*, revised edn., London: Duckworth, 1962.

    The Old Testament Against its Environment, London: SCM Press, 1950.

Wyatt, N., *Space and Time in the Religious Life of the Near East*, Sheffield: Sheffield Academic Press, 2001.

Zizioulas, J., *Being as Communion. Studies in Personhood and the Church*, London: Darton, Longman and Todd, 1985.

    'Towards an Environmental Ethic' in RSE, *The Adriatic Sea, 2003*.

    'Proprietors or Priests of Creation?' www.rsesymposia.org

INDEX OF BIBLICAL AND ANCIENT TEXTS

Christian Texts
[Works traditionally attributed to an
     author are not distinguished from
     works certainly attributed]

INDEX OF PERSONS, PLACES AND SUBJECTS